1976

competency-based education: a process for the improvement of education

Gene E. Hall
The University of Texas at Austin

Howard L. Jones
University of Houston

Prentice-Hall, Inc., Englewood Cliffs, N. J.

Library of Congress Cataloging in Publication Data

HALL, GENE E. (date).
  Competency-based education.

  Bibliography: p. 366.
  Includes index.
  1. Teachers, Training of.   I. Jones, Howard L.,
joint author.   II. Title.
LB1715.H27   370'.732   75-17564
ISBN   0-13-154864-6

Cartoons by Charles Shaw

10 9 8 7 6 5 4 3 2 1

Prentice-Hall International, Inc., **London**
Prentice-Hall of Australia, Pty. Ltd., **Sydney**
Prentice-Hall of Canada, Ltd., **Toronto**
Prentice-Hall of India Private Limited, **New Delhi**
Prentice-Hall of Japan, Inc., **Tokyo**
Prentice-Hall of Southeast Asia (Pte.) Ltd., **Singapore**

contents

foreword

Robert B. Howsam
Dean, College of Education, University of Houston

Hundreds of visitors each year come to see the University of Houston College of Education Building and the Competency-Based Teacher Education program that has been emerging there. They tour a unique building—one of few *planned* with innovative, instructional programs in mind. The tours vary according to who conducts them. Some guides know the full meaning of every detail of the facility and how it is designed to relate to program; others are less well informed. Predictably, tour variations according to the insight level of the guide have come to be lightly but meaningfully referred to as the two-bit, four-bit, or six-bit tour. The two-bit tour is a pleasant and worthwhile experience. The six-bit tour, however, is an educational experience at least and a revelation of instructional system at most.

The authors of this book take the reader on the six-bit excursion into the realm of CBE. The *why,* the *what,* and the *how;* the cognitive, the affective, the behavioral; all are manifested throughout. To use their own phrase, they "put it all together." They can do so because they have been there.

Each author is a teacher and developer at heart. Each has participated—and continues to—in the design, development, testing, and use of competency-based systems of instruction. Perhaps most important is that each, in the humanistic tradition, believes in—and practices—teaching as a highly human and personal act. This is the leaven needed if CBTE is to succeed in professionalizing teaching. There

iv

are knowledges, attitudes and beliefs, behaviors and skills that teachers must have, but these characteristics must be mediated through the individuality of the teacher. Teacher educators need both to exemplify and explicate this delicate admixture of the individual and the professional.

Hall and Jones are exemplifications of this balance in their professional lives. They have succeeded in achieving a similar quality in their book. Incident, example, concept, theory, research, and practice are merged into what should prove a very useful sourcebook for those involved in CBTE and textbook for those who wish to study it.

It would be less than honest to lead the reader to expect a highly polished work. Indeed, it would be a disservice both to authors and readers. Hall and Jones have taken enough time from the trenches to share their insights and experiences with others who share the pioneer effort in CBTE or who choose to follow it. The "mud on their boots," if there be any, is their legitimation; it needs no excuse.

There is a flavor to this work that excites the appetite and arouses the imagination. It induces the urge to thrust forward but cautions against simplistic approaches and naiveté. It shows how and reveals where we don't know how. The overall effect is affirmative, encouraging, and, above all, formative in its message. We *can* prepare teachers and we ourselves *can* learn.

preface

We each started out by attending a small, public, "teachers'-collegelike" institution. After work in public schools we completed our doctorates in science education-related fields. As we worked as full-fledged teacher educators in major institutions, we became somewhat disillusioned. If we got one thing from our initial experiences as small-school students it was the feeling that we could talk to professors; we wanted to do the same thing as teachers. Student enrollments, however, were staggering. The mass-production mode of teacher education made it extremely difficult; it seemed a never-ending rat race.

We recognized that concerted efforts by *teams* of faculty were most important. Fortunately, we have been where teacher education movements toward what we value—competence and personal contact with students—have been supported. At the Universities of Houston and Texas—and elsewhere—there have been exciting developments. Here, we share our excitement about them.

We chose the concept *competency-based education* rather than competency-based *teacher* education or competency-based *dental* education, for example, because we consider the concepts of CBE applicable to many different areas of education. By no means is CBE a cure-all or final solution to professional education; rather, we see it as a means to improve education, not the end.

We provide a more practical viewpoint than do many books on CBE or CBTE. Each of us is an in-the-trenches guy who works full time with students and faculty.

We recognize the theory and present it; however, it is intertwined with the missing link of past CBE descriptions—the practical side. It's all well and good to say that CBE efforts are modularized, but what does a module look like? What problems have people run into in building them? What are student reactions to modules and other parts of the CBE movement?

Where possible, we provide solutions to some problems inherent in any kind of change process and especially as they relate to establishing a CBE program. We want to try to save you some of the growing pains. We also share some of the implications and consequences of establishing a CBE program. It is very likely that there are many institutions and populations for which a CBE program is not the answer.

One of the major criticisms leveled at CBE is that you cannot take a professional and subdivide his skills into smaller parts—it's the gestalt that counts. We agree. We hope you will bear this in mind.

Chapter 1 is an overview of the CBE movement and of the balance of the book. It is more theoretical than practical and sets the stage for introducing a decision model that becomes our frame of reference. Chapter 2 focuses on objective and competency setting; Chapter 3 on assessment and evaluation difficulties; Chapter 4 on instructional activities (modules). Each of these chapters presents some in-depth examples from programs throughout the nation.

The second set of chapters reflects on global problems. Chapter 5 looks at personalization, and Chapter 6 makes a case for it. Chapter 7 deals with changing faculty roles. As CBE moves toward real-life situations, so does instruction; so Chapter 8 deals with field experiences or practicum. Chapter 9 focuses on management considerations, and Chapter 10 on programmatic evaluation—a keystone. CBE's self-renewing characteristics are some of its most important features, and we describe some ways to accomplish them.

In Chapter 11 program developers from six different, nationally recognized CBTE programs describe their experiences. To emphasize the importance of the student in CBE, a student who had just completed such a program shares his impressions and experiences in Chapter 12. We reserved Chapter 13 for our own thoughts and impressions on the place of CBE in the larger picture. This last chapter briefly explores various long-range implications and consequences that are likely.

One last note: Anyone who works with teachers recognizes that if he/she were to describe teachers with personal pronouns, the words "she" or "her" would have to be used—due just to the large number of female teachers. To give equal billing to the male counterpart, we could have used "his/her" of "her/his," or, as our friend Beulah Newlove suggested, invented a new pronoun such as "per." We run the risk of being chauvinist on one hand and sexist on the other. Therefore, we have made a conscious decision—to oscillate. Regardless of the personal pronouns, we hope the messages come through.

ACKNOWLEDGMENTS

All the missed deadlines and those pages that just didn't make sense are part of the agony of writing a book. Much of the joy emerges in discovering a fresh idea or writing a paragraph that says something better than it has been said before. It all is an intenese and highly personal experience. Coauthorship compounds the potential for problems, but it significantly increases the promise of the final product.

But the personal investment in this book is not limited to the coauthors. Dave Wilson, who edited the manuscript, faced a challenge, as did Susan Loucks, Nancy Via, Marilyn Fisk, and Rosemary Wetherold, who all demonstrated their proficiency at deciphering our typing and handwriting.

Susan Loucks was our content critic. Dave and Sue forced us to clarify our thinking and get out what we really wanted to say. Nancy, Rosemary, and Marilyn calmly—on the surface, anyway—typed the rough and final drafts. We greatly appreciate their assistance and cooperation. Ted Arnold and Alice Harvey of Prentice-Hall are to be acknowledged for their friendly, high quality work in producing the final product.

Thanks are extended to our colleagues, Ward Sybouts of Nebraska, Garry Hardy and Vern Wade of Brigham Young University, Pat DeMarte of SUNY-Geneseo, Bill Capie of Georgia, Dick Ishler at Toledo, and Blaine Parkinson of Weber State, for describing their programs—benchmarks of CBTE.

Thanks go to Bruce Thompson, who wrote the chapter on a student's reaction.

A special thanks goes to Bob Howsam for writing the Introduction. More than anyone else, he has influenced the CBTE movement. His extensive knowledge and enthusiastic commitment to education have been compelling factors in our professional development.

The personal involvements extend to our wives, Betsey and Renda, and to our children, Greg, Jeff, Kelly, and Stephen, who alternately left us alone to work on "The Book" and "helped" by insisting on having to use the typewriter —"NOW." Without their understanding and constructive cooperation our effort would not have been produced.

One final note to our counselor, Beulah Newlove: Beulah, we think we'll be OK.

to Frances Fuller,
a very beautiful person

CBE—*where did it come from, what is it, and how is it different?*

It belies the "all things to all people" appearance of teaching and learning and permits the resources of a system to be directed toward appropriate and accountable ends.

Old wine in new bottles.

Probably no educational movement of recent times has shown so much promise as this application of a common sense principle . . .

It sounds like a good idea if you can figure out what it is.

CBE—competency-based education—what is it anyway? The comments above, collected by Schmieder (1973) about competency-based teacher education, touch on the knowledge about and attitudes toward CBE that range today in the educational community. At the moment, about all any sizable group of educators can agree on with regard to CBE is that

- It has something to do with competence as an objective of education —a goal few seem to find fault in.
- It appears to be a relatively new movement; and, as a movement, it seems to be growing rapidly.
- It has a catchy name.
- The name is value laden, for when it is mentioned discussion follows quickly and loudly.

- It has divided the educational community into armed camps of Pro and Con.

- It is best known as something in teacher education, and heaven knows, some say, whatever it is they need it.

The temptation now is to toss out a neatly packaged, one-paragraph definition of CBE. To say CBE is thus and so would be a simple—and simplistic—way to build our soapbox, but the moment we stood on it to speak we would surely crash straight through its weaknesses and be left foolishly wallowing in contradictions and splinters. Our definition is to be found in the remainder of this chapter, and in the remainder of the book. Do not look for a single, ringing phrase to sum it all, but rather look for the answers in the totality of the process.

To us the goal of competency-based education is the development of learners who have learned, of programs that promote learning, and of instructors who can and do teach. The movement involves basic changes in philosophy, changes that could modify considerably the goals, means, and outcomes of education. As it is viewed in this book, the competency-based movement is *more* than a curriculum change and *more* than a change in instructional emphasis, although the movement impinges on both.

WHERE DID IT COME FROM?

The CBE movement has a long list of well-known precursors. At the same time it appears to have developed out of a less well known lineage of events in the evolution of education. The main thrust for CBE probably came from four separate and unrelated factors:

1. A teacher surplus.
2. A shift in expectations about college education by society and students.
3. Public demand for accountability in professional training.
4. The coincidental timing of research and development efforts related to instruction and learning.

Each of these factors developed independently, but in combination they provide an overlapping set of needs and solutions that lay the groundwork for a powerful and unique form of professional training. Let's look briefly at each.

Teacher Surplus

Until the late 1960s the primary demand on teacher education institutions was to produce *quantity*. Teachers were needed to fill the job market and needs of schools in the face of an ever-expanding enrollment of public school children. As a result, faculty at teacher education institutions were occupied with certifying large numbers of teachers, without adequate resources or time to assess the job they or their graduates were doing. No matter how many graduates were produced and certified, all of them found a job, and the tremendous pressure to produce still more teachers remained. Many teachers even functioned on provisional certificates to cover classrooms for which certified teachers were not available.

As the sixties drew to a close, increases in the classroom age population in the United States suddenly began to level off and the demand for teachers did an abrupt about-face. A surplus appeared in the supply of certified teachers. Many graduates of teacher education programs, even outstanding graduates, were unable to find teaching positions. Colleges were often caught unaware as their enrollments began to level off and the demands on teacher education began to decline. While the leveling-off process was unexpected, the event did provide colleges with opportunities to more carefully focus on their products, their programs, and their impact. Colleges were able to begin considering moving from mainly experience-based programs with varied outputs to competency-based programs, the graduates of which were expected to be effective professionals when they began their careers, not after five or more years' immersion.

Shifting Expectations for College Education

Other college graduates besides newly certified teachers were also unable to find employment at the end of the sixties. This reality was especially evident among science and engineering graduates when such major employers as the aerospace industry began to lay off workers with advanced degrees. Those same employees had spent most of the early part of the decade training and recruiting for the jobs that suddenly weren't available. In addition, a large number of young men were staying in school to avoid the draft, getting advanced degrees, and then exiting into a suddenly depressed job market where it was not uncommon for an applicant to be turned down as "overqualified."

The protest movements of the sixties led many young people into the counterculture and its social experimentation—communal living, drugs, and the revival of primitive arts, crafts, and lifeways. One observable outcome of these explorations was some intense questioning by many young people as to what the reasonable expectations for a college education should be. The postwar values that lay behind "go to college so you can get ahead" were being sternly questioned, as were the leaders of government and industry who exemplified those values. The consequence was that an increasing number of eligible young people began deferring college education for alternative experiences or rejecting it altogether as being neither a realistic meal ticket nor even a "relevant" situation. This consequence also provided a clear message to ongoing programs in areas like teacher education: look carefully at what you are doing; make changes or many good prospects are going to get away.

Citizen Demand for Accountability in Education

Another phenomenon of the late sixties was a steady increase in the burden of local, state, and federal taxes. Citizens began to seriously question the value bought with their tax dollars. There were many types of taxes, but one of the few places where an individual had a chance to exert direct influence on spending was in public school financing. Widespread rejection of school bond issues in the late sixties and early seventies were interpreted by many as a rejection of the work of the schools. Although the burden of taxation itself might have contributed to such defeats,[1] the public was also expressing concern over the failure of many children to learn to read or write. Lawsuits were even filed in several states and stand as testimony to the depth of this feeling. The result of this disillusionment with the products of education was an increasing demand from the public to require accountability of educational institutions—accountability not only for fiscal responsibilities but also for the goals of education valued by the taxpaying public. A direct consequence was increased experimentation, including alternative schools, performance contracting with private firms, and other innovative practices, all designed to increase accountability. The results were not always positive. Nonetheless, the climate for experimentation was present.

Timing of R&D Efforts

Another development in the 1960s was the emergence and acceleration of programmatic educational research and development funded by the federal government. This included the founding of twenty educational labora-

---

[1] An alternative explanation of the rejection of school bond issues is that such defeats were due not only to dissatisfaction and disillusionment with the schools but also to a protest against the general level of taxation. Richard Foster (1972) made the intriguing suggestion that the spending of tax dollars be changed so that the schools would receive the income tax revenues and the military would operate from the property tax. He stated that it would then be interesting to observe how taxpayers would vote on bond issues for the development of new military apparatus.

tories and eleven research and development centers beginning in 1965. Each of the R&D centers was associated with a major university; the laboratories were established as new nonprofit corporations.[2] These new institutions were scattered throughout the nation and were supported to do basic research and development in education. Various kinds of diffusion activities were also designed to translate research into effective classroom practice. Systems theory, including systemic planning and decision-making processes that had been developed in the aerospace industry, was a tool available to these program developers. New procedures and conceptualizations in the area of formative and summative evaluation of products and their learning outcomes were also developed and studied.

Many researchers were empirically examining the personal-psychological variables related to learning. Multivariate studies designed to identify what learner variables are related to learning outcomes under what forms of instruction increased in sophistication. A vast amount of development activity was initiated that began to relate learning theory, curriculum materials, and new developments in instructional media and teaching strategies. The National Science Foundation spent millions of dollars on curriculum development projects. "Behavioral objectives" became the big buzzwords as inquiry-oriented curricula found their way into the schools. Several of the educational laboratories were heavily involved in curriculum development, as were many school districts and intermediate education agencies through Titles I and III of the Elementary and Secondary Education Act.

Events Combine with Institutional Development

Each of the four events described above provided the basis, the opportunity, and the need for forcing improvement and dramatic change in professional education and training programs. The demand was for change from models that emphasized quantity to an emphasis on quality, and the resources were becoming available to effect such change. Probably the greatest single catalyst for actual development of competency-based education came in the federal initiatives to support planned development and change in teacher-training institutions. Most notable was the development of ten model teacher education program proposals (Burdin, 1969) supported by the U.S. Office of Education; other impetus came with the funding of Teacher Corps and Training Teachers of Teachers (TTT) projects.

---

[2] Each of the laboratories was originally given a regional focus, but they later evolved to deal with problems on a national basis, much the same as the R&D centers. By the early seventies the labs and centers were distinguishable chiefly in their organizational arrangements rather than in the focus of their work. However, the laboratories have generally been more lavishly funded and have had a more powerful dissemination apparatus than the research-oriented R&D centers.

MODEL TEACHER EDUCATION PROGRAMS.   In 1968 each of ten teacher education institutions was given the task of designing replicable, accountable, systemically controlled programs that would focus on the development of effective teachers. While each of the ten separate staffs designed unique programs, certain common threads ran through all of them. These common characteristics included (1) an emphasis on specification of learner outcomes in terms of behavioral objectives, (2) a heavy emphasis on both clinical and field-based experiences, (3) the use of interdisciplinary faculty resources, and (4) a heavy emphasis on evaluation of students during and after the training program. Part of this student evaluation was to assess how the graduate of the teacher education program would perform on the job. This information could then be used for the redevelopment of a regenerative teacher education program.

TTT, TEACHER CORPS, AND OTHERS.   During the genesis of CBE the U.S. Office of Education was channeling funds for the design and operationalization of quality teacher education through two major programs: the Training Teachers of Teachers (TTT) and the Teacher Corps.

TTT grants were provided to aid teacher education nationally by impacting personnel and organizational structures of college education programs. While most TTT funding was designed to aid educational personnel in acquiring advanced skills, efforts were also made to influence decision making by involving parents, local school personnel, and college educators in dialogues on educational problems and solutions of problems. Some TTT grants even went so far as to focus on curriculum development. The Texas TTT project, for example, used these funds specifically for development of competency-based teacher education programs at a small number of prototype centers of teacher education in the state.

Teacher Corps funds were targeted primarily toward the education of the disadvantaged through special programs, but the careful design of programs at several institutions enabled them to incorporate competency-based curricula and instructional strategies developed in Teacher Corps into their regular teacher education programs. Indeed, it was through the funding of Teacher Corps and TTT projects that the impetus was provided for many teacher education institutions to establish experimental competency-based programs.

During this same period, other groups of innovative educators were developing CBTE programs with little or no outside funding. Faculty accomplished these tasks by taking it out of their hides, by using intrainstitutional monies, and, in some cases, by forming linkages between several institutions for the purpose of sharing resources and expertise. Several associations or consortia were established for facilitating CBE program development. Agencies and groups involved included state education agencies (e.g., Multi-States Consortium), various teacher-training institutions (e.g., Southern Consortium), and local education agencies (e.g., in later cycles, school systems became the prime contractors for Teacher Corps grants).

Initiatives have also been made by professional organizations to aid communication, to clarify issues, and to catalyze further thinking and movement toward CBE. The American Association of Colleges of Teacher Education's Committee on Performance-Based Teacher Education has been a continuing source of literature and ideas. Task Force 72, a committee whose purpose was to explore future educational alternatives and to make recommendations to the U.S. Office of Education based on these explorations, has been yet another source of leadership and sustaining power behind the CBE movement. CBE-related presentations are also a regular feature of professional meetings and are found in professional journals.

The brief description above should give the reader some feel for the scope and resources that have led to and been committed to this effort in a relatively short period of time. Movement toward CBE is also being observed in areas other than teacher education. For example, educators working in the health sciences, including dental health and others, are showing an active interest in the movement and some programs are operational. Unfortunately, because of the lure of funding and, in some cases, the pressure of accreditation requirements, many educators have entered into CBE without fully understanding what implications the movement has for them, for their institutions, or for their profession. We hope this book will provide information that will allow prospective CBEers to identify and understand some of these implications. Toward this end, the rest of this chapter focuses on the conceptual characteristics and theory of CBE with some illustrations of CBE in action. This will set the stage for the remainder of the book, where we will look more closely at the various characteristics and examine especially how they impact the process of implementing CBE.

THEORETICAL STEPS

A variety of reasons heralded CBE's appearance at its particular time in history, in addition to those already listed. Elam (1971) cites changes in general societal conditions and institutional responses, the influx of large amounts of federal money, the emergence of private industry as a force influencing school decisions, and development of new concepts of management as just a few factors that made the CBE movement possible. We agree.

But we also argue that the following three theoretical developments were essential precursors of CBE's emergence to fill the voids then present in education:

1. The reversal of educational practice away from group instruction and group comparisons toward emphasis on the individual as the controller of his own learning.
2. The concept of mastery learning.
3. The redefinition of "aptitude."

Reversal away from Group Instruction and Group Comparisons

The trend away from grouped instruction and comparisons of individual achievement against group curves quite likely found its impetus in a reaction against the gray-flannel-suit regimentation and button-down minds of the fifties and sixties. The social pressure of compacting so many individual minds into corporate packages eventually forced some young people to seek escape and to begin searching outside the system for ways to "do their own thing." By the late sixties, students generally were demanding unique and relevant experiences in pursuit of individual goals. Moreover, educators and psychologists began, in theoretical arguments at least, to support the students' position. This same desire for personal meaning has existed among students since the beginning of formal education. The realities of formalizing education, however, in the absence of other solutions had forced an increasing emphasis on group education. Educators concentrated so intently on the *process* of education in order to get the job done that they eventually began to sacrifice quality in the product. The modern patterns of mass education appear to have effectively prohibited individualized and personalized instruction, or at least they have provided excuses in the form of "too much to be done."

This does not mean that mass education has been a total failure. CBE is not a negation of mass education, nor is it the formation of alternative schools. Rather, CBE focuses on the problem recognized by every person who has been involved in group instruction—that not all students in a group learn the same amount of material in a set period of time. Good instruction, regardless of the topic, still lies in structuring learning conditions for the learner, not the lesson.

CBE includes provisions to ensure that at least minimal achievement is reached by all students of specified goals and objectives. Student achievement is not evaluated by group comparisons on a normal curve. Instead, each student's achievement is measured against completion of objectives. Bloom (1971) points out the shortcoming of using the normal curve or other comparative statistical procedures in evaluating student achievement:

We have for so long used the normal curve in grading students that we have come to believe in it. Our achievement measures are designed to detect differences among our learners, even if the differences are trivial in terms of the subject matter. We then distribute our grades in a normal fashion. In any group of students we expect to have some small percent receive A grades. We are surprised when the percentage differs greatly from about 10 percent. We are also prepared to fail an equal proportion of students. Quite frequently this failure is determined by the rank order of the students to grasp the essential ideas of the course. Thus, we have become accustomed to classify students into about five categories of level of performance and to assign grades in some relative fashion. It matters not that the failures of one year performed at about the same level as the C students of another year. Nor does it matter that the A students of one school do about as well as the F students of another school.

The problem with the normal curve is that, by definition, someone has to fail. CBE attempts to reduce the failure syndrome, hopefully negating the factor identified by Glasser (1969):

> I believe if a child, no matter what his background, can succeed in school, he has an excellent chance for success in life. If he fails at any stage of his educational career—elementary, junior high, high school, or college—his chances for success in life are greatly diminished. . . . *Unless we can provide schools where children, through a reasonable use of their capacities, can succeed, we will do little to solve the major problems of our country.*

Concept of Mastery Learning

The development of the mastery learning concept is another key to the implications of CBE. Bloom (1971) notes:

> Most students (perhaps more than 90 percent) can master what we have to teach them, and it is the task of instruction to find the means which will enable our students to master the subject under consideration. Our basic task is to determine what we mean by mastery of the subject and to search for the methods and materials which will enable the largest proportion of our students to attain such mastery.

Bloom's position is antithetical to that advanced by many proponents of group learning. Mastery learning rests on the fact that most students can learn and that an instructor has the *responsibility* for working with individuals until they do learn.

The historical definition of "aptitude" in education and psychology has been that "some can and some can't." The function of many freshman-level college courses has traditionally been to screen out the can'ts from the cans. In rethinking the notion of aptitude, however, Carroll (1963) suggested that aptitude is the *amount of time* required by the learner to attain mastery of a learning task. Bloom (1971) noted:

> Implicit in this formulation is the assumption that, given enough time, all students can conceivably attain mastery of a learning task. If Carroll is right, then learning mastery is theoretically available to all, if we can find the means for helping each student. It is this writer's belief that this formulation of Carroll's has the most fundamental implications for education.

If the Carroll definition of aptitude is accepted, careful consideration must be given to the time required for a learning task. In CBE, in fact, time becomes a variable that is determined by the internal and external needs and capabilities of the learner. Mastery learning is the goal. In the traditional learning experience, time has been the constant and learning has been the variable. One strength of placing mastery learning in as the constant and time as the variable is that the strategy permits an observer to perceive education from other points of view.

CHARACTERISTICS OF CBE

The theoretical developments discussed above underlie the basic characteristics of competency-based education. Just how they are put into action varies greatly—in fact, variety is one characteristic that is most notable when examining different operational CBE programs. Despite this variety, however, there are common characteristics among CBE programs that permit us to label a specific program as competency-based and other ancillary characteristics that are generally used to facilitate the programs.

Basic Commonalities

Competency-based education, first of all, is education that focuses on students' acquisition of specific competencies. In other words, the educational program includes a set of learning objectives that are stated so that their accomplishment can be observed in the form of specified learner behaviors or knowledge. Minimum levels of achievement of these objectives are established as a criterion of success. Learning activities are geared to assist each student in acquiring at least the minimum levels of competence. Getting through the learning experience within a specified time period has no intrinsic value—acquiring minimum competence, regardless of time, is the valued end. This is a direct application of the concepts of mastery learning and aptitude as described above.

Competencies are composite skills, behaviors, or knowledge that can be demonstrated by the learner and are derived from explicit conceptualizations of the desired outcomes of learning. Competencies are stated so as to make possible the assessment of student learning through direct observation of student behavior. Learning objectives are known to the student as he begins a learning experience. The student also knows in advance the levels of mastery to be used as criteria of successful achievement. Such criteria are always explicit and are based on the specified objectives that contribute to the competencies being learned. Objectivity in assessment of achievement is sought by using the individual learner's performance as the primary source of evidence and by taking into account evidence of the learner's knowledge rather than relying solely on judgments.

Ancillary Characteristics of CBE

Once we get past the basic notion of competencies as learning objectives, we discover that CBE can take almost any form necessary to get the job done in a particular environment or for a particular purpose. Some of the more common accessories of CBE, however, can be cited to provide an idea of how such a program might be structured. These features include self-pacing, modularized learning experiences; learning resource centers; faculty teams; field experiences; personalization strategies; and communication facilities.

SELF-PACING LEARNING MODULES. CBE programs frequently use "modules" as delivery systems for instruction. A *module* is a learning unit with stated objectives, a pretest, learning activities to enable students to acquire competencies the pretest has shown to be lacking, and a competency evaluation to measure learning success. A module usually focuses on a single competency or discrete set of competencies, and the ability to demonstrate these competencies satisfies the requirements of the module, whether the learner performs the module's enabling activities or not. The learner usually works through modules individually or in small groups and at his own speed. Modules are typically self-contained so that the teacher is not always an essential element in the learning of the competencies specified for a given module. The instructor's role is that of an additional resource and guide to the learner, but many learners may not require the instructor's input at all to achieve module objectives.

Such self-pacing allows faculty the time for essential one-to-one interactions with students to ensure that students understand the gestalt of the learning experience. Faculty may also aid students in seeking unique ways of applying newly acquired skills, and they may urge students beyond minimum learning requirements. By having faculty spend considerably more time with students in one-to-one or small-group encounters, students come to know faculty better and faculty know students better. This change is not always comfortable—remoteness has traditionally provided some safety to both camps—but it does open doors to increased attention to the individual student's personal as well as cognitive needs.

LEARNING RESOURCE CENTERS.   Different use of instructional resources and classroom facilities provides for a variety of organizational patterns for CBE. At some institutions an LRC, or learning resources center, has become a central and popular part of the program operation. The LRC is essentially a library of written and media materials and other instructional resources that is open for use by students as they progress through modules and related experiences.

FACULTY TEAMS.   Interdisciplinary faculty teams allow for capitalization upon individual strengths and interests of faculty members while buffering the program and students from faculty weaknesses and dislikes. Teaming in professional training programs permits an integrated training approach with less redundancy and fewer gaps. At the same time faculty who plan and integrate their instruction together for the same students tend to share information about students, which benefits students through the faculty's more varied and balanced view of their needs.

FIELD EXPERIENCES.   Competency-based programs for professional training typically have a heavy emphasis on field-oriented experiences. This is particularly true in teacher education and the health sciences where the learners are, from early in their training, heavily involved with the clients of their future profession. Such field experiences entail close working relationships between inservice professionals and preservice students. Faculty members benefit through opportunities to become involved in the field experiences by staying abreast of the inservice realities for which they are preparing students and also in the increased knowledge such experience gives them about the entire scope and progress of the training program. Faculty also stay in closer touch with the developmental progress of each student. Field experiences can systematically involve both professional and lay communities in program development and evaluation activities. This is important, since these communities are the consumers of the educational product and, in many cases, sources of funds for establishment and operation of the program.

CBE, like any educational program, has the potential for churning out "graduates," instead of competent individuals.

PERSONALIZATION STRATEGIES.   By our definition a CBE program cannot be successful without some form of personalization. By *personalization* we mean more than merely individualizing instruction to meet the cognitive and pedagogic needs of the learner. Personalization means individualization of instruction that includes responses to the personal feelings and psychosocial growth needs of the learner as well. In attending to personalization, some CBE programs include special features and procedures, such as active participation of a specially trained counseling psychologist.

This attention to students' personal needs also requires utilization of techniques for assessment of such affective needs and their development.

COMMUNICATION FACILITIES. Self-paced instruction combined with faculty teaming and field experiences often requires the establishment of special communication channels to keep scattered faculty and students in touch with each other. Such communication strategies as bulletin boards and newsletters help take up the slack.

We could go on, but these are good examples of the common trappings of CBE. Other facilities and strategies can be readily found. We will discuss the examples given and others in more detail as this book progresses. The above should provide the reader with a general overview from which detailed study of CBE can progress.

WHAT DOES CBE LOOK LIKE?

The following stories are presented to illustrate some of the key characteristics of CBE. The stories portray different kinds of programs and students. As you read them, think about how you would feel in the situations depicted. Think also about how the situations compare with those with which you are familiar.

Situation I

It was 10:30 in the morning and Pete was preparing to work on his language arts materials. He had been in the class for two weeks, and his experiences had already been a lot different from what he had done the year before in another elementary school. The year before he had read pretty much what everyone else did, except for the books used by the kids in the slow group who always stumbled through the words. Since arriving in this new school he hadn't read with a group once, nor had he listened to others read.

The first thing his teacher had done was give him a long test that lasted several days and seemed to go on forever. Pete really did not like tests because he felt that he had to do better than anyone else. The teacher told him it was a pretest to find out where he should begin studying. That didn't make much sense, but he tried hard anyway.

After finishing the test, the teacher sat with him and outlined the things he could begin working on. This private conversation with a teacher made him feel a little guilty, but he couldn't figure out why because both he and the teacher knew he had done nothing wrong. She introduced him to some other kids who were studying the same things she had outlined for Pete. The teacher said that if they decided to work together they could do so, but they didn't have to. The other kids seemed to know what they were doing, so Pete followed along. The group decided to work on Skill 141, whatever that was. Pete followed the others to a part of the room where there were file cabinets and where one boy, Sam, asked for four copies of Module 141, one for each member of the group. They sat down to read what they were supposed to do. Pete couldn't figure out why the teacher wasn't telling them what to do, but she seemed busy with some other kids, asking and answering questions.

When they opened their module booklets the four students first found something called an objective:

> In order to complete this module you should be able to write a paragraph telling the moral or gist of a short story you have read. The paragraph must have a topic sentence and have no more than one spelling error.

The next thing they found was a description of why the kids were being asked to achieve this objective. Not everything in the paragraph made sense, but Pete was amazed—no one had ever before given him a real reason why he should do anything in school except that he would get a bad grade if he didn't.

The next thing Pete found was a sentence telling him that if he thought he could already do the objective he should see the teacher for a test. He didn't want any part of another test just now, but one of the other kids told him that he was going to see the teacher and take the test even though he wasn't certain that he knew what a moral or a gist was. Pete asked him if he was worried about flunking the test and getting a bad grade. No, the other kid said, he often took what he called "pretests" to find out the parts of a module he could skip. All of the kids decided to take the pretest.

The test was short—in fact, it had only two questions:

1. What is the gist or moral of a story?
2. Read the story below and tell the moral or gist of the story.

After taking the test the boys were talking, and Pete asked why the teacher had asked them to do the same things that she had told them to learn in what was called the objective. The other kids laughed and told him not to knock it—at least they didn't have to guess what was going to be on the test. Pete asked how the teacher ever flunked anyone that way, but no one seemed to care about that.

A quiet kid named George found out quickly that he had passed the test and announced he was going on to Skill 142. The other three, including

Pete, were a bit disappointed, but they decided to work as a group to get out of the module quickly. Besides, they still didn't know what a gist was and they weren't about to ask George.

They turned to the next page in the booklet and found several sets of instructions:

> You will probably want to know what a gist is first, so here are some things you can do:
> 1. Read your text, pages 34–35.
> 2. See filmstrip S-6.
> 3. Ask someone who knows—be certain he is right, though.
> 4. Ask your teacher—she probably knows.
> 5. Do whatever you think will help you.

"Do we have to do them all?" Pete asked. The other boys laughed and said no. The three all decided to do different things to make certain they would be able to find out the correct definition of a gist or moral. They went their separate ways about their assigned chores and then came back together to plan their next step. They compared their answers and talked about their definition and finally asked the teacher if they were right. She said they were.

The teacher then told them they could go to the library, pick a book, and read any story they wanted to. When they finished they were to write the moral of the story on a card and give it to her. The boys left for the library, planning how they would work together to . . .

Situation II

As they took their seats, the students in the beginning physics course really didn't know what to expect. The instructor and a lab assistant entered, and, as if by reflex, the students picked up pencils and opened note pads. The instructor began by passing out what he said was a list of objectives of the course. Three students smiled smugly, knowing that it was not unusual for objectives distributed early in the semester to be ignored.

The instructor woke them up, however, when he announced that the students would be held accountable for demonstrating all of the required objectives prior to receiving credit for the course. In addition, several lists of optional objectives were included. A daring student raised his hand in the back of the room and asked when the exams would be given. The instructor said that examinations would cover each of the objectives individually and could be taken at any time the students felt they were ready for them. But he recommended that students take the exams only when they felt they could pass them. "But how will we know whether we can pass the tests," someone wanted to know, "if we don't know what will be on them?" The instructor said they should read the objectives; when they could perform what was described in the objectives they would be able to pass the exams. The student reaction could best be described as mixed.

The instructor then handed out a two-page description of what he said was the first unit. In the unit description students were told to pick a partner and then begin. Bill and his partner were reading the instructions for this first unit when they noticed another student who was working on something different. They asked him why. The student said he had already been in the course for a semester and that he had not completed mastery of the required objectives so he had to return until he did. Bill asked if the instructor was really leveling when he had said they could take a test whenever they wanted to. The old hand answered, "Yes, but be careful. Last semester I really didn't know how to pace myself. I did term papers for other courses, figuring I could always wait until everything else was done to complete physics since there were no set deadlines. Needless to say, I didn't plan very well and wound up with an Incomplete." Bill wondered if he could have taken a *C* or a *D* and gone on to another course. "No," the student replied, "the instructor insists on mastery of all the objectives. And, you know, the more I think about it the more I like the idea. This way, when I start the next physics component I will have the background I need. And I can start that component anytime I finish this one. I hope to have my last three units completed by next . . ."

Situation III

Gladys knew that one of the key competencies she needed to work on for first-level certification as an elementary teacher was that of questioning. When she thought back to her days in public school she was amazed at how her teachers could ask questions. She even remembered that some teachers seemed to ask questions that called only for memory responses, while others could really zing students with thought-provoking questions.

Her instructor had given her a threefold prescription on questioning during her last videotape analysis:

1. Work on asking higher-order questions.
2. Work on asking probing questions.
3. Practice "wait time."

She could see from watching her videotape with her instructor that her questioning skills left a lot to be desired. She had worked on it, even making cards with questions noted on them in advance, but her lack of skill was still evident. She wondered how those teachers that she remembered had been able to come up with questions on the spur of the moment.

Gladys had already tested out of a module on identifying higher-order questions. She knew all about categorizing questions according to Sanders's and Bloom's taxonomies. That wasn't hard at all, not nearly so hard as asking those kinds of questions in a classroom.

Three modules that focused on the elements of her prescription were available in the bookstore, so she bought them and set to work. All the modules were pretty much the same in style. They began with a list of objectives, then had a prospectus telling why the skills were important (she already knew why they were important!). They then had written descriptions of classroom incidents where teachers used the skills. Gladys had a choice of viewing filmed classroom incidents, either elementary or secondary, showing teachers using the skills. Some practice exercises followed, and then there were instructions on how to pass out of the module by demonstrating the skill herself. In each case Gladys was to submit a teaching vignette on videotape that showed her using the skill. She knew from past experience that she would have to not only demonstrate the skill but also be able to identify when she employed them and why in the presence of her instructor while viewing the tape.

Gladys considered how strange she had found the testing procedures to be in her competency-based teacher education program. In other college courses she was expected to perform most of the time on written tests. In this program the instructors expected to see her teach using the skills she was supposed to be learning. When she entered the program she was given a blank videotape that one instructor had called a "circular blue book." She had more one-to-one contact with her instructors than she had ever experienced before with teachers. Just one videotape viewing session took forty-five minutes. It was no wonder the instructors had designed supporting modules that called for a minimum of instructor input.

Gladys also thought back to her concern that since the objectives were all written down and the same for everyone, she would have to teach like everyone else. She found that when she taught, however, she was unique and that her instructors did not try to make her teach like everyone else. In fact, her counselor kept insisting that she incorporate her own unique teaching style. The individual skills she acquired then became part of her own repertoire. Right now she knew she could lecture because feedback from her pupils on taped lessons had been excellent, but she didn't like to lecture, so she rarely did. She liked the school experiences, since they gave her opportunities to practice with live kids . . .

LEARNING-INSTRUCTING—SOME DEFINITIONS AND CHARACTERISTICS

A key characteristic of competency-based education is that there are minimal things that a student is expected to learn. As can be seen in the previous examples, learning and instructing appear to have special definitions in CBE programs. In CBE, *learning* is similar to Gagné's (1970) definition:

> Learning is a change in human disposition or capability, which can be retained, and which is not simply ascribable to the process of growth. The kind of change called learning exhibits itself as a change in behavior, and the inference of learning is made by comparing what behavior was possible before the individual was placed in a "learning situation" and what behavior can be exhibited after such treatment. The change may be, and often is, an increased capability for some type of performance. It may also be an altered disposition of the sort called "attitude," or "interest," or "value." The change must have more than momentary permanence; it must be capable of being retained over some period of time. Finally, it must be distinguishable from the kind of change that is attributable to growth, such as a change in height or the development of muscles through exercise.

Learning, in CBE jargon, is the change from *can't do* to *can do*. Goals, objectives, and assessment activities are all designed to focus on the student's achieving competence or his working until he does achieve it.

Elam (1971) describes *instruction* in a CBE effort:

> The instructional program is intended to facilitate the development and evaluation of [the learner's] achievement of competencies specified.

Instructing is not an act of a single teacher or a teacher plus text simply describing knowledge, but rather it entails skilled consultation, facilitation, and assessment of a student's acquisition of preset competencies. In short, the instructor is partially accountable for student learning.

Levels of Accountability

Regardless of how the goals and objectives are stated and by whom, one key to identifying a CBE effort is that there are built-in areas of accountability for learning and instruction. As viewed here, there are two such levels of accountability in CBE.

The first level is one stating that the learner will be certified, appraised, stamped on the forehead, or whatever, only after he has demonstrated performance of preset objectives. Finishing a model boat, spelling all forty words correctly, solving four out of five problems, getting along with his mother-in-law, tolerating spinach—whatever the outcome, the learner will not be "completed" with the program until he can demonstrate the objectives. This does not mean that the learner will not "learn" other things or that he cannot quit his attempt toward the goal at any time. It only means that the learner (actually a poor choice of words if he doesn't succeed) will not be certified competent in a given area *until* he has demonstrated competence.

The second level of accountability is even more interesting. The instructor/teacher is also held accountable. This means that the instructor has the responsibility for aiding a student *until* the student learns. An instructor, for example, can reinforce desired behaviors on the part of the learner, perhaps increasing the probability that the behavior will continue. The instructor can ignore, punish, pray for, cajole, prescribe, lecture, repeat, meditate, critique, and perform a host of other things. These actions are all external to the learner, but most are, nonetheless, important in learning. In addition, it must be remembered that the effectiveness of these external conditions will differ considerably for each individual, dependent to a great extent on his internal capabilities.

The ability of a teacher or an instructor to manipulate external conditions to bring about learning is the key to the definition of instruction in the competency-based movement. According to Gagné, "Instructing means arranging the conditions of learning that are external to the learner." It can be inferred that teaching or instructing has taken place when a prospective learner learns. Some examples:

"I can't do this #@*&% thing."
"Here, try . . ."
"Hey, that works! I *can* do it!"

"I like all animals."
"Here, pet this crocodile."
"I used to like all animals."

These simplified examples may seem strange, yet you could substitute any learning example you wish, from using agreed-upon child-rearing practices to applying Fourier transforms, and the definition still holds. If we accept the idea that teaching is dependent on *learning,* then competency-based education projects a different role for the teacher/instructor.

The instructor is free to use any form of action necessary to get the student to learn to perform the competency—lecture, coercion, punishment, praise, whips, bribery, slide-tapes, set inductions, threats, ridicule, warm fuzzies—anything. (Please note, this does not mean that an instructor *should* use these; we'll get back to that in a minute.) This level of accountability simply means that the "teacher" is placed in an awkward spot if he tries to cop out by saying "Dumb kids," "Lousy curriculum," "I don't get paid enough," "No equipment—can't . . . ," or that old standby "You just don't know these kids." If instructing calls for arranging the external conditions for learning, then the accountability level of the teacher is such that *he* must demonstrate accountability at least in part for having his prospective learners learn. If the objectives and goals of the effort are agreed upon by the instructor in advance, he has the responsibility for working with the students until they become learners.

"The boycott hasn't affected Miss Birdy's class—she teaches just as well without the students."

Specification of Competencies

As was mentioned, basic to learning in a competency-based program is the fact that there are certain minimal things that students are expected to learn. These are made public to the prospective learner in advance. In some programs the prospective learners are expected to perform objectives that are set in collaboration with an instructor. In these programs the instructors allow the students to "contract" for the completion of a unit of work by demonstrating negotiated skills or competencies. In other programs the instructors allow the students to do what they wish toward any goal they wish. Let's face it, the world is replete with people who learn best on their own. In most cases these people have set their expectations in advance. And usually the criteria are pretty obvious:

> I'm gonna make a million by the time I'm thirty.
> So help me, I'll put this swing set together if it takes me a year.
> I'm going to get along with my mother-in-law or it will kill us both.

Other instructors or certifiers set forth minimal competencies prior to certification. E. G. Dimond (1972), in discussing certification in the medical profession, states:

> Men who give their time and strength to serve on state licensure boards are essentially charged by the people with protecting the public from poorly prepared physicians. The license is, therefore, an endorsement (at that moment in time) that the physician is "safe"—that a citizen is "safe" in asking him for health care help.

Competency-based certification of medical personnel, then, calls for the identification of minimal "competencies" to be demonstrated by the prospective physician, dentist, nurse, and so forth, prior to licensing. Identification of competencies in this case is left to state licensing boards.

In the competency-based or certification efforts of educational personnel, identification of minimal competencies is an area of great concern and discussion. Part of this book will examine the types of competencies being generated and the individuals who have generated them in the field of education.

CBE—END, MEANS, OR END-MEANS

Many have mistakenly assumed that CBE is some sort of package or kit that can be bought, plugged in, and operationalized with the flip of a switch. This assumption may underlie many of the misinterpretations of competency-based education. People who have been intimately involved in the establishment of CBE programs know that CBE is more than something that is plugged in and its objectives achieved. They know that CBE is a means as well—a *process* for change. Rather than being a box of new curriculum materials, CBE is a set of tools both for building new programs and for dismantling old ones and putting them together in new and more flexible ways. As both a means and an end CBE still does not pretend to be a final utopia for education, however. We easily imagine the year when advocates of yet unnamed means and ends are complaining about having to overcome the resistance of "CBE traditionalists."

In the scramble to locate quick cures for the problems we face as educators, we focus too easily on products that may be simply purchased and adopted, like textbooks or media packages, and then assume that after the new materials have been used once or twice they will become a regular part of the program with no more need for thought about their role or integration. Sound program building is seldom so easy as this product-purchasing orientation would suggest. There are no CBE kits, and none can be made. No two established CBE programs are the same.

CBE can be a catalytic process for change and program development that embodies guidelines and ways of specifying many outcomes that any educator would find worthwhile and desirable. With a CBE program, different characteristics are specified, resources are allocated in a different way, and evaluation has a different frame of reference than with many experienced-based programs, but the focus is still on the learner. Rather than merely solving particular problems, establishment of a CBE program crystallizes the need for solutions to other problems. CBE program development also catalyzes the identification of additional ideas and procedures that need to be included as well as the identification of some existing practices that might be deleted.

In examining CBE programs to determine the appropriateness of the process to a given situation, don't stop after merely reviewing available materials. The materials are only the means, and you must also examine the ends; you must look at the total program—its assumptions, goals, and effects. Make contact with as many people as possible who have had personal experiences in establishing CBE programs. Talk with students who have been in CBE programs. Visit established programs. In doing this be sure to look for not only the weaknesses and problems encountered, as certainly there are many, but also the different strengths and unusual outcomes. At all times be extremely wary of the guy who claims to have an established, complete CBE program. This person needs to be listened to with caution, for it is extremely unlikely that a *process* such as CBE can ever become a finished, completely installed *thing*. If you find one with a little brass plaque commemorating its date of completion, then almost by definition it cannot be a CBE program.

WHAT'S TO COME

As you study the rest of this book you might find the model presented below to be a useful conceptual tool. The matrix shown in Exhibit 1.1 depicts the manner in which program development decisions in CBE can be made for each of three areas: (1) who sets the program goals, (2) who specifies the instructional alternatives, and (3) who evaluates whether or not a student has learned. The matrix also reflects how CBE program adoption is controlled by decisions in three areas: (1) how plans are made for program adoption, (2) how programs are implemented, and (3) how programs are maintained once implemented.

EXHIBIT 1.1 Decision Making in CBE Development/Adoption.

In CBE as we view it, each of the six factors can be addressed from one of five sources of input:

1. By the instructor
2. By the student
3. By the community
4. By the profession
5. Negotiated between two or more of the above

Any program developer will have to consider questions in each of the matrix cells. In some cases the programmatic decisions will be identified as the instructor's task; in other cases the decisions will be those of the profession. In still other cases the students will have to make the decisions. No formula for CBE dictates *who* will make the decisions.

Several critics of CBE argue that the basic tenets of the movement ensure dehumanizing effects. However, if a CBE program is found to be dehumanized and inhumane because its learners are denied options among goals, instructional alternatives, and evaluations, then the movement itself cannot be said to be at fault. One characteristic of a truly flexible system is that it can be flexed in less than ideal ways. Thus it is with CBE—which decision cells of the matrix are selected for the development of a given program will determine who makes the choices in that program. If conscious efforts are made to exclude input from significant parties and to ignore alternatives for learners and if evaluation is no more than a facade, then the resulting program will likely be on a par with such notably humanized strategies as mass lectures or any other required teaching (as opposed to *learning*) session.

In most cases the instructional staff will deal with the three program adoption factors of planning for adoption, implementation, and maintenance. Collaborative decision making, however, is a desirable process in CBE and can be incorporated into an effective management system. Also, CBE calls for as much preactive (advanced) planning as possible. Without sufficient attention to the program adoption process, the CBE program that is developed may require more dollars, personnel resources, and hardware and software than can be afforded. It may fail to be implemented or may be abandoned due to unanticipated affects, consequences, or requirements.

The remainder of the book, then, may be used as a guide to assist the prospective developer of CBE programs in considering all of the angles, in examining each of the cells of the matrix. We will be exploring in depth the various CBE program characteristics and how they relate to the decision-making process. We will continually be pointing out pitfalls and issues that need to be considered when implementing and maintaining a CBE program. We will attempt so far as possible to provide a view of CBE from the trenches. Theoretical elaborations already exist under other covers. There will be theory, for that is necessary before anything can be done. Our intent, however, is to describe how the theory applies when educators become involved in the reality of developing a CBE program.

2

identifying competencies, goals, and objectives

If we are going to get anywhere in talking about competency-based education, we will have to start with a mutual understanding of what competencies are. The specification of competencies to be learned is the keystone of CBE, and like any keystone it is the most vulnerable point in the structure.

Specification of competencies for bricklaying can be accomplished through a rather simple task analysis. Specification of competencies for effective teaching is a pole away, complicated by the infinite vagaries of the human experience. One of the most penetrating criticisms of competency-based teacher education is that no one can say which competencies are directly related to effective teaching. Some say that such correlations are impossible because effective teaching involves different behaviors for different teachers with different kinds of students.

Criticism of CBTE on the basis of complexity and lack of baseline data does not appear to us to be sufficient cause for abandoning the process. Non-CBTE programs suffer equally from a lack of hard data on what makes for consistently effective teachers. At least in CBTE one puts his cards on the table, says what he is striving for, and has some notion of his success. This makes it easier for the responsible educator to identify weaknesses in the program and to replace faulty components. The process that makes this possible is the explication of goals, competencies, and objectives. If nothing else, they help one to organize educational efforts into manageable components based on explicit assumptions and directed toward publicly stated goals.

Failure to examine assumptions and goals of programs can have serious consequences. We have witnessed several programs that never really got started simply because implicit assumptions and program goals were never made explicit. Team members responsible for building these programs experienced inherent conflicts that were never resolved, and these conflicts were the direct result of team members not working from a mutual set of assumptions.

If there is a major point to be made in this chapter it is that before you start modularizing, building elaborate self-pacing devices, or establishing cooperative field-based operations for students, you should lay out on the table where you are with your existing program, where you would like to be, and some alternative means for achieving your goals. In short, cooperative planning and communication are essential for program development. We recognize, of course, that you could spend the rest of your career talking and planning and never implement anything. This is not what we are encouraging. However, there is precious little time, manpower, or money to waste in ill-planned efforts and false starts. Program developers must take heed to avoid the trap reflected darkly in educational history in the words: "Having lost sight of our objectives, we redoubled our efforts."

Thus the focus of this chapter is on examination of the key conceptual underpinnings for a CBE program, that is, the identification of assumptions, goals, competencies, and objectives. Open communication about and explication of these dimensions are the initial key steps in the development of an effective program.

How to identify and select goals, competencies, and objectives is the topic of this chapter. Our schema is as follows:

Page	Heading	Questions
26	Overview	Why bother?
27	Distinguishing between Goals, Competencies, and Objectives	What do they look like?
34	Identifying Program Assumptions and Goals	What are some factors related to the selection of program goals?
42	Identifying Competencies	What are some factors related to the selection of competencies?

DISTINGUISHING BETWEEN GOALS, COMPETENCIES, AND OBJECTIVES

There have been any number of workshops offered, books written, lectures given, discussions held, and even one film made on the topic of goal and objective identification. Certainly Robert Mager's (1961) fateful book, *Preparing Instructional Objectives,* opened the door for portions of a movement in education that has been both rewarding and valuable and, at the same time, controversial and potentially damaging.

At this point it would be nice to insert a brief, concise definition of what a competency is and then present one or two illustrations to emphasize certain more subtle points of the definition. The CBE movement would be receiving much less flak if an acceptable definition could so easily be stated. However, defining a competency is not that simple, since competencies are not independent of the better-known concepts of goals and objectives and must be defined relative to those concepts.

Goals are the broadest statements one makes about the expected outcomes of a CBE program. On the opposite end of the continuum from goals are objectives. An objective is the most specific formal statement that is made about expected learning outcomes. Objectives are behavioral descriptions of learning skills. On the continuum of goals to objectives, competencies lie in the mid range. All three—goals, competencies, and objectives—rest on a base of assumptions.

A useful analogy might be to think of goals, competencies, and objectives as a series of fitted boxes, with goals being the largest box and competencies being slightly smaller and fitting inside of goals, and objectives being smaller still and fitting inside of competencies. A more complex arrangement, and more in keeping with reality, would be a group of competency boxes inside each large goal box and then a set of subcompetency boxes inside each competency box and then a set of objective boxes inside each subcompetency box. Already you must be sensing the complexities of definition. We have said nothing about scale. How large the goal box is— how broad our goal is—determines the size, or specificity, of the competencies and so on for each box in the series. Just how big the goal box is, how ornate it and the succeeding boxes are, how many boxes there are of each size, and the size of the smallest box (the ultimate preciseness of specificity) are all factors left up to the builder. The only thing constant is the hierarchical arrangement.

There will obviously be ranges in the degree of specificity that any particular goal statement has and also ranges of the breadth that is covered by the learning behaviors being specified in a competency and subcompetency (see Exhibit 2.1). However, the general idea is that competencies should be more specific than goals, subcompetencies more specific than competencies, and objectives more specific than subcompetencies. For any program there will probably be more competencies than goals, more subcompetencies than competencies, and more objectives than subcompetencies.

One part of our definition, then, would be that goals encompass com-

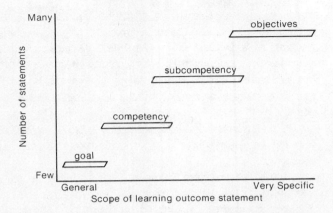

EXHIBIT 2.1   Degree of Specificity and Frequency of Outcome Statements.

petencies, competencies encompass subcompetencies, and subcompetencies encompass objectives.

Another part of the definition is that each descending step is more specific in terms of the ability of a learner to demonstrate its accomplishment. This difference might be most readily seen in the choice of verbs used in the statement of each. For instance, a goal statement might specify that the learner "will appreciate the aesthetic values of photography," while three objectives found in the smallest boxes inside that goal might specify that the learner "will (1) expose three sheets of photographic film focused on an 18 percent gray card at three successive f/stops, (2) develop all three sheets for the same time and at the same temperature, and (3) compare the resulting negatives, arranging them according to any observed order, and write a statement about the observed effects of that treatment." Obviously, "appreciate" is not as specific as "expose," "develop," "compare," and "write." Intermediate steps in this series might be a competency statement specifying that the learner "will be able to discuss aesthetic effects of control of exposure of photographic film," and a subcompetency specifying that the learner "will be able to describe the effects on film exposure of manipulating the camera's diaphragm."

The third characteristic of a competency is that although it encompasses many identifiable individual behaviors or skills that can be specified in behavioral terms, a competency is a statement that describes the observable demonstration of a *composite* of the specific skills. The learning of a large list of individual skills is of little value unless these skills can be combined and interrelated so that, with practice, the result is a capability for a composite performance by the learner that is greater than the sum of the individual skills. A competency statement, then, is a description of those performances that are based on the acquisition, integration, composite building, and application of a set of related skills and knowledge. These performances entail a growth process, a gestalt building, as well as the learning of individual skills. We feel that the learning of individual skills is not where the emphasis should be in any educational program. The emphasis in CBE, as the name implies, is on competencies, on the ability to develop and demonstrate a total performance, not just the mere learning of specific skills.

To illustrate what a competency is, let's consider some example competencies and how these competencies relate to goals, subcompetencies, and objectives.

Consider teaching in the field of language arts. One goal of language arts instruction is that all educated persons should be able to communicate. A necessary competency based on this goal is the competency of writing.

It is impossible, however, for a language arts teacher to teach a student to "write." It is much easier for a teacher to specify an area of writing and to help the student focus on that area. We'll call this area of writing a *subcompetency*. A subcompetency for writing that we might specify for this example is: "Writing paragraphs that include topic sentences."

This subcompetency is considerably easier to focus on than "writing." For a group of eight-year-olds, however, the topic would have a different meaning and relevance than for literature students in academically able classes at the senior high school level. Similarly, the teachers of each of these classes would have different expectations (specific objectives and criteria) for their pupils:

Fourth-Grade Student Expectation: After reading a given short story the pupil will be able to write at least one paragraph about the story. The paragraph must include a topic sentence.

Senior High School Expectation: The student will write a short essay comparing any two stories with respect to realism, relevance, and mood. Each paragraph in the essay will include a topic sentence.

It may help to look at some examples of goals, assumptions, competencies, subcompetencies, and objectives in other fields.

Field: Baseball

Assumption: You won't win many baseball games if you can't score runs.

Goal: To win!

A baseball player has to have many kinds of skills and clusters of skills if he is going to be successful at his game. He must know the rules of the game, he must be a successful batter, he must be able to field the ball, he must throw the ball accurately, and so forth. Each one of these job functions can be called a competency. For each competency there are a number of subcompetencies. If we look at the single competency "batting," one sub-competency could be identified as the *stance* that the batter takes in the box. Another could be described as the *swing* that the batter employs. Another subcompetency is the *selection of pitches* at which the batter swings.

For each subcompetency, more specific skills can be identified that can be described in observable terms. For the subcompetency "batting," for example, specific skills can be identified describing how the batter places his hands on the bat. A specific objective could be identified for the position of the batter's arms and hands at the beginning of the swing. An objective could also be written to describe the position of the arms, hands, and bat at the middle of a swing as well as at the end of a swing. Further analysis could lead to the identification of other important skills.

Although each major league baseball team has a batting or hitting coach, it is doubtful that he really teaches major leaguers to hit. One of the authors recognizes this, since he has been a Phillies fan since 1950. How-ever, in an attempt to help a player climb out of a slump, a major league hitting coach encourages a player to focus on subcompetencies like swing, stance, and selecting pitches.

A concept important to the understanding of the planning and opera-tion of competency-based education is that the parts do not always equal the whole. In batting, for example, the batter is not, by definition, a better batter because he has increased his skill in one subarea. Hopefully, the batter will improve, alleviate his slump, and help his team win. But there is a great deal of evidence that there is something more important than the acquisition of specific skills. A learner must focus on the gestalt. He must be able to master the total performance, not just the individual parts. In batting, this means that the hitter must be able to put all of the skills and subcompetencies together and effectively hit the ball. Being able to perform each of the skills independently does not guarantee competence. Hitting a high fast ball into the bleachers is a pretty good demonstration that competence has been achieved.

As it is viewed in this book, the most important function of the instruc-tor is that of helping the learner incorporate newly learned skills into his personal style, always aiding the student in keeping the gestalt of the opera-tion in mind. This personal style is highly important in baseball, for example. Though they each independently have the necessary batting skills, Billy Williams, Carl Yastrzemski, and Johnny Bench demonstrate their "compe-tence" in the area of hitting in personalized, unique styles. Similarly, a group of "competent" teachers will consist of individuals who each have unique, personal styles of teaching. Each has skills of classroom management, interactive procedures, affective responses that are uniquely his. But each is competent.

Let's look at another example, this time from the area of teacher education. Many assume that a positive interaction among students and teachers will increase the probability of learning taking place. Given this, a sought-after competency for teacher education programs might be: The prospective teacher creates a positive affective climate conducive to optimal learning.

It could be argued, of course, that all teacher education programs have this competency as an expected outcome for their graduates. However, few programs really focus on the competency more than just in passing. Probably only a few programs hold prospective teachers accountable for demonstrating the competency prior to certification. One of the reasons for this, of course, is the lack of definition of "positive affective climate." Without such specificity most beginning teachers would doubtless have difficulty in focusing on this affective area.

It might help teachers and observers of teachers to focus on these affective relationships if subcompetencies and skills with more specificity were identified. These might take the form of what a teacher could do in planning for the use of the competency (preactive indices), what a teacher might do while using the competency, or what pupils (learners) might do in a learning situation where the competency was evident. Exhibit 2.2 gives some examples of possible specific indices of the presence of the competency, although the list certainly is not complete.

The meanings of the indices on the list are considerably less open to argument than the meaning of the stated competency. In addition, if the reader wished, he could take the next step and identify objectives for the indices and train for them. For 1.42, for example, it might be possible to specify that "Given any classroom setting, the prospective teacher will use at least once the following types of responses: evaluative, interpretive, probing, supportive, understanding."

The authors do not see the value of such specificity, however. For one thing, the identified indices certainly cannot be expected of each teacher each minute or even each day. Teaching is a complex activity, and the gestalt of a competent teacher may not be identified if one focuses on the individual skills or subcompetencies of the teacher. This last sentence should not be read in such a way to discourage the use of such a checklist as that shown in Exhibit 2.2. Such checklists are best employed as formative devices, aiding the teacher to focus on his strengths and weaknesses as they are perceived by observers.

Personal style is a key point for certifiers and observers of teachers. It certainly cannot be expected that one style of teaching will be shown by all teachers. A number of styles of teaching will be demonstrated, but per-

Exhibit 2.2

Name _____ Date _____ School _____

Observer _____ Subject _____

PROFICIENCY ANALYSIS RATING

Classroom Climate

1.0 CREATES A POSITIVE AFFECTIVE CLIMATE CONDUCIVE TO OPTIMAL LEARNING

				Not
YES	Yes	No	NO	Observed

Pre-Active Indices	Active Indices	
	Teacher	*Pupils*

Pre-Active Indices

1.11 Describes and gives rationale for advanced planning for supportive social/emotional climate

1.12 Determines points in lesson at which maximum involvement can occur

1.13 Provides for individual recognition and group interaction

1.14 Analyzes responses and identifies them as evaluative, interpretive, probing, supportive, and/or understanding

Active Indices — Teacher

1.31 Appears to be comfortable and confident

1.32 Has pleasant facial expressions (smiles when appropriate)

1.33 Brings in isolate and encourages all to participate

1.34 Uses silence effectively

1.35 Calls students by name

1.36 Enjoys teaching and working with pupils

1.37 Appears to like pupils

1.38 Works with and helps individual pupils both in and out of class

1.39 Does not disengage himself from pupils (touch, life-space)

1.40 Encourages pupils to independent action

1.41 Is accepting of pupil as a person when mistakes are made

1.42 Uses the following types of responses appropriately (evaluative, interpretive, probing, supporting, and understanding)

1.43 Demonstrates authenticity

Active Indices — Pupils

1.51 Appear relaxed

1.52 Are attentive

1.53 Are actively engaged in learning activities

1.54 Appear to enjoy school

1.55 Seem to relate well to teacher and to other pupils

1.56 Do not disengage themselves from teacher

1.57 Work independently and help each other

1.58 Appear satisfied with teacher responses (do not appear uncomfortable or to feel as if they have been "put on the spot")

haps all styles can be improved by *focusing on competencies, subcompetencies, and skills.*

If a teacher is found to be lacking in a specific competency, most CBE efforts would offer instruction to help the teacher increase his proficiency. Some observers view this successive approximation strategy for increasing teaching skill with alarm. These critics raise the question of whether such an approach might result in all certified participants looking alike, with similar styles, attitudes, and behaviors in teaching situations. Of course, this danger might exist, especially in CBE programs that use goal determination by instructors and the profession as their sole input. This is hardly likely to happen in CBE efforts that call for negotiated goal identification and selection. In CBE programs calling for some minimal expectancies with the presence of additional options among and between competencies, such dehumanization hardly seems possible. Nonetheless, the potential danger remains and must be considered.

In essence, competency-based teacher education programs certify competent teachers, not teachers who demonstrate uniform individual objectives or skills. Effective CBTE efforts allow teachers to develop unique ways with pupils and unique ways of incorporating the competencies they have gained into a personal teaching style.

IDENTIFYING PROGRAM ASSUMPTIONS AND GOALS

A key to the development of a valid CBE program is the identification of the program assumptions and goals. For too long, most training or education "programs" for professional personnel have been the products of a *number* of professional trainers rather than the products of a *group* of professional trainers. This sentence implies more than a semantic difference. Few professional education programs are more than collections of courses and experiences. If CBE has one overriding benefit to offer professional schools, it is the opportunity to rethink goals, assumptions, and, in short, total programs. CBE efforts force faculty and students to make some key decisions about whether the assumptions on which past and present experiences are built are truly viable and valuable. If these programmatic assumptions are not made by the *whole group* involved and constantly checked, then we will probably be faced with a future of modified competency-based *courses* rather than competency-based programs. If total group involvement is not assured, then program assumption statements are doomed to the same demise as that claiming the Seven Cardinal Principles—to be memorized from musty texts and then quickly forgotten because of lack of use.

Our good friend Jack Gant, at Florida State University, has a useful way of looking at this problem in the establishment of competency-based education. To accept an educational change, Jack says, the potential adopter must be involved in identifying the goals for the change. If he is not involved, the assumptions and goals of the change will not be his, no matter what they are. Sides are chosen, lines are drawn, and two opposing factions end up in often needless fray. In the case of competency-based teacher education, for example, the two sides are slugging it out, each staunchly defending the same banner as the other—that teacher education programs ought to educate teachers who are able to function for the best ends of their pupils. If assumptions and goals can be laid out on the table for discussion at the beginning, before CBE adoption ever begins at an institution, then chances are that this split does not have to occur.

In using the term *assumptions,* we are speaking of value statements that may have little or no empirical basis. In some cases assumptions cannot be proved empirically. However, assumptions do set parameters within which goals and competencies can be specified. To be consistent and valid, each competency must be screened through the set of assumptions that has been explicated for that program.

It is only necessary to look at the effect of the National Science Foundation's science and mathematics programs of the 1960s to pinpoint a good example of assumption failure. The assumptions behind these efforts went something like this:

a. Science and mathematics education must be improved upon if the U.S.A. is to continue to hold a leadership position.
b. Scientists and mathematicians are needed on the writing teams for new curricula if the programs are to have validity.
c. Psychologists are necessary on the writing teams to guarantee that the programs will be learnable.
d. Classroom teachers are necessary on the writing teams to guarantee that the programs are teachable.

The developed programs were and are considered to be innovative—they reflect science and math as inquiry, use manipulative materials for learners (a la psychological input), and call for student involvement in not-always-memory topics. Of course, each of these procedures stemmed from another set of *assumptions* about learning and instruction—learning is an active process, one that proceeds from experiencing the environment.

The problem with the new programs soon became obvious when these latter assumptions were not found to hold in many classrooms. For example, in classrooms where *quietness* was considered an optimum condition for learning, the developed programs were quickly modified to something less than the original expectations of the curriculum builders. In school systems where science and math were assumed to be considerably less valuable in the curriculum than reading, money was not provided for the necessary manipulative materials. In classrooms where the teachers had selected topics of science and math that were based on other beliefs and values, the topics of the "new" curricula were modified. One teacher after viewing the contents and the procedures of PSSC physics is quoted as asking, "How can I teach this [PSSC] and physics too?" Hence, the science and math programs were modified to something less than the original expectations of the curriculum builders.

If such difficulties with communication and acceptance of assumptions are present in science and mathematics, it boggles the mind to think of the value and assumption differences when the subjects of sex education, drug education, value education, human relations training, and religious education are considered. Regardless of the topic, the first step must be the identification and public airing of assumptions by as many of those involved as is humanly possible.

Assumptions can have a profound influence on other curriculum and instructional decisions made by program planners. Assumptions and some concomitant generalizations were the basis, for example, for the development of the Model Teacher Education Programs sponsored by the U.S. Office of Education in 1968. The development of the program models was funded to focus on certain concerns about the education of elementary teachers. Some of these concerns were as follows (Boerrighter, 1970):

1. Rapid changes were taking place in society which were not being accounted for in elementary teacher training programs.
2. A great deal of instructional technology was available on a piecemeal basis for improving teacher training, but this technology was not being put together into a comprehensive instructional system; that is, more knowledge, training technology, and technical capabilities existed than were being utilized in programs for training elementary teachers.
3. Few programs were being developed for training teachers of the pre-schoolers.
4. Programs for training elementary teachers did not appear to have clear goals regarding what their graduates were supposed to be able to do.
5. Management information systems were not being widely utilized to help in individual instruction.
6. The concept of humanization was not being stressed in the training of elementary teachers.
7. The possibilities of new staffing concepts in the training of elementary teachers were being under-utilized.
8. Little was being done to further develop inservice training programs for teachers, and often inservice training programs did not build on preservice programs.

9. Inservice training for teacher trainers was limited; and built-in capability for self-renewal in institutions that train teachers was seldom evident.
10. Total programs for training elementary teachers were seldom fully conceptualized, nor did program models along with their specifications exist.

The model programs were developed by ten different groups (nine that were funded plus the University of Wisconsin, which performed the task without federal funding) and included teacher educators, teachers, and other educational personnel. Exhibit 2.3 depicts some of the assumptions and goals of three of the models. Information on the models presented here is drawn mostly from the book *A Reader's Guide to the Comprehensive Models for Preparing Elementary Teachers,* edited by J. Burdin and K. Lanzillotti, Washington, D.C., ERIC and AACTE, 1969. Further information can be obtained by searching the Phase I reports listed in our Bibliography.

EXHIBIT 2.3

UNIVERSITY OF TOLEDO

Assumptions:

1. Educational technology will play a substantial role in the development of teacher education programs in the decades ahead. This role of educational technology has heretofore not been adequately identified, but pressures both from within and without teacher education will increase its development.

2. The instructional organization of the elementary school will change markedly. In the model used, the instructional organization was the multiunit school as developed through the R&D Center at the University of Wisconsin. This emphasis on instructional organization was considered necessary in order to prepare adequately teachers for the elementary school of the future.

3. The contemporary learning-teaching process needs a reevaluation and its orientation should be more toward behavioral outcomes.

4. A multicultural society, such as our present society, requires detailed consideration of societal factors in preparing the elementary teacher of the future.

5. Research in education in the past has not been adequately incorporated into teacher education programs, and if research is to make an adequate contribution to the improvement of education, research findings must be incorporated into teacher education programs.

Goals:

In a sense, our primary task was to develop a broad performance model of the professional educator, a structure of teaching that would enable the creation of the ends and the means of the teacher education program. The basis of our rationale stems from the idea that professional performance can be described in terms of control over certain areas of reality that are essential to develop creative roles, rather than the ability to fill already-defined teaching roles.

SYRACUSE UNIVERSITY

Assumptions:

The model is based on six principal assumptions:

1. No one point of view regarding teacher education has been demonstrated to be most effective. Therefore, it is assumed that from a pluralistic open dialogue involving students, teachers, and researchers, hypotheses can be generated and tested that may tighten the circle around these ideas, activities, artifacts, and people, and that would constitute a more ideal teacher education program than that with which many of us currently work.

2. We live in a world where basic institutions and their value structures are changing at an exponential rate. Therefore, it is assumed that since we do not know with certainty what form that future world, its societies, and institutions will take, or how the children of such a society should be educated, teachers today must be educated to be continually self-renewing as they adapt to and play a major role in shaping the changes that seem certain to occur in the future world of education.

3. A model program that nurtures a pluralistic and self-renewing teacher education program must be an open system. It is assumed, therefore, that the model program can continue to be relevant to the changing world only if it has a built-in intention, action, feedback structure for processing ideas, generating hypotheses, and collecting data regarding the system *qua* system and the system in relationship to the changing world in which the program will exist.

4. Clearly, the requirements of a changing world call for self-renewing teachers as well as self-renewing teacher education programs. The "products" of teacher education programs must possess the disposition and skills to change during their professional careers if they are to be as effective in the year 2000 as they are now. Therefore, it is assumed that the development of self-renewing teachers can only be accom-

plished by a program that is a self-renewing one staffed by self-renewing teacher educators. Implied, then, is continuing inservice education for the professional program staff.

5. A model program must recognize human uniqueness. It is assumed that learning styles, learning rates, and what a person considers important to learn in part constitute the uniqueness of an individual. It is further assumed that providing a program that recognizes and accommodates these unique differences is one way of fostering the development of self-directed, self-renewing teachers. Thus, the model program is largely individualized and self-paced.

6. The education of teachers must involve not only the teacher education institutions, but also the public schools and the educational industries. Therefore, it is assumed that the optional functioning of the model program is dependent upon a condition of proto-cooperation that involves teacher education institutions, public schools, and educational industries working together in new ways.

Goals:

The model program has been created to help develop individuals to (1) become increasingly perceptive, (2) have a positive concept of themselves as teachers, (3) come to terms with themselves in respect to their motives for becoming teachers, and (4) develop a system of professional values and skills consistent with their personal integrity and the demands of the education profession.

FLORIDA STATE UNIVERSITY

Assumptions:

There will be continued and accelerated social change generally and a revised and intensified set of demands placed on education accordingly. Further, and in great part a response to these changes, it is anticipated that there will be a radically different elementary school, one transformed in both program and organization, by 1978.

Goals:

1. The teacher will plan for instruction by formulating objectives in terms of behavior that is observable and measurable.

2. The teacher will select an organized content to be learned in a manner consistent with the logic of the content itself and the psychological demands of the learner.

3. The teacher will employ appropriate strategies for the attainment of desired behavioral objectives.

4. The teacher will evaluate instructional outcomes in terms of behavioral changes.

5. The teacher will demonstrate the competence and willingness to accept professional responsibilities and to serve as a professional leader.

Once the general assumptions underlying a program are explicated, program builders must move on to state general goals. One example of the results of this process is in the assumptions and goals specified for the Personalized Teacher Education Program (PTEP) developed by the Research and Development Center for Teacher Education at The University of Texas at Austin.

Here are some assumptions of the PTEP (Farrington and Wallace, 1972):

> The tempo of change in the world makes it impossible for teacher training institutions to predict what schools will be like several years in advance; rather than anticipating what schools will require of their teachers, teacher educators have to produce teachers who will be responsive to the world they find rather than the world experienced by themselves and their instructors.
>
> Virtually every change designed to improve education is dependent upon the teacher as the chief agent in all planned change.
>
> The problem of fully utilizing *human* resources in terms of human potential and creativity grows larger and more pressing. Only an educational system that stresses personal interaction, individual growth, and institutional sensitivity can penetrate this problem. Otherwise, changes aimed at reducing the problem will simply be additional bureaucratic activity and economic waste.

The resultant rationale for PTEP reads as follows:

> Teacher educators are aware that while good teaching procedures can be determined and applied to the training of prospective teachers, the teacher's success with pupils does not necessarily depend upon the acquisition of skills alone. The teaching act, perhaps more than any other behavioral function, reflects the traits and dynamics of the personalities involved.
>
> For a teacher training program to be adequate to the needs of today's teacher, it must provide skills and knowledge through graduated experiences, including self-knowledge and satisfaction. It must penetrate the dynamics of human interaction so that the teacher may overcome barriers to effective communication with her pupils. But once the teacher has "reached" the pupil, has broken through whatever social or personal bar-

riers existed between them, she is obliged to have something more to offer than herself. For ultimately, the teacher's goal is to provide pupils with tools which not only help them to cope, but which give them the basis for further acquisition of skills and knowledge; the teacher is ideally the "manager" of an environment in which students can find motivation for learning through successful personal interaction.

Within this very general scope, then, the PTE Program can identify outcomes related to:

Increased self-understanding
Increased teaching competency
Increased awareness of professional and personal impact on pupils

The general goals of the program are as follows:

The teacher, having achieved a realistic understanding of the kind of person she is and the way she does her job, will presumably reflect an increased:

. . . freedom to concentrate on perfecting her teaching techniques without fear of criticism or failure.
. . . ability to center her efforts on understanding and assisting her pupils in their learning needs.
. . . ability to empathize with her pupils and cope with their personal needs and concerns.

A more mature concept of personal development is achieved by the prospective teacher as a result of having passed through a comprehensive analysis of herself and her characteristics. This maturity will presumably help the prospective teacher to:

. . . assess the feelings which motivate pupil behavior.
. . . isolate and identify the intellectual and social idiosyncracies which influence learning.
. . . apply treatments commensurate with individual needs.

A deeper understanding of the complexities and importance of interpersonal relations results from the prospective teacher's experience in the counseling/feedback sessions and having achieved an integration of values. The result is:

. . . an understanding of the motives and values which cause her to react in specific ways to social stimuli within the classroom.
. . . an understanding of the impact she has on different pupils.
. . . an ability to assess the results of specific kinds of teaching behavior.
. . . knowledge of which kinds of personal interaction will enhance the child's emotional welfare and ability to learn.

A knowledge of her own improvement as a result of a more realistic *self-appraisal* will give the prospective teacher these tools:

. . . she will encourage her pupils to seek self-honesty.

. . . she realizes the processes of self-evaluation and self-commitment are essential to the pupil's personal and intellectual success and will encourage her pupils toward these procedures.

. . . she sees the need for realistic self-appraisal as the primary step toward her pupils' emotional health.

The prospective teacher's release from self-concern and her awareness of her competency and impact combine to stimulate in her a greater creativity, which gives her:

. . . flexibility in seeking new ways to stimulate the learning environment for her pupils.

. . . a sense of excitement about learning and living, and the knowledge that they are the same thing.

Although specification of assumptions and goals is essential at the beginning of the program development phase it in no way should be construed that assumptions and goals should forever remain fixed in concrete, with no possibility of alteration, extension, or even replacement. It is certainly conceivable that goals will be altered as time goes on and reexamination of the program begins, but the consequences of major changes may be severe. For example, changing goals may mean dropping entire sets of competencies and related instruction and the addition of completely new sets of competencies and related instruction. Deliberation and group concensus will help prevent precipitous decisions.

IDENTIFYING COMPETENCIES

A number of approaches are used in identifying competencies, subcompetencies, and objectives. Before some of these approaches are presented one thing must be made clear: we do not recommend the specification of program competencies by changing all topics of existing courses to behavioral terms. Adding "80 percent," "four out of five," "given this," and "given that" to topics only generates objectives, not competencies. In addition, this is the surest way to fragmentize or atomize a program.

Competencies are generated from the assumptions that are held about the function of the learning task and the concomitant goals set for the learner. This is why we urge so strongly that assumptions be specified prior to the identification of goals and competencies.

There are at least eight sources from which to identify competencies: (1) existing lists, (2) course translations, (3) course translations with safeguards, (4) taxonomic analysis, (5) input from the profession, (6) theoretical constructs, (7) input from clients, including pupils and the community, and (8) task analysis. Each of these sources might be tapped exclusively, but a multisource identification process will probably yield the best results. The remainder of this chapter is devoted to brief descriptions and analyses of each of these sources.

Existing Lists

There are a number of lists of spelled-out objectives and competencies. Many curriculum textbooks now identify not only content topics but also statements of objectives. Before accepting published competencies and objectives at face value, however, remember to compare them with your own assumptions. After snickering at the naiveté or admiring the brilliance of the competencies listed by curriculum designers, you would be well advised to search for and investigate the assumptions of the program for which the listed objectives were originally intended. Perhaps the competencies you reject are integral to a small portion of a program that is an essential cog that cannot be adequately assessed apart from its intended context. Some examples of existing lists of objectives are discussed below.

Elementary science objectives are to be found in *The Behavioral Hierarchy of Science, A Process Approach*. The Instructional Objective Exchange (Box 24095, Los Angeles, Calif. 90024) is a good example of an exchange where curriculum builders can locate objectives and evaluation procedures for topics ranging from preschool to high school levels.

Groups sponsored by such organizations as the American Association for the Advancement of Science have developed prototype competency and objective lists that are now available. The objectives in Exhibit 2.4 come from a list proposed for prospective teachers of elementary school science.

EXHIBIT 2.4 Objectives for Elementary Science Teachers.

A. Ability to investigate. The teacher will demonstrate his ability to carry out an investigation when presented data or a question about a natural phenomenon.

   Given data about the melting of ice when salt is added to it, construct and carry out an investigation to measure the temperature of mixtures of different amounts of ice and salt.

   Given a question about the relationship of the color of the ambient light and the growth rate of plants, construct and carry out an investigation to measure the growth rate of plants in light of different colors.

B. Science as inquiry. The teacher will demonstrate his enthusiasm for teaching science as inquiry to children by emphasizing investigation over memorization of facts.

   When asked by a child why ice floats on water suggest an investigation through which the child might find an answer to the question.

C. Teaching science as inquiry. The teacher will demonstrate confidence in his ability to teach science as inquiry by selecting the inquiry approach rather than the show-and-tell approach.

When asked to teach some children the law of the pendulum, give the children string, steel washers, a stop watch, and meter sticks and suggest that they investigate the relationship between the length of the pendulum and the number of swings per minute.

Preservice Science Education of Elementary School Teachers, American Association for the Advancement of Science, AAAS Misc. Pub. 70-5.

There are any number of competencies and objectives available for professional school curricula as well. The Phase I reports of the model teacher education programs offer literally thousands of objectives, subcompetencies, and competencies for that discipline. Another source of competencies is *The Florida Catalog of Teacher Competencies* (Panhandle Area Educational Cooperative, Chipley, Fla. 32428). Other input for competency-based teacher education programs can be gleaned from lists of competencies and reports from prototype CBTE programs. Chapter 11 in this book identifies and describes some of these programs.

Houston (1972) in his book *Strategies and Resources for Developing a Competency-Based Teacher Education Program* lists thirty-four teacher education competencies that were generated by educators interacting on the question "What does an effective teacher do?" His list is comprehensive and is given in Exhibit 2.5.

EXHIBIT 2.5 Teacher Competencies.

The following list of teacher competencies are stated at a subgoal level; that is, they include a behavioral statement, but not the criteria for successful demonstration of the competence nor the conditions under which it is to be demonstrated.

THE TEACHER AND STUDENTS: DESIGNING AND EVALUATING (PRE-ACTIVE AND POST-ACTIVE)

Diagnosis and Evaluation

1. Administers and interprets standardized tests.
2. Designs and uses teacher-made diagnostic tests.
3. Interviews pupils using Piagetian techniques.
4. Describes environment, values, and needs of students; familiar with background and language of students.

Organizing Classroom

1. Groups students on basis of data.
2. Makes resources and materials accessible to students.
3. Plans for routine tasks.

Goals and Objectives

1. Identifies goals and objectives appropriate to student needs.
2. Organizes instruction around goals and objectives.
3. States criterion-reference objectives correctly.

Planning

1. Plans daily to contribute to long-range goals.
2. Sequences activities and experiences logically and psychologically.

THE TEACHER AND STUDENTS: ACTIVE INTERACTION

Communication

1. Counsels students with personal problems.
2. Asks higher-order questions.
3. Presents instruction using inductive and deductive procedures.
4. Gives clear, explicit directions to students.
5. Responds to "coping" behavior of students.
6. Identifies clues to student misconception or confusion.

Instruction

1. Establishes set (motivation, transitions, classroom environmental conditions) which are varied and appropriate.
2. Employs a variety of instructional strategies (programmed instruction, games, and stimulation).
3. Utilizes instructional materials and resources.
4. Individualizes instruction.
5. Plans activities with children.

Management

1. Uses positive reinforcement patterns with students.
2. Manages classroom environment.
3. Manages deviant behavior.

Interpersonal

1. Builds self-awareness and self-concepts in students.
2. Develops understanding of cultural pluralism concepts in students.
3. Demonstrates sensitivity to others.

Evaluation

1. Monitors classroom interaction and modifies plans on basis of feedback.

THE PROFESSIONAL TEACHER

Self-Improvement

1. Engages in a designed professional development program.
2. Evaluates teaching behavior using coded instruments (interaction analysis, checklists, etc.) and plans for change on basis of results.

Colleagues and Other Professionals

1. Works effectively in an educational team.
2. Evaluates effectiveness of school program and contributes to improvement efforts.

Course Translations

One source of competencies and objectives for a CBE program must be the present curriculum. Planning for competency-based programs should include a reexamination of the goals and assumptions of existing programs, but whatever the outcome, the strengths of ongoing programs cannot be forgotten. Schematically, the course translation approach looks like that shown in Exhibit 2.6. Course content is operationalized into goals, then competencies and subcompetencies, and finally objectives and skills.

Naturally, course translation is the easiest source to follow; all instructors have to do is to change the course content to a different format. On the other hand, even though it is easier, the course translation process is dangerous if it is the total input into a CBE program. In most cases courses have developed in curricula much like the patches on a patchwork quilt. The patches are often put together at random. The gaps and overlaps of the curriculum being used will continue to exist in a course translation approach to competency and objective identification.

Some common overlaps among courses in teacher education stick out like sore thumbs. A recent survey at a major university showed that graduates of its teacher education program felt that the skill they could

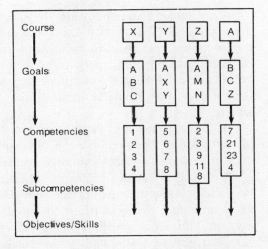

EXHIBIT 2.6 Course Translation as a Source for Objectives.

perform best was writing behavioral objectives. Subsequent examination showed that the topic of behavioral objectives was taught in six separate courses before student teaching. In this same survey it was found that students were often taught to write lesson plans six different ways. Piagetian theory was covered in a minimum of three courses (more if the students were psychology minors).

More serious than the overlaps in this program, however, was the finding that there was considerably less emphasis on classroom management techniques, the role of the administrators, school law concepts that might help or hinder teachers, how to individualize instruction, and how to communicate with parents. Survey input like this could obviously be invaluable in reducing program overlaps if it were rigorously applied.

Course Translations with Safeguards

Several procedures added to the course translation process can increase its value. One procedure is to have instructors specify projections of "ideal" competencies and objectives in addition to their existing course competencies and objectives. Negotiations could then be made among instructors for final content.

A second procedure is to have each faculty member rate, through some technique, the objectives and competencies submitted by other faculty members. A technique such as the Delphi technique might be useful. This technique was developed by Olaf Helmer and his colleagues at Rand Corporation in the early 1950s. As used here, this technique would pool informed, intuitive opinions of faculty through the use of a series of questionnaires.

The data from each questionnaire are analyzed and refined and fed back in the next questionnaire until a near consensus group opinion is reached. This procedure has been used extensively in predicting long-range developments in defense, automation, space research, and other scientific-technological areas and in the field of education. Several national organizations are at present using this technique to aid in the identification of teacher competencies.

Difficulties can arise in such processes as well. One very serious implementation problem occurs as faculty members start raising the question, "Are you telling me what to put in my course?" The answer to that question is, "Not really." But there must be trade-offs between courses. In a total individual parts of the program meet the assumptions of the total education effort there must be agreement with outside sources that the outcomes of program. This enforcement may appear to infringe upon academic freedom, but, in a professional school, professionals must identify those things for which they are going to hold themselves and their graduates accountable and then hold up the various ends of the bargain. There still remains a great deal of what Will Weber calls "wiggle room" for the instructor when it comes to the identification of enabling activities. However, instructors in CBE efforts must reflect upon the assumptions and goals of the total program—goals and objectives that they have agreed to.

Taxonomic Analysis

Another source for the specification of competencies and objectives is a taxonomy of competencies. This taxonomy is a bit different from those proposed by Bloom, Krathwohl, and others. It includes the following:

1. *Cognitive competencies,* which specify knowledge, understanding and awareness.
2. *Affective competencies,* which relate to values, attitudes, interests, and appreciation.
3. *Performance competencies,* which require the demonstration of behaviors.
4. *Consequence or product competencies,* which require the demonstration of the ability to bring about change in others.
5. *Exploratory or expressive competencies,* which provide experiences that may have value for prospective teachers even though specific expected outcomes from the experiences may not be identified or identifiable in advance.

Cognitive competencies and objectives specify the knowledge, intellectual abilities, awareness, and skills that are to be demonstrated. In teacher education, for example, such objectives may apply to the cognitive aspects of disciplines such as science or geography, to psychological theories or the knowledge of educational strategies, or to analysis of curriculum programs.

Affective competencies and objectives are not easily specified or evaluated. This may in part explain why so few of these are included in many programs. Although specification is difficult, objectives and competencies relating to such factors as teacher expectations for boys versus girls, the ability of a person to clarify his own values, or physician attitudes toward terminal patients seem to be crucial to the education and training of most professionals.

Performance competencies and objectives could include psychomotor skills in such areas as physical education or technological education programs. In teacher education, performance objectives include such things as setting up learning centers and asking questions. In most cases performance objectives have as a prerequisite some type of cognitive objective—knowledge of theory being prerequisite to demonstrating a skill, competency, or subcompetency.

Consequence or product competencies and objectives would hopefully be found in most professional school curricula. In such schools the curricula are designed to certify or license qualified personnel. "Qualified" usually refers to the success of the professional in changing others—properly defending a client, saving a life, bringing about learning in pupils. Assessment of consequence objectives is solely in terms of the changes brought about in the client, not what the doctor or teacher does to the client.

Exploratory or expressive competencies and objectives are considered by some as cop-outs. However, there are things that instructors want their students to *experience*. In teacher education, for example, it might be argued that all prospective teachers should attend at least one school board meeting. Attendance is an activity, not an objective (unless it is snowing and the roads to the board room are slippery). Yet many educators think that the school board experience is worth the effort for all students. Exploratory objectives can also be used as the basis behind rationales for internships in teacher education or medical school curricula. Some physicians have also noted the exploratory directive of the U.S. Army in inviting them to intern in the military after medical school.

Looking again at Houston's list of thirty-four competencies, we can see that most of them are either performance or consequence. The consequence objectives are especially evident when counseling techniques are considered. In assessing a teacher's competence it seems much more germane to assess what the teacher is able to do with his pupils than to assess his knowledge of counseling skills.

This points to still another difficulty with using present courses as total input or sources of objectives. Most existing courses emphasize cognitive and exploratory objectives to a great degree and include fewer affective or consequence objectives. The idea of assessing performance and holding students accountable for the objectives of teaching performance is something that has usually been accomplished only minimally because of logistical, monetary, and time limitations. In competency-based programs attempts are made to find the necessary time to emphasize performance and consequence objectives.

Input from the Profession

Another source of input for CBE programs is the membership of the affected profession. In other words, program planners should ask physicians what a preservice medical program should encompass, ask teachers and administrators what preservice programs for educational personnel should include, or survey lawyers on the content of law programs.

In professional schools this professional input might include (1) information on the kinds of objectives and competencies that practitioners wish they had had at the beginning of their professional experiences, (2) information on the needs of practicing professionals as they see them, and (3) information on projections for the future of the profession. However, do not seek this input unless the program developers are receptive. At least one state college of education faculty did not like the answers the local superintendents gave to their questions about the existing teacher education programs. After receiving their first volley of feedback, the faculty returned to the campus and have not ventured out again.

Input from the profession can be gained in a number of ways, not the least of which is the interview. At the University of Houston program developers have been interviewing public school teachers extensively since 1969 to determine the validity of program goals and assumptions. Their findings may be similar to the experiences of the reader. Teachers were typically very willing to share their ideas, but, as a number of teachers have indicated, "Although we'll share, we really don't believe that you are going to put our ideas into your teacher education program. We believe you are doing this just to be polite or to meet some kind of federal guidelines that you have."

With all of this, teacher input has been one of the most valuable assets in identifying the competencies that are included in the Houston CBTE program. If classroom teachers can see that teacher educators are sincere and that their suggestions are included in program developments, then the level of support can only be expected to increase.

Please be cautioned, though, that there may be difficulties if teachers think that everything they say will be included in the program. Often we as teachers are the last to accurately perceive the difficulties that we are having. We are also often the least able to identify the competencies we need to focus on. An example of this was found in an interview one of the authors had with a white teacher who had "crossed over" from a predominantly white to a predominantly black school. This teacher was in her first year of teaching in the black school after three rather lukewarm years at the other school. After raging for an hour over the difficulties she was having with her pupils, with parents, with her colleagues, and with the principal, it seemed that this teacher needed, along with the rest of the faculty and staff, some kind of human relations training. However, when she was asked about what kinds of competencies she would like to focus on for the future, she indicated, "I would really like to know how to run an overhead projector." Regardless of this example, the input that the teaching profession gives not only is valuable but is a necessary part to any teacher education program. Ditto for other professional schools.

Theoretical Constructs

Another area of input for the identification of competencies and objectives is that of the theoretical construct. In this area a theoretical position is assumed by program builders, and competencies can then be specified from the theory. This approach goes a long way toward avoiding one major problem associated with the development of educational programs for professions. If a program certifies a teacher, doctor, dentist, or lawyer for today's conditions, will these same practitioners be able to function in future settings? In addition, will they be self-renewing so that they can meet the needs of their future clients?

Some examples of this theoretical construct input might be useful here. Staff members planning the model teacher education program at Michigan State University generated assumptions and competencies that would be characteristic of teachers who were *clinical behavioral scientists*. At the University of Houston teacher educators use the definition of the *rational decision maker* and the *student of human behavior*. Each of these theoretical models is operationalized, and steps are taken to promote the operationally defined behaviors on the part of graduates.

In the examples cited in Exhibit 2.3 one can see how the different sets of assumptions for each of the model programs generated completely different goals for each. This is due, of course, to the different theoretical positions taken on teaching by each of the model-building staffs.

Projecting in this way keeps the teacher education program from being tied down to the present or the past and allows it to project into the future. We recommend that teacher education theorists do this in planning new programs. A potential difficulty with the theoretical construct approach is that if a "theoretical construct" teacher is certified by such a program, will he be able to fit into the present system? Competencies of self-renewal and acclimatization must be built into such programs as well.

Input from Clients, Including Pupils and the Community

Input from clients allows decision makers to obtain another perspective on professional competence. A good example of this kind of input was demonstrated in the model teacher education program developed at the Northwest Regional Laboratory. The process used by the Northwest lab program builders assumes that a direct relationship can be derived between the needs of pupils, subsequent teacher action's, and teaching competencies; it is depicted in Exhibit 2.7.

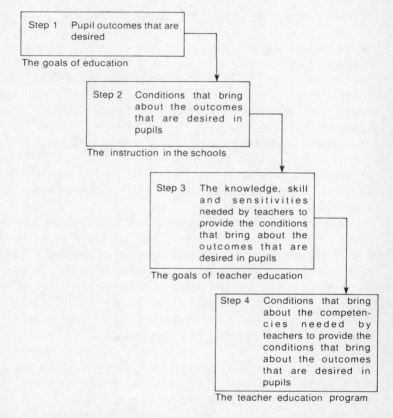

EXHIBIT 2.7 Sequence of Steps in the Systematic Design of a Comfield-Based Program.

A Competency-Based, Field Centered, Systems Approach to Elementary Teacher Education, Final Report, Project No. 89022, Contract No. OEO-0-8-089022-3318(010). Northwest Regional Laboratory, Portland, Oregon, October, 1968.

A similar approach was used by the model developers at the University of Georgia (Johnson, 1969):

> First, it was necessary to project, in the the next decade and beyond, the needs of society and its individuals. Such an investigation is concerned with the economy, technology, political theory, and the values of society. On the basis of this information, the next concern was to project the kind of elementary school that would be most effective in fulfilling its role toward meeting these societal needs as well as producing the kinds of individuals who, through their creative contributions, would be capable of aiding society and themselves toward improvement.
>
> Once the projected needs of society and its individuals were established and the nature of the kind of elementary school which tends to fulfill these needs was determined, the criteria for selecting the various components for the model program were able to be enumerated and the foundation for their justification evidenced.

Another example of this effort coupled with the sixth proposed input for objectives, theoretical construct, can be found in Weigand (1971), *Developing Teacher Competencies.* In this text, Weigand, as editor, postulates that the role of education is the development of students who are rational, inquiring individuals. From this assumption he then postulates five conditions required by the learner:

1. Freedom to explore
2. Time to explore
3. Freedom to make mistakes
4. Freedom to achieve closure at his own pace
5. Freedom to be judged on more than just verbal ability

Weigand and his coauthors then identify seven teacher competencies related to these conditions and offer instruction toward each competency.

Along a similar vein, Cooper, Jones, and Weber (1973) postulated what a teacher following Carl Rogers's ideas about teaching as facilitation might do (see Exhibit 2.8). Note, however, how they intermixed theory with the postulated needs of pupils in schools before identifying teacher competencies.

EXHIBIT 2.8

Assumptions

1. A person learns significantly only those things which he perceives as being involved in the maintenance of, or enhancement of, the structure of self.

2. Education should provide for the development of the personal qualities of the individual learner; it should provide opportunities for him to establish his self-identity; and it should help him pursue his personal objectives.

3. A supportive, nonevaluative environment reduces external threat and facilitates learning.

4. One cannot teach another person anything meaningful that will have significant influence on behavior; one can only facilitate his learning.

Desired Pupil Outcomes

We wish pupils to become individuals:

who are able to take self-initiated action and to be responsible for those actions;

who are capable of intelligent choice and self-direction;

who have acquired knowledge relevant to the solution of problems;

who, even more importantly, are able to adapt flexibly and intelligently to new problem situations;

who internalize an adaptive mode of approach to problems utilizing all pertinent experience freely and creatively;

who are able to cooperate effectively with others in these various activities;

who work, not for the approval of others, but in terms of their own socialized purposes.

Role of the Teacher

The role of the teacher in student-centered instruction occurs in two phases: the creation of an acceptant climate by the instructor, and the development of individual and/or group purposes. General guidelines for creating an acceptant climate are:

Encourage self-revelation rather than self-defense. Give each person a feeling of belonging. Create the impression that difference is good and desirable. Encourage children to trust their own organisms. Emphasize the existential, ongoing character of learning. Finally, acceptance requires the establishment of an atmosphere which is generally hopeful. Such an atmosphere gives the child the feeling that he can be more than he is—the feeling that he has something to bring to this business of education rather than the feeling that all of education means acquiring something from somewhere else for some unpredictable time in the future.

In the development of individual and/or group purposes, the teacher (or facilitator as Carl Rogers would call him) assumes the student's frame of reference, understanding but not judging the pupil's reactions while omitting his own concerns, and clarifies the pupil's attitudes by reflecting them back to the learner so that the pupil himself can be assisted in deciding what to do next. Further, the teacher organizes and makes available the resources that the pupils may wish to use.

Teacher Competencies

The following are some teacher competencies that are consistent with and derived from the role of the teacher as a facilitator of learning:

1. The teacher will clarify student's attitudes by reflecting them back to the learner.
2. The teacher will guide pupils through processes which will help them to clarify values that they hold.
3. The teacher will guide pupils in using a systems approach to solve a problem identified by the pupils.
4. The teacher will create a supportive learning environment that provides learning resources in response to the needs and desires of the pupils.

These attempts at a client-first approach are valuable assets to program builders, especially when the program is concerned with professional education's unique role with inservice professionals. Although certainly applicable in other professional schools, a real breakthrough in teacher education, especially in the inservice function, is seen in a study of the Needs Assessment Program developed at the University of Houston by Robert Houston and Richard Bain (1973):

> A needs assessment system provides an opportunity to receive input from and impact the various sub-systems related to the educational system. These targets of the change process include community (parents, business and civic groups, pressure groups, voters, board of education—both as individuals and as groups), professional educators (administrators, teachers, teacher trainers, and other educational workers), educational institutions (schools, teacher training institutions, and professional organizations), and students (both elementary and secondary). Any significant attempt to change the educational program in the school inevitably affects all of these various groups to a certain extent. Each will react in accordance to the way it perceives its interest. It may choose to agree or disagree, support or oppose, strengthen or weaken. Only through recognizing this commonality of interests and the systemic nature of change do needs assessment and planned change become relevant.

One value of the needs assessment, obviously, for the classroom teacher is the opportunity to view inservice programs as more than just 4:00 to 6:00 P.M. meetings after school. Needs assessment of inservice populations allows individual teachers to focus on their specific needs. It also promotes curriculum decisions that are more meaningful to local clients.

Before ending this part of the discussion, one other point must be made. A number of federal guidelines, especially in TTT and Teacher Corps programs, call for evidence of input from clients on program decisions. These attempts toward parity have been most successful in a number of cases and have aided in the generation of programs that are relevant to the needs of the community. We would hope that this same flavor could be imparted in other program attempts. Both authors can name a few places where attempts on the part of college curriculum planners have not been received with the most favorable reactions. In several of these cases the curriculum planners have subsequently curled up in their ivory towers and ignored any further outside input. This has always been a danger. With today's societal pressures, this avoidance reaction could be fatal to all professional schools. Let's invite and accept input—input that is a necessity for continued growth of all professions.

Task Analysis

Each of the preceding subsections has, hopefully, presented some ideas on how teacher competencies can be identified. Now for an embarrassing situation. We made the statement earlier that there is a vast amount of instruction in CBTE programs on the topics of behavioral objectives and lesson planning. The question that we are raising now is, *What relationship exists between a teacher who can demonstrate specific skills and his effectiveness as a teacher?* This question is in no small part a source of great wonder to program developers who ask the question, "What competencies are known to be demonstrated by effective teachers?"

The reader might think that this question would be an easy one to answer. Once an answer is obtained, the training program should be relatively easy to build. Joyce (1972) noted, for example:

> To build a training program for a functionary whose job is not very complex, one can frequently arrive at the specifications of the job and hence at the performances required of the functionary by doing a task analysis of what is required to get the job done.

But, Joyce continues, this really is effective only when viewing the job of a technician. When one views the tasks of a professional, it is quickly recognized that what separates technicians from skilled professionals is that the professional is a careful and successful applier of theory—knowing *why* and *when* in addition to *how*. Broudy (1972) lucidly makes this distinction between craftsman and technician in his critique of CBTE.

The difficulties with task analysis data on successful doctors, lawyers, dentists, teachers, and other professionals are such that we are left with very few identified key competencies that have a true research basis. Smith (1971), in observing this fact in teacher education, noted:

> . . . we are forced to conclude that there are few, if any, skills of teaching whose superiority can be counted as empirically established.

Cooper and Weber (1973) are even more adamant:

> Until recently, research conclusions about teacher effectiveness were so skimpy that educators may have been somewhat justified in basing their programs on tradition and speculation.

Of course, the complexity of teaching is only one reason why such research evidence is not available. Rosenshine and Furst (1971), in their comprehensive review of literature on research in teaching performance, make this point quite clear. Of the reviewed studies that used the learning of pupils as a criterion of teaching effectiveness, Rosenshine and Furst were able to identify only eleven teaching behaviors that have reasonable support as being effective:

1. Cognitive clarity of a teacher's presentation
2. The variety or variability of techniques, instructional activities and materials used by the teacher
3. Teacher enthusiasm
4. The orientation of the teacher toward the tasks of teaching, often the degree of businesslike manner in the learning situation
5. The opportunity provided by the teacher for the students to learn what was specified
6. The indirectness of the teacher; such things as using students' ideas in discussion, acceptance of student feeling and using praise or encouragement
7. Use of criticism by the teacher [note, however, that of the eleven identified variables this is the one that had a negative correlation between it and pupil learning]
8. Teacher use of structuring comments such as advanced organizers and set induction techniques
9. Teacher use of higher order questions
10. Teacher's ability to probe or help students probe into answers
11. The perceived difficulty of the course as noted by students, including challenge and the standards set by the teacher.

Of the eleven variables, Rosenshine and Furst note that the first five variables have strong support from the correlational studies and the last six have less support but do "deserve future study."

A point can be made here about the use of research data such as this in building CBE programs. Correlational studies, like those that generated the above data, provide only correlations, not cause and effect. It is also certain that a "good questioning" teacher with low or no "enthusiasm" might be highly ineffective. The key to CBTE efforts is to allow individual prospects to become their own style of teachers while aiding them by focusing on skills that might help them improve in certain areas.

3

assessment of competence

Friend and foe agree, a major problem in competency-based education is assessment of the acquisition of competence. Assessment may appear to the uninitiated as a deceptively simple process. Assessment of teacher education, for example, might seem to require only that one separate the "good" from the "bad" teachers. One merely has to identify the characteristics of "good" and "bad" teaching and then hold teacher candidates strictly accountable to those criteria. Educators who have tried to draw that "simple" line have more sweat than firm criteria to show for their efforts. Everyone seems to have a different definition of "goodness" in teaching. The evaluator must face reliability and validity problems with each instrument that would serve as his measuring tool. The political considerations of assessment can loom ominously whenever pay raises or promotions are at stake.

Anyone considering adopting a competency-based program must keep the problems of assessment firmly fixed in mind as he enters the planning process. The difficulties to be faced are considerable, but there are ways to meet them effectively. We would rather not debate the problems of assessment. We prefer to offer a rationale for effective CBE assessment and to propose some specific techniques that have been useful. We will also identify some research results that should be considered when planning the assessment of programmatic achievements.

A key point to be made in this chapter is that assessment criteria should be a clear reflection of the assumptions upon which the program is based. If, for example, a teacher education program is assumed to be heavily field oriented, then much of the assessment of teacher competencies should be made in school settings. If program builders work from the assumption that a primary object of teaching is to activate changes in schoolchildren, then assessment emphasis ought to be placed on the evaluation of consequence objectives. The assessment of other assumptions may be more or less apparent than in these examples, as we shall discuss in the following sections.

Another major point to be made here is that the use of value-laden criteria such as "good" and "bad" is a futile strategy. More appropriately, assessment must evaluate whether behaviors are "effective" or "ineffective" and whether they are "congruent" or "incongruent."

The schema for this chapter follows:

Page	Heading	Questions
60	Who Is a Good Teacher?	What are some major difficulties in CBE assessment?
63	Knowing-Doing—A Schism	What competencies should be assessed? What criteria exist for assessing competence?
67	Demonstration versus Acquisition	What do you do with the student who is already competent?
69	Summative-Formative Assessment	What is the basis for assessment, evaluation, and grading in CBE?
72	Assessing Cognitive Competencies	What instruments can be used to assess cognitive competencies? What are some problems?
76	Assessing Performance Competencies	How can performance competencies be assessed? What are some problems?
81	Congruence in Teaching	What is the role of the teacher? What do you look for in watching a teacher teach?
89	Assessing Consequence Competencies	How can consequence competencies be assessed? What are some problems?
91	Assessing Affect	How do you assess affect?

WHO IS A GOOD TEACHER?

Exhibit 3.1 describes various people's reactions to the same teacher. The "assessments" were different for each observer, ranging from some who thought the teacher excellent to others who thought her poor. Such ambivalence seems to have firm roots, for as Popham (1972) says, "One observer's Mr. Chips is another observer's Mr. Peepers." The problem is often one of perspective. Two people may observe the same teacher presenting identical lessons to matched pairs of pupils and yet report different levels of competence. This is why there are such things as computer programs to calculate observer "reliability" when using classroom observation systems in research. For the same reason the designers of such observation scales usually avoid subjective judgments like the plague.

EXHIBIT 3.1   A Subjective Description of Teacher Behavior

INTRODUCTION:

Often the only feedback teachers receive are in general terms made by various people. Compare these perceptions of the same teacher.

Superintendent:

This teacher is an excellent professional, she is involved in many extracurricular projects and is currently obtaining her masters.

Principal:

This teacher is involved in many new ideas and activities. She is an exciting person who is involved in many activities in the community, as well as professional. She can always be counted upon to start a project.

Parents:

What an involved person, she can always be counted upon to help with Girl Scouts or a church project. She gives so much of herself and her time. Sometimes my child complains about her being too rough, but my child needs to be told how to behave.

Student:

She is always yelling at me, and I really don't know why. My pencil was broken, so I went to sharpen it—she yelled at me and made me stay after school.

She never lets us do any fun things. Even the experiments are dull—she does them herself or sometimes she'll let one of her "pets" do it for everyone. Last year we got to do our own. She always is doing everything for us—we're not babies anymore.

From: Program of Instruction Specialist in Continuing Education (Vol. 2), CERLI, July 1969.

Researchers are not the only ones concerned with the difficulties of assessing, identifying, and rewarding the "professional" teacher. We have already discussed how taxpayers are showing their increasing discomfort with poor results in education. Much of their ire is directed at the individual teacher, the person with whom their son or daughter interacts in school.

Teaching apparently is the one profession that provides its clients with so little choice. Teachers are not selected by parents or pupils (except in the rare instances of private schools or tutorial arrangements). There is usually an attrition rate that is almost Darwinian for "unsafe" professionals in the areas of law, medicine, and dentistry. If a professional is not capable, his clients will not return. The unlucky clients who were the first to identify "unsafeness" are out of luck, but others learn from the misfortune of a few and generally put the unworthy professional out of business. Teachers, however, do not fall under this rule of survival. Few, if any, public schools actually permit students to select among teachers. Darwin's laws of selection processes therefore cannot typically hold for teachers. Teacher incompetence is tragic and painful and it keeps occurring. This point is even more evident when you consider Popham's (1973) amazing statement:

> A recent search of California's teacher employment records reveals that during the last 40 years not one California teacher has been dismissed on the grounds of incompetence.

Since the founding of the professional schools, program developers have made attempts to guarantee the success of their graduates. However, one would have to be quite naive to believe that the success of teacher education programs is the reason behind the above-mentioned forty-year statistic.

Certain nationwide developments have elevated teacher assessment difficulties out of the plane of intellectual exercise. For example, the California legislature proposed and passed a law in 1971 that fairly boggles the minds of educational assessors. The key stipulations of the law as proposed by Assemblyman John Stull are as follows:

> Each school district must establish its own objective system of evaluation for the annual appraisal of probationary teachers and the biennial appraisal of all other teachers.
>
> In devising its evaluation system the district school board must seek the advice of the local teachers organization.
>
> Each evaluation system must minimally include:
>
> —established standards and techniques for assessing student progress in each area of study.
>
> —assessment of teacher competence as it relates to the established standards.

—assessment of duties performed by teachers as an adjunct to their regular assignments.

—established procedures for ascertaining that teachers are maintaining proper control and a suitable learning environment.

A written evaluation plus a face-to-face meeting must be used to relay the evaluation to the teacher.

The evaluation must include any necessary recommendations for improvement (Popham, 1972).

To the professional educator, the Stull Act may be a stroke of naiveté. To the lay public, it may be a stroke of genius. One thing is certain: the act puts teacher evaluation to a very practical test.

KNOWING-DOING—A SCHISM

In competency-based teacher education there is heavy emphasis on the act of teaching. One factor that compels many faculty to examine CBTE as an alternative is the lack of any evidence that "book learning" makes any real difference in the effectiveness of a teacher's classroom performance. What a teacher *can do* is more important than what he *knows*. We would be mistaken, of course, to say that traditional, experience-based programs do not include performance as one barometer of teacher effectiveness. Rating of performance to determine course achievement, especially of student teaching, has been an important part of most teacher education programs. How then does assessment in competency-based education differ from assessment in an experience-based program? Here are at least three basic differences:

1. There is a much heavier emphasis in CBE on performance throughout the program, not just in the culminating student teaching experience.
2. Student achievement in CBE is not determined by comparing what the student does with other students but is measured by comparing what the student does against predetermined, public objectives.
3. The identification of competence is a more broadly shared decision in CBE. Teachers, paraprofessionals, and administrators as well as college-based teacher educators all share in decisions on competence.

Each of these differences will be expanded upon later in this chapter.

In looking at the assessment of competence in CBE versus experience-based efforts, it might be wise to reconsider the categories of goals and objectives identified by program builders. In assessing a teacher's competence, conscious decisions must be made to focus on:

1. What he knows (cognitive objectives).
2. What his attitudes, interests, and values are (affective objectives).
3. What he does (performance objectives).
4. What his pupils do (consequence objectives).
5. Combinations of these four.

Though most teacher education programs do assess students on each of these types of objective, there are variations of emphasis. To some, the consequence level is the keystone; therefore, heavy emphasis in their programs rests on the consequence objectives. To other program builders, the performance of a teacher over several years is the key to competence. Turner (1972) has generated a hierarchy of assessment strategies that might provide guidance in deciding on an assessment strategy.

Turner notes that a teacher must bring about desirable changes on the part of pupils. He places this at the top of his list.

Performance
+
Consequence
over an extended
period of time

Criterion Level 1. At the highest level, the criterion against which teachers (or teaching) might be appraised consists of two parts. The first part is observation of the acts or behaviors in which the teacher engages in the classroom. The observations must be conducted with a set of instruments which permit classification of teacher behaviors in both the cognitive and affective domains. The second part is systematic analysis of the level of outcomes achieved by the teacher with the pupils he teachers. Outcomes in both the cognitive and affective domains must be included. . . . To be placed at criterion level 1, the . . . appraisal of teacher performance must be conducted over a relatively long period of time, probably at least two years. . . .

Performance
+
Consequence

Criterion Level 2. This criterion level is identical to criterion level 1 except that a shorter performance period is involved.

Performance
only

Criterion Level 3. This criterion level differs from criterion levels 1 and 2 in that pupil performance data are eliminated from the criterion. Judgments about competence or proficiency are thus based on the observable behaviors of the teacher rather than on the pupil outcomes associated with these behaviors.

Performance   *Criterion Level 4.* This criterion level differs from criterion level 3 in that both the teaching context and the range of teacher behavior observed are restricted. The context might be a typical micro-teaching context involving a few categories in the cognitive or in the affective domain.

Performance   *Criterion Level 5.* This criterion level differs from criterion level 4 in that the teacher need not perform before live students (simulated students would be satisfactory). He must, however, be able to produce or show in his behavior at least one teaching skill, e.g., probing.

Cognitive   *Criterion Level 6.* This level differs from criterion level 5 in that the teacher need not engage in producing a performance, but rather, only show that he understands some behavior, concept or principle germane to teaching. Within this criterion several levels of "understanding" can undoubtedly be identified. These levels of understanding can be operationalized by varying the kinds of problems the teacher is asked to respond to in accord with some type of taxonomy, such as Bloom's.

What Does This Mean to Teacher Education?

Most teacher education programs do not include assessment of many competencies at Levels 1, 2, or 3. Performance of a prospective teacher during a student teaching or internship program is the highest criterion achieved in most programs. There are good reasons for this situation.

One major problem underlying the neglect of Levels 1 and 2 is the lack of instrumentation to check out criteria at those levels. Another is that most teacher educators are in situations where the assessment of consequence objectives is recognized as valuable but the program does not allow the time needed to assess competence in these objectives for one hundred students. Kennedy (1973) underscores this point when he notes:

> Another serious and very practical question is that of how much faculty time can a training institution afford solely for the purpose of making multiple observations of students. . . . For example, 16 hours of faculty time would be required for two instructors to observe eight teaching interns in two parent conferences which would last 30 minutes each.

In short, sometimes all we can do is make educated guesses about the performance of teachers and the consequences of their performance. Educated guesses are often aided by data on "objective" written tests. The reader should realize that attempts are made in CBTE efforts to free the instructor from the information-giving role and to place him in a more tenable position to be able to assess performance and consequence objectives. Through the use of interactive instruction, modules, and other aids to self-pacing, instructors should have more contact with individual students, and therefore more opportunities to assess competence in these areas.

Donald Medley and Robert Soar added still more fuel to the cognitive-performance-consequence issue at the 1974 AACTE Regional Conference in Phoenix, Arizona. They each noted difficulties with assessment measures. For example, while cognitive tests that are designed to tap a teacher's knowledge may be objective, practical, and even highly reliable, the validity of such tests must be questioned—Does knowledge make a more effective teacher? There is very little evidence that knowledge about teaching or about subject matter makes any difference in teaching effectiveness. The measurement of consequence objectives is equally gloomy. While the validity of the assessments of whether the pupils learn the objectives can be quite high and the reliability of individual instruments may be high, the impracticality of the assessments precludes their massive use for assessing teacher effectiveness.

A second argument against total reliance on consequence objective assessment as indication of teacher effectiveness is that there are any number of factors over which the teacher has no control that come into play in a classroom. Social status, parent attitudes toward school, and aptitudes and abilities of pupils all affect achievement.[1] Placing the teacher in a position of taking total responsibility for learning seems somewhat unfair and unrealistic. Both Medley and Soar propose that performance criteria be used as the *main* assessment procedures for teacher effectiveness. One reason for their suggestion is the greater practicality and objectivity of the assessment as well as the possibility of having reasonably high validity and reliability. A massive review of the literature by Rosenshine and Furst (1971) also indicates that there is some validity in using performance criteria as predictors of consequence outcomes.

One should not assume, however, that all competencies selected for inclusion in a program must have a validated research base. We are just not that sophisticated yet. While research findings are significant and must be integrated into program planning, the limited inroads that have been made into the thicket of human behavior leave a great deal of wilderness that we are simply going to have to navigate by dead reckoning and intuition. We know there are many competencies still to be tested, but rather than wait for

---

[1] See, for example, Office of Education, *Do Teachers Make a Difference?*, #HE 5.258.58042 (Washington, D.C.: Government Printing Office, 1970).

the final results we must get on with building programs using those components our experience tells us are "right."

Before going into examples of assessment research, one point must be made—Broudy (1972), in his critique of competency-based teacher education programs, makes abundantly clear that the distinction between teacher and technician is analogous to the distinction between artist and craftsman.

We do not mean to imply that a teacher in a classroom or a lawyer in a courtroom does not have to know how, why, and when to do something as well as to be able to do it. The point that is being proposed here is that knowledge, by itself, is not sufficient. To guarantee "safeness," some forms of performance and consequence objectives-competencies (Turner criterion levels 1, 2, 3, 4, and 5) must be demonstrated by the prospective professional. Care should be taken in the selection of objectives-competencies to ensure a balance between cognitive, affective, performance, and consequence objectives in a program. In a balanced program, the prospective teacher will be expected to explain the rationale behind and to predict the best place for as well as demonstrate the competencies and skills required of him. One without the other, however, is folly.

DEMONSTRATION VERSUS ACQUISITION

A key aspect of CBE is that students are held accountable *not* for the acquisition of a specific competency but for the demonstration of that competency. If we want "safe" professionals, we need not hold them accountable for how they acquired the skills, only that they have them.

No aspiring professional enters training without any existing knowledge or experience. Perhaps he has not studied the profession or had experience in it, but he does have some personal resources.

Such personal resources can be a help in getting through CBE programs, especially in being able to "test out of" instructional sequences. Let's look at some examples.

Upon encountering a module such as that shown in Exhibit 3.2, the student would read the prospectus (a rationale describing the value of the competencies) and read the objectives. Since the objectives are stated in advance, the student knows the ground rules for completing the module. If he has acquired the skills in previous experiences, he is *not* held accountable for how he acquired them. All he has to do is complete the preassessment to demonstrate his ability. If he demonstrates the objectives at the stated level of proficiency (90 percent in this example), he exits the module. If not, he may follow the prescription of an instructor or negotiate some other way of acquiring the skill.

In some modules, program developers add another dimension to the

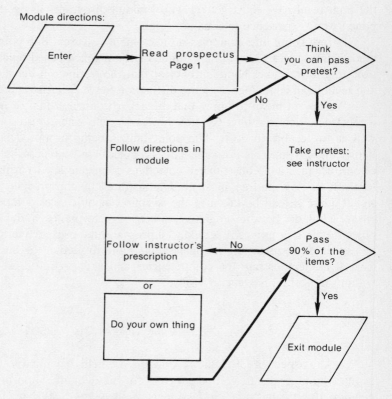

Competency: The prospective teacher states criterion-referenced objectives.

Skill: The student constructs objectives for lessons that consist of action, criteria, and conditions.

EXHIBIT 3.2 Example of Procedure for Students to "Test Out" of Instruction.

preassessment procedure. For example, suppose that *prerequisite* abilities expected of the learner before working on the module had been

a. Classifies objectives as cognitive, affective, or psychomotor (80 percent proficiency).
b. Classifies objectives into Bloom's categories in *The Taxonomy of Educational Objectives* (80 percent proficiency).

Items could be included in the preassessment to assess the student's achievement of these prerequisite skills. If the student did not demonstrate competency in one or more of the prerequisites, an instructor could prescribe additional instructional activities for the student.

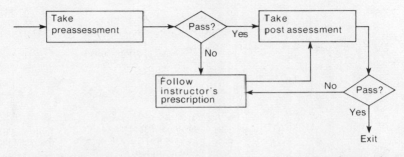

EXHIBIT 3.3   **Flow of Two Assessment Procedures for "Testing Out" of Instruction.**

Some program developers might specify two assessments before passing out the module, as in Exhibit 3.3.

In this case the module builder assessed only enabling objectives (subobjectives) in the preassessment. Perhaps there is evidence that a student could not perform the terminal objective unless mastery was achieved of the enablers. Such a strategy would permit assessment of the enablers in the preassessment, with the postassessment tapping the terminal objective.

Another way to route a student with existing competence is seen in Exhibit 3.4.

A key to this set induction module assessment is the demonstration of the performance objective of set induction. To demonstrate *set* the student must submit a taped episode of his demonstrating the skill with pupils. Of course, the student can make as many tapes as he thinks necessary and only submit for assessment the tape he perceives as the best. Once again, the student is held accountable for demonstration, not acquisition. If the student can perform without going through the module, he is permitted to do so.

SUMMATIVE-FORMATIVE ASSESSMENT

One question that must be raised here deals with the student who "fails" on a preassessment or postassessment. One assumption underlying CBE is that given enough time and instruction, most students can acquire mastery of skills. Unfortunately for many students, learning in most experienced-based programs is packaged into twelve-week quarters, sixteen-week semesters, or thirty-six-week "years." All students start a course with a variety of backgrounds and experiences and end with a range of knowledge and skill. All students go through a set of experiences designed to produce mastery. But mastery must be accomplished at the end of twelve, sixteen, or thirty-six weeks or else a grade of *A* is not acquired. In fact, this grading system is basically a summative, norm-referenced system.

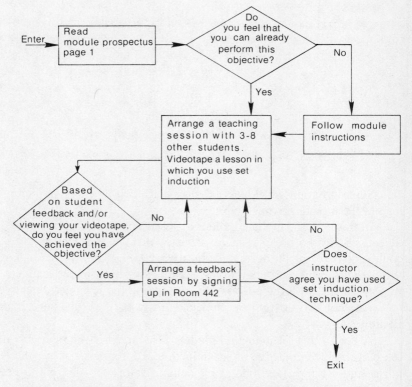

Competency: Establishes set (motivation, transition) that is varied and appropriate.

Skill: Demonstrates set induction techniques of the following types: motivational and transitional.

EXHIBIT 3.4   Example of "Testing Out" of Instruction in Which the Postassessment Procedure Can Also Be Used as a Preassessment.

Summative Evaluation—evaluation from which summary decisions can be made. Summative evaluations typically occur at the end of a unit, chapter, semester, program. Summative evaluation has as its primary goals "grading or certifying students, judging the effectiveness of the teachers, and comparing curricula" (Bloom, 1971).

Summative evaluation is also used in decision making, "go–no go" evaluation. Such tests as the Graduate Record Examination, the Minnesota Teacher Attitude Inventory, most achievement tests, and many observations of teachers (if the observations are made to certify, admit, hire, or fire) are examples of summative evaluations.

Norm-referenced tests and assessment items are called "norm-referenced" because students are compared with each other. A group norm is obtained and is then used as a yardstick to identify whether a given student is above or below the group average. This norm may be called many things —the median, mean, mode, the *C*, or the cutoff point. Norms are sometimes established before a test is given; at other times norms are identified using the test results as data. Teachers often "curve" grades to ensure that a "proper" ratio of *A*s, *B*s, and *C*s are found in a class, and in doing so they are simply comparing students, identifying the best, average, and worst. The responses to the resulting grades vary among students, parents, and teachers. We teachers sometimes respond by going to the movies on the night report cards are sent home.

Since mastery is the goal in competency-based efforts, time becomes subservient to mastery. Some students will take less time to achieve mastery than others (perhaps because of greater aptitude). Research results indicate that these late bloomers are no less competent in the long run. For example, Taylor, Smith, and Ghiselin (1963) showed that on-the-job performance of scientific researchers is not related to better college grades. In their findings the average college grades for the top third of the scientific researchers was a *B*—, the average for the bottom third was also *B*—.

In CBE efforts, program implementers typically are less concerned about comparing students with each other than they are about comparing student abilities against preset criteria. Their system is typically a formative, criterion-referenced system. *Formative evaluation* is evaluation from which prescriptive decisions are made.

> Formative evaluation, as the name implies, intervenes during the formation of the student, not when the process is thought to be completed. It points to areas of needed remediation so that immediately subsequent instruction can be made more pertinent and beneficial (Bloom, 1971).

In a *criterion-referenced* system, student achievement is compared not against other students' achievement but against prestated objectives.

In competency-based education programs, the distinction between summative–norm-referenced and formative–criteria-referenced assessment is more than just an intellectual exercise. In CBE, success is achieved only when the student demonstrates that he can perform the required objectives. The student does not receive a letter grade on the objective, but instead his achievement is recorded with a "yes," a "pass," a "completed," a "finished," or some other notation. If he cannot demonstrate the attainment of an objective, that fact is recorded with a "no," a "fail," a "not yet," an "incomplete," or something; he gets the opportunity to try again, perhaps after another prescription from an instructor. Robert Mager calls this the philosophy of the success-oriented school. In such settings total failure is infrequent because students are given more than one chance to learn. In fact, students get chances to learn until they *do* learn. This, of course, reflects on the definitions of aptitude and mastery learning described in Chapter 1.

Such "yes–not yet" records on individual skills, objectives, or subcompetencies or competencies do not preclude the use of grades in CBE efforts. In a number of institutions, the elimination of grades from a system will be next to impossible. Grades can still be computed by identifying a lower limit of acceptable skill as a *B* or a *C,* with higher grades being reserved for more proficient behavior. Similarly, since courses will consist of a number of subcompetencies or skills, course grades can be calculated by averaging "grades" on each of the enablers. The basic difference in grading with CBE is that the student knows in advance how grades will be determined, and he is aware that his grade will not be determined by comparing his behavior with that of other students.

ASSESSING COGNITIVE COMPETENCIES

Competency-based efforts typically do not lower the amount of cognitive information required of a student prior to certification or licensure. In fact, cognitive competencies are considered by most program developers to be prerequisite to adequate demonstration of performance and consequence objectives. Knowledge for knowledge's sake, however, is replaced with knowledge for action's sake. Nonetheless, cognitive competencies must be assessed, and they can be assessed in a number of ways.

One obvious method of assessing cognitive competency, of course, is the written test. For the teaching performance competency "Asks Higher-Order Questions," the teacher would have to demonstrate the higher-order questioning skill in a teaching situation. But prior to demonstrating this skill, the teacher would have to "know" what a higher-order question is. Enabling objectives such as the following could be assessed in written form:

Enabling Objective: Identify higher-order questions.
 Assessment: Check which of the questions below are higher-order questions. (A list of questions would then be given.)
Enabling Objective: State higher-order questions.
 Assessment: For each of the memory-level questions below, restate the question in terms of a higher-order question. (A list of questions would then be given.)
Enabling Objective: Classify questions into Sanders categories.

> Assessment: Label each of the questions below with the appropriate Sanders term. (A list of questions would then be given.)

The choice of enabling objective, of course, would be up to the instructor or program builder, who would also set the criteria (80 percent, four-out-of-five, etc.) in advance as well as let students know in advance what the criteria are.

Similarly, in a session in which the prospective teacher demonstrates skill at asking higher-order questions, he or she should be able to identify when and why the specific questions were used. This post hoc cognitive analysis is one method of aiding the reviewer of the lesson in assessing whether the prospective teacher has a rationale for, as well as skill in, questioning.

Suppose that a major assumption behind the program was that "teachers should be students of human behavior." Based on this assumption, program developers could decide to have students study the work of Piaget. This decision might be focused on this among other reasons: "To aid students in understanding more fully the cognitive development of human beings." The program developers might also propose that the student will be able "to demonstrate background knowledge of the cognitive development of children." This goal is obviously somewhat ambiguous unless it is operationalized—perhaps into the following objectives (from Jones, 1972):

1. As a result of this section you should be able to *describe, define,* and *give* examples of the following terms as they are related to Piaget's theories: Sensori-motor stage, pre-operational stage, concrete-operational stage, formal-operational stage, assimilation, accommodation, equilibration, states vs. transformations, centering, egocentrism, transductive thinking, identity, additivity, associativity, reversibility, class inclusion, conjunction, disjunction, negation, implication, conservation, causality, seriation, logical-mathematical, and physical properties.
2. Given a list of topics/content, *Identify* those topics suitable for teaching pre-operational, concrete-operational, and formal-operational children. (80% minimum)
3. Given a list of possible tactics/strategies for science teaching, *Identify* those tactics/strategies suitable for use with pre-operational, concrete-operational, and formal-operational children. (80% minimum)
4. Given a problem situation, *Predict* the responses of a pre-operational, sensori-motor, concrete-operational, or formal-operational child. (80% minimum)

Instruments, then, could be developed to assess each of the objectives. For example, Objective 1 could be assessed by having the student either describe, define, in his own words, or give classroom examples of each of the terms that is identified in Objective 1. For the last three objectives, assessments such as these may be appropriate:

Objective 2

Here are three stages of cognitive development:

P—Preoperational
C—Concrete-operational
F—Formal-operational

Below you will find five tasks, each of which describes a science topic that you might wish to teach to children. In the space to the left of each task, write the letter (*P, C,* or *F*) of the lowest stage for which the topic described would be suitable.

_____ *Task A:* Given a solid, 3-D shape, the child will be able to draw a 2-D drawing of the shape that shows the unseen back edges of the shape.

If you answered *P,* go on to the next task. If you answered *C* or *F,* circle the number of the statement below that best describes why the topic would not be suitable for the stage(s) of cognitive development that *precede(s)* the stage you selected.

1. No conservation characteristics.
2. Centering would cause difficulty.
3. Problem with states vs. transformations.
4. The content is mainly logical-mathematical.
5. No class inclusion.

(And so on through four more tasks.)

Objective 3

Below are five tactics that might be used by teachers working with elementary children. In the space to the left of each tactic, write the letter (*P, C,* or *F,* as outlined in Objective 2) of the lowest stage for which the tactic would be suitable.

_____ *Tactic A:* "Bill, I know you are upset that your frog died. But there are others just like him. We'll get another tomorrow."

If you answered *P,* go on to the next tactic. If you answered *C* or *F,* circle the number of the statement below that best describes why the tactic would not be suitable for the stage(s) of cognitive development that *precede(s)* the stage you selected.

1. Child does not have implication operation.
2. Child does not have identity operation.
3. Child is unable to use associativity.
4. Problem is with egocentrism.
5. Problem is with transductive thought.

(And so on through four more tactics.)

Objective 4

Below are five situations in which an adult is communicating with a child in a specified stage of cognitive development. In the space provided below each situation, predict (in one brief sentence) how you think the child might respond to the adult. Then, from the list of terms given below, select the term that best explains the child's predicted response. Put the number of this term in the space to the left of the situation.

1. Early class inclusion
2. Conservation of volume
3. Negation
4. Centering
5. Lack of class inclusion
6. Implication
7. Reversibility
8. Additivity
9. Transductive thinking
10. Conservation of quantity
11. Identity
12. States vs. transformation

_____ *Situation A:* A teacher gives two boys equal amounts of cola. One boy (four years old) gets his cola in a short, wide container. The other boy (concrete-operational) gets his cola in a tall, narrow container. The four-year-old protests that he has less cola than the other boy. What might the other boy say?
(And so on through four more situations.)

A few notes about assessing cognitive competencies must be inserted here.

1. Standardized tests are typically not very useful in assessing CBE efforts. Standardized tests are usually norm-referenced and used as summative devices. The assessment of CBE efforts is best considered formative

(try–try again) and criterion-referenced (compare with objectives). Unless the standardized instruments are such that the individual items or sections can provide formative data to help students and faculty with program decisions, it will be most difficult to use these standardized tests except to satisfy prospective employers who insist on comparative data (summative) on program graduates.

2. Don't write objectives if you aren't going to assess them, and don't assess objectives that students don't know are in the program.

3. In self-paced programs the question of cheating on cognitive tests is an important issue. The threat of cheating inspires the development of alternative forms of tests, security, and often an aura of mistrust on the part of students toward each other and certainly between faculty members and students. Part of this comes from habits associated with the use of norm-referenced criteria. When students are compared in order to identify grades, they must compete, and competition often leads to win-lose situations among students. Criterion-referenced systems establish a better climate for cooperation among students. In most existing CBTE efforts this cooperation is apparent.

Much of the distrust of student motives can be alleviated if faculty members will consider the function of cognitive competencies. Most cognitive competencies are included in programs because the knowing is prerequisite to the doing. Even if the student "fudges" a little on *Identifying Higher-Order Questions,* he still has to ask them of his pupils. If he cannot, then he is stuck.

4. To get around some of the testing difficulties, some institutions have developed operations centers where tests are kept. When a student is ready to take a test he reports to the operations center. Undergraduate and graduate assistants take care of administering and, often, of grading tests. In other schools, testing days are set aside and students are prohibited from taking the instruments except on those days. At Weber State College, to avoid the procrastination of students who wait until the last week before vacation to "complete" all their work, deadlines for testing were set. There are certain periods of time when no tests can be taken. One such period of time is during the week before and during final exams when students are completing finals in courses other than those in education.

ASSESSING PERFORMANCE COMPETENCIES

There seems to be a consensus that a key focal point for CBE assessment should be what the professional does in the performance of his profession. And, as mentioned earlier, performance assessment seems like a rather simple task . . . to anyone who hasn't tried it. Unfortunately, many people who *haven't* tried it get elected to school boards and to the legislature. Two chapters of *The Second Handbook of Research on Teaching* (AERA, 1973) are most useful to program developers who are interested in the assessment of performance criteria. The chapter by Barak Rosenshine and Norma Furst, "The Use of Direct Observation to Study Teaching," and the chapter by John D. McNeil and W. James Popham, "The Assessment of Teacher Competency," are excellent sources of information. In each of these chapters the authors describe many assessment instruments that have been used in past research studies to identify teaching performance. No attempt will be made here to add to the storehouse of information provided by these authors. However, we must emphasize that research studies are different from the development of programs. Having different assumptions, program developers might develop totally different criteria for assessing performance skills.

Whatever observation systems are designed for use in CBE efforts, there must be an attempt to make the criteria public—especially to the student being observed. The student should know what is being observed. Hidden agendas of observers can do much to engender mental (and sometimes physical, if the observee is bigger than the observer) damage, damage that may be irreparable.

Many observational devices have been developed for use in observing classroom behaviors. The most well known are forms of the interaction analysis technique developed first by Ned Flanders (1960). A modification of the Flanders system that we have found beneficial in competency-based efforts is the IAST Base system developed by one of the authors of this book (Hall, 1969, 1973). The IAST Base instrument consists of the following fourteen categories:

1. Accept feelings: recognizes and identifies with feelings of students (empathetic), nonevaluative encouragement or joking positive response.
2. Praise: a positive value judgment.
3. Acceptance of student's statements: a restatement of the student's statement, either written on the board or verbal. This category would also include short, nonevaluative confirmation such as "okay," "all right," or such responses as "no," "not quite," "maybe."
4. Question: all questions that require a student response.
5. Direction: giving directions and procedures; telling the students how to do something. This requires an *immediate* student response or behavior.
6. Initiate substantive information: lecturing, giving facts, calculat-

THELONIUS P. GARTH   636003   TAPE 3   LESSON 3

DATA
```
14101011101  4 9 9  9 4 9 9 8 6 6 6 6 6 6 6 5 5 9 9 9 6 9 9 9 3 8
 6  4 21212 912 9 91212121 81212131 6 6 6 911111 6 6 6 6 9 9 9 9 9
 6  5 512121212121212 913 913 912121213 6 6 9 9 5 5121212121213 911
13  8  9 913141212124 9 6 9 5 5 8 9 3 6 6 81212121513121212121 2
13  913 912  4 4 9 21010 1 9 5 5 6 6 6121212 913121213121213 913 9
 91212 412  4 9 9 9 6 6 6 8 5 5 4 4 5 914
```

TALLY MATRIX FOR   THELONIUS P. GARTH   636003

	1	2	3	4	5	6	7	8	9	10	11	12	13	14	15	ROW TOTALS
1	0	0	0	1	0	0	0	0	1	1	0	0	0	0	0	3
2	0	0	0	0	0	0	0	0	1	0	0	0	0	0	0	1
3	0	0	0	0	0	1	0	1	0	0	0	0	0	0	0	2
4	0	0	0	3	1	1	0	1	5	0	0	1	0	0	0	10
5	0	0	0	1	13	1	0	1	3	0	0	3	0	0	0	22
6	0	0	0	1	2	20	0	3	5	0	0	0	0	0	0	31
7	0	0	0	0	0	0	0	0	0	0	0	0	0	0	0	0
8	0	0	0	0	2	2	0	1	2	0	0	2	0	0	0	9
9	0	1	2	1	1	4	0	1	17	1	1	8	6	1	1	47
10	3	0	0	0	1	1	0	0	0	0	0	0	0	0	0	6
11	0	0	0	0	0	1	0	0	2	0	0	0	1	0	0	4
12	0	0	3	3	0	5	0	1	4	0	1	30	8	0	0	47
13	0	0	0	0	0	1	0	1	10	0	0	2	0	1	0	15
14	0	0	0	0	0	0	0	0	0	0	0	1	0	0	0	2

COLUMN TOTALS   3   1   2   10   22   31   0   9   47   6   4   47   15   2   199

CATEGORY	TALLIES	PERCENT		CATEGORY	TALLIES	PERCENT
1	3	1.5		8	9	4.5
2	1	.5		9	47	23.6
3	2	1.0		10	6	3.0
4	10	5.0		11	4	2.0
5	22	11.1		12	47	23.6
6	31	15.6		13	15	7.5
7	0	0.0		14	2	1.0

RATIO 1 (I/D)= 16/ 53 = .30   RATIO 2 (S/T)= 53/ 69 = .77   RATIO 3 (REVISED I/D)= 6/ 22 = .27

EXHIBIT 3.5

THELONIUS P. GARTH   636003   TAPE 3

THE FOLLOWING INFORMATION IS A PROFILE OF YOUR TEACHING BEHAVIOR BASED ON AN OBSERVERED LESSON YOU TAUGHT.
THE FIRST PART OF THE PROFILE IS A BAR GRAPH INDICATING THE PERCENT OF CLASS TIME SPENT IN EACH TYPE
OF TEACHING BEHAVIOR. IN THE DESCRIPTION OF THE BEHAVIOR CATEGORIES THE SYMBOLS (T) AND (S) ARE USED
FOR THE WORDS -TEACHER- AND -STUDENT-,RESPECTIVELY. EACH ASTERISK IN THE GRAPH REPRESENTS 1 PERCENT.
THE SECOND PART OF THE PROFILE IS A SERIES OF STATEMENTS WHICH REFLECT SOME GENERAL TRAITS OF YOUR TEACHING THIS SPECIFIC LESSON
THIS SUMMARY REPORT WILL,HOPEFULLY,GIVE YOU A BETTER PERSPECTIVE OF YOUR TEACHING.

CATEGORY NUMBER AND DESCRIPTION

1   (T) ACCEPTS STUDENTS FEELINGS   *
2   (T) PRAISES STUDENTS
3   (T) ACCEPTS STUDENT STATEMENTS   *****
4   (T) ASKS QUESTION   **********
5   (T) GIVES DIRECTIONS   ***************
6   (T) PROVIDES SUBSTANTIVE INFO   ****
7   (T) CRITICIZES STUDENT IDEA
8   (T) CONTROLLED SILENCE   ***********************
9   (S) MAKES STATEMENT   ***
10 (S) ASKS QUESTION   **
11 (S) GIVES AFFECTIVE RESPONSE
12 (S) INVOLVED IN ACTIVITY   **********************
13 (S) INTERACTS WITH STUDENTS   *******
14 (S) NONFUNCTIONAL BEHAVIOR   *

         ----
         0   10   20   30   40   50   60   70   80   90

                                      PERCENTAGE

ID1 YOU USED 5 TIMES MORE DIRECT BEHAVIORS THAN INDIRECT BEHAVIORS.

ST1 FOR EACH INCIDENCE OF STUDENT TALK,YOU TALKED 2 TIMES AS MUCH.

WT1 AFTER YOU ASKED A QUESTION, 16 PERCENT OF THE TIME THERE WERE AT LEAST THREE SECONDS OF WAIT TIME BEFORE A STUDENT RESPONDED.

GENE HALL AND CHARLES GOUGE---ATH PROGRAM--- R AND D CENTER FOR TEACHER EDUCATION--UNIV. OF TEXAS AT AUSTIN

EXHIBIT 3.5 (cont.)

79

ing, writing new information on the board, and review of information, including reading to students.

7. Justification or authority: disciplinary action and criticism of a student's behavior would be included in this category (determined by intent).

8. Teacher-controlled silence: periods of silence which would include teacher demonstration or a teacher examining her notes.

9. Student statements: this would include all student statements that are not questions.

10. Student questions: questions asked by the students of one another or of the teacher would be placed in this category.

11. Affective response: student responses that reflect student emotions or feelings about a certain topic; warm laughter.

12. Student activity: this would include such activity as students working in workbooks, reading silently to themselves or working with scientific apparatus, reading aloud, whole-group responses, non-verbal answers.

13. Division of student-to-student interaction: a mark for the separation between two students' interactions.

14. Nonfunctional behavior: behavior without direction or purpose where no effective instruction is occurring.

The observer uses the IAST Base system in a classroom by coding, every three seconds on an optical scan sheet, the identified code number reflecting his perception of what is happening. A computer program then uses the information prepared on the marked sense sheet to print out a matrix like the one shown in Exhibit 3.5.

Suppose that prior to a teaching session, a student asks an observer to focus on his question-asking skill. The student indicates that he will attempt to get (1) increased pupil involvement by (2) asking probing questions. Without analysis tools the observer would have to rely on his opinions and do the best possible job of sharing with the student his success or lack of success in increasing pupil involvement and asking probing questions. With systems such as the IAST Base, the observer can identify on a matrix whether or not it was likely during the time of observation that probing questions were asked. To demonstrate the skill of probing questions, the analysis would have to show a relatively high frequency of 9-4 (pupil response–teacher question) or 9-3-4 (pupil response–teacher acceptance of student response–teacher question) transition pattern. Similarly, the I/D ratio, a measure of the indirectness of teacher behaviors, would vary depending on the frequency of probing questions. In a classroom that had a large amount of student involvement, the I/D ratio should be higher than 1.00.

By themselves these measures are meaningless. There is no good or bad I/D ratio or degree of 9-4 categorizations. The meaning is only evident when applied in a formative sense. In a formative sense the teacher would be able to receive an organized and, in this case, quantified feedback to aid in identifying a *need* for modifying behavior, especially if a discrepancy is identified. However, if such instruments as the IAST Base are used as summative devices, then their effect is minimized. In essence they are useful instruments in determining congruence or lack of congruence. *Congruence* here is defined as the degree to which a teacher demonstrates predicted or predetermined performance.

Even checklists like those shown earlier in Exhibit 2.2 (p. 33) are useless when summative assessment stances are taken. In using the Proficiency Analysis Rating, the prospective teacher typically specifies the competencies that he wishes the observer to watch for. The observer then focuses on these competencies, helping the prospective teacher identify in postobservation sessions the success or problem areas that he perceives. In this illustration also, all of the data gathering and reporting is accomplished with a formative perspective—the "yes–not yet" philosophy holds for each competency.

The application of formative clinical supervision behaviors in providing feedback to teachers calls for a change in faculty role and value position. In other chapters in this book, this changing role is described in detail, but for the time being it is important to note a point made by Bowen (1973):

> The greater the psychological maturity of the supervisor, the more he will view such observational systems for non-oppressive ends. As a consequence of experiences in seeing himself, the teacher becomes a more autonomous person. The greater his autonomy, the greater value he will see in that condition for *his* teaching of children.

CONGRUENCE IN TEACHING

To the writers, one of the major difficulties associated with the assessment of teaching performance is that all too often the assessor and the assessee have different ideas about what is "good teaching." This is reflected in the following story told to one of us by an obviously upset student:

> You told me to get the kids actively involved in my science lesson. You told me to use manipulative materials so that the kids could discover some things on their own. So I did. I used a great motivation set induction and

then the kids went to work. My student teacher supervisor came in when the kids were working and I was helping out individual groups. I thought the whole exercise went beautifully, but during our conference he told me that during the next time he came out he wanted to see me teach, not the kids playing.

There are a multitude of effective teaching models and there probably is not one model that is *better* than another. Before performance can be assessed, it is important to make certain that everyone knows what is being looked at.

In *Models of Teaching* (1972), Bruce Joyce and Marsha Weil identify sixteen different models of teaching that are useful for both teachers and observers of teachers.

Joyce and Weil categorize the sixteen identified models into four families: Social Interaction, Information Processing, Personal Sources, and Behavior Modification. Each of the families promotes different goals, and each of the models provides some variation for achieving the goals with pupils. It is probably true that each teacher has an eclectic model, made of parts of several models described by Joyce and Weil. Teacher effectiveness can be construed if a teacher's pupils achieve preset goals. Similarly, a teacher's *congruence* of teaching behaviors can be assessed by comparing his performance with those competencies, subcompetencies, and objectives found in a model.

In the following descriptions of teaching models, we have tried to identify several significant teaching performances based on the Joyce and Weil categories. The identification may be useful to builders of CBTE programs in projecting competencies, subcompetencies, and teaching skills for their program. It should also aid program builders in assessing the teaching performance of prospective teachers.

FAMILY: Social Interaction
TEACHING MODEL: JURISPRUDENTIAL

In this model public issues are identified by teacher and learners, and the teacher promotes a dialogue through teacher-moderated discussion to generate solutions to the issues. There typically is a moderate-to-high structure on the part of the teacher; however, openness of the teacher to other opinions is important.

Necessary teacher competencies to promote the Jurisprudential Model:

a. The teacher accepts views toward controversial issues that are different from his own.

b. The teacher is able to promote group discussion toward solution.

An observer watching a teacher who is employing the Jurisprudential Model as a strategy might look for the following:

a. In what incidents did the teacher demonstrate acceptance and not rejection of "way-out" ideas?
b. How many students were really involved in the discussion?
c. Was there evidence that the pattern of interaction was teacher to student to student to teacher more times than it was teacher to student to teacher to student?
d. If Flander's interaction analysis techniques were used, were the I/D and modified i/d ratios considerably greater than 1.00?

A point here is that the performance of a teacher using the Jurisprudential Model cannot be assessed as either good or bad. However, the teacher's performance can be assessed by checking for congruity—Was the teacher's behavior congruent with the model? If so, the performance was satisfactory. Observers in a CBTE effort who view less than congruity still have the responsibility for helping the teacher become even more congruent.

FAMILY: Social Interaction

TEACHING MODEL: SOCIAL INQUIRY

In the Social Inquiry Model the teacher, in a moderately structured sequence, presents a puzzling situation to students and helps them develop hypotheses or solutions, explore solutions, and gather facts to support or reject the solutions suggested.

An observer watching a teacher using the Social Inquiry Model might look for the following:

a. Effectiveness of the teacher's set induction.
b. How many students were actually involved in this discussion?
c. Did the teacher help students focus on solutions by using probing questions?
d. Since the emphasis is on the student's inquiry, did the teacher reward the students for inquiry more times than for their correct answers?
e. Were the I/D and modified i/d ratios significantly greater than 1.00?

The reader might note here that there is a considerable overlap between the competencies and possible assessment procedures of the Jurisprudential Model and the Social Inquiry Model. Since both are from the same family

(Social Interaction), this may be expected. Yet there are also differences between the two models. The Jurisprudential Model is more of a debate; the Social Inquiry Model is one in which the teacher acts as a sharpener, focuser, and counselor to inquiry and helps students clarify positions through learning how to inquire.

Let's jump now to another totally different group of teaching models. Joyce and Weil refer to this group as the Information Processing Family, and all of the members of this family have one thing in common: ". . . their primary sources are the student's capacity to integrate information and to process it." The role of the teacher and the content selection in each of these models show a wide variance.

While Joyce and Weil describe six models in the Information Processing Family, for our examples we will present only three.

FAMILY: Information Processing

TEACHING MODEL: INDUCTIVE TEACHING

In this model, developed by Hilda Taba (1967), the attempt is made to help students develop and use categories. In essence, the approach is one of teaching inductive thinking.

Some examples of teaching competencies follow. The teacher should be able to

a. Sequence content and suggested learning experiences in terms of the pupil's background.
b. Ask divergent questions.
c. Ask probing questions.
d. Be nonjudgmental to pupils' responses.
e. Reinforce creative answers on the part of the students rather than "pat" answers.

Among other things, an observer watching a Taba lesson might observe to see if the leader

a. Uses the group background as input in planning the lesson.
b. Guides classroom discussion just by asking questions.
c. Responds and reinforces student questions by means other than "good," "that's right," and the like.

Compare the Inductive Teaching Model with the following.

In the Advance Organizer Model, Ausubel (1963) postulates that each discipline has an orderly set of concepts and that the structural concepts of the discipline can be identified and taught to students. This becomes the teacher's role. First through the use of *advance organizers* ("any idea, image, recollection, abstraction"), and then presenting the material in more specific terms, the teacher helps students focus on the important concepts of the discipline.

Some examples of teaching competencies:

a. The teacher is able to describe relationships with clarity.
b. The teacher uses set induction techniques for motivation purposes.
c. The teacher demonstrates a high degree of organization in presentations.

An observer assessing the competence of the teacher using an Advance Organizer approach would certainly have to reflect on the clarity of the set induction techniques and the organization of the strategies. Input from pupils who have gone through the lesson to these parameters of the lesson here might be a highly effective assessment procedure.

Note how both the Advance Organizer Model and the Inductive Teaching Model push students toward conceptualization. Note also that there are distinct differences in the models—one is deductive, the other is inductive.

Contrast these two models with a model representative of most science curriculum development in the past fifteen years.

In this model the teacher presents the student with an area of investigation from which the students identify a difficulty. Students are then asked to infer some explanations about the problems and to propose ways of clearing up the difficulty, often carrying out an investigation to test their inferences.

Some examples of teaching competencies:

a. The teacher uses motivational set inductions.
b. The teacher asks divergent questions.
c. The teacher uses probing questions.
d. The teacher places the burden of learning on the student and is

acceptant of students' answers that are congruent with the information the students have been given.

An observer in an inquiry classroom might look for the following:

a. In what ways did the teacher reinforce "good thinking" rather than "correct answers?"
b. Were a large number of pupils involved in the lesson?
c. Are interaction analysis I/D and i/d ratios significantly greater than 1.00?
d. Do students challenge evidence and criticize research designs instead of placing responsibility for the entire lesson, organization, and critique on the teacher?

Note that if an observer of a Science Inquiry Model classroom and an observer of a Jurisprudential Model classroom compared notes they might find some similarities. One basic difference between the models may be in their outcomes: in a Jurisprudential Model the outcome is one of group decision on a social problem; in a Science Inquiry Model the outcomes are increased inquiry skills of students.

It might be interesting here to postulate reasons for different reactions of students to teachers who each use a unique model of teaching. If a student spends ten to twelve years in a classroom in which his teachers follow a modified Advance Organizer Model and is then suddenly faced with a Science Inquiry Model teacher, it can be disconcerting. A teacher must recognize some possible difficulties with changing models. This latter point will be reinforced later when we discuss some difficulties of students who go through college following an Advance Organizer Model and are then faced with instructional systems in CBE that typically call for a different focus.

While some models of teaching reflect societal goals and those of individuals in society and others reflect information-processing outcomes, still another family of models reflects the individual person as a source of educational ideas. This is the Personal Sources Family. As Joyce and Weil note:

> . . . while the focus is on helping the person to develop a productive relationship with his environment and to view himself as a capable person, and although most of the model-builders in this group believe that the relationship between individual learner and his teacher is central to the learning process, it is expected that one of the products will be a richer interpersonal relationship and a more effective information-processing capacity.

Joyce and Weil identify five such models in this family, two of which will be described here.

A teacher using this model would adhere to William Glasser's tenets of Reality Therapy. The goals of the teaching strategies of Reality Therapy are to help the student deal with failure, with the emphasis being on the student's reaching success. The emphasis on interpersonal areas of self-understanding and self-responsibility of this approach contrasts greatly with the emphasis on Information Processing described earlier in this chapter.

Some examples of teaching competencies:

a. The ability to establish a climate of involvement.
b. The teacher being able to demonstrate a warm, personal, interested, and sensitive relationship with the student.
c. The teacher demonstrating a nonjudgmental characteristic.
d. The teacher's skill in discussion techniques toward topics relevant to students.

An observer watching the teacher using the Classroom Meeting Model might note

a. The degree of trust between the group and the teacher, e.g., the learners' lack of reticence in asking teacher's opinions and the amount of sharing of other than "school" topics.
b. The degree to which the teacher helps students focus on personal problems.
c. The follow-through of a teacher to push the student to meet with a negotiated contractual solution.

Note that the emphasis of this latter model is on the identification and solution of often unique personal problems or goals, not group solutions of social problems or the development of information-processing skills. A similar emphasis can be seen in the next model.

This model is derived directly from Carl Rogers's approach to therapy and is best explained in the book *Freedom to Learn* (Rogers, 1969). The emphasis of this model is on aiding the student toward self-instruction, and through this self-instruction, self-understanding, self-discovery, and self-concept.

Some examples of teaching competencies:

a. The teacher clarifies students' attitudes by reflecting them back to the learners.
b. The teacher guides pupils through processes that will help them to clarify values that they hold.
c. The teacher guides pupils in using a systems approach to solve a problem identified by the pupils.
d. The teacher creates a supportive learning environment that provides learning resources in response to the needs and desires of the pupils (Cooper, Jones, and Weber, 1973).

An observer watching a Rogerian teacher might note the degree to which the teacher

a. Puts the burden of decision making and choice on the students instead of making all the decisions himself.
b. Encourages self-revelation rather than self-defense.
c. Promotes a curriculum of problem solving.
d. Provides alternative learning activities for students, giving the students choices among options.

It can be noted that while Rogers's ideas follow the steps of self-instruction followed by self-understanding followed by self-concept, Glasser's sequence would be primarily directed at self-concept through success experiences.

Joyce and Weil note that the Behavior Modification Family is a one-member set containing only the Operant Conditioning Model of B. F. Skinner. In the Operant Conditioning Model human behavior becomes shaped into patterns by external forces. The learned patterns might take any form, such as "appropriate" social behavior or "correct" interpersonal skills or information acquisition. The Operant Conditioning Model is the basis for programmed texts and other such sources that are used in the development of cognitive and psychomotor skills and also for the affective development of students through the use of such things as tokens and other appropriate rewards. The key relationship in this teaching behavior is the reinforcement of approved responses by the teacher; and, as such, the competency of reinforcement is a key observable skill of an Operant Conditioning teacher. Of course, another key competency in this model is the teacher's ability to reinforce *v hen* reinforcement is needed.

ASSESSING CONSEQUENCE COMPETENCIES

Many teacher educators and also educators of other professionals appear to be somewhat shocked by the emphasis placed on the consequence competencies. For years certification and licensing have been at most targeted on performance and even on mere knowledge. Competency-based efforts force program developers to focus on the consequence level. That concern for the accountability level is not new and has been well stated by Merwin (1973):

> Throughout history schools have been a vehicle used by society to produce behavioral change (learning, skill development, etc.) in pupils. With few exceptions, the functioning of the school has been replaced by change in pupil performance, the purported *raison d'être* of schools, as the focus of attention. In spite of considerable diversion and attention to means rather than ends, there is a long history of concern for the ends as defined as performance and Horace Mann called attention of educators to some of the problems related to assessing performance many years ago.

Earlier it was stressed that the teacher cannot take total responsibility for pupil learning for the simple reason that he does not account for much of the variance. Parent attitudes toward learning, student emotional and physical health, student aptitude, and intelligence are all reflected in cognitive and affective growth in the classroom.

However, consequence objectives and the assessment of teacher competence by tapping consequence objectives cannot be ignored. The teacher does influence at least some part of learning that takes place in the class. Perhaps it is enough for CBE program developers to hold students accountable for some parts of learning; this move might provide at least some data on the prospective teacher's recognition that he has some responsibility for pupil learning. Consider this competency: Teacher helps students build self-awareness and self-concept. At the University of Houston, one module called *Psychological Foundations II, Phenomenological Learning* requires that prospective teachers demonstrate this competency. The module content reflects the work of the phenomenological school (especially the work of Arthur Combs) and how this school of thought might help teacher education students develop a similar rationale for use in their own classrooms.

In assessing competence, the student negotiates a target pupil or pupils with his instructor. The student is responsible for setting operational definitions of how self-concept or social desirability will be assessed. The student must also provide evidence of a positive change on the part of his pupil(s) before exiting the module. Module builders must recognize that students cannot be held accountable for *all* changes on the part of pupils; however, this module was developed to push students toward the realization that they could help pupils in developing other than cognitive skills.

A second form of accountability is shown in consequence assessment at both Brigham Young University and the University of Houston. To complete student teaching or internship, a student must provide evidence that pupils achieved the cognitive and affective objectives of an extended teaching unit. In other words, unit objectives are stated in advance, and the perspective teachers are not certified until they have demonstrated that each pupil has achieved minimal cognitive and affective growth. "Minimal" in this case is negotiated with each individual student for each individual set of pupils.

In preservice programs, one development may be quite useful in helping students to focus on the area of consequence objectives. Popham (1972) has developed a series of Teaching Performance Tests [2] that are now available commercially. There are forms for both peer teaching and teaching elementary pupils, and the format for each is the same. The teacher is provided with an objective he is to teach to pupils. In the adult forms the content is such that it is unlikely that the learners will have knowledge prior to the teaching experience. The teacher is also provided with an example posttest item and a descriptive narrative of the content. He is then instructed to develop a lesson to teach his pupils. After the lesson is taught, objective posttests are given to the learners, who must answer five to ten questions and also give some indication of their level of interest for the lesson. While formative performance feedback can be used to aid the teacher in improving teaching skills, the key to this assessment is the identification of how well the learners did on the tests.

Several CBTE efforts are now using these Teaching Performance Tests or are developing variations. One thing is certain, the tests do focus prospective teacher concerns on consequence objectives.

Whether or not the measurement of consequence objectives is a valid procedure in a teacher education program depends to a large extent on the assumptions under which the program is built. If the decision to measure consequence objectives is made, faculty have to recognize several things:

1. Outcomes from a given group of pupils must be negotiated with the student. Achievement of 95 percent of the objectives by all

[2] Two excellent sources for more information are W. James Popham, "Performance Tests of Teaching Proficiency: Rationale, Development, and Validation," *AERA Journal,* January 1971, pp. 105–17; and "Teaching Skill under Scrutiny," *Phi Delta Kappan,* June 1971, pp. 599–602.

pupils before certification is unrealistic *unless* that figure is part of the negotiation.

2. Since the student is responsible, and unless commercially available assessments are used, the validity and reliability of instruments will probably be low. Expect it. Accept it. Your emphasis is on accountability. If you want .90 reliability estimates, you are probably expecting too much.

3. Recognize that just as the students are accountable for bringing about predetermined changes in their pupils, you are accountable for aiding the student in the task.

ASSESSING AFFECT

At several points in this chapter there has been mention of the affective domain in teaching. No one can deny the importance of a teacher's attitudes, values, and commitments as they bear on his acceptance and success in teaching. Every student wants to be a warm, accepting, committed teacher. Every pupil wants to be taught by a loving, accepting, humane teacher. The question that is thrown in the laps of program developers is, "How do you know when a person has the positive affect that will allow him to function in positive ways with kids?"

The question is a difficult one to answer. Combs (1972) argues that

since humanistic objectives like values, feelings, beliefs, understandings, attitudes, and personal meanings lie inside people they cannot be effectively measured by any devices we now possess except through some form of inference.

We agree. We also argue that the safest guard against students' leaving a program with less than humanistic values is by providing constant and continuous and open feedback. One of the key reasons for the inclusion of human relations training in some CBE efforts is to promote honest sharing of feelings among people. One of the key reasons for the use of videotape or audiotape feedback sessions is to promote honest sharing between instructors and students. A person can make a conscious effort to change only if he knows how his actions are perceived by others and then consciously decides to change his actions. Furthermore, the decision to use behavior skills as a focus of CBE efforts comes from the fact that self-concept grows after success. Once a student sees that he can *do* something, he grows in self-concept. The use of competence motivation and a failure-free "yes–not yet" guiding system adds to increases in affect.

We must consider assessing the affective dimension of teaching even though the affective dimension is often exceedingly difficult to assess. On the other hand, we cannot forget the cognitive and performance areas of teaching. In short, even though many objectives and competencies stated in CBE efforts are vague, we feel that it is better to try to assess them at their vaguest than to be only changing all of our cognitive objectives to 80 percent, four-out-of-five, and in general trying to behavioralize the entire effort. The computer truism of GIGO—garbage in, garbage out—holds especially well in CBE program development. If useless skills, competencies, and subcompetencies are called for on the part of students, useless skills will be demonstrated by students. We are never going to get to a point where we are able to assess the truly important skills and competencies of teachers until we get around to trying.

There are no guarantees in using affect or in other objectives. Teaching and learning are human endeavors. All we can do is ensure human interaction. That may be enough.

4

packaging instruction,
or—what is a module?

Modules do not a CBE program make.

Modules receive a great deal of attention when competency-based education is discussed. Some of this attention may be disproportionate, however, for modules are not a necessity for CBE and there are potential disadvantages in their use as well as demonstrated advantages. In a sense modules are a new concept, but parts of the concept have been around for some time. In this chapter the concept of modules, their rationale, and their use will be explored. Value judgments about particular aspects of modules and their use will be kept to a minimum. The chapter goal is to present and describe various issues related to module development and use, to suggest some possible solutions to problems, and to offer some illustrations for consideration. The orientation will be toward the practical side rather than the theoretical. The following is the schema for this chapter:

Page	Heading	Questions
94	Why Modules?	What are the reasons and rational for using modules?
97	Modules Defined	What is a module and what are its components?
103	Selecting Enabling Activities	What factors should be considered in choosing enabling activities?

WHY MODULES?

Arranging instructional activities into a related set and organizing the activities and the associated instructional materials into some sort of "package" has become a common practice. In many cases the flurry and hustle of activity that surrounds the packaging of instruction seems to obscure the reasons for doing it and its expected outcomes. Module building can become the end rather than a means if program developers and package builders do not constantly remind themselves of why they are packaging instruction in the first place. There are at least five reasons why this form of instruction has become such a widespread practice:

1. The need to attend to the diversity in backgrounds, readiness, requirements, and personal objectives of learners.
2. The need to make more effective use of expensive human resources and to provide cost-effective, individualized learning activities.
3. The struggle to "keep up with the times" in the interest of institutional survival as students become more discriminating consumers of education.
4. An increase in the amount, quality, and availability of research on learning and instruction.
5. The demand for more than rote learning.

Diversity in Student Backgrounds

The diversity in student backgrounds, readiness, and goals can be readily observed. Students on university campuses are no longer solely from the middle and upper classes. Low-income and minority-group students are now attending college in larger numbers with support from scholarships, loan assistance, and work-study programs. In addition, four-year colleges and universities receive transfer students from community colleges and junior colleges, which in turn cater to an extremely diverse student population. The point does not need to be labored: the diversity in student skills, expectations, readiness, and aims is of such magnitude that it is just not possible to offer enough variety in conventional lecture and tutorial courses. One way to attend to the different entrance levels and needs of individuals is by packaging instruction with alternate learning routes.

Effective Use of Human Resources

The dollar resources are not available to most educational institutions to add instructional staff members simply because a new instructional need has been identified. Many highly skilled instructors on campuses are apt to be bogged down in spending most of their class time teaching the basics that students require before working with more sophisticated aspects of a given field. A way is needed to free these valuable staff resources while providing students with instruction in the basics at minimal cost. One common solution in institutions of higher learning has been to employ graduate students as teaching assistants (TAs). At a major university in the Southwest, nearly 65 percent of the contact hours of undergraduate courses are being taught by TAs. This approach may preserve faculty talents, but when TAs receive no training in teaching techniques and when they lack sufficient experience in the field of study, it seems unlikely that their students will become proficient in the course objectives. Packaged instruction is an alternative way to save faculty instruction time for high-level inputs and to implement reasonable economies in the teaching of basic skills and knowledge.

Keeping Up with the Times

As colleges face competition for a shrinking student population, alternatives to the mass lecture format are needed in order to recruit members for the freshman class. The students of the seventies have alternatives to formal schooling, and they insist on alternatives in educational formats as well. As a consumer group they are making calculated choices. Institutions that have attractive alternatives to mass education will draw the students, while those institutions that provide traditional course work and programs will lose enrollment. Packaging has always been a way to catch the eye of the consumer, but instructional packaging can mean even more if it provides students with viable, alternative routes to their personal goals.

Research on Learning and Instruction

Research on learning and instruction has yielded tremendous amounts of new knowledge during the past ten to fifteen years. Through use of tools like the Educational Resources Information Center (ERIC) and other computerized information systems, it is possible to use key "identifier" words to locate published research on any particular topic. This relatively easy access to research findings has made possible the design of instructional experiences that not only are based upon the professional judgment and feelings of the developer but also have a sound foundation in the research literature. Theories of learning reported in the literature, including the works of Piaget, Bruner, Gagné, Ausubel, Skinner, Bloom, and others, are available to serve as the basis for designing instruction. Also, various instructional approaches have been developed, expanded, and extensively studied. Self-paced instruction for the college level (Keller, 1968), audio-tutorial instruction (Postlewaite et al., 1964), and Individually Prescribed Instruction (the Learning Research and Development Center at the University of Pittsburgh) are three examples of self-pacing strategies available to educators. In using self-pacing techniques, instructors do not have to expend time providing cognitive information to students. The packages provide the information while the instructor works with small groups or individual students to help clarify and build beyond the basic concepts. Through this approach the learner is able to pace his own learning and make use of as little or as much instruction as he may need from the instructional packages and instructors so that he can master a set of objectives at the rate that best fits his learning style.

Demand for More than Rote Learning

Packaged instruction is not limited solely to use in basic courses. Instructional packages can also be of value to students who are working at advanced levels and seeking guidance in self-help toward personal objectives.

In theory, packages can be combined in a manner tailored to the needs and goals of each student, and totally unique courses of instruction can be offered. The negotiation process in company with alternative learning routes can make for a learning program that is quite diverse in instructional approaches and sophisticated in the degree to which it can be tuned to the needs of individual learners. Consequently, such programs do not find it necessary to require of students extensive memorization without application unless such memorization exercises are the goal in themselves.

In summary, many reasons, including diversity in learner needs and personal goals, cost-effective use of human resources, limited appeal of traditional approaches, and research and technological developments have accelerated the movement toward packaging instruction. Ideal instructional packaging reflects the need for faculty to provide the best possible experiences for students by utilizing the knowledge, skills, and experiences of all available resources.

But, what do the packages look like?

MODULES DEFINED

Instructional packages can have as many different faces as there are people who develop them. The packages have many names: Learning Activity Packages (LAPS), WILKIT (Weber State Individualized Learning Kit), IPAC (Individualized PACkets), Uni Pac (Unified Packet), and so forth. The general term for instructional packages that seems to be the most widespread is *module*. One brief definition of module is the following: "A module is a self-contained set of learning experiences intended to facilitate the student's attainment of a stated set of objectives" (Hall et al., 1973). This definition may seem simplistic or unsophisticated, and it certainly could be expanded upon, but it can serve as a beginning point.

Modules have different formats and organizations; some may have sections that others omit. In general, however, a module has the following five parts:

1. Prospectus—A statement of rationale to the learner.
2. Statement of Objectives—A behavioral statement of the most important learning outcomes.
3. Preassessment—A test to determine the learner's need and readiness for the instructional activities.
4. Alternative Enabling Activities—A multipath set of learning activities designed to facilitate learning the behaviors described in the objectives.
5. Postassessment—A test to determine whether or not the learner can perform the behaviors described in the objectives.

Different terms may be used in different programs and different organizational formats abound, but these five components should be contained in every module, no matter what they are called or where they appear. These components are also a good set of checkpoints against which to compare materials when reviewing modules for adoption or when examining the products of your own module-development effort.

Prospectus

The prospectus tells the learner why he is dealing with the set of objectives addressed in the modules, what kinds of experiences he will encounter, what kinds of materials and other logistical requirements will be needed, and what prerequisites he is expected to have completed before beginning work on the module.

The prospectus should contain a statement explaining why the learner is being asked to confront the module's objectives. For his modules, Will Weber has established a policy that if the prospectus cannot convince the student of the importance of learning the module's specified objectives, the student does not have to go through the module experience. In other words, Weber believes in the module builder's responsibility for convincing the learner of the relevancy of particular learning outcomes. Instructors who do not believe in negotiating with students will not rank this "sales pitch" so highly as a part of the prospectus.

Another part of the prospectus is an overview of the kinds of experiences and alternatives the student will face as he progresses through the module. This description should include some information about the types of activities he will encounter and the general flow of events. Sometimes a flowchart is a useful device for illustrating how the various activities, options, and sequences fit into an overall plan. This allows the student to map his progress through the module and helps him to plan his next step.

A list should be included in the prospectus outlining special material and logistical requirements of the module. The list should include materials and where to get them; special appointments, conferences, or field trip arrangements; and schedules of special events such as lectures. The Weber State modules contain a special checklist for this task. A rough approximation of pacing and time requirements may also be helpful to the students.

The prospectus may also include a statement of the prerequisite skills or experiences that the learner should bring to his participation in the module. In addition to obviously essential skills, such as demonstration of the ability to write instructional objectives before embarking on a unit on how to design enabling activities, the learner should be advised of more subtle prerequisites that occur in the module or program context, such as beginning nurses' ability to not faint at the sight of blood.

Statement of Objectives

The learner should be told at the outset what important skills, subcompetencies, and competencies he should expect to acquire as a consequence of working through the module. The objectives are descriptions of what behaviors or skills are to be demonstrated and by whom, including specification of the minimal degree of accuracy that will be accepted. Objectives should be stated as student objectives (i.e., "The student will be able to . . .") rather than instructor objectives (i.e., "The instructor will discuss . . ."). In designing modules, the developer can follow the categorizations and format for competencies, subcompetencies, and objectives that were described in Chapter 2.

As was pointed out in Chapter 3, preassessment activities can serve a variety of functions, depending on the module developer's intent. The module developer, therefore, should keep in mind exactly what function or set of functions he intends for the preassessment.

Preassessments can have at least one of four functions. The preassessment can (1) serve as a learning activity, (2) be employed to determine whether or not the learner has the necessary readiness to undertake the module, (3) determine whether the learner can already do what the module is designed to instruct, and (4) serve as an awareness- or arousal-building experience.

One of the effects of preassessment is that it can be a learning experience. Whatever intended functions preassessment may have in taking the preassessment and going over the desired responses, the student is apt to learn some of the material. Even when the preassessment is designed simply to assess the module objectives, the student may complete the preassessment and then upon reviewing the correct responses discover that he has learned enough or recalled material he once knew to the point that he will be able to demonstrate the objectives that have been specified for the module. Depending on the module design, this student would either immediately move on to the next module or take the module posttest and submit it for review by his instructor. In most cases, however, the preassessment will serve to make the student aware of what he does not already know and will arouse his interest and concern to work on developing those yet unlearned skills.

The preassessment, depending on the items that are in it, can also determine whether the learner has the prerequisite skills needed to begin work on the module. In many cases specific prerequisite skills are needed, and an assessment for these can save the learner the anguish of having a terribly difficult time with material he is really not ready for. Such diagnostic feedback can aid the student in selecting prerequisite instructional activities. For example, Ed Kurtz, at The University of Texas at Permian Basin, has consistently found that 10 to 15 percent of the college students taking freshman biology are unable to read a Celsius thermometer within plus or minus ten degrees. These students are immediately at a disadvantage in laboratory work.

The preassessment can be used to determine whether the student can already do the behaviors that are required for the module. In this case it is important to make sure that the preassessment items and the postassessment items are parallel, that is, that they are interchangeable. Instructors have been known to design preassessment items so that they are self-fulfilling prophecies—they use items that have idiosyncratic terms and misleading phrases that guarantee failure.

By taking the preassessment, the learner ought to become more aware of what he does and does not know about the particular content at hand. This awareness, in combination with the rationale for the importance of learning specific skills, should arouse the student to a high motivation level for acquiring the behaviors that are learning outcomes of the module.

The preassessment for many modules may not even be taken. Some students, just by reading the objectives or having gotten the "word" from fellow students, know that they can't demonstrate the required learning outcomes. Other students may wish to do all or part of a module, regardless of the preassessment results, because it looks like fun or because they may not be sure of the material or because they are uncertain about what they experienced in the preassessment. Unless the preassessments are prescriptive, that is, unless the results inform the student about which enabling activities he does and does not need to do, then completing the preassessment should be at the student's option. If he wishes to get on with the enabling activities, that should be his prerogative.

When faculty are entertaining the idea of employing preassessment measures, one of their concerns is that all of their time will be consumed in scoring them. Experience suggests that students should evaluate their own preassessment responses. An answer key and whatever discussion is needed can be provided either within the module text or elsewhere in the classroom. Only when a student is confused does an instructor have to become involved in scoring and interpreting preassessment results. Instructors may have to respond to the student's concern that he does not know the right answers. In this case the instructor need only remind the student that the function of the preassessment is to find out what the student can and cannot do and that this, in turn, will guide him in selecting the enabling activities to help him master the skills that he now knows he needs.

Enabling Activities

Enabling activities are those experiences that have been designed to help the student (or "enable" him) to attain the specified learning outcomes of the module. Ideally, a module will have multiple paths to the attainment of the stated objectives. That is, the learner should be able to choose from alternate enabling activities, depending on his own learning needs, style, and desires. In practice, most modules, at least in their early development, will consist of just one set of enabling activities, and the learner is limited to the choice of doing all or part of this set of enabling activities or designing an alternate set of experiences on his own.

The importance of a provision for student choice cannot be overemphasized. In competency-based programs and the modules they offer, the student is expected to decide how much instructional input he needs and then select from the available enabling activities those that he will use to facilitate his acquisition of the desired learning outcomes. How many of the enabling activities he does and which ones he selects to do are his personal decisions. If he chooses to do none of the prescribed enabling activities and to do something on his own instead, then this is within the realm of possibility. We would suggest that this is even desirable. The criterion of success is whether or not the student can demonstrate the desired learning outcomes, not whether he went through any specific enabling activities. The only exception to this might be for enabling activities tied to expressive or exploratory objectives, if program designers have agreed on the need for certain experiences and have made these public, thereby making the experiences into objectives in themselves. Such things as attending school board meetings, visiting halfway houses, or touring child centers might provide valuable input to students. Hopefully, the rationale for such exploratory objectives will be strong, however. In addition, the possibility of a student negotiating alternative experiences can add to the personalization aspects of a program.

The enabling activities or instructional strategies and tactics that are used for a given module should ideally have firm foundations in learning theory as well as in related research and development and instructional technology. Of course, use of each will depend on the available resources.

Contrasting types of enabling activities may be sequenced together within a module, or one module may employ only one type of enabling activity and the next module in the series may use another technique. Contrary to popular belief, enabling activities are not limited to readings and pencil-paper work, although in some cases module builders may be limited to these. In theory, however, there are many types of enabling activities, including lecture, small-group seminar, laboratory, field trip, programmed instruction, computer-assisted instruction, self-paced instruction, low-ratio teaching, simulation, role playing, reading, manipulated materials, and interaction with media programs such as slide-tape, films, videotapes, and so forth. The only limits on variation in enabling activities are resources and the creativity and adaptability of the module builder. However, the enabling activities selected for inclusion should provide the student with opportunities to practice the skills he is expected to demonstrate. Reading and writing about suturing will not very likely improve one's initial suturing performances.

The wise choice of a set of alternative enabling activities is an important key to individualized learning within optimal time limits. If, after progressing through a set of enabling activities, the student finds on the posttest that he is still unable to demonstrate the required behaviors, an alternate set of enabling activities should be available. Of course, the instructor and other types of "people help" should also be available to assist the student who is having difficulty with the packaged parts of the instruction. Modules are not legitimate reasons for instructors to flee the classroom. Indeed, when all the instructional people abdicate their responsibilities to the module, no matter how well it is designed, the whole thing will fall apart.

Postassessment

Determining whether or not the student can demonstrate desired learning outcomes is accomplished through a postassessment measure. This postassessment must test behaviors that are directly related to the publicly stated objectives of the module. Ideally, there should be a one-to-one correspondence between the individual assessment items in the postassessment and the stated objectives. Also, as mentioned previously, those preassessment and postassessment items that are designed for determining whether or not the student can demonstrate the desired learning outcomes from a particular module should be constructed in parallel form; that is, they should be interchangeable.

While preassessment tests may be scored and interpreted by the student, most postassessments are interpreted by faculty and staff members. The postassessment measure may be scored by the student and then discussed in conference with an instructor. In other cases, evaluation of the postassessment measure may be handled completely by the instructor.

As we discussed in Chapter 3, assessment items cannot always be of the pencil-and-paper variety. Students may be expected to bring in a videotape or audiotape recording of their behavior, such as teaching a class using specific strategies. Some modules may have consequence objectives, for which data will be needed of the student's effects on others.

Scoring the postassessment measures is another area where a great deal of instructor time can be consumed. Clerk scoring of cognitive tests has been used in some programs; in other programs instructor scoring may be desirable. Instructor scoring time can be more effective in a one-on-one situation where the instructor can use the time with the student to review and discuss the postassessment results and get to know the student better. The time can also be used for gestalt building. Sometimes postassessment results may be the stimulus for a special enabling activity. A student's taped teaching performance, for example, may provide the basis for a videotape feedback session that includes time for diagnosis and planning of subsequent instruction. During the module-design phase, the instructor's use of time must be considered. If adequate attention is not given to how the low-level, cognitive objective postassessments are going to be scored, the instructor will end up spending all of his time doing that job and will miss out on important opportunities to interact more personally with students and at more sophisticated levels.

SELECTING ENABLING ACTIVITIES

Selection of enabling activities is so important that some further discussion is needed. The array of possible combinations of media, group size, locations, technological aids, and other factors is almost infinite. For example, for a given set of objectives, enabling activities could be designed that included one or more of the following: lecture, lecture-demonstration, small-group seminar, laboratory, field trip, programmed instruction, computer-assisted instruction, low-ratio teaching, micro teaching, simulation, games, role playing, reading, manipulative materials, or interaction with media such as films, audio tutorial, slide-tape, videotape, and educational television. In reviewing the research, one finds that all the activities have been compared with the others, with the general conclusion that each is "as good as" the other.

The module developer should take a deliberate approach in selecting and designing enabling activities. Many people begin building modules with the assumption that they must develop everything from scratch and that only they will know how to modularize their course. This includes not only writing their own objectives and assessment items but also designing all of the enabling activities. The "finished" module that has been built by this process is often easily identified. A good description was given by a coed at a major university who, when asked about the module upon which she was working, replied, "Oh yes, this is the same stuff he used to lecture about, only now we read it!"

Since a goal of instruction in CBE is the provision of alternative enabling activities, reading an edited lecture script or attending the lecture does provide for alternatives. It does seem, however, that more variation and relevance could easily be achieved by use of other enabling activities.

When selecting enabling activities for inclusion in your module, you should consider the following questions:

1. Does the enabling activity provide the student with the opportunity for appropriate practice of the behaviors specified in the instructional objectives?
2. What materials already exist that could be used?
3. How much time does it take?
4. Can you afford the necessary logistics?
5. Will the enabling activity be of interest to the students?
6. Are there data on how similar students have done with similar activities?

Is There Provision for Appropriate Practice?

The key in identification of enabling activities is that each has what Popham and Baker (1970) call "appropriate practice," that is, the activities are related directly to the objectives. Enabling activities should facilitate students' acquisition of the behaviors expected of them. Students must have opportunities to practice the behaviors that the objectives describe. If the objective calls for a student teacher to demonstrate that he can ask probing questions, providing enabling activities that only ask him to read about types of questions and then classify a list of questions would not be adequate. Enabling activities should be included that provide the opportunity for the student teacher to actually practice asking probing questions.

Reasonable assistance should also be built into the enabling activities. If there is one paragraph in a book that will help a student acquire an objective, the module developer should identify that paragraph and should not have the student read 312 pages to search for what has already been identified by the builder. Similarly, most students respond better to synopses than they do to long readings. Synopses can be placed on audiotape or be provided in printed form.

What Materials Already Exist?

Module developers who work on the assumption that everything must be built from scratch are exerting a lot of effort for nothing. Many good and tested materials, some excellent materials, and a lot of salvageable ideas exist that can be adopted or adapted to fit most objectives. Use these existing materials as starting points whenever possible. The individual who refuses to do so is probably so ego-involved in module construction that he has forgotten its ends—effective instruction. Another side of this issue is that there are certain to be areas where no materials exist, usually because they are hard to develop for those areas. Conserve your time and energy for work in these difficult areas and beg, borrow (with permission when required), and adapt materials for those areas where materials exist. Don't overlook the many commercial materials available. For example, Far West Regional Laboratory, General Learning Corporation, and Vimcet have developed and tested many materials that are ready for immediate use as alternate enabling activities. Sources for existing materials will be described in more detail later in this chapter.

How Much Time Does It Take?

The time required to work through modules must be considered from several points of view. If an enabling activity requires a great deal of one-to-one instructor time, then the instructor cannot be doing other things, and perhaps proctors must be hired (not necessarily with dollars, there is always special course credit) to monitor student work. How much preparation time will faculty need during each week? If an instructor is going to be involved full time for a two-week period on one enabling activity, such as repeated "on call" videotape feedback sessions or a seminar, he can't be holding final conferences on another module. The use of limited faculty resources should be carefully planned and coordinated.

Time requirements should also be considered from the student's point of view. An excessive amount of student time spent on one enabling activity or for only one or two cognitive objectives that may not be that important in the overall program diminishes the amount of time students have for other objectives. A good example of this is one set of materials that requires an average student some forty hours to achieve approximately twenty-five relatively low-level cognitive objectives. With available learning time being as scarce as it is, selecting reasonably efficient and multiple-outcome enabling activities is essential. If it is judged important for students to experience certain activities, the developer must specify important competencies, sub-competencies, and objectives for those enabling activities if they are to occupy much student time.

Can You Afford the Logistics?

Many attractive enabling activities are available or can be designed. Many kinds of manipulative materials, media, and experimental procedures can be used for enabling activities. When selecting enabling activities, make sure that the logistical requirements do not become constraints due to un-availability, cost, high downtime of machines, or unrealistic demands on scheduling. For example, a piece of equipment that costs several thousand dollars, needs to be cleaned after every two hours of use, and has expensive parts that need replacement after every one thousand hours of use may not be a good choice for use in only one enabling activity. Furthermore, do not go out and spend all your budget on an exotic piece of equipment that is used once in a four-year program. The authors once worked with an innovative science curriculum that was being adopted by several school systems. Each school was allotted a modest budget for "consumables" at the beginning of the year. In one school the principal rushed out and spent all the money on four aquariums that would be used for a total of two weeks by two of the six grades. While this left no funds for the many little items that would be needed, the aquariums were very nice.

Will It Interest the Students?

Many enabling activities may look good to us as instructors but be of no relevance whatsoever to the students. Pick illustrations and enabling activities that are related to the students' frame of reference. An obvious example might be reflected in the selection of musical background for tapes; we might expect university undergraduates to be more in tune with Kris Kristofferson than with Lawrence Welk.

Are There Data on How Others Have Done?

The word soon gets around from student to student on what activities are worth the effort. At times, however, as an instructor you will want to aid students in selecting the activities that they may like best. Information on how students with similar learning styles attacked the problem in the past might be helpful here. Ideally, students should be able to compare their learning characteristics with the characteristics of other learners and then select an enabling activity, though as Allen (1971) pointed out in his review of instructional media research, prescriptive education is not yet that sophisticated:

> There is a consistent attempt by a number of researchers and theorists to discover the unique attributes of instructional media and their relationships to the performance of particular psychological functions with different kinds of learners. The study of this three-way interaction of stimulus, task, and learner is extremely complex, but some evidence is building up that could lead to a more precise understanding of the place of media in the instructional process . . . The time is far off, if in fact it ever arrives, when we can identify an instructional problem and then faultlessly select the proper instructional mix to solve it. Yet the significance of the present research is that careful investigation of the design elements in mediated instruction are being made and that these searches are being conducted within a theoretical framework, thus laying a foundation for a theory of instructional media.

Module developers do need information on how well enabling activities work. If you have a choice between one that has demonstrated that 80 percent of the students achieve 70 percent of the objectives and one where the results were 40 to 50 percent, your task will be simplified. We believe that there should be a truth-in-packaging law for educational materials that requires this type of information to be available for all materials before they are released for general use.

In summary, enabling activities should be selected with care. Careful consideration should be given to the time and dollar requirements for students and instructors. Also, thought should be given to the demonstrated track record of enabling activities when this information is available. In all cases, learn from what others have done. Don't be entering the starting gate when the rest of the world is already rounding the curve.

THE LEARNING RESOURCES CENTER

Whether modules are to be used just for parts of a course or the entire program is to be modularized, the resources needed for enabling activities must be organized and coordinated. If a module requires use of a Carousel projector and accompanying cassette tape recorder, easy access to this equipment must be provided. Manipulative materials will be required, and students must have easy access to these materials. For economy, materials should be organized in such a manner that the fewest duplicate sets of materials can serve the largest number of students.

In most CBE efforts, the facility for holding and organizing instructional materials is known as a "Learning Resources Center" (or LRC), although some prefer the name "Learning Center," feeling that the emphasis should be on learning rather than on resources. A Learning Resources Center may be one end of a classroom, or it may be an entire floor or several floors of a library or classroom building. Within the LRC the various instructional materials needed for a particular set of enabling activities can be packaged together in boxes, trays, or paper bags. These are cataloged and placed on shelves for easy access. Media equipment such as tape recorders, slide projectors, cassette tape recorders, and so forth can be set up in individual and small-group work spaces. If the LRC is being developed for an individual course, a classroom can be converted to include an LRC. The media equipment and shelves containing manipulative materials can be set up at one end of a room, while trapezoidal tables or other movable tables and chairs are used at the other end for seating and work surfaces.

When an entire program is going to be modularized, the logistics become more sizable and specialized facilities will be needed. Building an LRC does not necessarily require all sorts of new and exotic equipment; more importantly, it does mean pooling available resources and equipment so that they are used by everyone involved in a program rather than having a media depot where requests by individual instructors are serviced or having each "course" claim a classroom and develop a private LRC.

Peterson (1973) has given considerable thought to the concepts underlying a Learning Center and has identified seven premises for having such a center:

1. Media, regardless of their formats, should be viewed first for their informational and stimulus possibilities, and second for their format potential.
2. Schools provide an access to learning, not learning. The instructor is an engineer of learning environments, a manager of information, and a learning counselor.

3. Media extends an instructor, both buoying up his or her instruction and enlarging that instruction. At times, mediation may provide a peripheral and/or reinforcing stimulus and at other times it may provide all of the instruction.
4. Learning and instruction are not one and the same. A school provides for learning, and instruction is but one element in the learning milieu.
5. The wide variety in type and emphasis of stimulus media should be developed to maximize learning potentials. The multiplicity of educational goals and goal paths must be provided for through a plurality of stimuli.
6. An integrated approach to learning is most economical in terms of all human and nonhuman resources.
7. Though education is at best an imprecise science, a technology of instruction is now becoming available and that technology can best be introduced through a learning center.

In most operational CBE programs the LRC, or LC if you wish, becomes the nerve center of the program. This is where the paths of all students and instructors intersect. Here is one focal point for the activity of learning where all of the available supports and resources are at one's fingertips. All learning, of course, does not take place in the LRC, for much learning ought to take place in the broader environment. However, once the learner has mastered skills in the LRC, he is in a much better position to capitalize on the very rich learning opportunities that are found in the clinical and real-world settings.

POTENTIAL PROBLEM AREAS IN BUILDING MODULES

Modules are like icebergs—nine-tenths of each is not visible. The surface appearance of a module is all too easy to judge. Improving someone else's modules looks simple. However, once you build one (a module), you realize how complicated the process can be. Modules are not easily built. Programmatic development can be a real problem when heaped on top of everything else that an instructor is expected to do. The experienced module builder emphatically acknowledges that a finished module is not produced in one semester, for testing and revision through several cycles will be necessary before a module can effectively facilitate attainment of its specified learning objectives.

If you are planning to build modules, several questions will have to be thought through. In most cases we can't supply the final answers; you will have to work them out for your particular situation. However, the following list of questions that was drawn from an orientation workshop on modules and CBE (Hall et al., 1973) and our discussion of these questions should provide perspective for the task.

1. What arrangements will you make to have time to write, test, rewrite, and retest modules?
2. How are you going to reproduce and distribute your modules?
3. How will students gain access to films, manipulative materials, reference works, and other expensive components of your module?
4. If you establish a learning resource center, how will you handle staffing, hours, and security?
5. How will you arrange your classroom?
6. With students working at different rates, how will you monitor student progress? Why monitor?
7. How will you keep open a two-way communication system?
8. How will you aid students in developing the personal discipline required to complete your modules successfully?

Don't oversell your modules as the "final solution."

9. How are you going to assess student progress?
10. What means will you use for formative and summative evaluation?

How Will You Find Time?

Writing a module is not accomplished in one afternoon or evening. It takes time to outline, construct drafts, and try out enabling activities, to design a format that has potential, to test it out with some students, and then redevelop and retest. Where will the time come from? More than likely new learners will be available to try out the revised module only once each semester. Development time needs to be planned. Graduate students and work-study students may be of help.

Don't advertise the first draft as the final solution to instruction. It is probably better to undersell and warn students that the module is early in its development, expect points of confusion, and seek student feedback as a basis for revision.

How Will You Reproduce and Distribute Your Modules?

In many instances just getting an exam typed can be a difficult challenge for an instructor. In module building you will have to reproduce many kinds of printed materials, and the materials will have to be updated and adjusted after each stage of development. In many cases your materials will supplement or replace textbooks, so the cost of reproduction also becomes a problem. Will you charge your students a materials fee? Or is the program going to absorb the cost for production of the materials—assuming you locate a printing press? A distribution system is also needed. Will this be done through the bookstore, or will materials be peddled by the instructor at the beginning of each class?

Copyrighting materials you have developed is another ticklish problem. Be sure to include copyright notice on all editions of your product and on all copyrightable components. If you are restrained from use of copyright by a funding source, you can still publish in the public domain. Of course, you should not reproduce copyrighted materials without proper arrangements with copyright holders—this includes either photocopying or reprinting materials. It is OK to buy copies of materials to include in a kit.

How Will Students Get Expensive Components?

Be careful about building exotic equipment into the enabling activities of your modules unless it is really crucial that it be there. The cost of providing more than one copy of some exotic materials may be prohibitive.

Have you thought about what it will take to get your modules reproduced and distributed?

Organizing and locating equipment and materials in a way that permits easy access and yet maintains reasonable security can create a real dilemma. Videotape machines have been known to completely vaporize. Films, various kinds of manipulative materials, and reference textbooks can easily disappear. More than one student will need to use these, and when they are not available quite a problem results. Materials must be easily accessible to the students as they become ready for them or their learning time will be chewed up in obtaining and returning materials or they just won't bother to use them.

To accommodate for losses, several established CBE programs have built into their annual budgets a "loss figure" on the assumption that a certain amount of material will be damaged or lost. Since students are not buying textbooks for courses, charges can be made for module texts, consumables, and special references that may be needed. Many students in CBE programs buy a cassette tape recorder rather than a text, since so many of the presentations are on cassette tape. By simply punching out the record plug in the cassettes used in the LRC, rerecording on the tapes is made impossible, thereby reducing the desirability of removing tape cassettes from the LRC to use for rerecording. At the University of Houston if a student wants a copy of a tape, he can have one made in a matter of minutes if he provides the blank tape.

The use-life of a film is relatively short. With use, films break and tear. One solution is to obtain permission from the filmmaker to copy the film on videotape. Color videotape cassettes work well for this. Students then check out the videotape for viewing, and the film is stored until needed to make additional copies.

How Will You Handle LRC Staffing and Security?

In theory students should have access to materials in the LRC as they might in a library, at any time of the day or night. In practice this creates all sorts of difficulties. These include making clerical and perhaps guidance help available to students on call, making sure all the materials get back where they belong, and scheduling regular maintenance. Providing for this important set of requirements can consume quite a bit of development time.

Theoretically . . . students should have access to materials in the LRC at any time of night or day.

Decisions that need to be made about LRCs include the following:

1. Where is the space for the LRC coming from—a storage closet, a corner of a classroom, a whole classroom, or a section of the college library? Policies will need to be clearly stated and adhered to.
2. What will the hours be?
3. Which materials will be for open access and which will have to be signed out?
4. Will slide projectors and other media equipment be set up for unrestricted use or be checked out when needed?
5. What about maintenance?
6. For security will there be monitors, a search upon leaving, an open-door policy?
7. Do these policies mean hiring new staff or reassigning existing staff?
8. How does the LRC relate to existing libraries?
9. How will duplicating and copying services be provided?
10. How will students be "trained" to properly use the LRC?

How Will You Arrange Your Classroom?

How will rooms and spaces be arranged for modularized instruction? Is everything going to be done with fixed tablet armchairs, or will there be movable tables and chairs? Will there be large rugs on the floor with no other furniture, or will each room be filled with carrels equipped with media equipment? How will the space be arranged to provide for flexibility and to enhance the enabling activities that will be going on?

What will you do if the school schedules other classes in a room that you wish to have opened for students working on modules? One solution has been to block schedule certain rooms for related courses so that the students who use these rooms are only those who need the materials in them. In other cases instructors have had to provide carts that were rolled into a room for one hour and then removed, only to be rolled back later for another set of students.

How Will You Monitor Student Progress?

After the first hour of work on a series of modules, there is a high probability that each student will be at a different point. Unless it is unilaterally decreed, all students will rarely be at the same point again as they proceed through their competency-based programs.

Monitoring student progress and scheduling group events like seminars, special presentations, field trips, lectures, and assessments can be a big problem. Strategies that have been found to be effective include having students maintain file folders for records and notes on their progress and having sign-up sheets where the students can sign up for group activities. Group activities can be repeated at various times during a three- to four-week period, so that when students are ready for them they can sign up for one of several alternate times.

Monitoring of student progress also provides the instructor with information about those students who are having difficulty. Data are recorded so that students who seem to be unduly slow in finishing a particular module or those who appear to be non-self-starters can be identified. Information of this type allows the instructor to be more on target with his individual help.

A point should be made here about individualization. Use of modules does not necessarily mean that each student progresses completely independent of all others without any class contact or group activities. Students not only work independently with instructional materials but also combine in many instances to form small groups for seminars, field trips, and so forth; or they may work in pairs on the same enabling activities. The extent of independent work is determined by the module builder. In CBE, cooperation can truly be reinforced and encouraged. Thus in a group, the progress of each member is a concern of all rather than having individuals in the group be in competition with each other over who is going to be at the top of the curve.

Use of student teams in some programs has aided in student acceptance of modular instruction. In this approach students work together to acquire needed competencies. There are several side benefits for the instructor in this approach. First, groups of students stay together, making assessment and monitoring of enabling activities somewhat easier. Second, the student who has a difficult time accomplishing self-paced activities may be able to do better with group contact. Third, in helping each other toward successful demonstration of competencies, a less-competitive relationship exists. Students working in groups and knowing that they are not being compared with each other increase in their level of cooperation as they aid each other in reaching objectives. This type of group work also provides experience in teamwork that should transfer to future team situations.

How Will You Keep Open Two-Way Communications?

Since all of the students may be working at different points, communication is a problem. Students need to communicate with their instructors, the instructors need to transfer messages and information to the students, and communication is necessary just to maintain organization and supervision throughout the program. Some practical strategies that have been tried include using a bulletin board as a message center and establishing a newsletter or program newspaper that is distributed among students and faculty. Other operational strategies employed include what the KANTEX Program faculty at Kansas State Teachers College call the "home-base concept." Each of the instructors is assigned thirty students, and they hold a home-base meeting once a week in which the prime function is sharing messages as well as taking care of personal problems that may have arisen during the week. Functioning faculty teams, meeting regularly and having student representatives, can enhance communication also. Through teaming, each member of the faculty is in communication with other faculty members on a regular basis and individual students are less apt to be lost. In this setting, personal and program operations can be discussed, and plans made and changed before major problems arise. Student representation at these meetings often enhances the reality orientation.

How Will You Develop Student Self-Discipline?

As has already been mentioned, for many students, especially those who are non-self-starters, working through modularized instruction presents tremendous difficulty. For other students, particular enabling activities that have been specified may not be those that they find easiest to learn by, and for still others there may be a problem of task avoidance. These students are going to need special attention. What mechanisms will be employed to identify these students early? How will they be helped? Will there be an opportunity for personal counseling, alternate programs, and transfers to other schools, or will they be left to fend for themselves?

How Will You Assess Student Progress?

Postassessment measures will provide information on student achievement when modules are completed. But what means, if any, will you employ for checking on retention of once-demonstrated skills? Will assessment items from earlier modules be built into later module postassessments, or will some form of "check test" be administered occasionally for assessment of retention and diagnosis of learning needs? An alternative is to assume that once a behavior has been demonstrated, that is all that is needed. We hope the futility of this assumption is apparent.

What Will You Use for Formative and Summative Evaluation?

It is not enough to draft a module and assume that you have a finished product. The material must be used, information must be collected about its success, and then the material must be revised and evaluated further. The test-revise-retest process can continue for quite some time. Any module builder who talks as if he has a finished product needs to be approached cautiously. Evaluation of modules will be explored in depth in Chapter 10; we simply remind you here that evaluation of the module and its effects is vital to the success of a CBE program.

RESOURCES FOR MODULE BUILDING

The last thing the world needs is another module on writing behavioral objectives.

Many modules have been demonstrated as effective. Still other materials exist that could easily be adapted for a particular modular use. For many areas effective nonmodular materials have been developed and tested and would make developing a particular module easier. Various resources available to the module builder can aid him in learning what exists. Check these sources out before beginning.

Several catalogs provide annotated listing of modules and related materials:

HOUSTON, W. R. et al. *Resources for Performance-Based Education*. The University of the State of New York and the State Education Department, Division of Teacher Education and Certification, Albany, March 1973.

Annotated Listing of Competency-Based Modules. Florida Center for Teacher Training Materials. University of Miami, Coral Gables, Florida, December 1972. Addendum A, January 1973. May be purchased from Panhandle Area Educational Cooperative, Post Office Drawer 190, Chipley, Florida 32428.

Program on Teaching Effectiveness. Teacher Training Products: The State of the Field. Research and Development Memorandum No. 116, January 1974, School of Education, Stanford University, Contract No. NE-C-00-3-0061, National Institute of Education.

The PBTE Project of the American Association of Colleges for Teacher Education has established a PBTE Information Center that has extensive files on materials and resources. Plans are for the PBTE Information Center to serve as a clearinghouse and referral center to more comprehensive collections of learning modules and PBTE-related documents.

Example modules often are available from the colleges and universities where they have been developed. The University of Houston's Professional Development Center, funded by Teacher Corps and the Texas Council for the Improvement of Educational Systems, offers instructional modules (available for printing costs) developed at the University of Houston.

Newsletters have also been established to aid in communication of ideas and resources about CBE. The following newsletters contain teacher education ideas and information:

ABBOTT, A. R., ed. *Florida Center Review: A Report to Florida Teacher Educators on Competency Based Teacher Training and Protocol Materials.* Florida Center for Teacher Training Materials, University of Miami, Coral Gables, Florida 33124.

ANDREWS, T. E., ed. *PBTE.* Multi-State Consortium on Performance Based Teacher Education, New York State Education Department, Albany 12210.

BURDIN, J. L., ed. *AACTE Bulletin.* American Association of Colleges of Teacher Education, Washington, D.C. 20036.

Other instructional resources for teacher education are the protocol materials being developed under U.S. Office of Education funding at Bucknell University, Education Development Center (Cambridge, Massachusetts), Far West Laboratory for Educational Development (Berkeley, California), Indiana University, Michigan State University, Ohio State University, Oregon State University, San Fernando Valley State College, University of California at Los Angeles, University of Colorado, Utah State University, and University of South Florida. A listing of the available materials can be found in:

A Catalog of Protocol Materials in Teacher Education, 1972 Revision. Division of Elementary and Secondary Education, Department of Education, Tallahassee, Florida 32300.

Educators interested in resources for module building should not limit their search to their own professional territory. Other professional areas are involved in the development of instructional materials and establishment of CBE programs. This does not mean that they are actively involved in CBE as such but that they are doing work that is easily related to CBE efforts. For example, many universities are establishing "Instructional Development Agencies" (Alexander and Yelon, 1972) to support their faculty in developing new instructional approaches. To aid in communication and expansion of their work, instructional developers have established the Division for Instructional Development of the AECT (Association for Educational Communications and Technology). Many of the Instructional Development Agencies have their own newsletters (one good example being *Learning and Development,* the Center for Learning and Development, McGill University,

Montreal), and the AECT Division for Instructional Development also has a newsletter (AECT Division for Instructional Development Newsletter).

Several engineering colleges are renovating their programs to include more individualized, self-paced, and packaged instruction. Innovative programs for engineers that have received recognition are located at the University of Texas at Austin; the Technical University of Monterrey, Mexico; Worcester Polytechnic Institute, Massachusetts; Florida State University; and the University of West Virginia.

In the health sciences many schools are heavily involved in instructional development activities that include modularizing instruction. The Office of Medical Education Research and Development at Michigan State University is one of perhaps thirty instructional development units around the nation that have been created to aid health science faculties in designing innovative instructional programs. Several of the recently established health science centers, such as the University of Oklahoma Health Science Center and the University of Texas Health Science Center at San Antonio, hired experts in program development before many of the faculty were hired. The University of Texas Dental Branch at Houston has been developing a fully modularized, self-paced program for dental students. Its materials have been packaged, used, and redeveloped through several classes. The materials are organized along topical themes and allow the students increased opportunity for practice and study as compared with the one-shot lecture approach. Ohio State University's College of Pharmacy used a National Institute of Health grant to establish an Office of Educational Development in June 1970 to aid faculty in developing new instructional approaches.

These efforts are just a small sampling of the activity that is progressing throughout the nation. The intent here has been to illustrate the exent and diversity of activity, not to provide an all-encompassing list of the most important resources for each area. The concern for developing more effective and alternative forms of instructional materials and programs is widespread nationally and is found in many different areas of education. The reader must expand this list in his own area; hopefully, our brief discussion will provide a starting point.

For those interested in training in module building, various individual study and workshop style packages have been built. Two modules on building modules are the following:

Developing Instructional Modules (1972) by W. R. Houston et al. is designed for use individually or in a group setting. The materials include a self-paced text, three slide-tape programs, and one audiotape. The purpose is training in module-building skills. It is available from the College of Education, the University of Houston, Houston, Texas.

Modules and Their Role in Personalized Programs (1973) was developed by Hall and his associates at the Research and Development Center for Teacher Education at the University of Texas at Austin. This package is designed as a two-day orientation workshop to modules, CBE, and personalized teacher education. The workshop includes four slide-tape programs and a series of participant activities.

EXCERPTS FROM SOME MODULES

Now that some of the characteristics that a module should contain have been described and some of the difficulties in building modules and some of the resources that are available have been explored, it might be worthwhile for the reader to review some representative modules. In studying these materials you will be involved in two distinctively different roles; be sure to keep these two roles clearly in mind. One role will obviously be that of prospective module builder examining the materials to learn what kinds of enabling activities are included, how clear the instructions are to the learner, what the logistical requirements are, and how you think your students would like using these particular materials. The second role you will find yourself taking is that of being a learner involved in working with the module. You may become engrossed in doing an activity and start thinking about the consequences of use if this activity was included in your program. In participating in this role, you may want to be asking questions about whether you think the amount of time that you would spend as a student is the most effective use of your time and what kinds of incidental learning would occur besides the learning that has been identified through the objectives.

In reviewing these modules, continue to be aware of the two perspectives you are taking, that of a critical module builder and that of a learner participating in a module. Mixing up these two roles may confuse your picture of the strengths and weaknesses of the materials. Each of these modules has had some field testing and revision. This does not mean, however, that they are considered by their builders to be finished products. The module developers acknowledge their limitations and are willing to share these so that others will not have to start at ground zero. A point here is that even after materials have been field tested, an outside reviewer may find things that he believes to be weaknesses. One message for that reviewer is that, in many cases, it is impossible to tell what the strengths and weaknesses of a given module are until it has actually been tried out with students. Given a set of needs and a frame of reference, combined with his time in the program and previous experiences, the learner may perceive a particular module in an entirely different way than the module reviewer does. On the other hand, in many cases what we have written that is completely obvious and interesting to us as module builders may not make a bit of sense or may be confusing or boring to the student.

The following modules and those included elsewhere in this book are offered as samples of locally developed materials. Professionally developed modules should also be examined, such as the Minicourses being developed by the Far West Regional Laboratory and the previously mentioned protocol materials.

Module 1

Social Studies Education Learning Tasks
Edgar A. Kelley and Larry Andrews, editors
NUSTEP Learning Materials for Performance-Based Teacher Education

THE CURRICULUM COMMITTEE, NUSTEP, TEACHERS COLLEGE
UNIVERSITY OF NEBRASKA, LINCOLN, 1973

This module was selected to illustrate the variety of enabling activities that might be offered. It also illustrates the scope and sequence that is possible, even in a secondary teacher education module. We have included the Table of Contents for the whole series of learning tasks to provide an overview of their range and the Competency Statements section, which outlines expected learning outcomes for the tasks. A single sample Learning Task is included. A student would have access to the suggested reading either within the module package itself or through the Learning Resources Center. The program this module was designed for is described in Chapter 11.

Table of Contents

Spiral II Social Studies Competency Statements

An effective social studies teacher has been characterized as:

1. An effective citizen in a democratic society,
2. A specialist in the study of man (social scientist),
3. Effective in human relations skills,
4. Effective in inquiry/decision-making skills, and
5. A specialist in planning, conducting, and assessing learning activities to develop social science concepts.

To achieve these goals, the following competencies are established as Spiral II requirements for social studies students:

1. After analysis of New Social Studies (NSS) goals and trends, the NUSTEP social studies student will (a) state to a proctor the significance to you and to your students of at least four major NSS trends or goals, (b) state to proctor the significance to you and to your students of at least one NSS national project, (c) indicate to proctor at least three NSS goals which you hope to implement in teacher assisting and student teaching.

Means of achieving Competency 1:

a. Learning Task 20 is designed to assist you to achieve Competency 1. Completion of the "evaluation activities" in Task 20 will represent satisfactory achievement of Competency 1.

b. If you feel that you can achieve Competency 1 without participation in Learning Task 20, complete the checkout sheets or equivalent and have them approved by your proctor.

2. Each NUSTEP Social Studies student will describe at least four basic elements of an effective member of a democratic society and demonstrate each element in continuing activities throughout Spiral II and teacher assisting experiences.

Means of achieving Competency 2:

a. Learning Task 21 is designed to assist you in achieving Competency 2. It is important that you plan and assess your NUSTEP activities throughout Spiral II to present evidence of successful achievement of this competency.

b. If you have already completed Competency 2 through non-NUSTEP activities or current NUSTEP activities, present evidence of successful achievement to your proctor.

3. For a given student population (teacher assisting class or other group or individual population) the NUSTEP social studies student will develop an instruc-

tional plan which is approved by the proctor and/or cooperating teacher. This plan may be prepared individually or as a member of an instructional team, and should include (a) statement of concept, goal and problem, (b) instructional (performance-criterion) objectives, (c) generalizations to be developed, (d) learning activities to achieve objectives, (e) materials and media to implement plan, (f) assessment and plan evaluation, and self-assessment plan.

Means of achieving Competency 3:
a. Learning Task 22 is designed to assist you to achieve Competency 3. By completing the evaluation activities in Task 22, you will have achieved this competency.
b. If you are not a team member in a Learning Center, you may develop your instructional plan with approval of your proctor, completing the evaluation activities shown in Task 22.
c. If you have already developed an instructional plan which meets the criteria established for Competency 3, present your plan to your proctor for analysis and approval.

4. For a given student population (preferably teacher assisting class, but may be other class, group, or individual) the NUSTEP social studies student will conduct as least one learning activity and achieve the objective(s) established for that activity. The plan for this learning activity must be approved by the proctor prior to conducting the activity.

Means of achieving Competency 4:
a. Learning Task 23 is designed to assist you to achieve Competency 4.
b. If you are not a team member in a Learning Center, you may conduct a learning activity in a regular teacher assisting assignment, a laboratory or micro-teaching situation or arrange a special activity to be approved by the proctor.
c. If you have taped or coded evidence of a learning activity you have previously conducted, you may present such evidence to your proctor for analysis and approval.

5. For a given student population (preferably teacher assisting class, but may be other population), the NUSTEP social studies student will assess the student achievement of the objectives of the instructional activity or activities conducted for Competency 4 and report the findings to the proctor for analysis and approval.

Means of achieving Competency 5:
a. Learning Task 24 is designed to assist you to achieve Competency 5. By successfully completing the "evaluation activities" in Task 24, you will have achieved Competency 5.

b. If you are not a team member in a Learning Center, you may assess the student achievements in the activity conducted for Competency 4 through the use of audiotape, videotape, or live coding.

c. If you have previously assessed student achievement of specific learning behaviors, submit these data to your proctor for analysis and approval.

6. Based on student, proctor, and self-assessment data, the NUSTEP social studies student will develop and present to proctor a "profile" of instructional strengths and weaknesses. Using this "profile" propose a self-development plan for yourself including (1) a depth study, (2) a teacher assisting assignment, and (3) an elective program of Spiral III and Series 30-40-50 Tasks.

7. The NUSTEP social studies student will successfully complete the objectives established for *one* of the depth studies.

8. In Teacher Assisting, the NUSTEP social studies student will receive satisfactory or above ratings on *all* of the Teacher Assisting behaviors.

9. The NUSTEP social studies student will successfully meet the performance criteria established in any *five* Learning Tasks of the 30-40-50 series in Spiral II.

LEARNING TASK 20

The New Social Studies (NSS)

Problem area: New projects, new courses, and new methodology seem to be the major emphasis in social studies education today. This is not unique to the social studies area, nor are the changes occurring much different from those throughout secondary schools in general. And yet, it is difficult to pinpoint what trends are significant, how much change is actually taking place in different schools, and what will be the social studies program in the future.

Task 20 is an orientation task—to acquaint you with trends, programs, goals, and questions about your present and future participation in social studies education. It provides an opportunity for sincere dialogue on such questions as "What is social studies?," "How is the 'New Social Studies' different from the more traditional social studies?," and "What goals should I establish upon entering the field of social studies education?"

Performance objectives: Each social studies NUSTEP student will:

1. Identify and explain the significance of at least four major trends in the area of social studies education which constitute the "New Social Studies." This may be done in writing or orally to the proctor or Task 20 instructor.

2. Classify social studies content, process, and objectives into a "structure" which will be useful in planning, conducting, and assessing learning activities when given examples of content, process, and objectives from social studies materials.

3. Identify at least five curriculum projects available for use which exemplify the "New Social Studies".
4. Express his/her own feelings about the social studies instruction received and what he hopes to achieve as a social studies teacher.
5. Complete instruments for Curriculum Materials' Analysis System (CMAS) for one NSS project and for one secondary school social studies textbook.

Prerequisite(s): None.
Learning activities:

A. *Readings.*
   1. Learning Task 20 reading by Dan DePasquale and Lee Witters.
   2. "New In-Depth Evaluations of Social Studies Curricular Projects, Programs, and Materials," *Social Education* (36:7, November, 1972).
   3. Irvin Morrissett, W. W. Stevens, Jr., Celeste P. Woodley, "Origins and Development of the Materials Analysis System," *Social Studies Curriculum Development* (39th Yearbook, National Council for Social Studies, 1969).

B. *Activities for Classroom Practice.*
   1. In a small group, discuss the analysis of curricular projects, programs, and materials from *Social Education*, November, 1972.
   2. Individually or in pairs, investigate at least four of the national projects, programs, and/or materials identifying some major trends or significant principles related to New Social Studies.
   3. With the assistance of the Task 20 instructors, examine the CMA instrument, the rationale behind it, and how it is to be used for fulfilling Competency 1.

C. *Activities for Practice in Field Situations.*
   1. Using the CMA instrument provided with this Task 20, complete the instrument for (a) a social studies textbook used in the classroom where you are assigned as a teacher assistant and/or a textbook selected from the social studies resource centers, (b) at least one social studies curricular project, program, and/or materials.
   2. Participate in a seminar presenting a position paper that represents your analysis and synthesis of the major trends in social studies education, the significance of these trends, and compare the single textbook (model) method with NSS curricular models.

D. *Assessment Activities—activities to demonstrate achievement of Competency 1.*

1. In a proctor meeting or in a conference with your proctor, explain the significance of at least four major NSS trends or goals. Your explanation should use support data gathered through the use of the CMA instrument, the seminar position paper, and readings.
2. In a proctor meeting or in a conference with your proctor, present a statement which assesses a national social studies project and explains the significance of the project. Your CMA instrument may be used to present the basic data about the project.
3. In a proctor meeting or in a conference with your proctor, present a statement of three or more NSS trends/goals which you wish to implement in your teacher assisting and student teaching experiences.

Module II

Psychological Foundations II: Phenomenological Learning
Howard L. Jones and Wilford A. Weber, developers

COLLEGE OF EDUCATION
THE UNIVERSITY OF HOUSTON, 1972

We include this module to illustrate the kinds of enabling activities that can be used with consequence objectives. The module is also an example of a unit that focuses on educational foundations content. It uses diverse kinds of enabling activities and is tied to several prerequisites, which are identified. The module is suitable for both elementary and secondary teachers-in-training.

Before you start the module, we would like to understand some of your perceptions about schools. Below there is a scale from 1 to 11. Please circle the numeral which you think reflects your feelings about what is most important for pupils to learn in schools. There is no right answer; please be honest. If you feel strongly that the most important outcome of schools is increased knowledge and skills on the part of students, circle 1. On the other hand, if you feel that the most important outcome of schools is the increased self-concept of the pupil, circle 11. If you are somewhere in between those two positions, please number between 1 and 11 which most nearly reflects your feelings. Once you have done this, you are ready to start the module.

Most important   1   2   3   4   5   6   7   8   9   10   11   Most important
is the student's   is the student's
learning the   learning that he
content and skills   is important.
necessary for his   Increased self-
understanding (a)   concept is the
subject(s)   key to education.

PROSPECTUS-RATIONALE

According to many vocal observers of public schools today, there is a perceived gap between the wants and needs of pupils and what pupils learn in school. Reports from Silberman, Kozol and others as well as from the lay public and pupils themselves indicate that the relevance of school curricula and the effectiveness of pupil-teacher interactions are not what they should be—and must be.

Part of the undergirding reasons behind some of these perceived difficulties can be found in the schism that has appeared among those who would examine the role of the school in American society. There are those who believe that the function of the school is to transmit knowledge to pupils and to prepare them for the future by instilling the cogent concepts, principles, and skills associated with the various disciplines. They see cognitive and psychomotor outcomes as usually being more important than affective outcomes.

Others view the role of the school not as a preparation *for life* during which pupils collect information, concepts, and principles. These viewers—phenomenologists—see education *as life*, with the school reaching its goals only when students are given a chance to become more human. According to these proponents: "Whatever we decide is the nature of the fully functioning, self-actualizing individual must become at once the goal of education."[1] The most important outcomes of school from this point of view are goals such as the increased self-concept of pupils and goals which are more affective in nature.

While there has certainly not been open warfare between these two viewpoints, there are some philosophic differences of which any teacher should be aware if he is to function most effectively in the classroom during these times of quickly changing foci. The function of this module is to present some of the views of the phenomenological, cognitive field, and perceptual field schools of psychology to the prospective teacher. As a result of this module, the teacher education student should have a better understanding of phenomenological psychology and its possible impact on the teacher's classroom.

Objectives

Specific objectives for the module are noted below. At the completion of this module, the prospective teacher should be able to:

1. Define the following terms as they relate to phenomenological learning: self-concept, social desirability, perceptual field, competence motivation, intelligence, reality, perception, conscience, and discovery.
2. Name and/or construct and use at least two instruments or techniques for obtaining data about a pupil's self-concept or social desirability and/or about the affective relationship between pupils and the prospective teacher.

[1] ASCD, *Perceiving, Behaving, Becoming* (Washington, D.C.: ASCD, 1962), p. 2.

3. Demonstrate that as a result of his teaching, there is increased positive affective growth in self-concept or social desirability of his pupils or that there is increased positive affective relationship between his pupils and himself.

Instructional Activities

There are three basic instructional parts of the module. The first part consists of readings, a slide-tape presentation, and discussion sessions designed to give the prospective teacher enough knowledge of the phenomenological terms to apply them in a learning setting.

The second part of the module consists of a seminar, readings, and work sessions culminating in the prospective teacher's selecting, constructing, and using instruments to assess self-concept and affective relationships of pupils and teachers.

The third part of the module is the actual implementation of a planned strategy on the part of the prospective teacher to bring about self-concept or social desirability growth of his pupils or increased affective pupil-teacher relationships.

Prerequisites

1. The student should be able to distinguish between the cognitive, psycho-motor, and affective domains (Teaching I, 1.0).
2. The student should be able to distinguish between the eight Gagnéian types of learning (Psychological Foundations I).
3. The student should be able to distinguish the major characteristics of S-R theories of psychology (Psychological Foundations I).
4. The student should be able to identify attending behavior on the part of individuals in a learning setting (Teaching II, 11.0).

Materials

All readings can be found in Room 230 of the Education Building. Slide/tape is available in the LRC. For any seminars, please sign up in Room 230.

MODULE INSTRUCTIONS

Part I. Definitions

A. Read the Rationale-Prospectus on page 2. If you feel that you can already perform Objective 3 noted in the prospectus, skip to Part III.
B. Either:
   1. Read article by Arthur Combs "The Human Factor in Curriculum Development." [2]

---

[2] In H. L. Jones, ed., *Curriculum Development in a Changing World* (Syracuse, N.Y.: Syracuse University Press, 1969).

    2. View slide tape, "Humanizing Education" (LRC 363).

    3. Design your own activity.

C. Turn to the page called "Definitions and Questions" in this booklet. On this page are a number of terms and questions. Define and give examples of all terms. Answer the questions. If you need help with any of the terms or questions do one of the following:

    1. Read any or all of the readings on the Reading List, page 8.

    2. Call a seminar with an instructor (10 or more students). Sign up in 230ED.

    3. Design your own activity.

Part II. Constructing Instruments

A. Attend a seminar with instructor at time posted on bulletin board in room 230. Seminar should take no longer than two hours. Be sure to bring this booklet with you.

B. Read *Diagnosing Classroom Learning Environments* by Fox, Luszki, and Schmuck (copies in Room 230). Book is extremely helpful in identifying a wide range of appropriate instruments.

C. Construct at least two instruments (to be used in Part III) to assess self-concept or social desirability of pupils or to assess pupil-teacher affective relationships. Submit instruments to instructor. When you get instructor approval go on to Part III.

Part III. Consequence Objective

A. Plan and execute learning activities which you predict will bring about positive results. Using instruments constructed in Part II, gather data relevant to the results.

B. Meet individually with instructor to report results. When you get instructor approval, exit the module.

DEFINITIONS AND QUESTIONS

As you read or rap to garner knowledge of phenomenological psychology, try to focus on specific points. Some terms and questions are noted below. Add some of your own if you wish.

How would you define:

    1. Self-concept?

    2. Social desirability?

    3. Perceptual field?

    4. Competence motivation?

    5. Intelligence?

6. Reality?
7. Perception?
8. Conscience?
9. Discovery?

How would you answer these questions?

1. Who would make the decisions on curriculum in a classroom in which the teacher acts totally in accord with phenomenological psychology?
2. What is the role of behavioral objectives in a phenomenological classroom?
3. How does set induction relate to learning in a phenomenological classroom?
4. How would a phenomenologist react to this statement: "A teacher should aim to keep his students perplexed just short of frustration"?[3]
5. How does a phenomenologist view permissiveness in the classroom?
6. What is transfer of learning to the phenomenologist?

READING LIST

Note to student: Read or view any of the following (or others, if you wish) that you feel would be beneficial in aiding your reaching the specified objectives of this module. Keep in mind that it is not the reading or viewing that is important but your achievement of the objectives, both ours and yours. All books can be found in the CBTE library. Please return them quickly to the library after completion.

Film: "Eye of the Beholder." (Notes how perceptions from different points of view differ. Although it is not on campus this film can be gotten quickly if you do need it.)

ASCD, *Perceiving, Behaving, Becoming.* Washington: ASCD, 1962. Any or all of the book. (Some 20 copies are on reserve in the main library.) Available also in 230ED.

BIGGE, MORRIS L. *Learning Theories for Teachers.* New York: Harper and Row, 1964. (Especially pp. 49–83 and 175–242.)

FRYMIER, JACK. "Focusing Future Curriculum Development," in H. L. Jones (ed.), *Curriculum Development in a Changing World.* Syracuse, N.Y.: Syracuse University Press, 1969, pages 71–83.

GINOTT, H. *Between Parent and Child.* New York: Macmillan, 1965.

GINOTT, H. *Between Parent and Teenager.* New York: Macmillan, 1968.

GINOTT, H. *Teacher and Child.* New York: Macmillan, 1972.

HAMILTON, N. K., and J. C. SAYLOR. *Humanizing the Secondary School.* Washington: ASCD, 1969.

ROGERS, CARL. *Freedom to Learn.* Columbus, Ohio: Merrill, 1969.

SILBERMAN, C. E. *Crisis in the Classroom.* New York: Vintage, 1970. (Especially Chapters 6, 7, and 8.)

[3] M. Bigge, *Learning Theories for Teachers* (New York: Harper & Row, 1964), p. 234.

SNYGG, D. "The Cognitive Field Theory: New Understandings about the Person," in *Influences in Curriculum Change*. Washington: ASCD, 1968, pages 21–27.

MORGAN, RICHARD L. *Psychology*. Westinghouse Corporation
    Unit 10—"Theories of Learning." (LRC 361 is accompanying tape.)
    Unit 12—"Perception."
    Unit 23—"Ginott's Approach to Child Development." (LRC 362 is accompanying tape.)

Module III

Affective 12.0: Professional Ethics for the Educator
Sherry B. Borgers and G. Robert Ward, developers

THE UNIVERSITY OF HOUSTON, 1973

This module is an example of a unit with exploratory (or expressive) objectives. It deals with the ethics of teaching, content that is probably most relevant in the later stages of a preservice teacher education program when the student teacher might be expressing a greater number of impact concerns. You will notice the lack of provisions for preassessment or postassessment. These are not included because the module emphasizes participation in stimulus situations rather than the acquisition of specific learning outcomes. We present the whole module, excluding Appendix A, which is a copy of the "Code of Ethics of the Education Profession" from the *NEA Handbook, 1971–72*, pp. 105–7.

AFFECTIVE 12

I. Identifiers:
    A. Module Name:
        Professional Ethics for the Educator
    B. Compiled by:
        Sherry B. Borgers
        G. Robert Ward
    C. Area:
        Affective
    D. Number:
        12

II. Prospectus:
    A. Rationale:
        Every profession has a code of ethics which serves as a guideline for the professionals in that field. The code of ethics for the education profession is the National Education Association (NEA) Code of Ethics.

B. Purpose:

As a teacher you will be a part of the education profession; therefore, there is a need for you to be familiar with the NEA Code of Ethics. This module will introduce you to the NEA Code of Ethics.

C. Overview of Module:

1. Form a group of 20–24 people; contact instructor and set a time for a 90-minute seminar.
2. Attend the seminar and participate in the activities:
    a. Individually:
        1) Read NEA Code of Ethics.
        2) Read the Teaching Situations and decide what you would do if you were the teacher.
    b. Form a subgroup of 4–6 people and compare proposed actions.
    c. Participate in the total group discussions.

D. Terminal Objective:

This objective is exploratory in nature. Upon completion of the module you will have decided what action you would take if you were the teacher in the situations, and you will have also determined whether or not your actions are consistent with the NEA Code of Ethics.

E. How to Complete Module:

Form a group, attend the seminar, and follow the directions given by the instructor.

III. Prerequisites:
None

IV. Enabling Objectives:
None

V. Preassessment:
None

VI. Activities:

A. General Instructions:

This module provides an opportunity for you to become familiar with the NEA Code of Ethics. If you do not invest yourself, you will get little from the module.

If you have questions, if you have concerns, or if a particular task seems to be difficult for you, please contact the instructor. Remember to complete the module as honestly as possible so that you can gain the maximum benefit from the suggested activities.

B. Specific Activities:

    12.1 Form a group of 20–24 people, contact the instructor and set a time for a 90-minute seminar.

    12.2 Attend the seminar and participate in the activities.

        a. Read the NEA Code of Ethics (See Appendix A).

        b. Read the Teaching Situations (See Appendix B). Decide what action you would take if you were the teacher. Check to see if your actions are consistent with the Code of Ethics. Be able to give a rationale for your actions. Do this activity individually.

        c. Form subgroups of 4–6 people and compare your proposed actions with the actions suggested by other members of your subgroup. If there are different proposed actions, refer to the NEA Code of Ethics to see if all of the actions are ethical. It is not necessary that the members of subgroups agree; however, each of you should be able to give a rationale for your choice.

        d. After the subgroups have compared answers, the instructor will lead a discussion about the NEA Code of Ethics. You may wish to consider the rationale for the Code, the value of the Code, the relation of the Code to the teaching profession, the relation of the Code to human relations skills, and how you as a teacher might change the Code of Ethics. You may also wish to discuss what to do when there is no one correct action. As a teacher there are many times when you will have to do what you believe to be best without knowing if it is really the correct action. Questions or concerns that you may have about these or similar situations and professional ethics will also be discussed.

VII. Postassessment:

None

APPENDIX B

Teaching Situations

    I. *Situation 1.* You have been teaching in the same school for seven years. Your department has a supervisor whom you neither like nor respect. You said nothing earlier this year when you believed she overlooked your good qualities; now you see that she is doing the same thing to a new teacher whom she does not like.

    II. *Situation 2.* You know that the teacher next door is a poor teacher. A boy whom you know to be a good student comes to you and tells you he is in her class. He says that she is incompetent and that he is learning nothing. He pleads with you to write a note to the counselor saying that he has your permission to transfer to your class.

III. *Situation 3.*   You find a note in your box from the principal. He asks you to come to his office. When you get to his office, he is angry because he believes you have not been doing your cafeteria duty. You have been doing your duty; however, you know that the teacher who is supposed to relieve you never comes on time.

IV. *Situation 4.*   You have taken your students on a field trip. You see one of them steal an object from the museum. Her mother is a chaperone; you believe that she also saw her daughter take the object, but she says nothing.

V. *Situation 5.*   One of your students who is a senior tells you his girlfriend is pregnant. The school year ends in another month, and they plan to be married then. He tells you this in confidence. His girlfriend is also in one of your classes, and her pregnancy is beginning to be obvious. The school rules state that neither married nor pregnant students can attend classes.

VI. *Situation 6.*   One of your first grade students often comes to school with bruises and black marks on her arms and legs. She seems afraid of all adults. You believe her father abuses her, but you have no real proof.

VII. *Situation 7.*   You and three other teachers have taken a group of students to see a play. One of the teachers is gone for several minutes; when he returns it is obvious that he has been drinking. You and he came on the same bus with sixty junior high school students.

VIII. *Situation 8.* You believe in encouraging your students to express their opinions, and at times you state your opinion about a controversial issue. During Public School Week a parent comes to visit your class. At the end of the class he tells you that he is going to complain to the principal; he calls you a liberal and says that you are forcing your ideas on the students. He says that it is a teacher's job to be objective. Your students are still in the room, and they are looking at you, waiting for you to reply.

IX. *Situation 9.*   You have a boy in one of your accelerated classes. He is incapable of doing the work. You talk to him about transferring to another class where the work is less demanding. He tells you that his parents force him to take accelerated classes, and he knows he is not really smart enough. You feel sorry for him so you agree to let him stay in your class. However, he cannot compete with the other students, and the first semester he receives a "C". He then becomes upset because his parents are not happy with his grades. During the second semester he develops an ulcer. His mother calls you at home and tells you that her son has an ulcer; she also points out that you demanded too much of her son in your accelerated class.

X. *Situation 10.*   You are at a party. A lady whom you do not know tells a story about a teacher at the school where you teach. She does not have all the facts, and you believe she is being unfair to both the teacher and the school.

5

personalizing programs

Critics of competency-based teacher education have noted that while individual teachers can be taught to demonstrate specific skills related directly to the teaching act, these individual skills, by themselves, do not guarantee success in teaching.

We had a conversation recently with a CBTE student about the competencies identified by Rosenshine and Furst (1973) as characteristic of effective teachers (see Chapter 2). The student said that he had been using those skills for several semesters and was using them regularly at that time in his student teaching. What was important to him at this point was how he applied those skills in his own unique way. He also noted that while the Rosenshine-Furst skills were helping him to cope with most classroom management problems, they were not of much value when working through psychosocial problems with pupils.

Earlier in the program this student teacher had attempted a module on probing questions and his experience was an interesting one. In his own words:

The module was interesting. I had never thought about probing questions before as being anything that you can learn. The module was helpful, I read some things, saw some films and could identify them. Then I tried it with a small group of kids in MacArthur High School. My cooperating teacher kept finding me all kinds of things to do. Anyway, I really felt uncomfortable asking probes. I knew what they were. I knew how to do it. But it made me feel like I was putting the kids on the spot by probing their answers. Heck, I don't like to have people put *me* on the spot.

It occurred to me later why I felt uncomfortable. I was more interested in being liked than I was in teaching. When that realization happened, I really felt more at home in the classroom with kids. I still have problems, but I have strengths too.

The preceding anecdote is not an atypical story coming from students or instructors in teacher education. If a CBE program actually ignores the personal psychosocial needs of students in the program, it is doomed. This chapter focuses on how personalization can be built into a program, be it competency-based or otherwise.

Personalization is needed for growth on the part of individual teachers. All programs espouse the need for healthy, happy, loving pupils. Teachers should work with pupils to these ends. Yet, the basic premise is incomplete. Healthy, happy, loving *teachers* are a necessary prerequisite to being able to work with pupils toward the same ends.

We make a clear distinction between *personalization* and *individualization*. Individualization is the identification and sequencing of instruction according to the cognitive needs of learners. The individualization process is in force as instructors specify enabling activities and competency attainment by a student, or in the application of self-paced modules, or when students choose their own pace or learning activity. Personalization goes beyond this. Personalized instruction is relevant to the learner's inner personal goals and needs. Personalization helps the learner to become aware of his personal needs, potential, and limitations, and it offers instruction that is sequenced according to what we will call "concerns."

In this chapter we would like to discuss personalization theory and explore some practical applications we have observed that might help CBE adopters to personalize their own programs. Our schema:

Page	Heading	Questions
137	Personalization—Some Background	What do you mean by "personalization"? What are some key elements in a personalized program?
139	Psychological Theories	What are some ways of looking at the psychosocial development of preprofessionals?
141	A Conceptual Framework for Personalization	What are teacher concerns?

PERSONALIZATION—SOME BACKGROUND

Every curriculum builder likes to think that his effort provides some form of "personalization" for students. Every program builder strives for a realistic structure that is relevant to the needs of students. With all the commitment toward personalization, however, it still remains a seldom-reached goal, one that eludes most of us in professional education programs.

What is personalization? For one student personalization can be found in having the opportunity to select the experiences that he feels he needs. In CBTE, students spend a considerable amount of time in schools. One student may quickly note that he needs some help with classroom management procedures. Personalization takes place when the student's perceived need is met with some classroom management help. Another student may be given the task of working up a science lesson for seventh graders. Personalization for this student may be no more than having a science specialist sit with him to outline some possibilities. Personalization for other students can be seen when a counselor is available to talk with them on a one-to-one basis about problems or concerns, even if the concerns have little relevance to "becoming a teacher."

In short, the efforts that are made for personal contact with students and to enhance their personal growth are efforts toward personalization. If an instructional program is personalized, then more attention has been placed on the wants, needs, attitudes, and concerns of individual students. Personalization also calls for one-to-one contact between instructors and students. People contact is vital. In a helping profession, a professional must be able to interact with people in mutually rewarding ways. Personalized programs must reflect this. Personalized programs must also reflect the fact that different students might have totally different concerns, thus necessitating a totally different set of experiences. And even for those students who have identified similar sets of competencies or skills to work toward, the order of their acquisition of the competencies may be totally different. CBE allows us to look at the education of professionals in other than a mass-production manner; an additional emphasis on personalization will allow CBE to focus on unique programs for each student.

To meet more than just a few of the different needs of students who are on their way to becoming professionals is a massive task. Of all of the aspects of CBE, personalization is the most important. Selecting competencies, involving all affected persons, building modules and evaluation devices, creating a management system—these are all important. But without some form of trusting relationship between faculty and students, all these other efforts toward CBE are doomed. There is not an educator in the world who would argue against the assumption that one of the things we want out of all educational experiences is happy, healthy, loving, and accepting students. A logical extension of this is that for this assumption to come to fruition, we need happy, healthy, loving, and accepting teachers. To guarantee this result, a teacher education program must permit its students to look at themselves and how others view them. Yet no one in his right mind would be willing to take this risk without some kind of trusting relationship. The whole focus of the "yes–not yet" grading system of Chapter 3 is such that it permits people to make mistakes.

Often when building professional programs we overlook some basic tenets that many of us write about in our less hectic, more reflective moments. One such tenet is how self-concept and acceptance grows. Whether we talk about kindergarten children, high school seniors, or preprofessionals, the sequence does not vary. "I'd like to try that; I think I can do it; I can do it; I'm not such a bad person after all; I'm OK, you're OK." Whether it's learning to tie a shoe or presenting a lecture to a group of pupils, the sequence starts with some form of motivation, a willingness to try. This willingness to try in a "yes–not yet" environment leads eventually to "I can do it" satisfactions, which in turn lead to a feeling of self-adequacy. The last step is the key one for the teaching profession. Unless children are successful and have feelings of self-adequacy, they will never accept the adequacy of others. Unless teachers have these same feelings of adequacy, they never will accept others as adequate. Without that competency any program fails, for teachers, above all, must be acceptant of others.

Personalization is the key to self-acceptance. Personalization recognizes the sequence and plans for its fulfillment. For if the sequence is not respected we are doomed to hear again and again the plaintive cry of the education major: "I didn't learn a thing until I began teaching." In programs where students' concerns are not assessed, it is small wonder that the content seems less than useful, for students are receiving answers to questions they aren't asking.

In the remainder of this chapter we will be looking at some attempts toward personalization. Before proceeding, however, we would like to share seven assumptions that we feel can do much to lay the foundation for some form of personalization in a professional program. The assumptions have been developed by Richard Ford, president of Richard Ford Associates, a private consulting firm in Syracuse, New York. While you read them you might note your degree of acceptance or rejection of each assumption:

a. Most people, most of the time, want to do the best job possible.

b. People need to be taken seriously.

c. Leadership can and should be a shared function.

d. People who are closest to the action are the best sources for information.

e. People need to be involved in planning and decisions that will impact directly on their activities.

f. When there is trust there is validity in data; when there is low trust there is low validity in data.

g. In the absence of shared objectives there can be no accountability, only justification.

PSYCHOLOGICAL THEORIES

In Chapter 2 we discussed the importance of developing CBE programs on the basis of explicit assumptions. We said that your assumptions will influence your choice of competencies, enabling activities, evaluations, strategies, and, indeed, all phases of program operation. One basic set of assumptions that must be faced deals with the model of personal growth and learning that the program will follow. To personalize a program, one must necessarily have some concept of the personal development of the students it reaches. The psychological theory that a program ascribes to is therefore very important, but there is no one, "right" viewpoint. Psychologists have been picking apart and piecing together human development for years, and a variety of different theories have emerged from their labors. Several have been used with success by CBE developers. Three of the most notable theories are third-force psychology, operant conditioning, and human relations training.

Third-force psychology is well represented and described in the 1962 Yearbook of the Association for Supervision and Curriculum Development, *Perceiving, Behaving, Becoming: A New Focus for Education.* Representatives of the third-force movement, such as Carl Rogers, Abraham Maslow, and Arthur Combs, view growth of the self as being dependent on and shaped by one's interaction with others. One's growth is directly related to the quality, intensity, and diversity of these interactions. Growth also is related to the perceptual meaning that these interactions hold for the self.

The humanistic component of an education program based on third-force psychology would not necessarily be found in modules or other instructional materials, but rather in the assumptions and beliefs that the program developers and instructional staff hold about their students. No humanistic objectives can counteract the effects of the instructor who does not believe that students can be trusted with manipulative materials, media equipment, or perhaps even responsibility for their own learning.

Another point of view about people and learning is put forth by the Skinnerian school. The research and practice of this movement began with the early work of B. F. Skinner and his use of the Skinner box in the 1930s. In these early studies Skinner found that pigeons, rats, and other animals could be trained to perform specific behaviors by rewarding them for demonstrating these behaviors.

By the late 1950s many of the concepts and techniques of what has become known as operant conditioning were being applied in educational settings. It has been demonstrated that positive reinforcement of desired pupil behaviors can be employed to get pupils to perform tasks more quickly, efficiently, quietly, neatly, and so forth. In his book, *Technology of Teaching* (1968), Skinner explored various implications of his work for teaching.

Whether or not you accept either third-force psychology or operant conditioning as your basic psychological premise, there are some fascinating outcomes of each. Not the least of these is the fact that personalization steps in each may contradict each other. Operant conditioning places much more emphasis on outside stimuli for personalization, but third-force proponents look more for inner motivation. The two do not mix readily. The authors know of several school relationships that have been broken because of this schism. In one case, a principal insisted that CBE interns be removed from "his" school because they were issuing M&M's (rewards for "appropriate" behavior) to his pupils. Other principals, noting a need for more "quiet" and a heavier push toward the "basics" became rather adamant in discouraging teachers from using Rogerian methods to allow student self-decision about what would be learned. The point was made in Chapter 2: Assumptions must be shared. We make it again here.

A different approach to attending to the personal dynamics, skills, and needs of persons is accomplished through the varied strategies of Human Relations training. Such terms as "sensitivity training," "encounter groups," "retreats," "marathons," "O D (organizational development) workshops," and "T (training) groups" are used with much enthusiasm by some, with fear and trepidation by others, and probably with confusion by most.

Two general foci seem to underly the goals of Human Relations training. First, through personal interactions with groups—where immediate feedback and reinforcement are possible—a person can gain insight into himself and develop awareness of his interactions with others. Secondly, groups provide a setting in which the participants can learn more effective skills for team building and collectively working to accomplish tasks. The relative emphasis that any particular group has on increased self-awareness and/or increased group productivity capability seems to be dependent on the reasons for the group's existence, the agreed-upon goals of the group, and the functioning level of the group leader or trainer.

As will be expanded upon later in this chapter, a number of existing competency-based teacher education programs use retreatlike Human Relations (or "H-R") sessions to build trust relationships between and among faculty and students. During these retreats, group-building allows students to identify other students with whom they will associate throughout the remainder of their programs.

A CONCEPTUAL FRAMEWORK
FOR PERSONALIZED TEACHER EDUCATION

Personalization of instruction calls for a careful blending of education and psychology. The unique concerns, worries, and needs of students in preprofessional programs cannot be met with more courses or modules on teaching strategies or interaction analysis. Similarly, the perceived weaknesses of preprofessionals in teaching areas cannot be met with a psychology course.

An exciting convergence of psychological research and theory and educational research and theory has been accomplished by the staff of the USOE-NIE-funded Research and Development Center for Teacher Education at the University of Texas at Austin. At this R&D center, clinical psychologists and teacher educators combined forces and resources to first research mental health in teacher education (Fuller et al., 1969) and later to research and delineate a "Personalized Teacher Education Program" conceptual framework and to develop an operational program that took into account the psychological and educational research findings, theory, and practice.

The operational program is designed around seven components: (1) instructional modules, (2) interdisciplinary faculty teaming, (3) early and continuing field experiences, (4) assessment systems, (5) feedback systems, (6) time blocking, and (7) evaluation. Many of the salient features and products of this operationalization are discussed elsewhere in this book. At this point, we would like to present a description of the conceptual framework for the Personalized Teacher Education Program. This framework has been most thoroughly articulated in the writings of Frances F. Fuller, who has devoted her career to researching, conceptualizing, and practicing personalized education. The conceptual framework as described by Fuller (1974) is organized around two dimensions: (1) *concerns of teachers* and (2) the *principal processes of instruction.* A third component of the conceptualization is a detailed analysis and modeling of the process and dynamics of feedback to learners. This feedback theory will also be briefly described.

Concerns of Teachers

We are going to spend quite a bit of time in the remainder of this book talking about the concerns of teachers. What is a concern? To us, a concern is anything that is of consequence to a teacher. There is not enough paper. The chalk supply is gone. My mother-in-law won't get off my back. My co-worker has body odor. I can't get the kids to listen. I'm afraid of that one big kid who acts so hostile. My paycheck is not going to cover my expenses.

Concerns of teachers differ from teacher to teacher. Any principal who has had a staff member go through a traumatic experience (death in family, divorce) recognizes that for some period of time the needs of pupils will be secondary to the concerns of the teacher. Inservice training on IGE (Individually Guided Education) or "Science as Inquiry" directed at such a teacher might as well be fed to the gerbils in the science room.

Even the concerns of two teachers with the same amount of experience and not undergoing a recent trauma will be different. The differences of concern and satisfaction for experienced versus beginning teachers are even more revealing. Gabriel (1957) explored the problems and satisfactions of teachers in England. His results are seen in Exhibit 5.1. Problems for the beginning teachers were those of discipline and criticism from superiors. Contrast this with the problems identified by the experienced teachers: how to deal with the slow progress made by some pupils.

The satisfactions are even more interesting. While the beginning teachers expressed satisfaction from inspector praise and, of all things, holidays, the experienced teachers felt most satisfied when speaking of the success of their former pupils.

EXHIBIT 5.1 Concerns of Experienced vs. Inexperienced Teachers in England

	Who Is More Concerned?	p
Problems:		
Criticism from superiors	Inexperienced	.01
Maintaining discipline	Inexperienced	.01
Slow progress of pupils	Experienced	.05
Satisfactions:		
Praise from inspectors	Inexperienced	.01
Holidays	Inexperienced	.01
Success of former pupils	Experienced	.01

Adapted from John Gabriel, Emotional Problems of the Teacher in the Classroom *(London & New Zealand: Angus & Robertson, Ltd., 1957), pp. 197–99.*

The Gabriel study is just one of a number of fascinating studies of the concerns of teachers. If we accept the notion that if a person is concerned about a topic, then that topic is relevant, we will have the start of a good definition of *relevance* in education curricula. If we also accept the notion that the concerns of everyone are different, then the need for personalized curricula, based on self-pacing, becomes rather obvious. The mass-production model that we have been using in professional education really does not reflect any degree of personalization. On the other hand, we cannot forget that as educators who have responsibilities to our profession we must see to it that our students obtain the skills, competencies, and attitudes that they want *and* need. Personalized teacher education programs must reflect both.

Teachers' Awareness of Their Concerns

This section looks at the awareness or lack of awareness of concerns on the part of teachers. Assuming that concerns cannot be coped with until they are evident, then the arousal of concerns on the part of teachers is highly important.

There have been a few public statements of teachers' concerns that have made the best-seller list—*Up the Down Staircase* and *The Way It Spoze to Be* are notable examples—but even these expressions have been largely ignored. Probably the most ignored example is a twenty-plus-year-old book by Arthur Jersild, *When Teachers Face Themselves*. Jersild discusses teachers' self-understanding, emphasizing that it is common for teachers to be anxious, lonely, searching, hostile, compassionate, and even in need of sexual gratification.

Frances Fuller has been studying teachers' concerns for fifteen years, and we would like to present some of her ideas here.

The concerns of teachers, as seen in a Johari window, look like this:

SELF OTHER	Known to Self	Unknown to Self
Known to Other	Public A	Incongruent C
Unknown to Other	Private B	Unconscious D

In the first box A, the concern is known both to the person himself and to another person. For example, the teacher says to the class, "Let's be quiet on our way to lunch." The class knows the teacher is concerned about noise in the hall. That concern is *public*.

The teacher is also wondering whether the lunch menu will conform to her diet, and if it does not, whether she will eat the brownies. She does not tell the class though. This concern is private. The teacher (self) knows, but others do not know. Such *private* concerns are represented by quadrant B above.

INCONGRUENT CONCERNS

If we look at the diagram again, at box C in the upper right hand column, we see that concerns may be known to others but not known to the self. These are concerns we have, concerns of which *others* are aware, but of which we ourselves are *not* aware. Can we have concerns of which we are not aware?

Miss Smith is walking beside the class telling them to be quiet. As they approach the principal's office door, John notices several things. Miss Smith straightens up. Her shushing becomes a little more insistent, then stops after they pass. John knows that Miss Smith is concerned about the principal's good opinion. Miss Smith does not know, or at least she could not freely name, what she feels. It may be apparent to any observer that Miss Smith is concerned about the principal's good opinion. At the same time, Miss Smith might deny it and even maintain that she is not concerned about the principal's opinion.

A classic example of incongruent behavior is the loud, angry comment, "I am not angry! I am not shouting!" Congruence is awareness of one's own feelings, a good match between what one feels and what one knows about what he feels. Incongruence is lack of awareness of one's feelings. Incongruent concerns are those of which another person is aware, but of which I, the owner of the concerns, am not aware. These concerns are represented in C above.

UNCONSCIOUS CONCERNS

One kind of concern can exist that is recognized neither by the person himself nor by others around him. This is illustrated in cell D of the diagram. Consequently, there is no way of knowing what, if anything, is there until it "dawns" on the person or on someone else. If it dawns only on the person himself, it becomes private (A). If it dawns only on an observer, it becomes incongruent (C). For example, an experience from this sector may move to the private sector when some insight dawns. We say "I know now that was how I felt then, but I didn't realize it at the time."

A teacher may have a feeling something is amiss but not be sure exactly what it is. She may think she is concerned about one thing, a private concern perhaps, and actually be concerned about something else, something of which she is not aware, an unconscious concern. A common example is a student teacher's concern about discipline. She says, and truly believes, that she wants the class to quiet down. Still, she stands by helplessly when the class is unruly. Many alternatives are suggested to her that would achieve her expressed objective of quieting the class. But she does not accept the suggestions, or if she tries to do what is suggested, the suggested method fails. For example, she is told to be, and tries hard to be, "stern."

But her sternness is half-hearted. Her heart is just not in it. Then one day the truth dawns on her. She is not concerned entirely with discipline as she thought she was. She is concerned also with a quite different goal. She is concerned with winning the affection of the class. She wants them to like her. She fears that if she reprimands them, they will not like her. She is concerned both about a problem of which she is aware (discipline) and about a problem of which she is not aware (being liked). She was not sufficiently aware of this last concern to put it into words, but it was there. When the truth dawns, her concern moves from the unconscious sector to the private sector. No one else knows, still; but she does. (Fuller, 1970.)

Obviously, the more public the concerns are, the more open communication can be and the fewer hidden agendas will exist between people. Teachers who recognize their concerns are better able to make the decision to work on them.

In addition to identifying concerns, teacher education programs must begin to include procedures to address them. If programs are going to have students exiting with more than a mechanical ability to apply skills, students are going to have to perceive the need they have for the skills.

Personalized programs permit students to focus on ways of alleviating their concerns. Returning to the three psychological theories discussed earlier, it might be noted that both the third-force movement and proponents of human relations are emphatic about the arousal and handling of personal concerns. The Johari window example just presented is a convenient way of assessing self-growth for both camps. "Personalization" for each group would include allowing students to identify and work through their own unique concerns.

Making the job easier for teacher education curriculum builders is the knowledge that there is a sequence of concerns through which most teacher education students often progress. In other words, the concerns of teachers are often predictable. The sequence in which they normally progress is as follows:

Phase I—Concerns about Self
    Level 0—Concerns unrelated to teaching
    Level 1—Concerns about self as a teacher
Phase II—Concerns about Task
    Level 2—How adequate am I?
    Level 3—How do my pupils feel about me?
Phase III—Concerns about Impact
    Level 4—Are they learning what I'm teaching?
    Level 5—Are they learning what they need?
    Level 6—How can I improve as a teacher?

The first phase of concerns is essentially selfish. Neophyte student teachers usually come into the training program with no teaching experience and, consequently, no realistic view of teaching upon which to focus professional concerns. Their statements at this time are usually about concerns completely unrelated to teaching: "Will I get a date for this weekend?" "How am I going to keep my grade point average up?" "I don't have any decent clothes to wear when I'm teaching in the schools." We call this Level 0, because essentially there is nothing there related to teaching.

Given a dose of the real world of teaching with their backs to the chalkboard, neophytes will quickly begin expressing Level 1 concerns—concerns about self as a teacher. These are usually concerns about psychological and even physical safety in the teaching role: "How am I ever going to control a class. They'll see that I'm scared and they'll eat me alive!" New teachers are also worried about asking "stupid" questions and have to be reassured that no questions are "stupid" if one needs to know the answer. They also need orientation to aspects of school life that are often taken for granted: "Can I go into the teachers' lounge? Where is it?" "What do I do if a kid splits his head open?" "How do I handle the case of some other teacher's child misbehaving in the halls?"

Once the new teacher's orientation and survival concerns are adequately dealt with, she begins to express concerns about the tasks of teaching, or pedagogy. This is Phase II. The Level 2 concerns—"How adequate am I?"—are focused on one's ability to cope with the demands of instruction. A typical question might be, "What do I do when I don't know answers to their questions?" In Level 3 new teachers are concerned about being respected and liked by their pupils. They may begin to fall into traps of playing for the children's favor at the expense of discipline and control of the learning environment. Phase II is the traditional area targeted by most teacher education programs. It is the major phase for preservice teachers, provided that steps are taken to resolve Phase I concerns early so that Phase II can supersede them.

Much later, after concerns about themselves and their adequacy in the skills of pedagogy are at least tentatively answered, teachers' concerns move into Phase III, concerns about their impact on pupils. These are questions usually asked by highly regarded, experienced teachers: Level 4, "Are they learning what I'm teaching?" Level 5, "Are they learning what they need?" Level 6, "How can I improve myself as a teacher?"

As might be seen, if this sequence holds consistently, and there is evidence that it does for most professionals (Fuller, 1969), then it can provide the curriculum planner with a handle for beating the "lack of relevancy" game.

One relatively simple and yet profound strategy for personalizing a CBE program is to sequence the competencies and experiences within the program according to this developmental concerns sequence. This approach is equally useful in training other kinds of professionals besides teachers. One of the authors has been involved in an application of the concerns theory to a dental education program. Once competencies have been identified there is usually no great difficulty in sorting them by whether they address self, task, or impact concerns.

A DESCRIPTIVE MODEL FOR INSTRUCTION

The second dimension of the Fuller conceptual framework for personalized teacher education is focused on the instructional processes that a program must bring to bear:

> The educator's task is a complex one: gathering information to enable him to understand the student deeply as a person; gathering information which the student needs; translating the information for the student so that it will be maximally usable to him; feeding the information back to the student so that the student is aware of the real import of the information and its relationship to his concerns; gathering information which the student needs; confronting the student with reality; negotiating choices with the student to evolve a mutually satisfying set of developing goals; supplying for the student alternate routes and procedures for implementing these goals; and monitoring movement toward these goals. (Fuller, 1974.)

Fuller subsumes these instructional activities under four major instructional processes: *assessment, awareness, arousal,* and *accomplishment.* In a CBTE format, these four can be summarized as follows:

Assessment—A prospective teacher prior to certification must demonstrate certain minimal competencies. Assessment is made of how close the teacher is to this goal.

Awareness—Regardless of what a teacher educator thinks about the skills of a prospective teacher, somehow these thoughts must be translated into terms the student understands.

Arousal—Unless a prospective teacher can see a need to change his behavior, modify an attitude, or increase skills, the student will not change her present style.

Accomplishment—Once the prospective teacher has been aroused to change, she must still identify alternatives, implement a plan, and monitor her own movement.

In competency-based programs, this sequence plays an important part in each student's progress. Each student teacher is aware of her feelings of inadequacy with pupils; there is no need to arouse interest in working on instructional materials that are designed to help her conquer her inadequacy feelings. That's the easy part. But what do you do with students who cannot see themselves as ineffective even when all knowledgeable observers can plainly see their lack of competence? This is the hard part of CBTE. The difficulty is compounded when thoughts of personalization are considered. Providing supportive feedback to living, breathing, preprofessional students calls for humane ways of arousing concerns. The key is the student's acceptance of the validity of the data. Trust increases this validity.

Feedback

A basic premise so far has been that in order to see a need for change, the preprofessional must be aware of the present state of his skills, attitudes, and so forth. One blessing in most preprofessional programs is the existence of videotape recorders and television cameras. Anything that can be provided to increase the validity of data is a worthwhile tool. Videotape can be invaluable.

Fuller and Manning (1973) provide the most complete review of research literature with respect to feedback in teacher education and videotape feedback in particular. In the past, microteaching projects at Stanford and other developments throughout the nation have provided evidence that people can change when they are confronted with their performance on videotape and audiotape. Videotape feedback of students performing teaching skills is used in many existing CBTE efforts to focus students' attention on their teaching styles. Students in some programs use videotapes like blue books to demonstrate competence and achievement of objectives. When a student is ready to demonstrate a skill such as probing questions, he brings an example of his teaching on videotape to an instructor.

There are, however, some potential dangers in self-confrontation. Under certain conditions and with certain students, self-confrontation can have no effect; and in other instances, it can even have harmful consequences. Many people are astonished, shocked, and even frightened by the self-confrontation experience. Persons with low self-concept are less able to discern discrepancies between what they experience and what they observe on the videotape, consequently they are less likely to be aroused to change. Dogmatism and body image also influence the effect of self-confrontation. A person who has poor body image may not be able to see beyond this or he may obtain confirmation via the feedback process, while more dogmatic people are apt to be less open to change.

Fuller (1972) has proposed a paradigm for viewing the dynamics of feedback. This paradigm can be represented by a triangle. The points of the triangle represent three perspectives that the student can bring to the feed-back session. The top of the triangle represents the ideal goal (*G*) that the student is attempting to achieve. The second perspective is represented by the experience (*E*) that the student recalls. This point represents his re-membered feelings, his perceptions, his thoughts about his performance. The third point (*O*) represents what is observed when the student views himself on videotape. Goal (*G*), Experiencing (*E*) and Observation (*O*) then become the three points of a triangle.

EXHIBIT 5.2   A Representation of Posited Discrepancies and Their Conceptual Bases.

   The relative length of the sides of the triangle represents the degree of discrepancy between each of the perspectives. From one frame of reference the student experienced (*E*) his performance, and from another frame of reference the student observes (*O*) his performance. The degree of differ-ence between these two perspectives is represented relatively by the length of the *E–O* side of the triangle. This side represents the amount of awareness and realism that the student has about his performance. The more objective and realistic the student is, the shorter the side.

   The relative length of the side of the triangle between what the student observes and his goal (*O–G*) represents the student's perception of how far he has to move to make his behavior congruent with his ideal. If the distance is moderate, the student will feel that the change that is needed is reasonable and that he can easily handle the change. If the distance is extremely large, the student may feel that sufficient change is hopeless, or that his behavior is out of control, or that he simply has a long way to go.

   The third side of the triangle (*E–G*) represents the size of the dis-crepancy between how the student feels about what he did and his ideal.

Discrepancies on this side of the triangle represent how satisfied or dissatisfied the student feels about his performance. Dissatisfaction can be a purposeful motivator for some students, while for others it may lead to discouragement and withdrawal.

As has been pointed out by Newlove and Pendleton (1974), once the approximate size and shape of a student's *EOG* triangle has been assessed, several questions need to be asked and analyzed. What is the impact of the discrepancy on the student? How satisfied is the student? Does the student feel motivated to change or is he too discouraged?

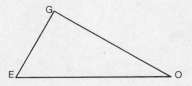

This triangle represents Adolph, who is not realistic (long *E–O*). He is reasonably satisfied with his experience, feeling that it is relatively close to his goal (short *E–G*). However, there is incongruence between his goal and his observed performance (long *G–O*). He fails to see the discrepancy between *O* and *G* and *O* and *E* by ignoring, doubting, repressing, or forgetting behavior he observes when viewing his performance. His performance is poor, his perceptions are distorted, and yet he is not disturbed. In a feedback session he is not apt to change based on hints and mild suggestions. Whether change is even possible is something that will need serious consideration. Will Adolph realize that his actual performance is greatly different from his ideal? Will he become depressed and discouraged, or will he be able to accept the revelation and deal with it? These questions need to be thought over by the instructor conducting the feedback session.

Another example is the triangle representing Judy.

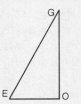

This triangle is tall and thin, which suggests that she sees things realistically (short *E–O*). However, there are large discrepancies between Judy's present level of performance and her ideal (long *O–G*) and between her experiencing and her ideal (long E–G). Since the distance between her experiencing and her goal is great, she is probably dissatisfied. The great distances may be due to poor performance, or they could be due to setting unrealistically high standards. Before Judy is confronted with her performance by videotaping, there should be assurances that that there is hope for improving her performance, otherwise there is strong likelihood that Judy may become discouraged.

Other shapes of triangles obviously exist and have other interpretations. The implications of self-confrontation need to be considered in developing any CBE program, since assessment and feedback are such crucial processes.

In Fuller's conceptualization of personalized teacher education, the concerns of teachers coupled with the four principal instructional processes as applied through self-confrontation procedures make for a powerful representation of the highly complex process of personalizing the education of professionals.

OPERATIONAL STRATEGIES FOR PERSONALIZING A CBE PROGRAM

As was pointed out in the introduction to this chapter, personalization of education means the individualization of learning experiences based not only on the cognitive needs of the learner but also on his personal needs. The psychological assumptions that underlie a particular CBE program will determine the objectives and desired effects of various personalizing procedures. Even more important, the psychological assumptions that an outside observer brings to viewing a particular CBE program are going to color his interpretation (if he is not careful) and influence judgment of whether or not a particular program is or is not personalized. What is highly personalized to the operant conditioner may appear to be nonhumanistic and mechanistic to the perceptual-psychology-oriented educator, while both may view a group-oriented program as not attending to individual needs. Personalization is in the eye of the beholder.

The remainder of this chapter is devoted to brief descriptions of various operational strategies for use in personalizing CBE programs.

T-Groups, Encounter Groups, and Sensitivity Training

Let's look for a moment at the function of doing "group work" with prospective teachers, doctors, lawyers, and other professionals. As we view it, there are a couple of choices:

1. Group work to focus trainees on how they interact with others. In

such a group the trainer would help trainees focus on interactive styles. In teaching, for example, it is assumed that the better a teacher interacts with pupils, the more conducive the environment will be for learning. Prospective teachers need to get honest feedback on their interactive styles before they can make a conscious effort to modify them, if need be.

2. Group work to build groups. Most existing CBE program managers are faced with the fact that many of the students are not able to self-pace. Recognizing the safety of the group, some programs run sessions where students identify other students with whom they would like to work for an extended period of time, perhaps as long as four years. Group work allows students to make the choice of subgroup membership. Experiences can also be provided that focus on group cohesiveness. In program operation, students can self-pace or group pace; it's their decision. There is always the group membership to fall back upon.

While group work may sound like a useful method to utilize in personalizing a program, the reader must not forget the need for a qualified trainer. Having gone through human relations training (H-R) experiences does not qualify a person to be a trainer. It must also be remembered that some H-R exercises are better for group building than others; some are better for decision making than others. A useful manual for program builders once they have identified their objectives for H-R is *Human Relations Development, A Manual for Educators* by G. M. Gazda et al. (Boston: Allyn & Bacon, 1973).

A source of already developed exercises for teacher education is the *Interaction Laboratory for Teacher Development* (ILTD) produced by the Technical and Educational Group, Economic Development Operations, Thiokol Chemical Corporation, Ogden, Utah, in cooperation with Weber State College (1971). The laboratory is designed to provide future teachers with a human relations model that is oriented toward the realities of their future teaching situations. Four aspects of teacher human relations skills are dealt with: *basic communication* (exercises related to the complexities of the communication process as it is found in the school setting), *group interaction* (exercises related to facilitating feedback from student peers and understanding of group process in the classroom), *interpersonal skills* (exercises targeted toward expanding role flexibility and providing opportunity to test and practice new teaching related behaviors), and *professional problems* (exercises dealing with professional problem solving). All the work is centered around one basic premise: "Teachers are primarily people interacting with other people in a specialized way" (J. J. Kampsnider,

1971). Activities are built around such skills as one-to-one communication, listening, rumor, feedback, group consensus, teacher-pupil interaction, decision making, and problems with parents.

The laboratory exercises provide students with an opportunity to analyze and practice the various role patterns that they will be meeting as they deal with pupils, parents, and fellow teachers in their careers.

The Retreat

Retreats are increasingly being used with CBE programs. Usually these retreats occur at the beginning of the program and involve both students and faculty. In a few cases retreats occur at other points in a program as well. Program developers who employ retreats believe that isolating faculty with a new group of students provides a valuable opportunity for everyone to get to know and trust each other early in the program as well as presenting an opportunity for the participants to get to know themselves better. By being off on a retreat, all participants are involved and telephone calls and other interruptions are minimized.

Normally retreats incorporate various human relations training activities. Whether the exercises are more self-awareness or interpersonal-skill oriented depends on the orientation of the human relations experts who are involved with the program.

One of the most innovative retreats is the opener to the ISTEP (Individualized Secondary Teacher Education Program) at Brigham Young University. Regardless of the time of year, the students and faculty begin the ISTEP by going on a three-day survival camp in the Rocky Mountains. Many of the standard human relations training exercises such as the "blind walk" are employed, as well as Outward Bound type activities such as rope climbing. Value clarification processes include preparing a meal, beginning with slaughtering a live animal. The ISTEP is based on several different categories of objectives ranging from required to optional to student developed. On the retreat helping to prepare the meal is required, as is a swim in a mountain stream. Eating the prepared meal is optional.

A basic assumption behind such a retreat is that through these kinds of experiences students get to know themselves, other students, and faculty better than they would by only attending classes and doing the more conventional modular instruction. Following the retreat, students return to the campus knowing their fellow students and the faculty on a first-name basis, and they are ready to participate in the remainder of the program.

Organization Development

Another source of interpersonal communication skill and group process exercises are the materials and activities devised for organization development or OD. Each of these exercises has been devised or adapted for application in school settings. The following references for organization development exercises include a wide range of tested activities as well as some theory and rationale for their appropriate use.

JUNG, C., R. PINO, and R. EMORY. *RUPS: Research Utilizing Problem Solving.* Portland: Northwest Regional Educational Laboratory, 1970.

JUNG, C., R. HOWARD, R. EMORY, and R. PINO. *Interpersonal Communications.* Portland: Northwest Regional Educational Laboratory, 1971.

PFEIFFER, J. W., and J. E. JONES. *A Handbook of Structural Experiences for Human Relations Training.* Iowa City: University Associates Publishers and Consultants. (Vol. I, 1969; Vol. II, 1970; Vol. III, 1971; Vol. IV, 1973).

SCHMUCK, R. A., et al. *Handbook of Organization Development in Schools.* National Press Books, 1972.

Value Clarification

The theory and strategies entailed in the processes of value clarification that Louis E. Raths, Merrill Harmin, and Sidney B. Simon have been researching and developing for use in schools seem to also have utility as a personalization strategy in CBE programs. These researchers suggest that children and many adults have difficulty in making value decisions. The manifestations of this indecisiveness are not limited just to inability to make quick and clear decisions but also show up in schools in the form of "behavior problems" and inconsistent decision making. The reasons for this dilemma are many, including a lifetime of exposure to so many different and contradictory events and scenes through newspapers, comics, television, movies, peers, parents, institutions, and their own encounters. This bombardment does not leave a person feeling that he has alternatives to freely choose from but rather leaves him confused and uncertain and facing more to decide than he is able to handle.

Raths, Harmin, and Simon suggest that values are not hard and fast and that decisions are seldom all right or wrong, very clear, or totally uncertain. Values are developed and are changing depending on the experiences, events, and growth of the individual. They suggest that for something to be of value it must meet seven criteria that, in combination, compose the process of valuing. Values must be (1) chosen freely from (2) among alternatives, (3) after thoughtful consideration of each alternative and its consequences. A value must be (4) prized and (5) affirmed by the actions of the valuer, and (6) values must affect choices in living, and (7) they must be repeated.

The researchers do not suggest what values a person should hold but do suggest that instruction in the process of value clarification can be an important part of education. In their writings they suggest teaching strategies and behaviors that can be employed in helping students learn the process of valuing. Many of these suggestions (ranging from relatively simple clarifying responses that a teacher can make in response to a child's statements on up to full class activities) are easily adaptable to and have been used in CBE programs.

The following references are a good starting point for information about value clarification:

RATHS, L. E., M. HARMIN, and S. B. SIMON. *Values and Teaching*. Columbus, Ohio: Charles E. Merrill, 1966.

SIMON, S. B., L. L. HOWE, and H. KIRSCHENBAUM. *Values Clarification*. New York: Hart Publishing Co., 1972.

CURWIN, R., and B. FUHRMANN. *Discovering Your Teaching Self*. Englewood Cliffs, N.J.: Prentice-Hall, Inc., 1975.

With the authors' permission we present as Exhibit 5.3 a table from the latter book. This is one exercise from *Discovering Your Teaching Self*. It focuses on having students identify what classroom qualities they value. After individual students have made their choices, group sessions are used to aid all students in sharing and clarification.

EXHIBIT 5.3   Values in the Classroom

Below are twenty-two values that might be displayed in various ways in a classroom. In your ideal classroom, how would you rank them? Place a 1 next to the quality you value most in your classroom, a 2 next to the second most important, and so on through 22, which will represent the quality you value least.

_____ Freedom		_____ Dogmatism	
_____ Rigidity		_____ Orderliness	
_____ Self-Direction		_____ Favoritism	
_____ Disorder		_____ Creativity	
_____ Quiet		_____ Alienation	
_____ Chaos		_____ Respect	
_____ Laughter		_____ Privacy	

_____ Passivity   _____ Equality

_____ Concentration   _____ Dominance

_____ Fear   _____ Fairness

_____ Purposefulness   _____ Love

Analysis of Teaching Behavior

In teacher education, feedback to developing teachers about their teaching behavior is crucial. Several techniques have been developed and are employed that provide more systematic feedback than that often received from supervisors' subjective notes. In combination with supervisor feedback, some of these techniques have been quite effective in making teachers aware of their behaviors.

Probably the most extensively used system for quantifying information about teaching behavior is interaction analysis. The process has received extensive use and adaptation since the original ten-category system was developed by Flanders (1960). An excellent review of this early work and subsequent research and modification is Amidon and Hough's *Interaction Analysis: Theory, Research and Application.*[1]

The authors have found a fourteen-category system of interaction analysis, the IAST Base (Hall, 1971) to be effective and well received by preservice and inservice teachers. The IAST Base includes verbal and nonverbal categories of behavior for both teachers and students and has several built-in "extras" that provide additional data. A Category 13 makes it possible to isolate interaction that goes on between two students without intervening teacher behavior. Another category is used for recording student-initiated questions.

One problem with most interaction analysis systems is that once the teacher has coded his teaching, he still must go through the error-prone drudgery of constructing a matrix. Once the matrix is constructed, the relatively sophisticated task of interpreting the data still remains. The result is that many students and teachers never use the technique once training is complete, or they are unable to easily interpret the resultant data.

With the IAST Base a computer program and an optical-scan scoring sheet have been developed (Hall, Pennington, and Gouge, 1973) so the computer does the drudgery work and some of the interpretation. This

[1] E. J. Amidon and J. B. Hough, *Interaction Analysis: Theory, Research and Application* (Reading, Mass.: Addison-Wesley, 1967).

process increases teachers' use of the system and eases data interpretation problems. The IAST Base categories and a sample printout are included in Chapter 3 (see pp. 78-79).

Personal Assessment Feedback

A procedure for personalizing teacher education that has been extensively researched and developed at the R&D Center for Teacher Education is that of employing a specially trained counselor as a member of the undergraduate program's faculty team. This trained counselor employs an Initial Assessment Battery (Veldman, 1970) that consists of five specially designed and researched personality inventories to assess the personal dynamics and concerns of each preservice teacher.

The Initial Assessment Battery is administered to preservice teachers at the beginning of their professional education program. The counselor, with computer assistance, then assesses the battery and prepares for an hour-long Personal Assessment Feedback (PAF) conference with each student. The aim of the conference is to provide feedback to the student about her personal dynamics and provide her with some insights that she may wish to be thinking about as she considers her potential career in teaching. It should be pointed out that the Initial Assessment Battery is not designed as a screening device, but rather as a means for enabling a specially trained counselor to develop a quick, tentative picture of the student that can be tested out in conference and used as a basis for providing feedback throughout the program. This analysis of the student's personality is not from a solely therapeutic point of view, but from the point of view of facilitating reasonably healthy education majors to utilize their utmost potential and to develop their own personal styles of teaching.

The specially trained counselor, in addition to conducting Personal Assessment Feedback sessions, is available in a consultation role to the faculty in their planning educational experiences for those same students. This again is an attempt to ensure that effective attention is paid to the personal needs and personality dynamics of individual students. Of course, this particular role requires a great deal of skill, since the confidentiality of the information on a student must be preserved. At the same time, the sharing of information can help make the student's education more personalized. If the operational design of the program permits, the counselor may also be available to the student at subsequent times throughout the teacher education program, including while the student is working as a teacher in schools, and for three-way videotape feedback sessions including the student, counselor, and the curriculum supervisor.

In describing this approach to personalization, Veldman (1970) says:

The central thesis of this system is that there *is* no "ideal teacher"; there are individual teachers who are making more or less use of their potential for exerting benign influences on children. To maximize the potential of an individual during a teacher education program, it is essential for the staff to know each candidate as a unique person, so as to tailor experiences in the program to fit individual needs and talents.

General personality characteristics, attitudes, and interests are quite well established by the end of the second decade of life. No teacher education program can hope to cause significant changes in such general characteristics. Rather, teacher education should seek to *develop* individual potentials for optimum performance in what is for most students a new *role*. This implies that "optimum performance" may be quite different in appearance for various students who complete the program. We are convinced that children benefit from exposure to a variety of teaching "styles"—that no one style is best for all children under all circumstances. We also believe that the best teachers are those who have learned how to make the most of their own natural styles.

Supervisor Feedback

Probably the most frequently used form of feedback is that given by a supervisor. Supervisors are normally experienced professionals who are supposedly wise from years of field-based experience and ready to pass on to the preprofessionals their accumulated learnings. However, years of experience as a practitioner does not mean that one is well prepared and skilled to serve as a supervisor of others or to give effective feedback. Fifteen years as a defensive tackle in the National Football League does not necessarily qualify Gerald Mountowski to become a coach. Other skills, training, and techniques are needed. Sensitivity to skill development and the personal needs of other adults does not always come about simply because one has been through the process.

Students want direct and specific feedback. To be personalized, this feedback needs to be just that—direct and specific and also paced and interrelated with the personal needs and feelings of the student. The feedback needs to be based on observational data and should be delivered as soon after the performance as is possible. The content of feedback should also be congruent with the student's ability to make constructive use of it.

One strategy that has been highly effective in helping professionals to grow and also improve communication is the conducting of three-way conferences. In teacher education, for example, a supervisor's instrument such as the Teacher Evaluation Form (Veldman, 1964) can be completed by the cooperating teacher and the college supervisor based on observation of the student teacher. The student teacher also completes the same form on himself. A three-way conference is then held in which each party can share his observations and perceptions, and the completed observation forms can be studied and compared for areas of agreement and areas where there are discrepancies between what is observed and what is ideal.

Other observational forms can be used. These might include interaction analysis systems like those discussed above and lists of behavioral indices such as the Proficiency Analysis Rating form found in Chapter 3. All of these are hypothesized to be indicators of the presence or absence of certain competencies and are often useful. These data sources provide the supervisor with structures that will aid in focusing the supervisory feedback process.

Feedback from Clients

One data source that is all too commonly overlooked is what clients observe and perceive of their experiences with developing and practicing professionals. In the health sciences, for example, patients can be asked to evaluate their contacts with student nurses, doctors, and dentists. The exact questions that are asked will depend on the competencies being considered.

In teacher education, teachers need feedback on how pupils see them, in addition to feedback on what pupils learn and what supervisors observe. Two interesting instruments that facilitate such pupil feedback are the Student Evaluation of Teaching (SET) forms I and II.

The data obtained in these instruments are not intended to serve as summative evaluation but rather as formative feedback to developing teachers. What the recipient of the data does with the information is up to him with guidance from his supervisor.

The SET I (Veldman and Peck, 1970) is a ten-item pencil-and-paper instrument intended for use by pupils at the fifth-grade level and above. Five factors result from processing the data: (1) friendly and cheerful, (2) knowledgeable and poised, (3) lively and interesting, (4) firm control, and (5) non-directive. A copy of the SET I and a computer-generated report are presented in Chapter 6, pp. 180-82.

The SET II (Haak, Kleiber, and Peck, 1972) was developed for use with younger children who are not yet able to read or write. The SET II can easily be used with kindergarten and primary-grade children. This instrument includes six cards with a simple statement and a different symbol (a ball, a star, etc.) on each and an envelope that has two pouches. On one pouch is a drawing of a mailbox and on the other is a drawing of a waste-paper basket. To administer the SET II, each child is given a set of the six cards and an envelope. The test administrator then asks all the children to find the card with a picture of "balloons" on it. The administrator then reads the statement on the card identifying it by its symbol, and if the child thinks it is true of his teacher he "mails" the card to his teacher by placing the card

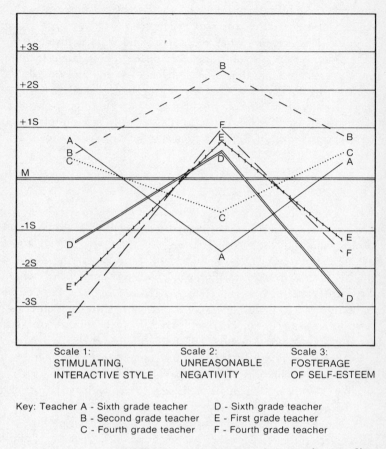

Scale 1:   Scale 2:   Scale 3:
STIMULATING,   UNREASONABLE   FOSTERAGE
INTERACTIVE STYLE   NEGATIVITY   OF SELF-ESTEEM

Key: Teacher A - Sixth grade teacher   D - Sixth grade teacher
     B - Second grade teacher   E - First grade teacher
     C - Fourth grade teacher   F - Fourth grade teacher

EXHIBIT 5.5   A Comparison of Six Teachers' Profiles.

in the pouch with the picture of a mailbox on it. If the child thinks that the statement is not true then the card is dropped in the wastebasket pouch. The resultant data are then processed to yield three factor scores in addition to the six individual item scores.

The factor scores are (1) stimulating, interactive style, (2) unreasonable negativity, and (3) fosterage of self-esteem. Haak and her associates have found that children can distinguish between teachers who have a temporary reason for being "disagreeable" and teachers who are just plain hostile all the time. Haak has also found that over a period of years with different classes some teachers are consistently rated high on the factors while other teachers are consistently rated low. (See Exhibit 5.5.) By processing the boys' responses separately from the girls', as is illustrated in Exhibit 5.6, it is quite commonly found that the boys' perceptions of the

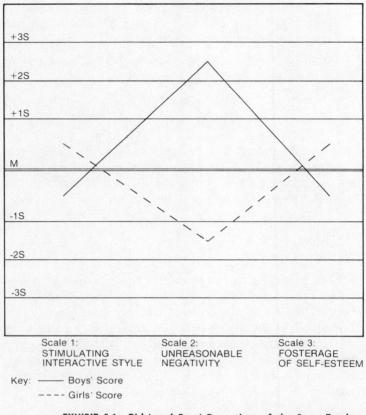

Scale 1:	Scale 2:	Scale 3:
STIMULATING	UNREASONABLE	FOSTERAGE
INTERACTIVE STYLE	NEGATIVITY	OF SELF-ESTEEM

Key: ———— Boys' Score

— — — Girls' Score

EXHIBIT 5.6   Girls' and Boys' Perceptions of the Same Teacher.

teacher are diametrically opposite from the girls' perceptions. When information of this type is shared with developing teachers, they are better able to organize their approach and identify specific goals, such as striving for the same perceptions from both sexes.

Affective Modules

Another operational strategy that has been employed is the development of specific modules that have expressive and affective objectives built in as their major criteria. The assessment of learning outcomes is not based upon demonstration of particular behaviors, but rather the affective modules are provided as stimulus and thought-provoking experiences for the students. Sherry Borgers and G. Robert Ward (1972) have developed a series of affective modules that are employed as a regular part of the CBTE program at the University of Houston. These modules include such titles as the following:

Module 2: Awareness of Self and Others
Module 6: Communication One Way and Two Way
Module 9: Decision Making III
Module 11: Teacher Interaction
Module 13: Group Process

These modules provide stimulus situations that the students read individually or in small groups. Following reading and other preparatory enabling activities, discussions are held concerning the implications and consequences of what the students have been reading.

SUMMARY

The preceding pages represent a small sampling of the materials and strategies that exist for personalizing education. Others are discussed elsewhere in this book. Still other materials exist that are ready to use, and many more materials and strategies are available that could be adapted to a particular CBE program's assumptions and goals. The preceding pages are offered as documentation to support the contention that whether or not a CBE program is personalized is not influenced by any absence of research, theory, or developed or adaptable materials.

6

the program: sequencing instruction and feedback according to concerns

The September 9, 1973, edition of the *Houston Post* carried the following feature story:

> The word would not go away. It was too right.
>
> Dr. James M. Thompson, 28, two years out of Baylor College of Medicine, sat in the library of the Champ Traylor Memorial Hospital playing the medical detective game.
>
> Only this time the fat medical books were not open for an exercise in differential diagnosis. There in Port Lavaca there was no teacher to check his diagnosis.
>
> There was only the man in the hospital room dying, his body so exhausted that the diarrhea had stopped because there was nothing left to come out . . .
>
> The man had been there since early morning. His private doctor's tentative diagnosis was gastroenteritis—inflammation of the stomach and intestine that could be caused by many things.
>
> In the middle of the afternoon the nurses, becoming alarmed, called Thompson, "They said the man was very sick and wasn't getting any better. I went to see him. He was critically ill."
>
> As Thompson examined the patient he felt sure this was no gastroenteritis. The temperature was below normal, and there seemed to be no blood pressure at all.

"I was scared," he admits. "The man was not responding to treatment. He was dying and I didn't know why."

Thompson had ordered symptomatic treatment and laboratory tests. Then he had come here to the library.

"I gave up on all the various insecticide poisonings, the heavy metal poisonings, the food poisonings." He reviewed the bacterial diseases, the viral diseases . . .

Again he reviewed the symptoms—the severe leg cramps, the absence of pulses in the arms and legs and the way they were turning blue, his inability to detect blood pressure, the shock and the rapid heart beat and the "rice water" diarrhea . . .

Vibrio cholerae. The bacterium produces toxins which cause circulatory collapse, pooling the blood in the major vessels, leaving the peripheral ones oxygen-starved.

"The man must have cholera because nothing else fits," he told himself. "This is a classic case of cholera, though there hasn't been a case in the United States in over 50 years . . ."

"The only way to prove cholera is to get a culture of the stool on a special media which we didn't have." Even then it would take days to get results.

He returned to the wife, saying nothing of his suspicion. "I questioned her very closely about the type of well they had, the septic tank, the connections . . . There was a possibility that the well water was contaminated."

Again as the minutes passed he went over the facts in his mind.

"When a man is dying, you've got to do what you think is right . . ."

"Baylor teaches if the patient's getting worse you're either treating for the wrong thing or the treatment's not the right treatment.

"They're very strong on not being afraid to ask questions, on going to the library and checking it out . . . Sometimes you have to go out on a limb."

He took the pen in his hand. As he wrote the word down on the chart, "I thought I'd be a laughing stock."

Then he picked up the phone and called the patient's private doctor.

"He said this was a pretty doubtful diagnosis since we hadn't had any cholera for more than 50 years and nobody else in the community was sick.

"I said did I have permission to treat the man as if he had it. It wouldn't hurt the man and it might benefit him. You have to give the doctor credit. He told me to use my judgment."

The doctor, an older man, probably thought he was a fool, a young upstart living in the Never Never Land of academic exercises, Thompson realized.

Maybe two hours had passed since the nurses had called him to the patient. Now he had his diagnosis, right or wrong, and he headed for the patient's room.

The antibiotics the man had been given would not be effective against the cholera bacterium. Another category of antibiotic, the tetracyclines, would.

"The man quit breathing for a moment just before we started treatment." They resuscitated him as he lay there, fluid from a bottle dripping down a tube, entering his vein to replace what he had lost from vomiting and diarrhea.

Thompson began the new antibiotic.

Meanwhile a stool sample was sent to Victoria, and eventually on to Austin and to the Center for Disease Control in Atlanta . . .

"By the next morning the patient looked like he was going to live." He continued to improve through Sunday, whether because of the treatment or by chance, Thompson did not know . . .

Ten days later Dr. Jack Weissman of the Center for Disease Control [contacted] Thompson . . .

"He congratulated me. I almost fainted."

The diagnosis was in—and nobody was laughing.

"Cholera." [1]

By any criteria, this young physician demonstrated competence. That competence might be attributed to some innate qualities on his part, but he gives a lot of credit to the curriculum and faculty in his medical school. We were most impressed by the statements "Baylor teaches . . ." and "They're very strong on not being afraid to ask questions." As strong as this story's recommendation of the young doctor is, we believe the recommendation for his school is equally strong. The curricula of professional schools that turn out people with such ability do not just grow; they are the result of decisions made by people.

The young professional was probably able to use what he had learned in a meaningful way because he had learned it in a way that was meaningful. This is more than just a nice twist of words. If you want someone to learn something that you believe is vital, you had better make sure your student is motivated to learn your content before you teach it. This idea lies at the heart of Frances Fuller's (1969) concerns theory discussed in the preceding chapter, and the use of this theory to make professional training curricula relevant is the theme of this chapter.

This chapter is organized around the sequence of developing concerns levels, beginning with self-concerns and moving to impact concerns. For each level of concern we will expand on the description of the dynamics presented in Chapter 5; we will outline content that is relevant to that level, including some enabling activities; and we will point out some implications of student concerns for instruction and program management. The final section of the chapter will discuss the operation of feedback to students. Feedback is a process that deserves separate consideration outside the context of a particular concerns level, since it is needed at all points in a pro-

---

[1] *Miriam Kass,* "Doctor's Unlikely Cholera Diagnosis Saves a Life," *Houston Post,* September 9, 1973.

gram. The discussion here will focus on the dynamics of audiotape and videotape feedback, using transcripts of actual feedback sessions.

The schema for the chapter is as follows:

Page	Heading	Questions
166	Programs and Relevance	What does it take to make a program relevant?
168	Using the Concerns Model in Building Programs	What would CBTE look like if modeled on the concerns theory?
187	Providing Students with Feedback on Their Teaching	How can I make effective use of the feedback tools available to me, especially videotape?
194	Some Further Thoughts about Early Program Formative and Summative Assessments	What kind of assessments need to be made of students entering a personalized program?

PROGRAMS AND RELEVANCE

What does it take to put together a relevant program?

The real strength of CBE lies in how *programs* are built. The key is in the word *program.*

There are actually very few teacher education programs, for example. There are many teacher education curricula and degree plans that specify education courses for students. These do not measure up to our definition of program.

In a program, students receive a carefully considered sequence of experiences designed to influence them at teachable moments, prerequisites mean something, and students are held accountable for minimum levels of achievement before going on to advanced goals. There are various managerial and organizational structures that will support viable programs. Some are discussed in Chapters 9 and 11. But, as we view program building, a key element is the ordering and sequencing of instructional materials for students. That is our focus here. We assume that you have already identified which competencies, objectives, and activities you want to include in a program.

Smorgasbord

Obviously, one way to order the elements is to have students decide on their own sequence. In present course structures this is essentially how students get registered. Modular or component offerings provide more pieces than larger courses, but the smorgasbord effort can work. The advantages are more student flexibility and choice. The one obvious disadvantage is that certain logical orderings would provide a more relevant experience for students. Perhaps student teaching should come before some other experiences, for example.

Many programs use prerequisites to enforce a sequence of experiences for students. The advantages here are ease of record keeping and commonality of experiences for students entering a new phase of the program, making it easier for instructors to tailor their offerings. The disadvantage is that student choice is often forgotten.

A compromise between ordering and choice might be possible. We would like to propose that such an ordered choice of experiences be offered around Frances Fuller's concern model, which is described in detail in Chapter 5. Fuller (1969), in work done at the Texas R&D Center for Teacher Education, noted that there is an ordered sequence of concerns that most professional teachers pass through. An adaptation of this order (Wilson et al., 1973) is as follows:

Phase I—Concerns about Self
    Level 0—Concerns unrelated to teaching
    Level 1—Concerns about self as a teacher
Phase II—Concerns about Task
    Level 2—How adequate am I?
    Level 3—How do my pupils feel about me?
Phase III—Concerns about Impact
    Level 4—Are they learning what I'm teaching?
    Level 5—Are they learning what they need?
    Level 6—How can I improve as a teacher?

According to Fuller, the concerns are developmental: most teachers will not be concerned with impact questions until they have dealt effectively with self and task concerns.

Assessing concerns of teachers can be accomplished quite easily through the use of a relatively simple instrument that consists of nothing more than a page that has the following written across the top: "When you think about your teaching, what are you concerned about? (Do not say what you think others are concerned about, but only what concerns you *now.*) Please be frank." The remainder of the page is left blank, providing space for the respondent to do his writing. The resultant statement can then be judged as to the concern levels that are reflected. The procedure for scoring this concerns statement is outlined in a manual available from the R&D Center for Teacher Education.[2] A more quantitative fifty-one-item concerns checklist has also been developed (George, 1974). In her work, Fuller has found that 60 to 64 percent of preservice teachers' concerns are in the self-to-task areas of the concerns development progression, while 60 to 64 percent of inservice teachers' concerns are in the task-to-impact areas— which suggests that many needed competencies may not be considered as such by preservice teachers.

USING THE CONCERNS MODEL IN BUILDING PROGRAMS

What would a teacher education program look like if it were modeled after Fuller's concerns theory? For one thing, careful study would be made of the concerns of entering students. Careful consideration would also be made of the order of competency attainment. The ideal, of course, would be to permit students to acquire the skills and competencies they were concerned about or those that would help them alleviate their concerns when they needed to.

There are, of course, other models that can provide the skeleton for program development. The work of Robert Gagné particularly cannot go unmentioned. Gagné (1970) attempts to order skills according to the probability of their successful attainment by students. Hierarchies like that in Exhibit 6.1 are subject to validation and can be used to provide estimates of successful terminal objective attainment. To build a teacher education program on such a model would require the identification of skills necessary for teaching. The skills would then be arranged in order, and instructional material would be specified to foster student attainment of the skills. The one major difficulty we find in Gagné's schema (other than the mathematical analysis necessary for the validation of the hierarchy) can be seen in the logical sequence: (1) the student identifies probing questions, (2) the student uses probing questions.

Questioning, especially the use of probing questions, is one of those special few competencies identified by Rosenshine and Furst (1973) as being a skill demonstrated by effective teachers. The use of probing questions must obviously be preceded by knowledge of what a probing question is, thus the sequencing above. But the question remains, When should a

---

[2] F. F. Fuller and C. Case, *A Manual for Scoring the Teacher Concerns Statement* (Austin: Research and Development Center for Teacher Education, University of Texas, 1972) ($1.00).

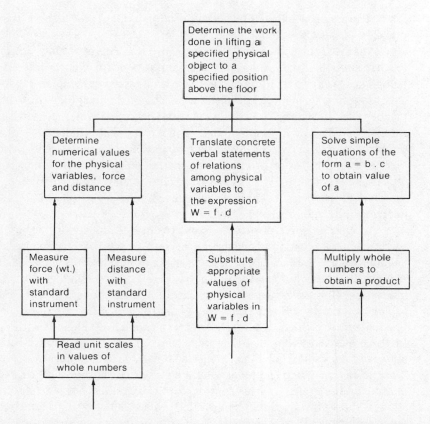

EXHIBIT 6.1 A Learning Hierarchy Pertaining to a Science Topic (After Gagné, 1970).

student teacher be expected to acquire these skills so that they will be of maximum benefit? It is true that almost anybody could be trained to identify probing questions in a relatively short period of time. Asking the questions might be a slightly more difficult skill, but certainly not beyond the realm of possibility. But look at what the Fuller model implies for the prescription of learning this skill.

The student who is still at Level 3 of the Fuller model—"How do my pupils feel about me?"—would be most hesitant to *use* probing questions in a teaching situation. This is not so much because he doesn't know how to ask them as it is because by asking them he is placing his pupils in a position of possible embarrassment and awkwardness, of not knowing the answer. Consequently, rather than ask probing questions, many beginning teacher education students and beginning teachers are satisfied to answer their own questions or to ask another pupil rather than embarrass one who has answered incorrectly or who they think doesn't know the answer. The point is, it's not so much whether a teacher education student *can* learn a skill; the question is, *Will he use it?*

Another excellent example of the Phase II concern coming into play in teacher skills is in classroom management. A student who is interested in being liked, who wants to be the nice guy, will have a difficult time enforcing classroom management rules. In this case it's not so much the "tricks" that a teacher uses to "control" a class as it is the degree to which he will enforce rules, regardless of how unpopular he becomes with students. Without a doubt, a sample of any 1,000 teacher education students at random would include 975 who were primarily concerned with classroom management. Our opinion is that the "tricks" of classroom management work only when the student becomes concerned with his impact on pupils. This usually happens quite late in a teacher education program.

Another example of how the concerns model reflects on the futility of some teacher education curricula can be seen in the perceived value of the beginning teacher education courses in history and philosophy of education. Admittedly there are instances where these courses can be vibrant and interesting. But for the beginning student, primarily concerned with self and asking questions such as "Where do I stand?" and "How adequate am I?" the content of such courses rarely affects the student's behavior with pupils. In the concerns model such historical and philosophical points would be perceived relevant only by the teacher who had reached mature concerns. In other words, maybe the content should be reversed. History and philosophy might be more useful later in the program or once a teacher is in service.

In the following discussion we have made attempts to identify some other content and experiences that may be useful for program builders as they view total program decisions. We are making the assumption that your faculty are making a team decision on the identification and ordering of competencies. We are further assuming that the major competencies and some subcompetencies have been identified, at least tentatively, and that you are searching for a sequence. In the remainder of the chapter, each concern phase is described and mention is made of some possible topics and enabling activities that could be employed at each phase.

Phase I—Concerns about Self

LEVEL 0—CONCERNS UNRELATED TO TEACHING. At this level the subject has few realistic concerns about teaching or about himself as a teacher. Students think of teaching primarily in terms of their own experiences as pupils and as college students. In short, the concerns are not those of teachers as professionals. They are not about the tasks of professionals.

This is the concerns level of many teacher education students when they arrive in the first education course. In some programs where students do not get education courses until completing some initial liberal arts experiences, this level may not be as lasting as in other programs, such as those experienced by both the authors, who began their "Introduction to Education" courses as freshmen.

The question must be raised, what is important enough to be learned by beginning students? One key might be to focus on some experiences that would provide students with realistic information on what the school is like. In many present programs students are placed in schools early to act as teacher aides, clerks, or tutors. Although these experiences can be most valuable, care must be taken to ensure that students know *why* they are in the school and to ensure that teachers and principals in the schools can use the students' aid to mutual advantage for them and the students.

There are a variety of formats for observing-tutorial-aide work in programs throughout the nation. In some programs students are assigned to schools because it is easier to assign than to permit individual choice. In some programs students are expected to find a school and make their own arrangements for observing and then must report back to an instructor after thirty hours or so of observation has been completed. In other programs that are designed to produce more and better inner-city teachers, experiences are provided in drug-abuse clinics, halfway houses, and preschool day-care centers. Attempts are made early to acquaint students with ethnic experiences they may not have had before. "Observing" is sometimes limited to videotaped examples, closed-circuit TV, or readings. Some colleges have large student populations and few schools to handle all observing-micro-teaching-student teaching requests. In field-centered CBE it is difficult to imagine any part of the program not involving students in some form of fieldwork, however.

In their observation experiences, students must be told much more than "Go observe." Particular student or teacher behaviors and/or learning environment might receive attention, but this is not the time to provide twelve hours of training in interaction analysis. If steps are made to promote the movement of concerns of students from self to impact, care must be taken to assess and arouse in students an awareness of the need for changing concerns.

As important as the school experiences are, the instructional design used in conjunction with them cannot be overlooked. What kind of content could be included in on-campus or in-school seminars? Several things come to mind.

As distasteful as it is to some, the use of interpersonal training must be considered for students who have zero-level concerns. These students need to see that they can make mistakes and that they have unique strengths and the same hang-ups as others and can communicate their concerns to someone who may be able to help them. Students need to see that teacher education calls for them to be understood and to be understanding.

In Chapter 5 justification was made for human relations training exercises, and some examples of these experiences were identified. It is with Level 0 concern students that such exercises can be most helpful. Some programs consider the human relations experiences so valuable that large portions of the beginning efforts are set aside for such activities.

In the experimental CBTE program at Houston, a three-day retreat was held in an off-campus retreat center. Based on the assumption that an effective teacher education program gives students the opportunity to relate with and engage in activities that are designed to allow freedom of expression of concerns about self and teaching, the retreat focused on sharing and team building. The teams that were built for the most part existed throughout the remainder of the program, and the members of each team provided a supportive and constructive source of release for students.

While some teacher educators argue against the use of time-consuming efforts to focus on human relations, the time spent on the efforts might be a most valuable asset later in the program. In a teacher education program where students see continuity, even so much as continuity of faculty, these early experiences are an asset in saving time, stopping game-playing, and generally increasing communication.

A few other topics of interest might be useful for students. Because of the shortage of teachers in the past we have really not tried to discourage students from entering the profession. Now, however, students need to know quickly and early whether they have a chance of making it as a teacher. A module used at the University of Houston, called *Employment Opportunities* (Dillner, 1973), focuses on job opportunities for teachers. The module doesn't screen students. It provides data on how past graduates have fared in finding teaching jobs. The realities brought home in this module have been effective in stimulating students to "deselect" themselves from the teacher training program or to change their training emphasis.

Dave Wilson, our alert copy editor, read the above paragraphs and suggested an interesting double-edged version of the *Employment Opportunities* module. Instead of having students in the program study information on past graduates, have them *collect* such information in follow-up interviews. Assign each student a list of program graduates representing a cross section of several past years, and require him to contact and interview them on certain specific points. The student would then compile a report that would be pooled with the surveys of other students both for the students' information and for the use of the college in its own follow-up evaluation of the program. The students would learn about the realities of the post-graduate life of student teachers and would have an opportunity to deal with a lot of early concerns in their talks with the veterans. The college would also benefit by a cost-effective data collection technique for long-range program evaluation.

Program control steps can even reflect the "Self as a Teacher" concern. For many students, the self-paced or group-paced CBTE program is the first time that they have had to make decisions about when tasks would be accomplished or even taken the initiative to call for a seminar with an instructor. These decisions are the domain of the instructors in most programs. Personalization, in this instance, often calls for instructors to monitor progress of some students, pushing some, shoving others, ignoring still others who don't need or want their assistance.

In summary, actual teaching experience arouses new concerns with teaching. But concerns about self are still strong. The question in Phase I was, "Where do I stand?" The second question is, "Where do I stand *as a teacher?* What are the rules in this new situation, the real rules? Who has the power to decide? What kind of behavior is *really* rewarded? What is expected of me? What am I supposed to do? How do I find out when I have succeeded and when I have failed? Where do I stand, in this new situation as a teacher?" (Fuller, 1970).

Phase I—Concerns about Self

LEVEL 1—CONCERN ABOUT SELF AS A TEACHER.   The subject is concerned about the new situation in schools and the expectations of principals and teachers. He is concerned about the ratings he is given by the teachers he works with and he is apprehensive about what to do when a parent arrives.

The students at Concerns Level 1 are asking a variety of questions. Frances Fuller describes them:

> They literally sit on the edges of their chairs, waiting to find out about their assignments, the school, the grade level, the supervising teacher, the university supervisor, the rules of the school, the orientation of the principal, and especially the expectations of supervising teachers, the requirements of the task and the limitations, both verbalized and tacit, upon them.
>
> Students are concerned with the problem of discerning real expectations, the behaviors for which *real* rewards are given as opposed to those that just get lip service. They search for the *real* power structure.
>
> Pre-professional students have reported being criticized as "unprofessional" because they avoided the teachers' lounge. Elsewhere, the telephone as well as the lounge is explicitly forbidden them. One principal may feel that student teachers who send pupils to his office for punishment are abdicating their responsibility; another may back them up and invite them to witness the paddling. If they ignore noisy members of another class in the hall, they might be judged irresponsible; if they take action, they might be told to stop "interfering." Evaluating the subtle cues on which such judgments could be based calls for social sophistication and sometimes two-

faced inconsistency. Many otherwise dedicated, knowledgeable student teachers won't "play it smart." "The kids need me more than the principal needs a new bulletin board! Well, maybe I can get a job without his recommendation."

During this stage, some students merely worry about their grade, but most try to discern how parents, supervising teachers, principals, and others evaluate them (Fuller, 1970).

Another question that many beginning students ask themselves is, "Why am I in education?" As instructors we have often assumed that everyone in our classes is there because he wishes to be. But students sometimes go into teaching for the strangest reasons. There is a great variance in commitment toward teaching by beginning students. Some go into teacher education for the money (will they be surprised!), the prestige, or the power of directing others. To us, effective teachers become teachers because they enjoy helping others. We feel that early in a teacher education program the student should be given the opportunity to find out *why* he is in education. The reader might note that this statement differs somewhat from the usual— that the beginning student should find out whether he wants to teach. This difference is intentional. The level of concern here must be, "Am I in teacher education for the right reasons?" "Right" must be operationally defined by the student in much the same way that an unconscious concern becomes conscious. One way of opening up a group of students to this question has been described by Curwin and Fuhrmann (1975). The exercise that follows is an example procedure that allows students to focus on concerns.

WHOM WOULD YOU HIRE?

Directions. Imagine that you are an elementary-school administrator with responsibility for hiring new teachers. You have four positions open in grades one through three and eight applicants from whom to choose. You have interviewed all eight, each of whom impressed you favorably. Read through the brief descriptions below, and select the four you would hire. (Admittedly, these sketches are briefer than you would have in reality, but no matter how much material you have, it would undoubtedly never be enough.)

Candidate 1: Forty-year-old female, single, lives alone. Eighteen years' outstanding experience, highly successful with typically unsuccessful students. Possible lesbian relationships.

Candidate 2: Twenty-four-year-old male, single, two years' experience in ghetto school. Near genius, outstanding recommendations. Leader of local black-power group; his students use African names and openly reject "slave" names.

Candidate 3: Thirty-five-year-old male, married, father of six. Community-minded, interested in Cub Scouts. Known for having very well organized, planned lessons and classes. Ten years' experience.

Candidate 4: Forty-year-old male, single, living with aged parents. Extensive experience as local businessman before returning to college for credentials. Just completed requirements, and received $5,000 grant to work with junior-high-school students in distributive education.

Candidate 5: Twenty-six-year-old female, divorced, supporting self and three small children alone. Highly creative; three years' experience; outstanding recommendations on professional capability.

Candidate 6: Forty-eight-year-old male, highly respected former minister who left pulpit to work full time with children. Has just completed teaching credentials.

Candidate 7: Fifty-eight-year-old female, widowed. Twenty-five years' experience, including three years in the Infant Schools of England. Wants to incorporate Infant-School concepts here.

Candidate 8: Twenty-two-year-old female, single, one year experience, excellent recommendations. Voluntarily tutored all four years in college, including full time in the summers. Living openly in the community with a man of another race.

When you have selected four, collaborate with other members of your support group (three to six others in a group is preferable) in order to function as a personnel committee for the school you choose to represent. Establish ground rules for the operation of your committee, including a possible chairmanship, the decision-making process (majority vote or consensus), and whatever other considerations you feel important.

When your group has selected your new teachers, post your selections and compare your choices with those of other groups (if there are other groups). A spokesman for each group might summarize the reasoning behind each group's choices.

QUESTIONS

(Answer both individually and as a group.)

1. What qualities or characteristics in elementary teachers do you value most highly?
2. What qualities or values have little or no relevance for you?
3. Would your choices have been different for high-school teachers? How?
4. Were you protecting anything in yourself in the choices you made? If so, what? Do you want to continue protecting that?
5. How would you have fared in your committee if you had been one of the candidates?

Discussion in seminar sessions using these materials allows students to form groups according to their similarities of values and then to look at which people would be hired by each of the groups. Each student might then consider which applicant he most resembled.

Concern levels in Phase I, for most students, are reasonably short. Often beginning teacher education students can focus on these concerns and quickly go on. This is not to say that the concerns are ever completely resolved. It means that the student can look at himself, size up the situation, and know that he can cope.

Phase II—Concerns about Task

LEVEL 2—HOW ADEQUATE AM I? The student expresses concern about self-adequacy as a teacher, about discipline, about what to do when a pupil asks a question to which he doesn't know the answer, concern with seeing himself teach and not liking what he sees.

The two major topics of relevance for teacher education students at this concern level would be classroom management and preliminary methods experiences with pupils. The emphasis here *must be on the practical.* As much as we as teacher educators get sick of answering practical questions, if our students are engaged in school experiences with pupils they need to be able to cope; coping to them at this level of concerns focuses primarily on classroom management and "What do I do to teach reading, science, math?"

Any discussion of the concern level "How adequate am I?" must, therefore, include at least a short section on classroom management and discipline. Many beginning teachers choose to work at the preschool and primary grade levels because they are afraid of the abuse they believe secondary teachers must face from the older and bigger pupils. They are often aghast when pupils three feet two inches tall start acting like gargoyles. Frances Fuller has discussed the situation:

> New teachers have few means of controlling the class. Their repertoire of "staring them down," snapping fingers, making pupils "freeze," writing names on the board and so on, works only temporarily. As all experienced teachers know, remaining in control is more complex than merely keeping order. The teacher's degree of control is influenced by many factors: by her status, the situation past and present, her relationship with the class, their opinions about appropriate behavior, their age, social class, mood and a host of other factors. The same class behaviors may be problems to one teacher, in one situation and not to another. "Problems" can be symptoms of boredom, frustration, or joy; of discrepant behavior standards, or they may have nothing at all to do with the teacher's behavior.
>
> But the view that discipline problems, like a fever, are merely a symptom, is relatively infrequent among beginning teachers. Discipline problems are usually treated as discrete events susceptible of cure by prescription, although the symptom hypothesis is given lip service. Student teachers feel there must be some trick to it. No one will tell them what the trick is!
>
> The reason for this conviction seems to be that, once class control is admitted to be a product, possibly of emotional interaction between the teacher and class, what the teacher *feels* (and cannot change quickly, if at

all) instead of what the teacher *does,* is subject to inspection. Subject to inspection too, would be many values of doubtful lineage, unexamined feelings, shaky convictions. In the area of discipline, it is not possible to abstain. The teacher always does something. Even doing nothing is doing something. In fact doing nothing is often doing something very important!

This first concern of Phase II, "How adequate am I?" evidences itself mostly in comments about class control and discipline. This is the concern with which students most want help. But since the problem of discipline is more complex than it appears to them, they are also concerned (though unaware of these concerns) about their professional roles, about the satisfactions of teaching, and about their own relationships and lives outside the class (Fuller, 1970).

Handling the classroom management problem is often as difficult for the teacher educator as it is for the student going through the "How adequate am I?" stage. Students tend to look at classroom management as if it is a trick to be learned. Teacher educators are confronted by angry students when they will not tell the novices how to do it. There *are* some "tricks" that students can learn. Several excellent books on working with individual pupils might be very useful especially to students who are working in one-to-one tutoring situations early in the program sequence.

The following materials also focus on group classroom management problems:

CARTER, RON. *Help! These Kids Are Driving Me Crazy.* Champaign, Ill.: Research Press, 1972.

COLLINS, MYRTLE T., and DWANE R. COLLINS. *Survival Kit for Teachers and Parents.* Pacific Palisades, Calif.: Goodyear Publishing Co., 1975.

GINOTT, HAIM. *Teacher and Child.* New York: Macmillan, 1972.

HYMES, JAMES L., JR. *Behavior and Misbehavior, A Teacher's Guide to Action.* Englewood Cliffs, N.J.: Prentice-Hall, 1955. (In at least its twenty-sixth printing.)

Inner-City Simulation Laboratory. Chicago: Science Research Associates, 1969.

JOHNSON, LOIS V., and MARY A. BANY. *Classroom Management: Theory and Skill Training.* New York: Macmillan, 1970. (An excellent source of study which views classroom management as a group process. Examples and exercises focus teachers' attention on developing group process skills.)

NEISWORTH, JOHN T., STANLEY DENO, and JOSEPH R. JENKINS. *Student Motivation and Classroom Management: A Behavioralistic Approach.* Newark, Del.: Behavior Technics, Inc., 1969.

The *Inner-City Simulation Laboratory* works particularly well. It consists of a simulated inner-city school. The participants assume the role of Pat Taylor, a teacher, and practice solving classroom problems. Each of the problems is presented on film, through role playing, as a written incident, or in some combination of these techniques. Faculty handbooks, cumulative record files, sociometric data, case studies, and other reports are provided in the kit.

Frances Fuller aptly summarizes the discussion of this level:

> Obviously the concern "How adequate am I?" can be very broad. It can include concerns about everything from a shaky voice and one's professional commitment on the one hand, to sexual adequacy on the other. Concern about discipline is the neophyte's rubric for this question, but concern with adequacy in many areas may underlie expression of concern about discipline. *One concern is with subject matter adequacy.* What do you do when a child asks about the past tense of "lie" and "lay" when this is something you've never been clear about yourself? What will the class think when you have to say, not the first or fourth, but the tenth time, "I don't know" or "Let's look that up."
>
> The first concern of Phase II then, is really not just concern about discipline, but concern about one's adequacy as a person and as a teacher on many criteria (Fuller, 1970).

Phase II—Concerns about Task

LEVEL 3—HOW DO MY PUPILS FEEL ABOUT ME? The student is concerned with social and emotional relationships with pupils. He is concerned with pupils as individuals and their unique feelings.

In the development of a professional teacher this stage is one of the most difficult, yet rewarding, experiences. For the neophyte it seems to be an impossibility. For the experienced teacher who has gotten there it is a benchmark.

Note that this is the first stage where true concern about pupils comes into play. Frances Fuller describes it:

> At this point education students become concerned about personal, social and emotional relationships with pupils. They are concerned about pupils as individuals and about the feelings of pupils. They have seen individual faces, learned names. They start to wonder what is going on behind the faces they are just learning to distinguish. They feel a relationship growing within themselves. They wonder whether pupils share their feelings, what pupils think about them, why pupils act as they do, where they live and what their lives are like outside the class.
>
> Although this concern involves pupils, self is not forgotten. Students say, "I'm attached to every child" or "Maybe I am becoming too personally involved with the children." "Do they think I am just a rich college kid?"

Still, they notice individual pupils, particularly the "problem" pupils and their strange behavior. At this stage, the concern is less with means to resolve the pupil's problem, although solutions would not be unwelcome. More often it is the teacher's own feelings about the child which are troublesome to the teacher, not the child's feelings about himself.

There is some concern about understanding the pupil, but still some concern about self, about *my* feelings about how he is. Self-forgetfulness has not yet occurred (Fuller, 1970).

Although self-forgetfulness has not totally occurred (and it never will), the neophyte teacher starts viewing the classroom environment differently. For many teachers who have not reached this stage of development, the classroom is one of teacher versus pupil. When the neophyte walks into the classroom, the student becomes a teacher. Those teachers who have reached this more mature level of concern, however, no longer have to put on their "teacher face," but instead can remain themselves.

At Level 3, students start focusing on what makes pupils tick, and this investigation can provide valuable insight into a classroom of cooperation. Obvious topics for study here are adolescent and child psychology. Consideration must also be given to skills that enforce the translation of the cognitive knowledge of psychology to the performance skills of the classroom. In Chapter 4 we described a module that forces the student to make curriculum decisions based on Piagetian theory. Such a module would be most useful at this point of concern. Glasser's *Schools without Failure* and *Reality Therapy* as well as any of Haim Ginott's works (*Teacher and Child, Between Parent and Child, Between Parent and Adolescent*) would also be useful here because in each of these "practical books" the author has attempted to tie theory to practice. Similar statements could be made about the use of transactional analysis in the classroom.

Feedback instruments for obtaining information from classes are also useful for students. One such instrument is the Student Evaluation of Teaching developed at the R&D Center for Teacher Education (see Exhibits 5.5, p. 160; 5.6, p. 161; and 6.2, p. 180). After a class of students completes the forms, they can be machine scored, and computer-printed feedback like that in Exhibit 6.3 can be provided to the teacher. Such information can help the teacher to focus on skills needed to alleviate any perceived areas of concern. In the example cases, Teacher 1 might consider what he is doing to give the students the impression that he gets mixed up. Teacher 2 might think about being the same nice guy but at the time time think about what might alleviate his being considered such an "easy touch" by the students. This identification and any reactive decisions, of course, remain the teacher's responsibility.

Other feedback instruments on the impact of the teacher can be useful at this level. One source the CBTE program developer might study is

STUDENT EVALUATION OF TEACHING

D. J. VELDMAN and R. F. PECK

TEACHER'S LAST NAME: _____

SUBJECT: _____

SCHOOL: _____

CIRCLE THE RIGHT CHOICES BELOW

Teacher's Sex: M   F

My Sex: M   F

My Grade Level:

    3   4   5   6   7   8   9   10   11   12

DO NOT USE

CIRCLE <u>ONE</u> OF THE FOUR CHOICES IN FRONT OF EACH STATEMENT.
THE FOUR CHOICES MEAN:

F = Very Much False
f = More False Than True
t = More True Than False
T = Very Much True

This Teacher:

F f t T   is always friendly toward students.

F f t T   knows a lot about the subject.

F f t T   is never dull or boring.

F f t T   expects a lot from students.

F f t T   asks for students' opinions before making decisions.

F f t T   is usually cheerful and optimistic.

F f t T   is not confused by unexpected questions.

F f t T   makes learning more like fun than work.

F f t T   doesn't let students get away with anything.

F f t T   often gives students a choice in assignments.

EXHIBIT 6.2

```
        SUMMARY OF STUDENT EVALUATION OF TEACHING (Teacher I)

TEACHER IDENTIFICATION = STEWART

    THE 25 STUDENTS IN THIS CLASS SAID THAT IT IS
VERY TRUE THAT THIS TEACHER IS ALWAYS FRIENDLY TOWARD STUDENTS,
RATHER TRUE THAT THIS TEACHER KNOWS A LOT ABOUT THE SUBJECT,
RATHER TRUE THAT THIS TEACHER IS NEVER DULL OR BORING,
VERY TRUE THAT THIS TEACHER EXPECTS A LOT FROM STUDENTS,
VERY TRUE THAT THIS TEACHER ASKS FOR STUDENTS' OPINIONS BEFORE MAKING DECISIONS,
VERY TRUE THAT THIS TEACHER IS USUALLY CHEERFUL AND OPTIMISTIC,
RATHER FALSE THAT THIS TEACHER IS NOT CONFUSED BY UNEXPECTED QUESTIONS,
VERY TRUE THAT THIS TEACHER MAKES LEARNING MORE LIKE FUN THAN WORK,
RATHER TRUE THAT THIS TEACHER DOENS'T LET STUDENTS GET AWAY WITH ANYTHING,
VERY TRUE THAT THIS TEACHER OFTEN GIVES STUDENTS A CHOICE IN ASSIGNMENTS.

PAIRED ITEMS SUGGEST THAT THIS TEACHER IS
    VERY FRIENDLY AND CHEERFUL,
   RATHER POISED AND KNOWLEDGEABLE,
    QUITE LIVELY AND INTERESTING,
    QUITE FIRM AND DEMANDING,
    VERY DEMOCRATIC IN PROCEDURE.

IN GENERAL, THIS CLASS HAS A FAVORABLE OPINION OF THIS TEACHER.
```

EXHIBIT 6.3

Diagnosing Classroom Learning Environments by Robert Fox, Margaret Luszki, and Richard Schmuck (1966). This booklet is invaluable for the teacher in designing assessment instruments to tap self-concept of pupils as well as the interpersonal relationships between students and between pupils and teacher.

Planned instructional activities can also be helpful in arousing prospective teachers' Level 3 concerns. One module, *Phenomenological Learning* (Jones and Weber, 1972, see Module II in Chapter 4), has as its objectives:

```
            SUMMARY OF STUDENT EVALUATION OF TEACHING (Teacher 2)

TEACHER IDENTIFICATION = PIPER

    THE 29 STUDENTS IN THIS CLASS SAID THAT IT IS
VERY TRUE THAT THIS TEACHER IS ALWAYS FRIENDLY TOWARD SUBJECTS,
VERY TRUE THAT THIS TEACHER KNOWS A LOT ABOUT THE SUBJECT,
RATHER TRUE THAT THIS TEACHER IS NEVER DULL OR BORING,
RATHER FALSE THAT THIS TEACHER EXPECTS A LOT FROM STUDENTS,
VERY TRUE THAT THIS TEACHER ASKS FOR STUDENTS' OPINIONS BEFORE MAKING DECISIONS,
VERY TRUE THAT THIS TEACHER IS USUALLY CHEERFUL AND OPTIMISTIC,
RATHER TRUE THAT THIS TEACHER IS NOT CONFUSED BY UNEXPECTED QUESTIONS,
VERY TRUE THAT THIS TEACHER MAKES LEARNING MORE LIKE FUN THAN WORK,
RATHER FALSE THAT THIS TEACHER DOESN'T LET STUDENTS GET AWAY WITH ANYTHING,
VERY TRUE THAT THIS TEACHER OFTEN GIVES STUDENTS A CHOICE IN ASSIGNMENTS.

PAIRED ITEMS SUGGEST THAT THIS TEACHER IS
    VERY FRIENDLY AND CHEERFUL,
    VERY POISED AND KNOWLEDGEABLE,
    VERY LIVELY AND INTERESTING,
  RATHER FIRM AND DEMANDING,
    VERY DEMOCRATIC IN PROCEDURE.

IN GENERAL, THIS CLASS HAS A FAVORABLE OPINION OF THIS TEACHER.
```

EXHIBIT 6.3

1. Define the following terms as they relate to phenomenological learning: self-concept, social desirability, perceptual field, competence motivation, intelligence, reality, perception, conscience, and discovery.
2. Name and/or construct and use at least two instruments or techniques for obtaining data about a pupil's self-concept or social desirability and/or about the affective relationship between pupils and the prospective teacher.
3. Demonstrate that as a result of his teaching, there is increased positive affective growth in self-concept or social desirability of his pupils or that there is increased positive affective relationship between his pupils and himself.

To complete the module the student must demonstrate the objectives. An enabling objective of the module is the design of assessment instruments to tap self-concept or interpersonal relationships. The Fox, Luszki, and Schmuck book is used by many students in their instrument development.

Before leaving this brief description of the "How do my pupils feel about me?" concern, a note of caution must be injected. There is an inherent danger at this level that causes many beginning teachers some difficulty. This danger is in doing things in the classroom to be liked rather than doing things that bring about real learning on the part of the pupils. This is a danger for beginning teachers and is one that program developers and co-operating teachers should be aware of. All human beings like to be liked. Teachers often become teachers to be liked. This is not a disease; it's a fact of life. Awareness of this need is usually enough to help the teacher keep curriculum and instruction decisions in perspective. At times, however, the constant effort to be liked can get in a beginning teacher's way. A competitive situation frequently arises in a classroom when a student teacher cannot enforce the rules. The cooperating teacher then becomes the bad guy in the eyes of the pupils for always enforcing the rules. Of course, the student teacher who is overly concerned about being liked cannot function as a teacher because she needs the votes of the pupils and cannot act in a way that might lose votes.

Frances Fuller identifies some other concerns that beginning teachers express about disciplining pupils:

> Prospective teachers from K through 12, but particularly in junior high school, talk about "discipline." *Resolution of the need, on one hand, to be liked by pupils and, on the other, to frustrate their impulses in the interests of socialization,* causes discomfort to most beginning teachers. For some, however, attempts at class control are deeply traumatic. For a student teacher who was a lonely only child, "discipline" may mean alienating potential "playmates" in the class or even "brothers" and "sisters" whose late arrival makes them more precious still. For the rebel, class control may be "going over to the enemy." Unconsciously hostile student teachers sometimes may panic in fear of their own rage; passive ones cry, narcissistic ones can be titillated and manipulated.
>
> In addition, discipline in teaching is vastly complicated by the presence of a supervising teacher. First, his standards, if even slightly different regarding tolerable noise level and impulse expression, add another dimension to an already complex situation. More important, his aims and those of the student are often at odds: the teacher's aim is success for his pupils. As we will see later, the experienced teacher is concerned about his pupils. He does not like them to suffer either by omission or commission. He wants good teaching. The student teacher on the other hand needs the freedom to fail (Fuller, 1970).

Regardless of the symptoms shown, program developers and implementers have the responsibility for helping the student identify some areas of this level that may get in his way while he teaches. Videotape feedback is useful here, as is the use of such instruments as those presented earlier in this section.

Phase III—Concerns about Impact

LEVEL 4—ARE PUPILS LEARNING WHAT I'M TEACHING?   Now students are concerned about pupil gain in knowledge and to some extent gain in pupils' understanding, application, synthesis, and evaluation of what is being taught them. Students are concerned with teaching methods that help pupils learn what is planned for them, usually cognitive gain. What is to be learned by the pupil is decided by the student in his role as teacher. In this phase, students say, "Am I getting across to them? I mean, *really* getting across to them?"

Level 3 above showed the first glimmer of concerns about pupils and their needs. In Phase III we find three levels of concern that all focus on impact on pupils. The main difference between the Phase III concerns and the Phase II, Level 3, concern—"How do my pupils feel about me?"—lies in whose needs are being met. For example, a teacher is considering dismissal of a problem pupil from her class. If she is considering dismissal primarily out of her own frustration at not being able to handle his problems, then she is concerned about her needs and is in Phase II. On the other hand, if the teacher is considering dismissal as the best alternative for the pupil or for the welfare of the rest of the class, then she is in Phase III.

These impact concerns are not at all typical of a preservice teacher population. They are distressingly uncommon even among experienced teachers. More than likely, however, teacher educators will deal with these concerns more frequently at the inservice level.

Preservice teachers who expressed Level 4 concerns would be ready for a unit on accountability like the module on Phenomenological Learning described above and in Chapter 4, p. 126.

Other relevant materials might include enabling activities that deal with questioning skills (a good way for teachers to evaluate pupil learning) and planning for instruction. The Teaching Performance Tests developed by James Popham (1972) can also be valuable experiences for students at this level. In these exercises teachers are given a topic, an objective, some information, and twenty minutes in which to teach a group of peers the objective. This is a good firing-line test of how well a teacher is succeeding in helping pupils to learn.

Phase III—Concerns about Impact

LEVEL 5—ARE PUPILS LEARNING WHAT THEY NEED?   Now students are concerned not just about pupils' absorbing and regurgitating what has been taught them. Gain in knowledge was their concern when they asked, "Are pupils learning what *I'm teaching?*" The new concern—"Are they learning what *they* need?"—is quite different. The needs of *pupils as persons* are of concern.

> The concern is not only with cognitive gain, but with affective influences and affective gain as well. Students are concerned with procedures to achieve that kind of pupil gain. They say, "I am trying to decide whether moving Mary to another fourth grade would help her. She seems afraid of me."
>
> Sometimes the concern shows itself more clearly in an action than in expression of a concern. "The rest of the class was doing arithmetic, but he was drawing a test tube, probably because of the science lesson this morning. Still, he had not put pencil to paper all year until today. I was so glad he was doing *something,* that I gave him a *bigger piece of paper.*" This teacher has translated her concern into action. She disregards what she is teaching, arithmetic, to consider what is possible for the child to learn. She accepts what he is able to do, what *he* can learn, instead of demanding what *she* wants and what he is not able to give. She even enlarges his efforts, truly "personalizing" her teaching.
>
> Teachers with this concern are trying to figure out how the world looks to a pupil, what the pupil is trying to do or where he is trying to go. Such teachers are trying to discover the pupil's concerns. They are asking, "Are pupils learning what *they* need?" (Fuller, 1970.)

The teacher at this level of concern is not one from whom you will hear the lament, "It's not in the syllabus!" This teacher probably spends as much time doing needs assessments of her pupils as she does checking out the syllabus. This is the teacher who is responsive to inservice training that she sees as being useful in her classroom, especially in individualizing instruction and doing needs assessment. She is also the one who really doesn't mind giving a pupil to another teacher, especially if the teacher might be able to help. In short, she is the professional, the one who focuses on the needs of the learner. She may not always be the most popular person in the building with administration or with fellow teachers, but she is the one who will be remembered by the children.

Preservice and inservice teachers at this level are not likely to need special concerns-arousing activities before instruction. They are probably actively searching for information, ideas, and resources to assist them in helping pupils. Instruction in needs assessment, diagnosis of learning difficulties, and interpretation of individual tests and measures will be perceived as relevant. Instruction in educational psychology subject matter related to child growth and development, theory and implications of research on the self concept of pupils, and strategies and materials for individualizing instruction and sources of alternative enabling activities for pupils are all on target. Training sessions in the use of affective-oriented instructional strategies such as those for teaching for values clarification suggested by Simon, Howe, and Kirschenbaum (1972) are also relevant at this concern level.

Phase III—Concerns about Impact

LEVEL 6—HOW CAN I IMPROVE MYSELF AS A TEACHER? Although these words are spoken often, this concern is so rare that our conceptualization of it is drawn from only a few observations of it. Hence this description is highly tentative. This concern is self-forgetful. The teacher is unconcerned with her own protection, pleasure, or gain. She is concerned with anything and everything that may contribute to the development not only of the pupils in her own class but of children generally. She may be concerned about herself as an instrument of change, as an interpersonal influence. She says, "What do I do that influences pupil development?" "How does what I *am* change them?" "What changes, anywhere, are possible to facilitate the development of these children?"

> Although the concern is broad, it manifests itself in specific questions and decisions. "Should I tell Mrs. Moss her son's I.Q. score?" "This school lunch program needs to be extended to breakfast. Hungry children cannot learn." "I am looking for a science workshop. I feel my science teaching is not what it should be."
>
> The rarest and possibly the most mature concerns of all involve attempts by the teacher to examine her personal impact on pupils, perhaps to bring to conscious awareness aspects of her impact of which she is only dimly aware.
>
> Interactions of which the teacher is not aware can occur between her and a child. One example was given earlier of a teacher's conscious concern with discipline and her other concern with being liked, a concern of which she was not aware. Such a concern with discipline might be thought a concern with self. It *is* of course, a concern with self-protection *if* the teacher remains concerned with discipline. But if the teacher becomes concerned about bringing to her own conscious awareness possible pre-conscious aspects of her relationship with the class, her question is, "What do I do that influences them?" This is a very different concern, a concern with pupil gain, even if such concern involves the risk of new and possibly painful insights into one's self. (Fuller, 1970.)

While, from the above description, it might appear that this teacher would be amenable to any training, a few specific things come to mind. This teacher would be the one who would be most amenable to trying out alternative ways of instruction and would be most receptive to experimental effort, if she thought the efforts could help pupils. This teacher would probably be the one looking for new things to do as well, just for something else to do, *if there were some predictable degree of pupil satisfaction evident.*

Since this teacher would constantly be searching for meaning, she would be most amenable to study of the history and philosophy of education, especially as it related to how her school functions.

Summary Thoughts on Concerns

Obviously, the concerns model provides a structure for *continuing* teacher education.[3] We would expect preservice teachers to exit a well-planned CBTE program with solid task concerns and the beginning of concerns about their impact on pupils. We believe CBTE goals and objectives ought to reflect at least that level of achievement while in the program. We would also hope that the program would provide students with self-resources to use in growing into the impact concerns as they gained experience as teachers. Follow-up evaluation of program results should examine how graduates have progressed in their concerns.

There are many implications here for inservice training and support for teachers. We expect and hope that teachers will continue to grow upon graduation and employment. Some do not. Some even regress to survival concerns, find a way to cope, and become fossilized in that position. One of the most important things a teacher can learn in preservice training is how to become a self-evaluating, self-actualizing person who can continue to grow even in the absence of supportive resources. How to use feedback is an important part of this lesson.

PROVIDING STUDENTS WITH FEEDBACK ON THEIR TEACHING

In Chapter 5 we made the point that before a student can change a teaching style, method, or whatever, there is a sequence of *assessment, awareness, and arousal* that occurs. Before a student can identify a strategy to change, he must be aware of a need for it. One key enabling activity in this feedback sequence is the use of videotape or audiotape feedback.

---

[3] For further insight into the concept of concerns and related issues in teacher education as seen by Frances Fuller, see the chapter, "Becoming a Teacher," by F. F. Fuller and O. H. Bown in the 1975 Yearbook of the National Society for the Study of Education.

Videotape feedback can serve in any number of ways. The techniques to be described here are in use at several CBTE sites. As part of the initial sequence of education experiences, students at one site are expected to focus on teaching skills; for example, higher-order questioning, set induction, stimulus variations, reinforcement, congruency of nonverbal behaviors, and handwriting. After the student has been instructed on lesson plan format, he might teach a lesson of his own choice to a group of four to seven peers. The lesson length is limited to some fifteen minutes. Videotape analysis is made of this lesson by the students with their instructors. The feedback sessions are conducted in groups or individually. In the sessions the instructor has the role of helping students to focus on concerns and skills that may encourage them despite the results seen on the tape.

As an example of what a videotape feedback session might look like, consider the transcribed session below. The student, obviously, is in lower-level concerns. Before she can make the move toward focusing on the needs of her students, she will have to have satisfactorily answered such questions as "Am I safe?" "Where do I stand?" "How adequate am I?" The transcript is a good example of how the instructor attempts to aid the student not only in answering these questions but also in focusing on the need for new skills. Note that neither the instructor nor the student has seen the videotape before. Therefore, no concerns are stimulated about the instructor's having already made up his mind about the tape or the student.

Instructor: Before we get started let me tell you something about my function. You are the expert. You know more about yourself than I ever will so I am not going to tell you about your good and bad qualities. You are you and I won't try to compare your behavior with others. My major responsibility is to help you focus on some teaching skills that may be important to you in your teaching. As you know, it is my job to check you out on these eight skills sometime in the next semester or so. OK? Any reactions to your teaching before we see the tape?

Student: I was nervous.

I: Did your nervousness get in your way of teaching?

S: Ya. I've never seen myself on videotape before. In fact, I've never been asked to teach before. I didn't sleep at all the night before.

I: Will I be able to see your nervousness on the tape?

S: Ya.

I: Let's look together. If you think it might help, while you watch, jot down a description of those things that went well and also of things you would do differently, next time.

The videotape is of the student teaching some painting technique to peers. There is no interaction; the lesson is pure lecture, and the student's nervousness even makes the viewer nervous.

I: What do you think?

S: I didn't know I sounded like that! I looked like I thought I would, but I didn't know I sounded like that!

I: The first time we see and hear ourselves can be quite surprising. We seem to sound differently than we think we do. . . . Did you look nervous?

S: Not as much as I thought I would.

I: Let me ask you this. What did you list under the things that went well? I note that you didn't write much of anything.

S: There really wasn't much of anything; it was bad.

I: What about your knowledge of your subject? You were mentioning some things that I didn't dream existed.

S: Ya, but I've been doing that stuff since I was in junior high school. I should know it.

I: It came through. I was also impressed by your organization of content. Everything that you mentioned seemed to be right in place. I'll bet you are organized in everything that you do.

S: Most people tell me I'm too organized.

I: Can you see where this organization of yours might be an asset in teaching?

S: Yes.

I: I've mentioned a couple of strengths. You name one.

S: Well, I did make all of those things that I showed. I remember some teachers who would just tell you about things. These, I actually showed.

I: True. And especially working with primary children—they need all the concrete experiences they can get.

The point of the beginning portion of this interview is to show how one student who is obviously unsure can be made to focus on some perceived needs. If CBTE programs exist only for an instructor to check off a list of skills when demonstrated by a student, then personalization cannot exist. In this interview the instructor saw quickly that the student was in lowest-level concerns. Any attempt to tell the student that she had not demonstrated one of the required teaching skills would have placed the student in a win-lose situation with the instructor, probably prohibiting the helping relationship to grow. A key is the identification of positives on the part of the student. Any student who cannot see anything good about himself certainly cannot focus on teaching strengths. The outside influence of the instructor can enforce the search for good qualities. Once this is done the student is in a better position to realistically focus on some skills that might help him deal with those things he thought were detriments. Look now at a later portion of the interview when the student was less anxious about assessing her performance.

I: OK, we've noted some real strengths. How do you feel?

S: I'm waiting for the other side.

I: A little apprehensive, huh? Suppose I asked you what prescription you would give the teacher you just saw on tape. What would it be?

S: Everything.

I: What do you mean?

S: Everything; there is an awful long way to go for the teacher.

I: For all of us. Seriously, let's look at some of the skills you might want to focus on. . . . Were your students involved with you in the lesson?

S: They paid attention but I couldn't get them to talk.

I: What did you do to get them to talk? Did you ask any questions to force them to talk?

S: No, except once I asked them if they understood.

I: Yes, and once you asked Sally to hold the painting while you talked about it. One part of my prescription would be to focus on your question asking. Modules 4 and 5 focus on this skill. Try them.

S: Will they teach me how to ask questions?

I: They will allow you to see how you might ask better questions. I really don't know if you can't ask questions. All I'm saying is that in this tape you didn't ask many.

S: OK.

I: How did you start the lesson? Do you remember?

S: Yes, I told them I wanted to tell them about . . .

I: One of the skills that you might want to consider is that of set induction. Module 6 will help you with this. Set induction is a method of getting the students actively engaged in the lesson. It's a motivation device and can be very effective in getting and holding your students' interests. If you were starting again, how would you start it?

S: Well, knowing what I know now I think I would show them some of my paintings and ask them how they were made.

I: That's a start. Teaching sometimes calls for seduction on your part. You've got to convince your students that what you are about to teach is worthwhile. . . .

The instructional specialist obviously would not tell the student to focus on 350 different skills at once. In fact, with a student at the level of concern of the one illustrated above, the questioning and set induction prescription is probably enough until the next tape. This successive approximation technique can be a valuable one for students who have to go slow in order to see that they *can* function. In a *program* the student will make any number of tapes or get feedback from a large number of field experiences. This long-range view of growth throughout the program is paramount. Too much, too soon, can gag. A second thing to remember about a true program is that the teaching skills not demonstrated by students by the end of a semester can be shown in succeeding semesters. Everything does not have to be accomplished in one semester or in one videotape feedback session.

Another point that should be discussed here is the use of peer-teaching experiences. Certification programs using a competency-based mode certify only when teachers can teach pupils in public schools. However, the value of peer teaching should not be underestimated. If students are in the low levels of concern, their needs are going to be met much easier while working with colleagues whom they trust, rather than with unpredictable pupils. Just avoiding classroom management problems can help the beginning student to focus on teaching and not control. In a *program* these in-school pupils experiences will come soon enough and in this sequence will be an even bigger boost toward helping the student reach higher-level concerns. However, the student cannot make the move from intermediate-level to higher-level concerns until he has made the move out of the lower level.

It might be worthwhile to consider how quickly some students can jump out of self-concerns through planned experiences. Several programs use the Teaching Performance Tests developed by James Popham (1972), which were mentioned earlier in this chapter. A videotape-peer lesson is conducted after an instructor has prescribed the lesson to be taught. Afterward, the peers are tested over the content. These tests are scored by the instructor, and some indication of the student's ability to bring about changes on the part of learners is obtained from looking at the test results. The effectiveness of teaching performance is reviewed by the instructor and student by watching excerpts of videotapes made while the peer teaching was in progress. The versatility of videotape feedback sessions and the teaching performance materials is again illustrated here, since the instructor is able to focus on issues related to the concern level of each student. The following discussion is from another feedback session with the student met earlier.

I: I have the test results of your students here and also some ratings that they filled out on their feelings toward you. How do you think the ratings are going to look?

S: Pretty good. We did five of the lessons the day I did mine and I felt as good about my performance as any of the other students'. I felt sorry for Angela; she really had a tough topic. Who selected them anyway?

I: I selected them but they were assigned randomly. You may have just been lucky.

S: I don't know. The first time I saw the thing I panicked. After my initial panic I focused on how I could get a set induction in and on some questions that I might ask. You know, I felt more comfortable this time—they were involved.

I: So I should look more for their being involved? How did you get them involved?

S: For one thing you really put us under the gun. We knew that you were going to give those blasted tests at the end so I knew that I would have to check out the students. Questioning helps. The module on set induction techniques helped also. I felt they were motivated to go.

I: Sounds like you did well; let's look at the tape and while we are doing that we'll peek at the test results.

The lesson is a big improvement. As the student reported, the questioning is reasonably good and the set induction seemed to be appropriate, albeit a bit long. During the tape the test results are shared with the student. Her pupils scored 83 percent on the test (above national average) and gave her "very interesting" ratings.

I: All right, you critique the lesson. You noted earlier that your questioning was good. How do you feel now?

S: OK, I did get a little confused at one time when Joe gave me that answer I wasn't expecting. It was obvious that I didn't want that answer.

I: I would prefer that you stuck with the good points, but since you mentioned it, I noticed the same thing. Do you think that it was a major problem?

S: No, not really. I just wasn't expecting his answer.

I: That's the beauty of higher-order questions—they force you, the teacher, to be open-minded. Students come up with all kinds of answers you wouldn't expect. How did you respond to Joe?

S: I laughed, sort of. But I went on to someone else.

I: How about the other interaction with students? Was it mostly teacher-student-teacher-student? Or was there some teacher-student-student-teacher interaction?

S: More teacher-student-teacher.

I: There is nothing wrong with that, especially with the objective you had for the lesson. It is good that you recognized it though.

The feedback continues, focusing on specific parts of the tape.

I: One thing that I must mention before we go on. Your questioning is OK, your set induction is OK. I also felt good about the way that you were moving around in the group—you didn't rivet yourself to the front of the room this time. In fact, I saw you as a teacher on this tape. Frankly, during the first tape, you looked more like a person *acting* like a teacher instead of a person teaching. Why so relaxed?

S: The group—I've been with them for four months.

I: I don't believe that's it totally. In fact, if I gave you the assignment to do the same lesson with four students of my choice, people you have never met before, I'll bet you would be closer to the person I saw on this tape than the person I saw on the first tape. Right?

S: Ya. Practice does help.

I: But it's more than practice. You seem to have a lot more confidence now as a teacher. I have a feeling that the next set of materials that you focus on will come a lot quicker. Which brings me to the point . . .

S: I knew you would get to that.

I: Always do. I would like to see you focus on your reinforcement skills for next time. I think that the module on basic reinforcement might help you over the difficulty that came up with your uneasiness with Joe's answer. Ever hear of positively qualified reinforcement—telling a person he's OK, but his answer isn't quite?

S: No.

I: You will. A second thing. I felt a little uncomfortable at times while watching the tape that your questioning sequences, while very good, always ended up with "right" answers. Try the module on divergent questions— you'll focus on asking questions that have no right answers. The next tape you do, remember, will be with kids in your school. Let me know if I can help set up . . .

A few points about the interview. First, the instructor again tries to be supportive of a student who has made a first step out of self concerns. The Popham materials helped this, but in addition to the materials, the atmosphere of feedback is most important. The system still has to be "yes–not yet." Feedback sessions that are viewed as punitive and summative rather than formative can be bad news. Of course, not all students make the growth that was seen in this student. Second, the growth process continues with a new prescription each time. Although it would be better if the student identified the needed skills—and this often happens—anyone who has given videotape feedback can attest to the fact that not all students are capable of self-prescription. Third, note that the student was not focusing on voice, diction, or looks in the second experience. The instructor was viewed as an insider rather than an outsider, and the safety necessary for movement out of first-level concerns was evident.

In addition to focusing on the skill development of teachers, videotape feedback sessions also provide an important opportunity to attend to the personal growth needs of students. The following excerpt illustrates the kind of discussion that can result when the student is relatively open about her feelings and the instructor is receptive to discussing personal growth and impact concern-related issues.

I: You seem pretty cautious about getting involved with those in your class.

S: If you mean really close I think that is true. I was in love once and I don't want to jump in that cold water again.

I: Cold water?

S: Yes. I felt like I was going to lose my freedom somehow. Yet I don't think I ever got close enough for that. It didn't bother me but it made me curious why he didn't really turn me on.

I: Curious? Then your relationship was neither warm nor cold—just indifferent?

S: I don't quite understand what you mean by that.

I: I am checking something out with you. I get the feeling you were pretty indifferent to him and his feelings.

S: Well—I don't like to think that, but I'm sure I was pretty indifferent.

I: I think you may have felt scared, but maybe the fear was too deep to feel.

S: I think I was and that helps me understand a lot. I think I wait for someone to make me feel good and if it doesn't happen I turn them off. That's awful. I'm *still* acting like a helpless, unloved child.

I: And maybe you aren't all that helpless?

S: Yeah! I'm really not. I just didn't see what I was doing.

I: You know if you try to change you'd better get set to feel some rejection if people don't respond when you reach out.

S: Yes. I can almost feel it, but at least I would feel like I was growing up. And I love kids and I just don't have any choice. They are not supposed to have to make *me* secure.

In a personalized CBE program attention must be given not only to the skill-related concerns but also to the personal growth and impact concerns of the developing students. Most discussions about the personal part of teaching will not be this open or handled this quickly; however, this student was open and concerned about her impact on children. As the reader may have realized, instructors participating in this kind of feedback session may also need to develop new skills.

SOME FURTHER THOUGHTS ABOUT EARLY PROGRAM FORMATIVE AND SUMMATIVE ASSESSMENTS

CBE efforts rely on the assumptions that (1) exit, not entrance, requirements are those most useful for identifying professional skills, and (2) aptitude is a measure more of time needed to achieve competence, and less of whether or not a preprofessional can achieve competence. Given these statements, it is difficult to understand why educators are constantly trying to identify sets of predictive tests that can be used in advance to screen students. Obviously, the answer lies in resources. With limited resources, every program implementer wants to find the best people to work with.

Given the resource crunch, the many students wanting to be in preprofessional programs, and the decreasing need for people in some professions, namely education, what predictors are available? This is an exceedingly difficult question. One thing is certain, common sense does not always hold. McClelland (1973), for example, notes a significant *negative* relationship between finger dexterity and the income of dentists.

In teacher education there have been several key studies relating teacher characteristics (the so-called presage variables) and teacher effectiveness as measured by student achievement (product criteria). Such research still continues as psychometric instruments become more refined. Up to this point, however, the research evidence has been scanty. Cooper and Weber (1973) reviewed this research:

1. TEACHER ATTITUDES

Gage (1972) summarized several reviews . . . [focusing on the] Minnesota Teacher Attitude Inventory. His conclusion was that the research on the MTAI has yielded positive results as consistently as any other research on teaching and will predict with better than chance success how well an elementary school teacher will be liked by her students.
Smith (1971) states that there can be little doubt that a teacher's attitudes toward himself influence his classroom behavior. . . . Smith also asserts that there is good reason to believe that the teacher's attitudes toward his pupils . . . will influence their achievement.

2. TEACHER'S VERBAL ABILITY

Guthrie (1970), reviewing the Coleman Report, states that it [verbal ability] is the most significant variable in explaining student achievement [measured by a vocabulary test].

3. OTHER

Mood (1970) speculates that there may be as many as fifty teacher attributes related to pupil achievement . . . [Mood] lists six major categories of attributes: dedication to the educability of all children; ability to communicate; ability to motivate; ability to organize and manage a class; ability to create learning experiences; and knowledge of subject field.

With the small amount of replicable evidence it is no wonder that most preprofessional efforts rely on the candidate's grade-point average in other courses for any screening that is done. In short, there seems to be no single or multiple set of factors predictive of teacher effectiveness.

In CBE efforts, it is anticipated that there may be more self-screening possibilities. Competencies and expectations are stated in advance. Students know more clearly what is expected of them. Perhaps test results could be used to aid students in focusing on their strengths and weaknesses with respect to teaching and CBE. At several CBE program sites, such testing is included as part of initial experiences. At Houston, for example, the following five instruments are given to students in the first two weeks of the program: (1) Minnesota Teacher Attitude Inventory, (2) Edwards Personal Preference Schedule, (3) Work Motivation Index, (4) Opinion Scale, and (5) Vocational Preference Inventory.

Counselors in the Houston CBTE effort chose these instruments for several reasons: the instruments tap a variety of psychological variables, they are norm-referenced, they allow quick computer scoring and group feedback to large numbers of students, and the results are easily describable to students in nontechnical jargon.

It must be mentioned that the results of the tests are not used to remove students from the Houston CBTE program; the results are fed back to students who must make any decisions. The test results, coupled with school experiences and seminars with peers, have aided a large number of students in choosing other careers before it was impossible for them to change.

While information on each of these instruments can be obtained from its publisher, a few comments must be made here about a set of scores. It is hoped that the scores reflect not only teaching-related attributes but also program-related attributes.

MINNESOTA TEACHER ATTITUDE INVENTORY.   The score on this instrument reflects a prospective teacher's concern with children—the principal factor being an assessment of how restrictive or democratic the teacher is. (Available from Psychological Corporation, 304 East Forty-fifth Street, New York, New York 10017.)

EDWARDS PERSONAL PREFERENCE SCHEDULE.   This instrument taps fifteen different factors. Some factors, like *order, nurturance,* and *dominance,* can be related to the needs of the classroom. Other factors, like *endurance, change, autonomy,* and *abasement,* reflect some evidence about a student in a self-paced program. One interesting set of data seems to note that those students who have low endurance scores (seldom finish what they start) and high abasement scores (feel overly guilty) have problems with CBTE at Houston. They seldom get things done and they then feel guilty. The cycle causes frustration which eventually causes some students to drop out, often rather painfully. (Available from Psychological Corporation, 304 East Forth-fifth Street, New York, New York 10017.)

WORK MOTIVATION INDEX.   This instrument assesses, with some high degree of accuracy, a student profile along the lines of Maslow's hierarchy of needs. (Jay Hall and Martha Williams, Teleometrics, Intl., P.O. Drawer 1850, Conroe, Texas 77301.)

OPINION SCALE.   This instrument assesses the dogmatism of a student and the degree to which he believes that he, versus others, controls his destiny. In later portions of many CBTE programs the student will be faced with situations where he will need to look at himself and how others see him with respect to a skill, competence, and so forth. The degree to which the person is open to outside opinions may affect his success in teaching (Kleiber, Veldman, and Menaker, 1973).

VOCATIONAL PREFERENCE INVENTORY. This instrument allows a student to identify how well his selection of a profession fits with others in the same profession. (Available from Consulting Psychologists Press, 577 College Avenue, Palo Alto, California 94306.)

One last note. The test results by themselves are useless. Students in most CBTE efforts are responsible for their decisions to remain. The test results provide only additional data.

IN SUMMARY

In this chapter we have focused on some aspects of operationalizing a personalized CBE program. We have attempted to show how a program that appears relevant to students and effective to professionals can be organized around the concerns theory introduced in Chapter 5. In the last two sections of this chapter we have made some points that we believe are important about two vital aspects of personalized programs—feedback and assessment. In a sense the focus of these last two sections summarizes the thrust of the whole chapter: if you know where your students are, and what they need, and if you help them to understand those facts, and organize the program to facilitate these actions—then you are on the road to personalized education.

7

differing faculty and student roles

Just as learners' styles and paces differ, so do educators' skills. Any educator could spend hours telling about the roles that he has been asked to play in his professional experience. Each of us has been information giver, seminar leader, remedial aid, counselor, friend, colleague, committee member, organizer, and administrator.

Some of us are excellent administrators. Others abhor paperwork but excel in lecture situations. Still others work well with media. A special few are excellent counselors in working with students in one-to-one situations. Others do their best in seminar situations, raising thought-provoking questions and helping clarify difficult issues. Still others prefer working in field or clinic settings as models for students and handling the real-world, day-to-day tasks. Some educators consider themselves content specialists. For example, content specialists in such fields as science, reading, mathematics, and social science maintain their professional identities in these areas while working in teacher education. Still others in growing numbers are focusing on generic skills—skills that cut across disciplinary lines.

In this chapter we attempt to identify the need for and to point out some of the consequences of faculty and student role changes in CBE. It is our contention that one of the best ways of organizing faculty for maximum impact is the use of interdisciplinary faculty teams, teams that amplify the strengths of individual faculty members and minimize the weaknesses. Students also experience role changes, and we wish to explore some of these changes as well as to identify some of the problems that might arise. To accomplish these objectives the chapter is organized around the following questions and topics:

Page	Topic	Questions
199	The Need for Interactive Faculty Roles	How will faculty cooperation as required in CBE affect faculty roles?
203	Interdisciplinary Faculty Teams	How can teaming facilitate interactive faculty roles?
213	Role Transition for Students	What problems will students face in the transition to CBE?

THE NEED FOR INTERACTIVE FACULTY ROLES

There are any number of faculty roles in CBE. What kind of role is best for an individual faculty member to assume? The answer to this question, of course, lies with the individual faculty member, simply because each is unique in his teaching style and has special strengths and weaknesses. The assumption in CBE programs is that there is no single "good" teaching role. There are roles that are more effective for some people than for others, and some roles are more appropriate than others for the acquisition of certain goals.

On the other hand, few professional educators are prepared to assume all the roles they recognize as necessary in education efforts. In planning an individual course or a total professional program, educators are cognizant of the need to have students acquire knowledge and skills that will make them more effective professionally. The rub comes when enrollment figures arrive. We would like to have one-to-one contact with students to provide feedback on their teaching in classroom settings. However, in all cases, except possibly student teaching, enrollment figures of thirty, fifty, or three hundred for each faculty member preclude any such effort. Often the best we can do is to provide cognitive input and hope for the best. We lecture.

In CBE the need to focus more on the performance and consequence areas has to be responded to. The entire function of modules is to provide ways for students to acquire information on their own or in groups, saving faculty contact time for those things that faculty are really needed for. What is the function of having a skilled professor lecture on Piagetian technique when the lecture can be placed on slide-tape, videotape, or audiotape? The students can see or hear the presentation at their convenience and hear it as many times as they wish. Valid instructor input comes when the student needs feedback on his success or lack of success in demonstrating a Piagetian interview or in seminar settings where the professor can answer questions related to readings or a taped lecture. This description of professorial time is distasteful to a number of our colleagues who believe that when you take a skilled lecturer from his students and replace him with a tape you might as well have the students send their tape recorders to listen.

These critics are missing one important aspect of the mastery learning idea. In any program that makes use of the mastery learning concept, the decision is consciously made to ensure that individual students will reach mastery before going on to another area of study. Yet the acquisition time for one student to achieve mastery is rarely the same as that of another. At the end of a fourteen-week semester students show a remarkable range of achievement. Traditionally, the constant has been time; the variable, achievement. Grades were determined by rating student achievement against the achievement of other students; this is basically a norm-referenced system, a system that is inconsistent with the criterion-referenced assumptions of CBE.

For this reason, mass instruction via the lecture is suspect if it is the *only* mode of instruction projected for a CBE program. This will not make lectures and seminars extinct. There is a place for the lecture, even in CBE, and the technique can provide outstanding results. Some lecturers can weave a complex subject together beautifully and can make clear, cogent points that stick with a large portion of the audience. But something needs to be done in a mastery program for that portion of the audience that even the good lecturer misses and to facilitate application of the lecturer's message. This is why we question the value of the lecture as a *sole* strategy.

A most viable form of instruction seems to be a variation of combining self-instruction and interactive instruction. The modules described in Chapter 4 are attempts at such instruction. Some are written for self-instruction. Directions are given for appropriate sequencing, and the student is held accountable for demonstrating specified objectives when he feels he can do so. Some of these modules require little, if any, instructor contact with students. The materials are kept so that the student can use them and even test out of them without the assistance of an instructor. At Weber State, for example, a clerk-librarian at a resource center has the responsibility for testing students when they have completed cognitive objective modules.

There is a lot more to modules than just self-pacing, and they are certainly more than teaching machines, but the main point we want to make here is that modules release faculty for more interactive instructional roles. In this role the instructor can clarify, amplify, prescribe, cajole, coerce, support, or even push a student to achieve an important objective or competency. Self-instruction may be all that is required for most cognitive outcomes. Faculty input is usually needed for performance and consequence outcomes.

Since there are not enough hours in a week to conduct a "normal" (i.e., mass instruction) class and maintain close contact with individual students, most module builders substitute a form of sequenced instruction to release the faculty time for one-to-one contacts. Exhibit 7.1 is a flowchart of such a unit that seeks to enable students to ask higher-order questions.

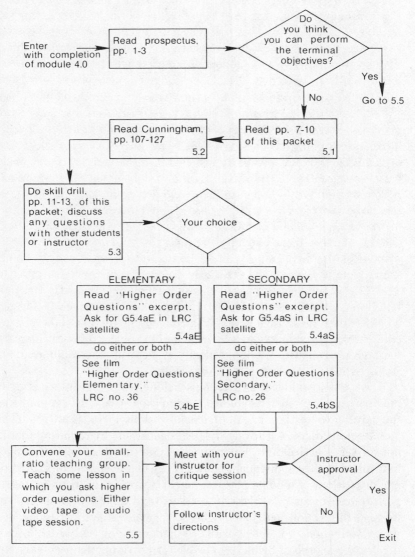

NOTE: *Since you would not be involved with this module unless your instructor prescribed it or unless you were interested in it, there is no preassessment option provided.*

EXHIBIT 7.1   Flowchart for Module on Asking Higher-Order Questions.

In this example the student reads about, studies examples of, and hears about higher-order questions until he feels that he is ready to use them in a class setting. He then schedules a teaching session which he conducts and has videotaped. He evaluates his effort and then sits down with the instructor to review his progress. In a "normal" course the instructor might lecture on higher-order questions and then require the students to distinguish them from others on a test. But the objective of this activity is that students be able to demonstrate that they can *use* higher-order questions, not just recognize them. The module replaces the instructor's lecture time with time spent with individual students for review and feedback on their progress toward the objective. While one student is receiving feedback, others are at other stages in the module or are moving on ahead to other objectives.

As an aside, we must tell the following story as a warning to program managers not to make overconfident assumptions about how well self-paced instruction is going to be used by faculty members. At one college we know of, a CBTE program was being installed using modules. Several weeks into the pilot semester student dissatisfaction was beginning to surface and was becoming quite shrill. Some students were getting further and further behind the projected pace. A quick investigation pinpointed the difficulty. One instructor was holding classes as he always had, complete with attendance checks. He was then assigning the modules as *homework!* Students were responsible for his lectures and his tests, *and* for satisfactorily completing the module objectives. We obviously do not recommend this procedure.

The variety of study activities in Exhibit 7.1 indicates that students differ not only in their rate of learning but also in their style. Some would rather read, others prefer mediated instruction, others are more confortable in seminars or even in lectures. Some work best alone, others need group support. Working effectively with all these different learning styles requires a variety of teaching skills.

As was mentioned earlier, the teaching skills and interests of faculty members vary as widely as student learning styles. A CBE program can take full advantage of the variety of teaching skills in its faculty and accommodate the variety of learning styles in its learners by requiring that faculty not all serve as lecturers but rather become involved in interactive roles best suited to their individual abilities. They can lead seminars, hold one-to-one discussions of module postassessments, provide feedback on videotaped performances, serve as gestalt builders and fellow-professional models through interaction with individuals and small groups of students. All of these interactions take place with the student being accountable for learning and the instructor being responsible for providing the necessary environment and constructive feedback on a personal and individual basis to facilitate learning. All faculty members will have strengths that can be capitalized upon, but no one faculty member should be expected to do everything well.

INTERDISCIPLINARY FACULTY TEAMS

The best arrangement we know of to take advantage of the variety in faculty skills is the interdisciplinary faculty team. In the faculty team each team member shares his strengths and has his weaknesses buttressed by the strengths of other faculty members. The team arrangement lends the following strengths to the program:

1. People working together are more productive than individuals.
2. The strengths of individuals are maximized.
3. The weaknesses of individuals are minimized.
4. People are more apt to take creative risks when they don't carry full responsibility for a task.
5. More and a greater variety of resources are available for solving problems.
6. Satisfactions for successful teamwork accrue in addition to opportunities for personal and professional growth.
7. Duplication of program components and effort is minimized.
8. Teaming encourages a more holistic approach to the program goals and objectives.

Faculty teaming is a viable and visible component of CBTE programs at the University of Georgia, the University of Houston, the University of Toledo, Weber State College, Brigham Young University, and other institutions.

Organizational Formats for Teaming

In essence, faculty teams can operate in one of the following formats:

1. VERTICAL TEAMING. The faculty team works with a group of students throughout the entire program and is responsible for total input.

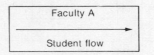

Advantages: Students and faculty get to know each other well. Continuity of the program is ensured because faculty work with the same students throughout their term in the program.

Disadvantages: Input is limited to only those faculty members on the team. If interpersonal problems arise between faculty, between students, or between faculty and students, they must be dealt with successfully because personal contact will be necessary throughout the program.

2. HORIZONTAL TEAMING. As students go through a program they meet with different teams of faculty that are responsible for specific portions of the program.

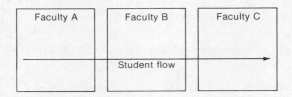

Advantages: Faculty members can specialize and can, in theory at least, become proficient in smaller areas of study. This will result in more up-to-date and valid content. Close coordination within each team is retained, but students are permitted contacts with a wider variety of faculty inputs.

Disadvantages: There is substantial danger of fragmentation of students' programs over the length of their professional training. Gaps and overlaps can occur if there is not sufficient communication and coordination between faculty teams.

3. COMBINATION FORMAT. This is a combination of the two formats described above. Faculty team *A* works with a given student throughout his professional training, offering specific help in generic areas. Team *A* faculty also act as "brokers" for students in contracting with specialist team faculty (*B, C,* and *D*) for assistance in attaining other competencies. Individual faculty members may serve both on a generic team and on a specialist team.

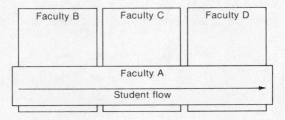

Advantages: This format blends the best from both the horizontal and the vertical format. Faculty members can focus on their specializations and other faculty can pick up the ball in other areas, but the student retains a constant "home" team throughout his time in the program.

Disadvantages: Most of the difficulties are managerial.[1] Faculty members will find it hard to serve on two different teams with overlapping responsibilities without some loyalty problems. Care must be taken to aid faculty in serving adequately the needs of both teams.

We have a lot of confidence in the combination format if the managerial problems are well controlled. We would like to point out an additional source of problems, however, in the "broker" role that "home" team faculty members must play. This requires communication among all faculty involved in the program. In one program brokers did not have sufficient knowledge of what fellow faculty were doing or of what they could offer students. They were thereby crippled in their efforts to determine when and to whom students should be referred. In addition, the brokers did not have confidence in the capabilities of several of their colleagues to provide the desired inputs (a situation probably aggravated by the lack of communication between them). The result was that the brokers were screening their students away from experiences rather than directing them toward broader horizons.

At the University of Houston a version of the combination format is used. Since students are not permitted to enroll in professional programs until their junior year, they typically participate in a four-semester professional sequence. Students register with one of five faculty teams that start each semester. There are teams for secondary, elementary, elementary–early childhood, elementary–special education, and all-level (including health and physical education, music, and art, which are K-12 endorsed). Each team has three to four faculty members, and the student technically registers for one of the faculty members' course sections. Some twenty to twenty-five students register with each faculty member. Each team has liaison with eight to ten schools in which field experiences are conducted.

The Houston program has four phases. During Phase I, students register for three hours and focus on introductory human relations exercises, generic skills (questioning, etc.), and teacher-aide experiences in the school they choose. At the completion of the skills and competencies of this Phase I, the student goes into advanced work in Phase II. In Phase II, the student registers for another three hours *with the same instructor,* plus twelve to fifteen hours of other education work. Components in educational foundations (psychological and cultural), multicultural education, art, music, and health are offered by teams of specialists. Meanwhile, during Phase II, the original instructor works with the students in advanced generic skills (classroom management, teaching models, and the like). This longi-

[1] The discussion of matrix management in Chapter 9 is relevant to this topic.

tudinal contact with one team, one school, and one instructor is designed to help students acquire a gestalt of education instead of a set of unrelated experiences.

In Phase III the student is involved in methods courses. Typically during this time the students are still engaged in enabling seminars with their original team and instructor. During Phase IV, Internship, the student completes the equivalent of student teaching. Here graduate assistants work with the student; however, the graduate assistant works under the direction of the original faculty member. Consequently, the clinical supervision activities are coordinated with experiences in earlier phases.

At Houston, faculty members can be specialists, generalists, or both. Some generic instructors work with students throughout all phases. Other instructors meet students only in their specialty areas where, along with other faculty members, they aid students in developing specific competencies, for example, in reading. Still other instructors work both sides; they work in the longitudinal teaming phases and are also team members of a discipline. A faculty member can be on two teams, one generic and one in science education for instance.

Economics and Logistics of Faculty Teaming

The organizational format employed for a given CBE program is dependent on economic constraints and existing collateral in terms of course numbers, available FTEs (Full Time Equivalents), number of students, and faculty load requirements, as well as theoretical implications. The consequent compromises between realty and the theoretical ideal have resulted in interesting and in some cases novel solutions. For example, at the University of Toledo, where a horizontal teaming format is used, five faculty members are assigned half time for four quarters (students can usually complete the program in four eight-quarter-hour semesters). In many institutions, twenty students must be enrolled to justify a course. Using this ratio (20–1) as a guide, faculty can be assigned half a load if students register for two courses per quarter (five sections of twenty students each multiplied by two courses equals ten courses). Toledo effectively uses this formula, as does the University of Nebraska. Toledo also has options and extra courses for those students wishing them as electives. In this way Toledo justifies course load for floaters. *Floaters* are faculty members who aid the teams in rush weeks (when everyone wants feedback), school assignments, and other special areas.

At Houston a similar argument is made to justify course credit, even though teaming is a combination of both horizontal and vertical concepts. A typical semester for a faculty member who serves on a generic team (horizontal) and a special team (vertical) includes:

One-half time generic team (two course equivalents, usually one beginning section of twenty-five and an advanced section of twenty-five)

One-quarter time special team, e.g., reading (one course equivalent, often working only with those students whom he taught as part of his generic team)

One-quarter time graduate course

Similar attempts have been made to justify course equivalents at other institutions. Whatever plan is selected or designed by program builders, it is folly to ignore monetary restraints. Let's face it—if more money is needed, more credit hours will have to be generated.

Fiscal responsibility and justification of course load are only a part of the problem for CBE program designers. Faculty time other than course load is an invaluable resource. A program that specifies that a faculty member will spend forty hours per week with four different preparations will soon find that it is losing. Faculty loads must be carefully considered. In some cases the graduate course assignment for the faculty member is teaching clinical supervision or other subjects to public school teachers who are also working with students in the CBE program.

Faculty loads change with the installation of a CBE program because of definitions of courses. To teach a three-hour course under the old plan, the faculty member is responsible for three contact hours with students per week, plus selected office hours, exam proctoring, and homework and assignment grading. In a program with self-paced mastery learning, scheduling is modified, often to a system in which faculty members are on call. "On call" may sound appealing to some students and faculty, but it has been less than viable at institutions where it has been tried. At Brigham Young, Weber State, and several other places, program developers recognized that self-pacing means that students will reach seminars points or assessments at varying times. They also found that such a system presented them with the responsibility for being open for business twenty-four hours per day, seven days per week, and even over holidays. Faculty dissatisfaction under such circumstances is understandable. Getting student phone calls at home night after night can pall quickly.

At BYU and Weber State, and also at Houston, scheduling for seminars and feedback sessions has been found to be a necessity. Scheduling at Weber State is accomplished through a central area. Faculty submit an agreed-upon number of hours per week to be on call, and students schedule their sessions through the central scheduling area. This system, coupled with faculty-scheduled seminars and communication through newsletter and mailboxes (at Houston each of 2,200 students in the program has an assigned mailbox), can do much to keep up the communication and reduce the constant flow of students through faculty offices.

Some Phenomena of Team Working

The team concept may sound inviting to the reader. The rationale is sound; however, the problems are many. It is easy to note instructional difficulties in teaming operations, for if team members do not have the necessary skills, content difficulties obviously arise. However, greater than the cognitive and performance difficulties are the interpersonal difficulties.

Functioning as a member of an interdisciplinary team is a complex role involving personal, pragmatic, and student concerns. Faculty who have been recruited and rewarded because of their individual and independent efforts must change a great deal to function effectively as team members. Basic to the change are the team member's interactions with other members of the team. Team members must develop such communication skills as paraphrasing, perception checking, and giving and receiving feedback. Each member must have opportunities for input into the team's discussions and must feel that he has had a part in decision making. Attaining these skills is so important that several workshops have been developed to train for these skills. One such workshop has been expressly developed and oriented toward higher education faculty.[2]

Each team of faculty and students will differ from other teams and will have different skills, personalities, problems, strengths, weaknesses, and concerns. Some groups consist of members who barely tolerate each other. Other groups are so cohesive that it is difficult to tell one member from another. Most groups fit some middle ground. Regardless of the personal dynamics of a group, if the group is to function effectively one thing is most clear: team members must give up individual proprietorship for system ownership. In everyday language, a team works toward common goals, not individual advancement at the expense of other group members. This sounds like common knowledge; we wish it were.

> *Item:* Faculty member X decided that the modules developed by his team colleagues were worthless. He let students know about this. Result: team splintering and much resentment, causing an almost unhealable wound in faculty and faculty-student teams.

> *Item:* Faculty members were assigned arbitrarily to work together on a team effort by a departmental chairman who used the philosophy that the team operation would be good inservice training for less-qualified faculty members. The other faculty members resented the

[2] Research and Development Center for Teacher Education, *A Workshop for Interdisciplinary Faculty Teaming* (Austin: University of Texas, 1974).

move. The team dissolved within three months, leaving one hundred angry students and four very unhappy faculty members who resolved never to be part of another team.

Item: One faculty member decided, without clearing it with other team members, to research one aspect of the program. The research was completed and published under the name of the one team member. Resentment was rampant.

Item: A faculty team decided as a group that it would coauthor all developed and printed materials including modules. With everyone's name on each module, ownership was shared to everyone's satisfaction.

As a minister we know once said, "It's amazing how much you can get accomplished if you don't care who gets the credit." [3]

What does make a good faculty team? We know that it is possible because we have seen effective teams in action. We would like to list some of their characteristics here.

1. TEAM MEMBERS PERCEIVE OF THEMSELVES AS HAVING SHAPED THE PROJECT IN SOME WAY.   Major difficulties in team operations arise when faculty members see someone "laying on" a curriculum. Cries in defense of "academic freedom" are heard throughout the halls when people believe that. However, team operations that call for agreement on *team* assumptions, competencies, objectives, and activities are really no threat to academic freedom. The team member who has had abundant opportunity to put in his two cents but has not done so has little reason to cry for academic freedom. But if the opportunity for input is *not* provided, that is a different story.

College faculty members are usually most hesitant to use other people's material in instruction. For this reason the attempt to implement an already-developed CBE program from another college or team is an exercise in futility.

2. TEAM MEMBERS KNOW THE PRICE THAT WAS PAID FOR AN EFFECTIVE PROGRAM.   The investment in teaming by faculty is heavy. By *investment* we mean more than just monetary investment. Anyone who has developed a program knows the sweat, tears, and struggle that it takes. Program development, whether it is initiation, legitimization, or maintenance, is hard work. Team building calls for honesty and openness as well as for having to justify your input to colleagues. Investment in the legitimization stage calls for placing a professional reputation on the line.

One thing that effective teams usually exhibit is a willingness to make

[3] Pastor Jack Lien, Memorial Drive Lutheran Church, Houston, Texas, 1974. See, Jack, someone *does* listen to your sermons.

the effort work. Team members who feel that their ideas will work come hell or high water will see their efforts work. This is especially evident when one looks at the results of CBE efforts by generation. First-generation efforts stand the best chance of working. It may be the Hawthorne effect; it may be that key faculty members are determined that it will work. Teams that follow often do not have the commitment, even though they are free to modify assumptions, competencies, and activities to meet their own personal value systems. With the value of hindsight, following teams are quick to identify places where originators goofed. Originating teams usually wind up with bruised shins. They must expect it and share it as a team. The game of "Blemish" is played well by most college faculty. Successful teams acknowledge the legitimacy of making mistakes.

3. TEAMING USUALLY EXTENDS BEYOND THE TASK. Teams that are effective professionally seem increasingly to act as teams in other parts of their lives. They start boring spouses to death with shoptalk at parties.

4. THERE IS OFTEN A MISSIONARY ZEAL IN EFFECTIVE TEAMS. When things work we want to share them. It's only natural; yet there is great danger if carried too far. Effective teams like to share their success with others. Sometimes they oversell; often they get burned. If they seem to be having all the fun most of the time, then others will not support them, participate with them, or come to their aid.

Actually this is where this book came from. Both authors recognize the dangers of overselling. Yet we feel good about our experiences in teaming with CBE efforts. We have more than a few scars from our sharing and expect a few more from readers of this gospel. We'll take the bruises if our ideas help at least one reader and his or her students.

5. EFFECTIVE TEAMS PRACTICE COLLECTIVE BARGAINING. Administrators take warning. A four- or five-member team is more persuasive and can muster more support to back a request than can isolated individuals. Effective teams will present a united front and draw in others to support a program and provide for its being. Where individuals could not, teams have been known to get campus classrooms, faculty, and courses from other departments and special equipment assigned to programs. Increased communication is not limited to programmatic issues. Communication of ideas and issues related to the larger institution are also enhanced.

6. EFFECTIVE TEAMS PROVIDE A CRITICAL MASS FOR SELF, AS WELL AS GROUP GROWTH. The potential resources within a team, if they can be tapped, can do much to improve not only the education of students but also the growth of the team and its members. By capitalizing on these available resources and developing feedback procedures, a team can learn from itself and make in-process adaptations to further its goals. Analyzing a team is most difficult, especially from within, but many relatively simple and quick measures exist that can aid a team in processing its functioning.

The following technique is borrowed from Emily Girault (1974) and may give some indication of your team's functioning. First, have each member place the names of other team members across the top of a piece of paper. Then number down the left-hand side from one to thirteen. For each question, each person named can then be assessed by placing a plus (+) below the person's name along with the number if the question is very true of the person. Assign a minus (−) to those names for whom the question is not true at all. Blank spaces can be left for those who fall in the middle.

1. Who spends the most clock hours per week working on the project?
2. Who spends the fewest clock hours per week working on the project?
3. In team interaction, who does the most initiation of interaction?
4. Is there anyone who never seeks out team members for interaction on project or other business? Who?
5. Other than yourself, which person would you choose to explain the project to a group?
6. Who are most interested in project concerns?
7. Who are least interested in project concerns?
8. Whom do you most often seek out for advice?
9. Whom do you most often ask for lunch or coffee?
10. Who is the most open to your influence?
11. Who is the least open to your influence?
12. Who tells you what he thinks?
13. With whom do you spend the most clock hours?

If you want to see your team operation from a different vantage point, have each member complete the above questions and share them in a group. This technique is often painful, yet it is one that can quickly identify those who are interested in the project and want to involve themselves in project success.

7. EFFECTIVE TEAMS HAVE MECHANISMS FOR PROVIDING SHORT-TERM AND HIGHLY SPECIALIZED INPUT. One very special example of this is in the team composition developed by the Research and Development Center for Teacher Education at the University of Texas. A specialist team member in the R&D center experimental program is a counseling psychologist. This

team member has special responsibility for aiding the students in focusing on their personal as well as cognitive growth. To accomplish this, the counselor uses a variety of assessment and feedback techniques, which also provide input to the team.

Brown and Menaker (1972), in their case study of a counselor, describe the working relationship of a teacher education team both inside and outside the team meetings as follows:

> Throughout the semester, the counseling psychologist was able to consult with faculty members about the various subjects in the program. The faculty members also provided information to her. Occasionally, she would make a statement in a general meeting to the faculty as a whole, but usually discussion took place with small groups of two or three faculty members. While consultation was available for all the faculty, meetings were informal and information was usually exchanged with those faculty members involved in the first phase of the program.
>
> The counselor never revealed confidential information such as the content of an interview, but rather sought to point out what the teacher was concerned about, or what changes she might need to make in order to achieve a special goal. The information she gave was always pertinent to the particular situation being discussed, e.g., a possible problem in interpersonal relationships in the classroom or with the faculty. Consultation generally dealt with some obvious difficulty—usually not a severe problem but, characteristically, an idiosyncratic one. Strengths of the student-teachers were also the focus of consultation. In giving information the counselor stressed that her interpretations were tentative, based on her impressions from analyses of the test battery and personal contact. She often gave indirect suggestions about how information might be utilized, but never tried to tell the faculty what to do directly.
>
> One of the ground rules of the counselor's interaction with the faculty was that whatever information was shared between them about the students was held in strictest confidence. No staff member quoted another to a student, or even to another faculty member, without permission to quote first being requested and *freely* given. Thus, while the students were aware that the counseling psychologist consulted with the faculty, they knew nothing of the content of consultation and seemed unaware, or at least unconcerned, that the interactions dealt with them personally.

As may be obvious from the above description, the teaching skills specialist helps the student to focus on demonstrating competence in one or more areas of pedagogy. The counselor helps the student to learn about his own being and becoming. Sometimes the counselor is almost a referee. At one moment he may help an instructor clarify a point. At another time he might be protecting the student from too much feedback too soon.

The benefits to all concerned are substantial. The advantages to students are obvious, but the team members also benefit. Some of the best inservice training to be had comes from colleagues. The counselor can teach faculty members a lot about interpersonal skills, and the faculty can teach the counselor a lot about teaching.

ROLE TRANSITION FOR STUDENTS

The problems of adapting to new roles are not limited to faculty. Students in CBE programs need to behave differently and work differently than they probably have before. As with faculty, the role transition for students is not always easily accomplished. In Chapter 5 Fuller's identification of the developmental levels of concerns about teaching that teachers appear to progress through in their professional training was presented. Her research has demonstrated that when preservice and inservice teachers think about teaching, they have various kinds of identifiable concerns. Hall, Wallace, and Dossett (1973) hypothesized that faculty and students also have concerns about their involvement in innovative experiences—in this case, their CBE program. In other words students involved in CBE programs not only have concerns about their chosen profession but also have identifiable concerns about their role, their performance, and the effects of their participation in a CBE program. These concerns need to be anticipated, accepted, and dealt with as a part of student growth in the program.

As with faculty, students bring to the CBE program preferred learning and work styles as well as extensive experience in certain styles that were preferred and rewarded by past instructors. Most of these learning and work styles, without some modifications and additions, will not be adequate for their involvement in a CBE program. One or more of the following orientation problems may contribute to students' having intense concerns and being in need of special assistance if their participation in a CBE program is to be the most successful possible. In most cases a special program orientation module or a short conference will be sufficient. In other cases more concentrated and extended input will be needed.

1. IN A CBE PROGRAM STUDENTS ARE CONTINUALLY CONFRONTED WITH ALTERNATIVES. Students must choose between alternative kinds of enabling activities within modules. They must determine which modules to do at any given point and also select from alternative field sites. They must decide when to solicit faculty assistance. In some institutions they even must choose between alternative CBE programs. They should realize that making and living with the consequences of these choices is not always easy.

2. STUDENTS SET THEIR OWN PACE FOR MANY PARTS OF THE PRO-GRAM. How fast a student moves through a module or a set of modules is decided upon primarily by the student. Only the student can determine how much of a particular enabling activity he needs to do. If he really needs to fill in every blank in a programmed instruction activity, it will take him much longer than if he were to skim through the material filling in the blanks only in those areas where he is confused about what he has read. Learning to accept the stated objectives as being the "real" criteria and pacing oneself accordingly is new for most students. Learning to pace oneself takes practice. Maybe there are some students who never will learn how to pace.

3. STUDENTS NEED TO REACH OUT. Reaching out is not just the psychomotor skill of getting a slide-tape program off the shelf in the LRC. Students must personally reach out to their instructors and their fellow students as well as to the clients they are or will be working with as future professionals. Reaching out is not something that comes easy to most students. Most of their past experience has been in waiting for instructors to approach them. In a CBE program instructors reach out to students, but students will also have to reach out by articulating their questions and needs and reporting on their progress. They will not be able to remain lost in the crowd.

4. STUDENTS WHO ARE NOT SELF-STARTERS WILL HAVE DIFFICULTY. Throughout a CBE program students are in control of much of their work and of themselves. Students who are able to determine easily which enabling activities they will do and how much of them they need to do to learn the skills and competencies involved will be able to pace themselves and reach out when they require additional assistance. For those students who have difficulty in making these decisions, special inputs will be needed. Conferences with individual faculty members, input from counselors, and perhaps even an alternative program or career choice may be required. In many cases it is the student who previously had "straight *A*'s" who has the most difficulty in CBE. Often it seems that the "bright" compulsive student who read all of the assigned books, wrote the library research paper, and recalled all of the information presented by the instructor has great difficulty in a CBE environment. There are no longer instructors setting the pace and the limits on the assignment. Now the student is expected to do this himself. Giving up a way of working that has always paid off is not easily accomplished. A supportive environment with reasonable expectations will be needed.

5. STUDENTS ARE TREATED AS DEVELOPING PROFESSIONALS. In many CBE programs that are already operational, a shift in perspective is ob-

served. The student is less apt to be seen and treated as some sort of second-class citizen, and he is interacted with more as a person and a developing colleague. This requires of the student a new maturity. The assumption is explicit that the student is concerned about becoming a highly effective professional who is concerned about his clients. Students who have entered teacher education more as a way of gaining employment security than as a way of becoming professional teachers may find this stance difficult to maintain.

6. STUDENTS WORK WITH FELLOW STUDENTS AS PARTNERS RATHER THAN AS COMPETITORS.　The climate shifts from hiding the single copy of a key library reference to deliberately reaching out and making the reference available to others. In a CBE program one student gains nothing by the failure of his peers. More likely he will lose something when fellow students don't make it. Working collaboratively with trust and openness for the purposes of all learning and growing, when put into practice, is not as easy, as efficient, or always as comfortable as one would like to believe.

7. GRADES ARE NO LONGER THERE AS TROPHIES TO BE COLLECTED. Working for the accumulation of grades is not practical in CBE, since all students will be evaluated based on what they do, not on how well they do in relation to their classmates. The learning and the experiences must have meaning in and of themselves instead of being done because they will result in a better grade.

8. STUDENTS IN CBE PROGRAMS TEND TO BE "OVERWORKED."　Especially the first time and probably the first few times that a CBE program is operationalized, the faculty will develop and require more work than the students can accomplish. Even when the mean pace is within reason, many students will have difficulty in pacing themselves and making sure to spread their work over the time period rather than starting the period light and having it all stacked up at the end.

9. STUDENTS ARE MEMBERS OF A PROGRAM.　This statement sounds rather shallow; however, prior to their entrance into a CBE program, most students will not have been involved in a large team effort. Especially at larger institutions they will have been taking independent courses from faculty who were not sharing knowledge and resources. It is quite easy and often there is no option but to go unnoticed. Besides having to shed anonymity, becoming a member of a program group means having responsibilities for other group members as well as for oneself. It also means that many of your peers are going to get to know you closely and on a day-to-day basis. This experience is not always comfortable or necessarily rewarding for all students at all times.

These nine points have been listed to illustrate some of the facets of the role changes and concerns that students will experience as they begin and participate in a CBE program. These are not atypical kinds of problems that only a few students have—they will be experienced by most students and in varied forms. The purpose here is not to list these points so that one can judge them. Rather these points are presented to demonstrate that students will experience these or similar problems and concerns. They need to be acknowledged, accepted as existing, and accounted for in developing and adopting a CBE program.

As a graphic illustration of what students in CBE programs face, look again at Exhibit 7.1 (p. 201), the flowchart for a module. In this module, students have no less than four decisions to make about their next major steps within the module. They must determine how much of each and which of eleven enabling activities they will do. They will experience at least six different types of enabling activities. Their first required contact with an instructor is to schedule a feedback conference based on a tape that they have just made. If this were the first module in a CBE program, students would not be able to select, pace, schedule, and manage themselves through the module with few or no problems. Although this kind of self-management is not mentioned as an outcome, it can be a spin-off benefit of the CBE environment.

As with faculty, students involved with CBE find that there are many new expectations made of them as well as the opportunity to use previously unused skills and to develop new needed skills. Assumptions and goals about learning also shift. Mastering these newly required skills, making decisions, accommodating the role transition problems, and developing new perspectives as a result of these changes and expectations are in themselves important learnings that both faculty and students will take with them long after the program is completed.

8

school–college
relationships

To our knowledge there are no teacher education programs that do not have some kind of field experience included as part of the training package. Normally, in addition to spending many hours in observation and in tutorial arrangements, students are expected to do some work with larger groups of pupils, and, eventually, to take over responsibility for entire classes of pupils in a "student teaching" phase.

We doubt that anyone who has been involved in teacher education would underestimate the value of such experiences in the development of teaching skills. Supporters and critics of teacher education alike are unanimous in their assessment of the value of field experiences.

> To the extent to which they value any aspects of their professional education, teachers generally cite practice teaching as the most valuable—sometimes the only valuable—part. Critics of education, too, all agree that whatever else might be dispensable, practice teaching is not. (Silberman, 1970.)
>
> The first consensus of . . . new teachers was the need for teacher training programs to provide earlier occasions for experiences with children. Most often participants criticized the fact that the teacher trainees were not allowed to be with children. (Bruner, 1968.)

Despite such support for "practice" teaching, however, the notion of expanding the concept to include more liberal use of field experiences throughout professional training is met with some resistance.

The experience of a friend of ours comes to mind. A major publishing company asked to review a series of instructional modules of his, and, as is usual, the materials were sent by the publisher to several "expert" reviewers to pass on their salability. One reviewer noted that while the content of the modules was fine, and was excellent in some instances, there was one major problem regarding marketing of the material. Our friend had included a heavy emphasis on field experiences. The problem noted by the reviewer was that neither he nor any of his colleagues would consider the use of field-based materials.

We don't know if this "expert" worked on the innovative frontiers of his field, but somehow we doubt it. We do know that the days of running college-based teacher-training programs with little or no contact with the real world of public schools are numbered. We also believe that for preservice and inservice education programs to grow and meet the needs of teachers, closer working relationships must be built between colleges and schools. This is the focus of this chapter.

Our agenda is as follows:

Page	Heading	Questions
218	Field Experiences—The Intersection of Theory and Practice	What is the present state of field experiences? Where are we going?
220	Field Experiences in CBTE	What field experiences can be used in CBTE operations?
225	Building the College-School Relationship	What are some hints on developing and maintaining college-school relationships?

FIELD EXPERIENCES—THE INTERSECTION OF THEORY AND PRACTICE

Throughout this book we have made comparisons between competency-based teacher education and the potential uses of CBE in other professional training programs for doctors and dentists, among others. In the area of field-based experiences, medical training schools provide a model of the form of internship in which the trainee works with a professional as part of a team. During internships the learner is expected to meld theory into practice under the watchful tutelage of experienced and competent professionals. The same theory lies behind teacher education field experiences.

In teacher education, however, there are few truly cooperative efforts involving both professional theorists (teacher educators on college campuses) and professional practitioners (teachers and administrators in public schools). School personnel have felt exploited by college people coming to the schools, doing their research, and then retreating to the "safety" of their towers.

Silberman (1970) describes a classic example in which almost unlimited funds were available for a teacher education college to "adopt" a low-income junior high school and transform it into a model school. The college faculty spent a great deal of time in the school, working with both teachers and students. Within a year, however, the project was abandoned as a failure. The college explanation of the defeat was to blame the principal who had "administrative difficulties" in implementing recommendations from the professors and to blame the teachers for being "preconditioned to what the system demands of them." For his part, the principal blamed what he called "the dilettantish approach" of the college faculty. "The forces brought in by the project just didn't sit down long enough to comprehend what they were walking into," he said. "They were dabbling with our children. We were simply a training ground for the university."

The teacher educator is in a difficult spot with respect to working in the field. Most colleges and universities provide rewards on the basis of a system that gives little weight to field experience. Professors are typically rewarded for research, publications, and university administrative service. Silberman also described the plight of the teacher educator who must balance a reputation as a "knowing scholar" against that of "skilled practitioner." One of Silberman's "items": "I went to school to become an anthropologist, not a teacher," an anthropology professor observed. "I'd resent taking time out from my work to study teaching."

In fact, to be effective in the role his profession has bestowed on him, the teacher educator must be the middleman between theory and practice. If the promise of field-centered and field-oriented CBTE is to come to fruition, the teacher educator must be the key person in the game. Few professors who work in liaison with schools are able to commit the time and effort it takes for success both in the field and in the typical campus reward activities. Those college administrators who expect their professional staff to be successfully involved in field operations must provide a reward system that is consistent with that desire. For example, Emporia Kansas State College has obtained approval for a weighted funding formula for student teaching supervision.

Despite all of these problems, there are successes in field-based teacher education arrangements. These successes are usually related to a recognition by both sides in the collaboration of the advantages and strengths in working together. School administrators can benefit from the opportunities for firsthand observations of student teacher capabilities and potential, a definite aid in recruitment of new personnel. Teachers recognize that field-based training will make available a few extra hands in the classroom; this permits more personal contact with pupils and means welcome help in noninstructional chores. Teacher educators can use the intimate and up-to-date knowledge of reality in the schools to help them provide more relevant programs for their student teachers. There are other advantages of inservice training, equipment sharing, and personnel crossovers that lend efficiency to both the school and the campus operations.

Teachers and teacher organizations certainly are not totally accepting of CBTE or expanded field operations for teacher education. Nonetheless, the American Federation of Teachers, the National Education Association, and the United Federation of Teachers *have* demonstrated interest in the concept of teacher centers and have published position papers that include model suggestions (Yarger and Schmieder, 1974). One impetus for this interest is that field-centered training operations may offer opportunities for certification of practicing teachers. In some CBTE programs, prospective teachers are certified only after approval by a team of classroom teachers. This move is making a reality of D. D. Darland's (1968) suggestion, along with others, that the teaching profession should have the right to license and certify teachers. Silberman (1970) discussed this point:

> Teachers have always wanted, but have never had, this kind of autonomy and control, for laymen have refused to recognize their professional knowledge as either essential or esoteric. For all the importance attached to public education, Americans, . . . have been unwilling to put teachers on any kind of pedestal. . . . Thus the tradition of lay control has been too strong to permit the kind of delegation of the licensing power to the professional associations of teachers or administrators that has characterized medicine and law.

FIELD EXPERIENCES IN CBTE

Integration of field experiences into a workable CBTE effort may be the hardest task of any of the formidable efforts needed in effective teacher education programs. There are many skills and competencies that students cannot acquire in other than real-world situations. Shostak (1973) notes that the experiences can be divided into two types:

> Type I experiences are those which do not require direct participation by a trainee in a teaching situation. These kinds of experiences include such

things as interviews with teachers, students, parents, administrators, community service personnel; formal and informal observations; attendance at teacher's meetings; and participation in curriculum planning sessions.

Type II experiences are those which require the trainee to participate directly with pupils in the classroom setting. These kinds of activities include tutoring, microteaching, and small and large group instruction.

The ideal teacher education program would have neophytes who were not able to demonstrate required competencies striving to acquire that competence through a well-sequenced and coordinated set of field experiences. By "well-sequenced" we mean that it would seem much more humane to introduce neophyte teachers to more manageable units of experience, such as tutorial work, before expecting them to take over total responsibility for a whole class. Such planning is behind the CBTE effort at Western Kentucky University.

As a first milepost in developing their program, the faculty and staff at Western Kentucky examined closely the developmental sequence of field-based roles that they expect student teachers to assume. The sequence of roles they identified is depicted in Exhibit 8.1.

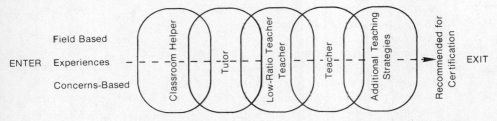

EXHIBIT 8.1   Roles of Preservice Teachers in the Western Kentucky University CBTE Program.

The program developers also identified experiences to be offered for students as they progress through the program. Their list follows and has been reproduced with their permission (Western Kentucky University CBTE Steering Committee, 1974):

A. CLASSROOM HELPER

The classroom helper engages in a number of pre-teaching experiences that will help the prospective teacher become more aware of himself as a person and of himself as a teacher.

As a classroom helper, the student may:

Observe the preparation and use of the teacher's instructional plans
Assist in categorizing and storing instructional materials
Observe and discuss the use of various teaching methods

Assist in reproducing instructional materials
Design and build an instructional aid
Grade papers
Discuss evaluation procedures with teacher
Evaluate the useability of instructional aids
Identify and observe guidance activities performed by the teacher and the counselor
Take roll
Assist in supervising laboratory experiences and extra-curricular activities
Observe and report on the professional image of teachers at work
Discuss the role of supporting school personnel
Observe and report teacher-pupil personal interaction in a variety of circumstances
Discuss the vocational and professional background of the teacher

B. TUTOR

The tutor uses the knowledge and skills gained at an earlier point and facilitates learning processes, typically with one student at a time.
The tutor may:

Interact with pupils on informal basis
Work with guidance counselor and teacher to analyze data of case studies
Diagnose a variety of pupil needs
Prescribe learning activities for a pupil
Implement learning prescription
Evaluate and assess a learner's progress
Manage physical learning environment for a pupil
Develop good working relationships with teachers, school administrators, and school staff
Demonstrate knowledge of the legal and ethical practices of a professional

C. LOW-RATIO TEACHER

The low-ratio teacher builds on knowledge and skills acquired and applies these to small group teaching.
The low-ratio teacher may:

Prepare and interpret sociograms
Use group dynamics
Formulate behavioral objectives for a unit and a lesson for a small group of students
Prepare a short teaching unit designed for a small group of students
Select and develop instructional content, teaching strategies, and teaching materials for a lesson
Teach a lesson using appropriate methods and techniques for a small group
Supervise study and laboratory experiences and co-curricular activities

Formulate a unit grading plan that is consistent with departmental and
  school policy
Evaluate and assess learners' progress
Interpret cumulative student records and use data as a basis for providing
  for individual differences
Manage physical learning environment of a small group
Observe a parent-teacher conference
Identify and display some of the behaviors, personal habits, and attitudes
  of a professional teacher
Demonstrate knowledge of ethical procedures of a professional

D. TEACHER

The teacher integrates the knowledge and skills of earlier roles and
assumes and accepts the total responsibility for the learning environment.
  The teacher may:

Formulate behavioral objectives for a course, a unit, and a lesson
Construct a lesson plan
Select appropriate teaching methods and techniques for a class
Teach lessons using appropriate methods and techniques
Design and supervise pupil study experiences, pupil laboratory experiences,
  and co-curricular activities
Evaluate pupils' work and progress
Formulate a term grading plan which is consistent with the departmental
  and school policies
Recommend term grade for pupils
Assist students with personal, scholastic, and vocational problems
Refer students to qualified personnel for educational and vocational infor-
  mation
Maintain desirable learning environment and classroom control
Provide for the management of physical facilities
Develop professional working relationships with school staff, parents, and
  pupils
Conduct effective parent-teacher conference
Demonstrate the ethical procedures of a professional
Participate in professional organization activities
Role play a job interview with a school administrator

E. PROFESSIONAL DEVELOPMENT

The students will evaluate their present strengths and needs as teachers
using feedback received during their work in each preceding role. At this
time, the students will be asked to describe their professional goals. Considering the evaluation of their strengths and needs in light of their professional goals will allow each student, assisted by appropriate university and
public school personnel, to plan and implement a sequence of experiences
which will increase their ability to reach their professional goals.

Sequences might include increased knowledge of and experience in one or more of the following areas as:

Differentiated staffing
Team teaching
Open concept schools
IGE schools
Diagnostic/Prescriptive programs
Urban schools
Rural schools

Anyone who has been involved in planning for student teaching is probably shaking his or her head in amazement at the overwhelming problems associated with just placing students in field positions. Shostak (1973) notes:

> Plans for the management of some 1,000 students seeking field experiences that are a part of any one of many different courses require a good deal of careful thought. The logistics of this are formidable. Not the least of our concerns here is reconciling faculty workloads which require much greater than usual time commitments in the field (managing student placements, assisting supervising teachers, participating in inservice education at the center) with resource generating formulae that are geared to student credit hour generation.

It is difficult. Yet it can be done and it has been done successfully in a number of places. Even in colleges having access to relatively few local public schools, the problem has been alleviated. Colleges located in small towns have developed centers of operation in larger towns. In these centers, field professors (staff members) from the college work in developing and maintaining relationships with schools while assisting students in instruction. Such sites, often several hundred miles from the main campus, have been useful in developing inner-city teacher skills as well. The University of Massachusetts and Indiana University even have similar arrangements with Indian schools in western states.

One difficulty must be cited here, however. Faculty members, instead of accepting this field task as a reward, may consider the job as tantamount to being sent to Siberia. In several universities field-based supervision is delegated to graduate students. The task is important enough, however, to be done by effective professors, not persons low on the totem. The reward system of the college must reflect the importance of field service. Unfortunately for teacher education, many colleges' and universities' reward systems probably do reflect their priorities.

BUILDING THE COLLEGE-SCHOOL RELATIONSHIP

We would now like to present some ideas about how colleges might consider starting the courting procedure in a college-school developing relationship.

While the formal setting up and operation of teacher centers may be a matter of little choice, since the state usually establishes guidelines, field-centered operations still must be negotiated on the local level. Regardless of who makes the move, the schools or the colleges, cooperative relationships must be built. Since the first move historically has been made by the colleges, this section proposes some ideas on how a group of instructors might develop at least beginning relationships with local schools. Much of what is said may be bringing coals to Newcastle; however, we would like to present our collective ignorance that we have based on reports of colleagues who wish they had done it differently.

The question raised in this section is, How can we avoid pitfalls in setting up field-centered operations?

One possible set of answers to this question has been proposed by Rutherford (1973), who identifies an eight-step sequence:

1. University readiness for program change
2. Forming a university team
3. Selecting a school
4. Approaching a school
5. Preplanning—or the courting stage
6. Implementing the program—the honeymoon
7. Continuous program monitoring
8. Program evaluation and replanning

At this point we have made the assumption that your program assumptions, tentative objectives, enablers, and assessments have been identified, if not constructed (Step 1). We are also assuming that the groundwork has been laid for faculty roles and that any teaming that will be done is at least started (Step 2). Let's look at the next steps as outlined by Rutherford in detail.

Selecting a School

It would be nice to be able to announce that many school staffs will undoubtedly be jumping at the chance to become involved with a college on a project. Such a statement would probably be a lie. Usually, someone must sell school personnel on the idea. But before selling can take place, the school will have to be identified.

One excellent way of identifying prospective schools is having instructors involved in the college end of the program identify those with which they have had successful experiences in the past. Friends who are principals, a cadre of teachers who were students at the college, and schools that professors' children attend are all good starting points. Program implementers must remember that approval must be obtained from the general administration of the schools. In large cities, schools may need to be identified by approaching the general superintendent who, in turn, has his area superintendents identify possible schools. School cooperative efforts can be more easily explored with individual principals and staffs who know that their superintendent is interested in the project.

Whatever process is used to identify possibilities, hopefully there will be a number of schools among which to choose. In some college towns one school gets all the college-related efforts, be they research, development, or training programs. You will probably not want to link with schools that are involved in a large number of innovative endeavors. Commitment to a new program or effort under such crowded circumstances is often minimal.

A second thing you will want to look for in narrowing down your choice of schools is the collective needs of the involved parties. What needs does the college have? Do you want schools that offer multicultural experiences for students? Are there schools that have some of the necessary equipment you might require? It would be considerably easier and cheaper if there existed a school with videotape facilities already in operation. Is location important? Are all students in the field-centered program commuter students? Can they get to the schools in cars? Are they dorm students? Is distance from campus an important variable? Will there be reimbursement for faculty travel if it is necessary that faculty be in the schools several times a week? Will buses be required? One of the neatest tricks in implementation can be seen at Purdue where program developers run shuttle buses to take dorm students to and from distant schools.

Other questions must also be raised. What kind of hospitality have others experienced in the past? Will there be space provided for instructor-student conferences, or will all feedback sessions have to be given in the teachers' lounge under the watchful eye of a gaggle of other teachers? Are there classroom facilities for professional instruction in the schools? Is the teaching staff effective? Will college students have good models? Are the teachers planning on being in the school for at least several more years, or is there a high rate of turnover of school personnel? For an extended cooperative effort to start and continue, there must be stability of key staff members.

What is the principal's philosophy? His philosophy will often determine the school philosophy. Is the philosophy at least semicompatible with the philosophy underlying the college's program assumptions?

Don't forget the school's needs, however. If the school feels it is doing the college a favor, you're both in trouble. Can the school benefit from your cooperative efforts? What are its needs? Does it need more staff members for a differentiated staff effort? Does it need preservice students to help with instruction, or will these preservice efforts get in its way? Are there inservice efforts identified as necessary or nice by the school staff? Can they be provided by the college personnel?

Remember, at this point you are only looking for potential schools. You will have to determine the ranking of the schools that you have identified from your criteria of importance.

Approaching a School

Selecting the cooperating schools is almost like the first steps of courting—you narrow the field down. The next step is the proposal. You want to make it good, which means trying to do as little wrong as possible. It takes careful planning.

A key in this step is remembering the chain of command. School principals need to be seen by their faculties as having decision-making powers. Area superintendents are reported to by principals. Area superintendents report to superintendents who report to the school board. Teachers are members of teacher organizations. There probably is no one right way to get inside the chain of command. Most past experiences, however, lead us to believe that if the principal is excited about the possibilities of a project, the chances are better than average that the project will at least be tried by the teachers.

However you approach him or her and under whatever authority, the principal is the first person to contact at a school. After explaining the effort and the involvement to the principal, you will want to meet with the teachers to explain the proposal. If the principal agrees, the meeting should be set. There are conflicting theories as to where such a meeting should be located. Some argue for bringing teachers to a college-related area, or for giving a "prestige glow" to the meeting (like meeting in church). Others (and we agree with them) argue that the meetings should be held in the school where the cooperative efforts will take place if the teachers agree to it. School is the teachers' home ground, so you can expect them to be more at ease and more themselves. You, as the college person, are an outsider. You have to do the selling, and you must do it in a short period of time.

Readers of Eric Berne's *Games People Play* are often fascinated by these college-faculty meetings. The meetings are interesting because the university representative who was once a schoolteacher now becomes a salesperson. The salesperson can expect at least three games to be played:

1. Gee, You're Wonderful, Professor
   Translated—"It's wonderful having you here and we surely are happy to have you here and we would like to cooperate any way you want."

Admittedly, this reaction is never universal, but there are always a few teachers who assume this position. The problem is that the professors want cooperative efforts, not do-anything-you-want submissiveness.

2. Blemish
   Translated—"This college cat doesn't know what it's like in this school. Let him talk on; he'll soon find out how much of his help we can use. If he could hack it he wouldn't be in college teaching."

Now here's a tough one. The writers have had few experiences in groups, be they college faculty, school personnel, or students, that have not started out with at least one group member insisting on this game. In cooperative efforts, it is important that everyone know where the other is coming from. It is exceedingly difficult to explain the benefits of an effort to a person who is looking for personal blemishes on the part of the "salesperson."

3. You've Got to Listen
   Translated—"I want to be heard. I want assurances that you will listen to my point of view."

This is a positive stance. Teachers may note that they do not want to be involved unless . . . As much as possible, their conditions should be heard and accepted. This is the first step toward cooperative efforts. We hear; we explain; we begin negotiations.

Of course the game of "Kiss Off" is sometimes played, effectively ending any attempt on either side to negotiate. However, rejection—or the opportunity for it—is one possible outcome of this step. This is the time to propose, not to seal a compact.

In any exploratory faculty meeting, the college representatives should set their best foot forward, coming to the meeting prepared to listen and learn. They should not come with a well worked-out final proposal that is formally presented for the school faculty to accept or reject. No final decisions should be expected at a first meeting. Both faculties should share ideas and take notes on the discussion to be used in designing any tentative plans of action. Based on the open solicitation of ideas and concerns from the school faculty about the possible establishment of a teacher center, the college and school faculty can go away and design a proposal to be brought before the next meeting for consideration and input. What we are suggesting is that before the teacher education program is fully designed and locked in, the school faculty should be involved. They should have the opportunity for input, and, if they so desire, they should have the opportunity for actively working on the proposal that is to be brought before the school and college faculties for operationalization.

One thing about the school-college negotiations. Make certain that the final decision is made by the teachers. Do not under any circumstances allow the principal to make the final decision for the faculty. Similarly, make certain that each individual faculty member has the opportunity to say no, even if the majority of the teachers want to go along with the project.

A useful strategy here might be to have the teachers leave the first meeting and submit to the principal their concerns about the effort. These concerns can be answered by the college team if possible, and, if not, they can be incorporated into any final negotiations with the teachers.

It is important that both the school and the college identify those points that are nonnegotiable. These points might include such items as "no more than one student teacher per class" or "regular hours must be set and maintained." In one CBTE program it was found that parents objected to having their children taught by "students." They wanted to be certain that a teacher was around. Teachers in another CBTE program insisted that a visitation schedule be adhered to so that the help they valued so much would be available on a dependable schedule.

Preplanning Stage

When schools have been tentatively selected, the next move determines the initial and long-range success of the cooperative project. Preplanning is necessary to ensure that the project is managed on a proactive basis rather than a reactive one. That is, decision making should take place *before* crises arise, rather than during or after them. Programs that operate on a reactive basis are usually brief and exhausting, and they frustrate everyone involved.

The preplanning step calls for an in-depth look at the details of the operation. Up to this point teachers and administrators recognize that students will be in classes and on the school grounds for a given number of months and that they will be involved in microteaching, observing, aide work, and so forth. How will all these steps be integrated?

One rule is the key: there must be consensus acceptance on both the college side and the school side of all significant program components. Times, places, roles, procedures, and expectations must all be agreed upon. In addition, all nonnegotiable items must be specified. One approach that works well here is a joint committee made up of school and college staff members that works toward mutually acceptable solutions.

Role expectations can cause difficulty. Teachers need to know their roles in grading student teachers, for example. As a rule, we have found that teachers are uneasy about providing negative feedback directly to students. This role is a crucial one to CBTE if certification is to be more in the hands of teachers, but the authors have found that, if anything, cooperating teachers are usually more positive in their reactions to students than are principals, college personnel, or the students themselves. It might be expected that teachers would share the responsibility for arriving at student grades. Details on this effort must be determined and criteria made public. The joint committee can be an immense help here.

Role expectations can be clarified if the lines of responsibility are clear. The communication linkages must be established and maintained. Policies regarding the removal of a student from a school for any reason must be made and adhered to. This action is as much for the student's good as anyone's. Students need to know the rules under which they are in the school. One effort toward CBTE faltered in one school when teachers, not permitted to wear pantsuits because of the school board policy, became incensed that students from the local college were wearing them. Policy regarding the status of the students was changed, making the dress code for students identical to that of teachers. In another school teachers expressed concern over students "overrunning" the teachers' lounge. Overcrowded parking lots have also been known to jeopardize programs. Joint committee decisions and discussions with both teachers and students regarding these matters have prevented any additional problems.

Policies regarding students play an important role in promoting positive attitudes toward school experiences. Parking facilities, lounge accommodations, and cafeteria policies must all be provided if students are to consider themselves part of the school. If the effort is really cooperative, few "we-they" problems will exist. However, planning for them will help ensure successful solutions if they do occur.

One "we-they" problem that is a direct result of school experiences must be mentioned here. In the past, teacher educators have used school and school personnel in research efforts, usually on an "outsider" basis. In cooperative CBTE efforts, all research must be cleared with school personnel. The joint committee is a useful forum to review proposed research efforts. "Our" research is the outcome here—research that might positively affect the school operation, thereby providing positive experiences for both the professor and his sample.

"Our" program is also the result of sharing the preservice curriculum with teachers in the school. In many teacher center operations, representatives from the teaching profession must approve of preservice curricula before they are implemented. This does several positive things. First, it gives a reality base to the experiences. Second, since teachers will be working with students in the preservice effort, they need to know what the students are working on. This can be of great help in keeping the air clear. One program ran into trouble early because during an observation phase, the students were requested to watch their cooperating teachers and notice how they worked with classroom management problems. Teachers complained, stating that they did not appreciate students' making judgments about classroom management efforts. It also appeared that they didn't like to have someone sitting in the rear of the room making notes. One basic rule for students that would help alleviate this problem would be: "Do nothing until you clear it with your teacher."

It is unlikely that any joint committee will identify all possible areas of difficulty that might arise, nor will they have planned so well that there will be no need for curriculum changes. However, the more care that is taken in this step, the higher the probability for program success.

Implementing the Program

The first several weeks of any new program are going to be the most difficult. Strange new faces are seen in the building by the principal, the teachers, the secretary, the custodian, and the cooks. One of the strange new faces that must be in the building during this time belongs to the college representative(s). One certain way to destroy excellent planning is to send students to the schools and then not follow them to see what happens. Memos to teachers and principals are nice and do present some record of contact, but personal contact is better.

The role of college faculty members is one of positive negotiation and liaison. The students are usually going through early self-concerns, and they need as much constructive support as possible, from both the teachers and the college faculty. One nice "stroke" for the student comes when the teacher introduces him to the class as an "assistant teacher" instead of a "student." For this same reason the use of "internship" rather than "student teaching" is helpful. Teachers also need their "strokes." The worst thing a college person can do is critique, either publicly or privately to a student, a cooperating teacher's classroom behaviors. There will be an underlying distrust of the college person on the part of some teachers anyway. Positiveness has to be the rule of the day.

The college person must push teachers for feedback on students. It was mentioned in the preceding section that this is something teachers are often hesitant to do if the feedback can be construed as negative. However, if behavior changes and growth are to be accomplished by the student, some feedback must be provided. Although three-way conferences are often helpful in clarifying some problems, they fail if negative feedback is necessary and the teacher wants to maintain an image as a "nice person."

College people need to monitor student success in the affect as well.

It is imperative to identify those cases where students are doing nothing but grading papers and sitting in the back of the room watching a teacher. These latter problems are especially typical of secondary school experiences. While elementary schools have groups and individuals working on different things, many secondary curricula are conveyed in "lectures." There is a need for extra help in most elementary classrooms. Secondary teachers sometimes view another person in the classroom as a pain rather than a help. Students' satisfaction in their experiences will, to a large extent, be determined by the things they are doing and finding success with. The problem is as bad, if not worse, in cases where once the student arrives, the teacher disappears and stays in the coffee lounge for hours at a time. Most beginning people are unable to cope with such situations, often winding up with some very sharp feelings of inadequacy.

The two problems mentioned in the preceding paragraph might well be alleviated in the planning stage. However, if they are not, the college person needs to negotiate a settlement without placing the student in the position of "squealer." It means that the college person must make some firsthand observations.

The "Our School" spirit for students can be encouraged in several simple moves. Students wearing neatly printed name tags can become known by teachers in the lounge and in the hall. (It also relieves them of the embarrassment of being asked to show their hall passes in high schools where many teacher education students look as young as the juniors and seniors.) A student bulletin board for notes helps with information flow. A sign-in sheet (either with the cooperating teachers or separate) helps them focus on their needed presence. Calling the school when an absence is required is also a nice touch. While the student should contact the cooperating teacher either at home or early at school if there is an unavoidable absence, the school call focuses on the you're-part-of-this-school syndrome.

Contact with the principal is also a key to ensuring a smooth operation. The principal is in charge of the school. He must be in on all planning and decisions. Coffee discussions weekly with the college representative can be the source of needed refocusing efforts. Principals will hear much more candid faculty reaction than will be heard by college representatives. If these general reactions need to be shared for positive program movements, the principal will share them.

Continued meetings of any formed committees such as the joint college-school committee should of course be a permanent fixture of the program.

Continuous Program Monitoring

In his description of program development, Rutherford (1973) refers to this stage as "after the honeymoon." It is a good choice of words, for this is the arduous time of implementation and seeing how well the plans are working.

The odds are pretty good that all efforts have not worked as well as they looked on paper. Continuous program feedback will reveal the need for changes, sometimes quick changes. A rule of thumb here is to make only those imperative changes and then only after consulting with the involved parties. In the planning stage hopefully someone or some group has been identified as the final decision maker in emergencies where the joint committee cannot meet. Changes that will help the program but are not critical should be saved for revision time before the next group starts the program.

This same rule of thumb applies in conflicts between teachers' wants and needs and those of students. The college person must be the arbitrator. If certain expectancies on the part of the program for students are not within the value structure of the teacher, there can be trouble. A good example here can be viewed in programs where students are expected to demonstrate "inquiry" science teaching. Such a teaching model calls for student activity that may be a level above that of many classroom science experiences. Classroom management problems can be anticipated, as can some early confusion as pupils focus on interactive problems. Teachers who do not value such behaviors in a classroom may well frown at students using such techniques. The college person must be able to negotiate a settlement, even if it calls for changing the college curriculum or placing the student in another classroom.

This is a good time to point out that the problems and complaints that students express will not always be legitimate, nor will they usually represent the whole story. Student teachers may deliberately set up conflicts and problems in an attempt to gain the college instructor's support against the classroom teacher. Students may have unrealistic expectations or may not fully understand the needs of the pupils or the classroom teacher. The student may be so involved with problems of his own that the needs of the school, pupils, and teachers are not considered or at least are not seen clearly. The college instructor's role is one of attempting to clarify issues and to collect information for processing by all parties. His role is not to take sides and thereby become viewed as a biased advocate of only one position.

Personal contact must continue. While it may not be necessary that the college staff be in the schools each day, some contact must continue. Students will want to know how they are doing with respect to grades. Teachers will want to know if they are providing the needed experiences for students. Principals are going to want to know about student absences. The questions are endless. Simple problems can be solved quickly. If they are not solved, simple problems grow until the "our" program once again becomes a "we-they" program.

"Stroking" needs to continue as well. Teachers need to experience a "thank you" every now and then, as do principals. Appropriate gifts, cards, cookie and punch parties, and flowers for janitors, administrators, and staff members at holiday times or during family crises are appreciated. Some programs make it possible for principals and teachers to make presentations to students and faculty as part of a college instructional program. This move does much in showing school staff members that they are being heard.

Constant review and feedback during this stage is critical. This does *not* mean a constant flow of paperwork for teachers who do not have time to fill out a questionnaire a week. It does mean that efforts are made to search for successes and failures of the program effort. Beware, however, of accepting the comments of a few students or teachers as being representative of everyone. Also be on the alert for "just-blowing-off-steam" comments. People have bad days. Don't make a crisis out of an "I'm tired" comment. One rule here is to listen and count to a large number (somewhere above ten) before reacting. At one program, the faculty use a sheet on which the student or the faculty member can write a comment if he or she wishes. Before writing it, however, he or she must check one of three boxes: *Take care of it, See me, Just blowing off*. One very nasty comment recently came in telling the college person that the writer "refused to do it." She and everyone else considered a specific task a waste of their and their pupils' time. The next day another note arrived from the same person. "Sorry about the note. I see your point and was just having a bad day yesterday."

The one problem that a college person can get into that can be most damaging to relationships is that of overprotectiveness of program efforts. It hurts when someone tells you that a module or a school experience that you think is valuable is a waste of time. Our only advice is, Be prepared—you're going to hear about it (especially if the decision making on school experiences is a joint venture). Also remember that teachers and students are constantly going to be playing "You Gotta' Listen to Me" with you, just to see if you are really serious about sharing the responsibility.

Program Evaluation and Replanning

Toward the end of the project or if the project includes several distinct breaking spots, efforts must be made to assess progress toward originally set goals. You are going to want to ask all involved groups to identify their likes and dislikes. You are also going to want to go beyond the likes and dislikes and search for recommendations for program changes.

You need to know if the arrangements, both physical and operational, were adequate for the effort. You are going to want to know if the expectations that the planning group had were also congruent with the expectations and successes of students in the schools. You are going to want to know if the physical and organizational structures were the most effective. You are going to want to know if there are personality conflicts that need to be focused on either through discussions or, in some cases, through "de-partici-pation." You are going to want honest feedback from students on their reactions to all phases of the effort.

Much of this information will be easily shared by teachers in one-to-one conferences. Other information may have to be identified through anonymous questionnaires. If the decision is still "involvement only after volunteering," arrangements should be made to allow a teacher to withdraw as well as to enter into the next phase of a project. Cooperating teachers ought to be allowed to get "out" painlessly as well.

The decision may also be that the total school experience is to be stopped because of a school decision, a college decision, or a joint decision. Ending a project amicably is as difficult as getting one started. Often the severing of a relationship is construed as being punishment to one side. Each side then takes on the job of telling why it didn't work. Usually, the reasons deal with the "other side's" inadequacies. This does not have to happen, however. In some instances things just don't work out, because of policy conflict, grant money termination, or whatever. Planning for the end during earlier planning stages can help when the end comes.

If the end does not come and plans are made to renew the relationship in succeeding semesters or years, renewal plans must be operationalized. The cycle starts over again. Only this time the planners know a lot more about the successes and failures that they had. They also know a lot more about each other. This latter point can be of great benefit. The second time through there is usually less game playing and much quicker progress toward goals. However, this also means that constant monitoring continues. Field-centered or field-oriented programs never run by themselves. It still takes the field professor to make them go and to ensure relevant and realistic efforts for both college students and school personnel.

managing
CBE program adoption

Even if you agree with the basic tenets of CBE and have made plans to implement an experimental program, the questions still nag: "How will we manage this thing? Can we operate it economically and logistically?" A quotation from Bill Tikunoff is relevant:

It is difficult to change when your back is to the future.[1]

The preceding chapters have focused on the theory and conceptual aspects of CBE. Such operational aspects of CBE have been described as interdisciplinary teaming, modules, and what an operational CBE program looks like. However, simply identifying CBE conceptual development, describing what a CBE program should look like, and discussing what existing programs do look like will not insure the ability of others to make their own program plans operational.

So far the emphasis has been on the left side of the Program Decision Model outlined in Chapter 1. The right side of the decision model, which focuses on the program adoption process, is equally important. A plan of action for actually getting the CBE program adopted must be designed

[1] Comment made to Howie in a bar in Albuquerque, New Mexico, in November 1973.

along with the conceptual development of the program. Planning, implementation, and maintenance of an operational program are essential to the adoption process.

The use of the term *adoption* does not mean that an educational institution is adopting someone else's CBE program; rather, the term refers to the assimilation of the CBE program being developed by the adopting institution. Ideally this CBE program includes "adapted" components from other programs as well as development of unique components. Regardless of the origin of the component innovations, the job still is to get the "box" into effective and widespread use within the institution.

Strategies for and consequences of planning, implementing, and maintaining a CBE program (that is, "adoption" of CBE) and managing this process are the focus of this chapter. If a CBE program manager has time to read nothing else, we hope he takes time to read these pages. Managing the adoption of a developing CBE program is not an easy task. The four to five years it takes to accomplish it are trying enough without floundering through the same change-related problems that others have encountered and resolved. Adoption of CBE is the biggest challenge—not development of the rationale, operational strategies, and other trappings. Getting the stuff usable and used, anticipating problems, considering the advantages and disadvantages of alternate change strategies and interventions is where the struggle is won or lost.

The first two phases, planning and implementing, are the most interesting for most faculty and staff. Once the program has become conceptualized, assumptions identified, liaisons established, components designed, and modules built—*then* the program's operation begins in earnest. The preliminary stages are vital, difficult, and interesting. The less visible, more arduous, and sometimes boring part of the program is its maintenance.

This latter point is underscored by every CBE director we have talked with. Several of the program descriptions contributed in Chapter 11 (pp. 296-331) make reference to this point. Ward Sybouts's description of the Nebraska NUSTEP is typical:

> Staff members can get "burned out" physically and emotionally. Once the Hawthorne effect is gone . . . it becomes necessary to carefully design renewal strategies into the process.

One thing is certain; no CBE program can be expected to succeed unless care is taken to insure a workable managerial system *before* implementation. A CBE managerial system may not always seem congruent with the system it displaces. This, needless to say, causes more than a few problems. Program implementers in teacher education face particular problems, since they work in institutions that are notably resistant to change. A common educational motto seems to be, "But we've always done it this way."

In this chapter we outline some alternatives for program management and in general, try to put it into some kind of logical perspective so that decision making can be based less on past history and more on present goals.

Our schema is as follows:

Page	Heading	Questions
238	Perspective on Change	What is the general order and pace of innovation adoption?
240	Decisions, Decisions—Systems Talk	What is a management "system?"
242	How Management Develops	What are the factors that influence the form of a management system? What are some alternative types of management systems?
248	Planning for Your Management System	What advice do experienced program managers have for you?
255	Managing Within the Costs of CBE	How do you keep a program running on a real-world budget?
257	Some Other Concerns	Are there any other ideas related to program management?
261	Guiding Principles for the CBE Program Manager	How can I, as a program manager, be most effective in facilitating the adoption process?

PERSPECTIVE ON CHANGE

An extensive body of literature exists on what can loosely be called the study of change. This literature includes contributions from researchers, theorists, and practitioners from many different academic tribes. In education the general term *change* has been employed to allude to what happens when new ideas are tried out in educational institutions. Other disciplines use different labels such as knowledge utilization, innovation, communication, organizational development, technology transfer, growth, or diffusion and dissemination. As in any field of study, references have been written that summarize and synthesize much of the documented research and experience. The references below will provide the reader with background information and summaries of the theories and findings of change research as well as references to other related work.

BENNIS, W. G., BENNE, K. D., & CHIN, R. *The planning of change.* New York: Holt, Rinehart and Winston, 1961.

BHOLA, H. S. Configuration of change. An engineering theory of innovation diffusion, planned change and development. Paper presented at the Ohio State University—USOE Conference on 'Strategies of Educational Change,' November, 1965.

CARLSON, R. O. *Adoption of educational innovations*. Eugene, Oregon: University of Oregon Press, 1965.

CHARTERS, W. W., JR., EVERHART, R. B., JONES, J. E., PACKARD, J. S., PELLEGRIN, R. J., REYNOLDS, L. J., & WACASTER, C. T. The process of planned change in the school's instructional organization, CASEA Monograph No. 25, 1973.

HALL, G. E., WALLACE, R. C., JR., and DOSSETT, W. F. A developmental conceptualization of the adoption process within educational institutions. Austin: Research and Development Center for Teacher Education, the University of Texas, 1973.

HAVELOCK, R. G., GUSKIN, A., FROHMAN, M., HAVELOCK, M., HILL, M., & HUBER, J. Planning for innovation through dissemination and utilization of knowledge. Center for Research on Utilization of Scientific Knowledge, Institute for Social Research, the University of Michigan, Ann Arbor, January 1971.

MAGUIRE, L. M. An annotated bibliography of the literature on change. Philadelphia: Research for Better Schools, Inc., July 1970.

MILES, M. B. (Ed.) *Innovation in education*. New York: Teachers College Press, Teachers College, Columbia University, 1971.

ROGERS, E. M., & SHOEMAKER, F. F. *Communication of innovations—A cross-cultural approach*. (2nd ed.) New York: The Free Press, Collier-Macmillan Ltd., London, 1971.

SCHMUCK, R. A., RUNKEL, P. J., SATUREN, S. L., MARTELL, R. T., & DERR, C. B. *Handbook of organization development in schools*. Eugene, Oregon: National Press Books, 1972.

Much of the best work on the study of change has been done with agricultural extension agents as they introduced agricultural innovations to farmers. The introduction of pharmaceutical products to physicians is another area that has had extensive study. These and other research studies are summarized by Rogers and Shoemaker. Havelock has done an excellent synthesis of the more established theories of knowledge development and utilization. These theories explore the relationships between critical variables and hypothesized sequences of events and activities that occur as new ideas are created, researched, applied to developmental products, and disseminated to practitioners. Carlson and Charters have conducted case studies and surveys of innovative practices in school settings. By contrast, little has been done or even attempted until quite recently to study change in institutions of higher education.

Some of the more utilitarian studies and research on innovation adoption are being conducted by the NIE-funded Procedures for Adopting Educational Innovations Project at the Texas R&D Center. This project has been heavily involved in the study of adoption of teacher education innovations by teacher training institutions. The research has been centered around the Concerns-Based Adoption Model (Hall, Wallace, and Dossett, 1973), which focuses on the concerns of individual innovation users and what they actually do in support of innovation adoption. These studies have generated guidelines for leadership styles, hypothesized time lines and phases of the adoption process, and facilitated the development of hypotheses about the development of individuals as they adopt educational innovations. One directly related finding (Hall, 1974) is that it appears to take five to seven years for a teacher training institution to fully implement a CBE-like program. Much of our frame of reference in this chapter is based on the work of that project.

DECISIONS, DECISIONS—SYSTEMS TALK

We are going to spend a lot of time later in this chapter discussing a variety of specific strategies that can ease the burden on program managers. It might be tempting to simply file these suggestions and leaf through the strategies when a problem arises. It might be tempting, perhaps—but not at all in the spirit of a management *system*. Systematic planning for management and systematic application of that plan are important keys to a well-maintained program.

The foundation of a viable CBE management system is *proactive decision making*. Many colleges today are trapped in a vicious circle of *reactive* decision making. Decisions are made in the heat of battle. They need to be made quickly; so they are processed in haste and with little in-depth thought. The consequences of the hasty decision soon appear to haunt the administrator and another reactive, kneejerk decision is made. The administrator's time is so occupied with putting out fires that he never seems to get ahead with planning.

The other way, *proactive* decision making, is becoming a concern of more and more administrators. Proactive decision making is essentially contingency planning. Provisions are made in advance for the means to handle sudden decision situations. Firm rules are established for making choices. As many decisions are made as far in advance as possible, and provisions are made to amend them without undermining the logic that supports them. Proactive decisions are made on the basis of explicit assumptions, and their effects are monitored and fed back to help refine the system.

The CBE management system has one main function: to increase the effectiveness of the program by constantly weighing the products of the program against the goals of the program. This is a process of discrepancy evaluation. Program builders or operators identify what their products will be, and an assessment is made to determine whether those products are being produced.

CBE management should be primarily a closed system. Exhibit 9.1 is a simplified representation of this system. This loop of input to process to output and then feedback to input and process is the same for program-wide decisions as it is for components and subcomponents decisions, such as what enabling activities to recommend for a particular competency. A detailed representation of a total CBE management system would depict a large closed loop of the type in Exhibit 9.1 filled with a myriad of identical but smaller loops or subsystems and subsubsystems. The net effect is a complex, integrated, ecosystem in which any decisions made about one part have an effect on all the other parts. The key to preventing dissonant ripples in decision making is to base all decisions on the same set of explicit assumptions about the program and its goals. Once again you see why we made such a big deal about specifying assumptions in Chapter 2.

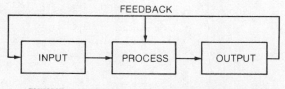

EXHIBIT 9.1   Systems in Competency-Based Education.

The most vital part of the loop is the feedback process. Feedback on outcomes is among the most crucial data for decision making about new input. Most educational programs do not really use information about the output of their efforts to change those parts of the program that need changing. Decisions are going to be made about program components, be they decisions to change or not to change (for even a decision not to change is a decision). Program managers can control whether or not those decisions are made from reality-based information. Decisions will be made with or without sufficient information and anticipation of consequences. Proactive decisions are made *with* information. It is a crucial function of the program manager in a proactive system to keep the feedback loop open and operating.

Exhibit 9.2 shows how specific program subsystems might be plugged into the management loop.

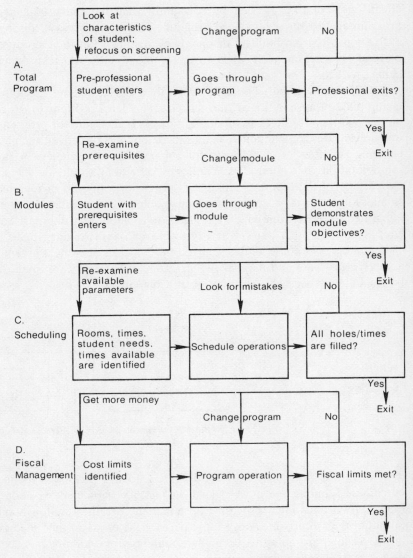

EXHIBIT 9.2   Subsystems in CBE.

HOW MANAGEMENT DEVELOPS

An examination of existing CBE programs would show that most of them began at the instructional level. A few instructors, perhaps even one, made objectives public and developed and installed the first modules, self-paced courses, mastery sequence, or whatever. Even in several cases where deans have been cited as project directors, the bulk of the work was accomplished under the direct leadership of faculty members. Of course the dean's myriad administrative responsibilities are ample reason for leaving the main thrust of experimental work to subordinates, but it is important to note that success appears to have been dependent on involvement of faculty members who demonstrate the highest level of concern and usually the highest level of use. Given, then, that the faculty must do the main pioneering work, what is the organizational environment that they must contend with?

Program Management and Departmental Politics

The realities of college and university administrative structures have a considerable influence on the choice of CBE program management organizations. We have noted that a consistent hurdle in CBE implementation has been that of bucking established systems that exist to support departments, not programs.

The college department provides a home for faculty members. The department provides rewards of released time, salary increments, promotions, and "ticket punches" toward advancement into the stratosphere of administration. In all of this, departments serve important functions, but their vested interest in the system is usually so strong that they often get in the way of interdisciplinary program innovators. Frankly, for all its strengths, the departmental system is designed to perpetuate the status quo, not to foster change. As Howsam (1973) notes:

> In traditional organizations precedent is king and continuance is the rule. Thus departments expect last year's budget plus an increment (How zero budget throws us!). They expect and get replacements for faculty who separate. Programs and courses continue in perpetuity as long as they "make" and the department doesn't move to change them.

Most existing "programs" are bundled into departmental courses. Unless you are interested in developing competency-based courses or a program within the confines of a single department, there is little in the departmental structure to encourage CBE, for there is nothing in the system that allows for interdepartmental, interdisciplinary cooperation or collaboration.

The interdisciplinary teams of faculty that develop and implement CBE programs usually cut across several departments. This raises a number of tough questions: Which department is the program housed in? Which department administers the program funds? Which department gets the course credits? Which department gets the faculty positions for next year?

Because CBE priorities relate to *program* needs, not departmental needs, a system must be devised for program management that sidesteps

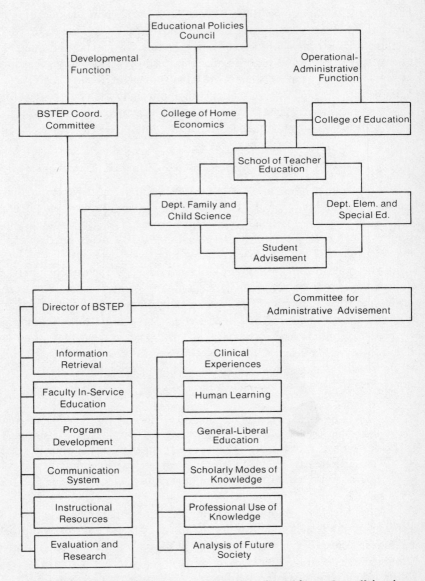

EXHIBIT 9.3   Administrative Organization Design for Michigan State University—Model Teacher Education Program.

departmental politics. This is not to say that academic politics will not be a factor under any new arrangement; they will, but at least they can be program politics, not departmental politics.

Exhibits 9.3, 9.4, and 9.5 depict management schemata proposed for three of the model teacher education programs (Feasibility Studies, 1970).

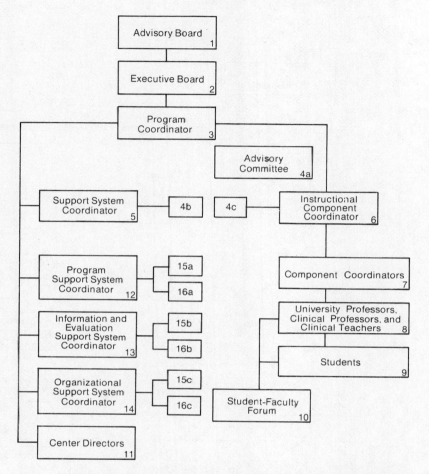

EXHIBIT 9.4 Recommended Management Structure for Syracuse University Model Teacher Education Program.

Each schema shows a single manager or director; note that not one of these directors is accountable to a single department or department chairman.

The director in Exhibit 9.3 is accountable to a coordinating committee and works with two departments. Some concerns about whom he answers to about what may plague this director, but still the leadership is not within a single department. The organization structure in Exhibit 9.4 calls for the director to be accountable to an executive board. Instructional and support components, in turn, are accountable to the director. In Exhibit 9.5 the director of teacher education is accountable directly to the dean, and he has a director of operations accountable to him.

There are, of course, many possible variations. Teacher Corps guide-

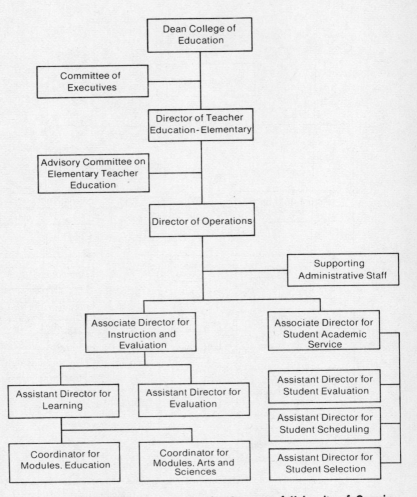

**EXHIBIT 9.5 Administrative Structure of University of Georgia—
Model Teacher Education Program.**

lines, along with some other guidelines for federally supported projects, require a director who is accountable to an executive board composed of school system representatives, parents, and college personnel.

One stumbling block inherent in management systems like those charted in Exhibits 9.3, 9.4, and 9.5 is the danger of creating and perpetuating an army of bureaucrats. College faculty have traditionally been given credit for their teaching roles, and program management time has come out of their hides. If care were not taken, the maintenance of management systems like those depicted might require more management than teaching.

Keep in mind that the organizations shown are from paper versions of model programs, few of which have been implemented in their proposed form. Real-world CBE management as it exists in current programs does share some of their characteristics, particularly the avoidance of single-department ties. In most CBE programs established to date, a director or a program manager has been appointed and has been made accountable to a decision-making body rather than to a single department.

The Matrix Management System

The organizational systems described above, whether traditional in their goals or not, have all followed traditional organizational patterns. They are simply variations of the hierarchical organization chart depicted in Exhibit 9.6. A different concept is shown in Exhibit 9.7. This is a matrix management system in which each program or project manager is accountable directly to the dean, as are the departments. The program manager is responsible for program goals and evaluation of outcomes, and he must justify his use of departmental staff resources as being in keeping with the public objectives of the program.

Actual attempts at such matrix systems are rare, but there is optimism about their potential for success with CBE programs. The advantages are apparent: continual vertical *and horizontal* accountability, departmental security for faculty, and provision for autonomous programs rather than series of courses. But most colleges view matrix management with great caution.

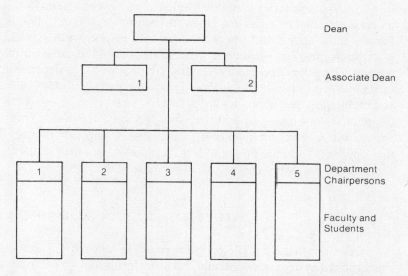

EXHIBIT 9.6 Traditional Organization Chart.

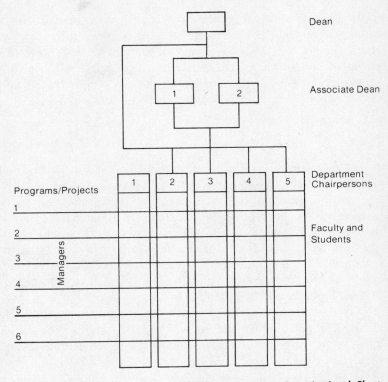

EXHIBIT 9.7   Matrix Organizational Chart.

Perhaps one reason for this caution is the commitment to the system that is required of its members. Open and constant communication is a must. Faculty must understand where they are with respect to the system. When working for program operations they are responsible to program managers; when working in nonprogram roles they are responsible to department chairmen. The department is the logical agency for personnel decisions, but the chairman must use input about a faculty member's effectiveness in the program when making decisions regarding salary increments, promotions, and tenure. Another problem is resolving nonnegotiable differences between the department and the program. If a third party (i.e., the Dean) makes the decision the precedent can permanently destroy the parity.

PLANNING FOR YOUR MANAGEMENT SYSTEM

Odds are that the CBE program you plan will require changes in the management system now operating in your institution. We cannot tell you what your new management system should be, for there is no single model of management that will fit every program's needs. We can, however, offer some guidelines and relevant thoughts that you would do well to keep in mind.[2]

CONCEPT *1*. MANAGEMENT IS NOTHING MORE THAN THE USE OF COMMON SENSE WITH PEOPLE IN WORKING TO ACCOMPLISH A TASK. Most people seem to think of management systems as a maze of diagrams, PERT charts, systems analysis designs, and worse. That's not the system, however—that is just one way of talking about it. Yes, charts are dehumanized, but people acting out the roles depicted on charts do not have to be so. How you use the system is what counts. All the flowcharts in the world will not help the manager who cannot work with people. Competency-based education lends itself well to systematic management because it has easily identifiable tasks. When you know the tasks that a system is to accomplish, then the system and the program can be evaluated by whether or not those tasks are accomplishd, by whether or not explicit goals are met. It is in such evaluation that the true value of a management system and the effectiveness of its components are revealed. It is in the use he makes of such evaluations that the true worth of the manager is revealed.

CONCEPT *2*. TRY, WHENEVER POSSIBLE, TO WORK WITHIN THE CONSTRAINTS OF THE EXISTING MANAGEMENT SYSTEM. Remember that it is a characteristic of a system that whatever changes occur in a subsystem will affect the whole system. Colleges of education, for example, may be subsystems of universities. If management decisions with regard to a CBTE program are made in the college, they had better be compatible with the university environment or the decisions will have been made in vain. This is similarly true for subsubsystems like departments within colleges or faculty within departments.

For example, we know of at least three institutions where, after careful consideration, an "*A*"–"Incomplete" grading system was decided upon for CBE programs. The rationale was that since CBE is a "success–not yet" process, grading should reflect that process in awarding an "*A*" for success and a no-penalty "Incomplete" for not yet achieving success. The logic seems irrefutable, but the new grading scheme lasted only one semester at one institution where it was shot down by administrators who claimed rather vehemently that the new form of grading was subverting the university system. At another institution the CBE program managers held off for several years in order to gather support for their impending confronta-

---

[2] These concepts have been derived from a number of sources. Two excellent sources of managerial principles are C. G. Gentry, *Heuristics for the Development of a CBTE Program,* University of Toledo, Fall 1971 (mimeo); and *Mutable Principles of Organization,* Public Administration News, Management Forum, Vol. 17, No. 1 (February 1967), Sec. II.

tion with the registrar over grading. When they finally entered his office they were greeted by the registrar stating that he had been expecting them to come several years before and was ready to assist. The moral is, be sure you understand where and what the *real* constraints are.

CONCEPT 3. WHEN CHANGES MUST BE MADE IN THE EXISTING SYSTEM, BE CAREFUL TO USE EXISTING PROTOCOL. While it can be argued that a system will be the least likely to recognize its own need for change, systems have been known to change themselves upon being given sufficient cause.

There are two ways to attempt to change a system: from the outside with loud banging on the doors and firebrand threats, and from the inside with steady argument and constructive logic. One guess as to which method makes the fewest enemies.

Protocol seems to be particularly important for CBTE programs when establishing field operations in a public school system. Attempts to circumvent teachers' organizations, for instance, can result in nothing but bad will. In one program we know about there was no money to pay cooperating public school teachers. One such teacher wrote a note to the program managers demanding to know whose work she was doing; that university person surely must make more money than she did, she reasoned, and she wanted a cut of the take. Some extra time ensuring effective communication with all levels of personnel in this project would obviously have been well spent.

CONCEPT 4. WHEN BEGINNING AN EXPERIMENTAL CBE PROGRAM, BE SURE TO BEGIN WITH A STAFF OF INTERESTED AND WILLING PEOPLE. Your experimental CBE program will be looked to for proof of the viability of the approach in your institution. With this much riding on the success of the experiment, you should be careful to staff the program with committed people. Small groups of dedicated workers can do wonders with an innovative program because they share a feeling for their work and they can communicate easily.

Be warned, however, that small dedicated groups can be a hazard to the growth and spread of the program in your institution if they are not open to new people. A closed group is bad policy. You should never give the opposition the chance to claim that they had no opportunity for participation. At the same time don't shanghai unwilling participants in an effort to ensure broad support; reluctant workers will only weaken your efforts.

CONCEPT 5. KEEP YOUR PLANS OPEN AND ON TOP OF THE TABLE. PROVIDE CONTINUING OPPORTUNITIES FOR INPUT AND DECISION-MAKING PARTICIPATION BY STAFF FROM OUTSIDE THE EXPERIMENTAL GROUP IF

THEY WISH TO BE INVOLVED. The key to success in a beginning CBE operation is openness. This is a point we made in Concept 4 above, but it bears repeating under a heading of its own. To protect the program from charges of "elitism," all planning and decision making must be done out in the open.

We know of a small staff cadre in one institution that is working on assumptions, competencies, and a prototype management system for a new CBTE program. Two department chairmen and an associate dean are among the other participating staff. Each time a task is accomplished, such as the identification of a set of assumptions, a written version of the action, in proposal form, is sent to the total faculty and to student and school representatives. The information is sent on ditto sheets for feedback. (The ditto format connotes something less final than mimeographed or other more polished printing.) Those who wish to provide input to the committee do so. Those who don't can't say they were never given the opportunity.

Another aspect of openness is the necessity for making sure that people involved in the program know what is going on and what is expected of them. An example of the consequences of not adhering to this principle occurred in our experience in the University of Houston CBTE program. A decision was made by the program developers and local public school administrators to allow program students to choose among the schools for the location of their field experiences. The students were to be allowed to visit several schools of their choice, talk with principals and teachers, and then decide in which school they would work for the next three semesters.

The rationale was solid. The problems were many. New area superintendents replaced some of those who had agreed to cooperate with the program. The students' search for a school threatened the teachers. Reports of student "spies" filtered to the area superintendents. The confusion that was tolerable in a pilot program brought the process to a grinding halt with implementation of CBTE to the total undergraduate education population. The reasonable system was junked, and students are now assigned to schools.

CONCEPT 6. BE EXTREMELY WARY OF INSTALLING CBE OR ANY OF ITS COMPONENT PARTS BY MANDATE. We are concerned about forcing people in any way with regard to CBE. Several states now mandate competency-based criteria for teacher certification, effectively requiring that all teacher education institutions in those states install CBTE programs. There are many who go along wittingly. Others cannot see anything of value in CBTE. For those who would try it and see, no trial is possible, at least no real trial with the option to reject the new system. Frankly, we think the mandate is one of the worst things that has befallen the CBTE movement. The movement has enough going for it to succeed without a mandate, so why stimulate the emergence of a whole army of organized opponents?

If you want to sell CBE, prove its viability with a well-managed pilot program. Let the enthusiasm of students, faculty, and cooperating professionals have its effect on the rest of the institution and you will probably end up with a full-fledged, voluntary CBE operation.

CONCEPT 7. GOAL ACCOMPLISHMENT IS THE FINAL TEST OF A CBE PROGRAM'S EFFECTIVENESS WITH STUDENTS. THE SAME STANDARD APPLIES FOR FACULTY INVOLVED IN PROGRAM DEVELOPMENT.   During all phases of program development and implementation, and even continuing with program maintenance, strive to keep faculty and staff workers task-oriented. Work to achieve specific goals before specific deadlines. Don't assign tasks to committees; assign people to tasks with agreed-upon deadlines.

Find ways to give faculty the time to accomplish assigned tasks. Faculty members will always have other things to do. It is impractical to expect a faculty member to develop and implement an experimental program in addition to teaching a full course load, working on a half-dozen committees, and supervising fourteen student teachers, plus worrying about a pregnant wife and a sheep dog that's nearly itching to death. Find ways to provide the poor guy with released time.

But don't just give people released time without negotiating contracts for work to be done and what the supports will be. An exception would be an award of free released time for a faculty member's accomplishments done on his own time.

CONCEPT 8. TO ENSURE PROGRAM SUCCESS, MAKE CERTAIN THAT EVERYONE INVOLVED KNOWS THE FULL EXTENT OF HIS ROLE.   Based on their past experiences, students, cooperating teachers, and faculty may bring faulty assumptions about their roles to the new situation. Students, for instance, often do not realize the responsibility they have for decision making with regard to what objectives they will seek to achieve and what instructional activities they will pursue in seeking those objectives. This is a new role for students who have always had such educational decisions made for them. Some students have problems with this role, and program developers may wish to provide help for them. At the University of Houston and in some other teacher education programs, affective modules have been developed for use with students who appear to have difficulty getting things done autonomously. Some commercial materials, like the College Entrance Examining Board's (1973) *Decisions and Outcomes,* have also been used effectively to help people increase their decision-making abilities.

Cooperating teachers in CBTE programs may have difficulties in the role of managing student teachers in their classrooms. Some public school teachers enjoy having student help; others don't know what to do with it. Student teachers "get in the way." This situation usually results in students' becoming dissatisfied because they aren't doing anything and cooperating teachers' becoming upset because of all the "free" help that is going to waste. Usually, this situation is symptomatic of a program in which the cooperating teachers have not been involved in deciding what their role will be. One important part of that role should be a lion's share of the say in the certification of new teachers. A number of teacher centers are operating on this assumption, but many cooperating teachers either do not recognize or are not willing to accept that role. Many teachers are not willing to reject a student for certification.

College faculty sometimes have problems with their roles as team members. Being used to making autonomous decisions about their courses, they sometimes have difficulties in subordinating their teaching to a set of objectives. They sometimes lose sight of their responsibility to help students achieve some specified competencies and they might even strike out on their own to change their part of the curriculum, losing sight of the ripple effect such decisions have on the whole fabric of an integrated CBE program. A good strategy to forestall such precipitous decision making on the course level is to establish a central curriculum committee that has the responsibility for approving changes in curricula.

CONCEPT 9. MAKE CERTAIN THAT THE NUMBER OF INDIVIDUALS RE-PORTING TO ONE SUPERVISOR IS NEITHER TOO LARGE NOR TOO SMALL. This concept is a corollary to the notion of proactive rather than reactive decision making. If a supervisor has direct responsibility for one hundred faculty members and twenty-five operations, he won't be able to do anything except fight fires and maintain a reactive holding operation against a daily onslaught of student complaints, faculty moans, missing modules, stolen tests, and broken equipment. Of course, if a supervisor has too few responsibilities, he may be able to plan ahead easily, but he is inefficiently used and the program is risking fragmentation into a lot of tiny noncommunicating groups.

One way that some larger CBE operations handle the staff-supervisor ratio problem is through teams. They establish teams of faculty, students, and cooperating institutions. A team may consist of five or six faculty and 100 to 150 students who work in five to ten public schools, for instance. The faculty group has a leader or manager, and they are responsible for most of the instruction and all field relationships involving their students. Each faculty member is a "broker"; either he helps a student with a competency, module, school experience, or other problem or he finds someone who can. This also provides a role for "floaters," faculty members who provide teams with help in specific areas when called on. Team leaders meet regularly and exchange ideas and experiences.

CONCEPT 10. TRY TO AVOID OVERLAPPING FUNCTIONS. There is

so little wiggle room for management in budgets that you must try not to duplicate efforts. Careful sharing of assumptions, goals, and competencies can do much to avoid miscommunication, but additional steps are needed to make sure that the same task is not done by several people.

Each faculty and staff member must know to whom he reports and who reports to him. Be certain that staff members are not accountable for the same task to more than one supervisor.

At first glance the matrix system may appear to be guilty here. However, the department chairperson and the program manager should have different functions to negotiate with the faculty member. In any case, the faculty member must be given the opportunity of buying into or out of a project based on what is expected of him. The department chairperson's responsibility to the faculty member is one of protecting him.

In one existing CBTE effort *one* office handles all correspondence with central school administration offices; *one* learning resource center handles the storage of books, articles, films, and so forth. *One* center handles all duplication materials so that a running account is kept of who ran how many copies and where the extras are located.

While we are on this topic, we might mention that there is a threat implied when a CBE effort decides to take on a task already accomplished elsewhere. In one CBTE effort, the decision was made to provide a mini-library for students in the education building. Five or six copies of selected books were purchased with student book-use fees and kept in this mini-library with printed materials and modules. No student texts were required unless students wished to purchase their own copies. Students could use the mini-library on two-day checkout. A problem arose when the head librarian heard that the College of Education was starting its own library. Negotiations were required in order to demonstrate that a duplication of function did not exist, nor was any attempt being made to subdivide the university library.

CONCEPT *11*. MAKE CERTAIN THAT THE RESPONSIBILITIES GIVEN TO THE PROGRAM MANAGER AND KEY FACULTY MEMBERS ARE ACCOMPANIED BY THE AUTHORITY TO PERFORM THE FUNCTIONS.   Just in case the reader cannot generate twenty to thirty examples of where this statement has been ignored, think of the responsibility and authority of most college committees. Committees in most efforts are advisory only. There is nothing wrong with this function unless the committee is being held accountable for program decisions and operations. CBE calls for giving committees some teeth. Curriculum committees need to be able to *enforce* a ruling stating that a certain curriculum exists and will continue to exist until individual or groups of faculty justify a change. Similarly, ethics committees for the safeguard of faculty and students need to have authority.

Student grievance committees need ways of ensuring that students are getting appropriate attention.

In a matrix management system, program directors must be sure of their authority. Budget and personnel decisions are made by department chairpersons. This leaves the program manager in a bad situation if he has no power, no money, and no staff. If the matrix system is used, program managers need the authority to ensure that the task is done without having to beg department chairpersons for funding.

CONCEPT *12*. REMEMBER THAT YOU ARE WORKING WITH PROFES-
SIONALS. MAKE CERTAIN THAT THEIR JOBS IN THE SYSTEM DO NOT BECOME
SO SMALL THAT THE PERSON FEELS LESS AND LESS SIGNIFICANT.

Enough said.

MANAGING WITHIN THE COSTS OF CBE

Most critics looking at CBE gag loudly when discussing the cost necessary to plan, implement, and maintain a CBE program. To most who take a cursory look, CBE is too rich for most colleges and universities.

Part of this impression comes from the Phase II model feasibility studies of the model teacher education programs. Each of these studies noted budgets well in excess of the budgets of entire colleges, including graduate school. For one-year operations, estimates of $4 million to $6 million were not uncommon. In these days of zero budget increases, such talk is indeed folly.

One basic problem with cost estimates as they apply to teacher education programs is that no one knows what it takes to educate an effective teacher. Few of us know what it really costs to turn out a *certified* teacher. We can describe budgets (albeit always too small), identify what the money was spent for, describe the exact date when the ditto paper disappeared, chastise faculty for too-high phone bills and overextended photocopying budgets. We can identify the need for more faculty support, and increased secretarial services.

Without any indication of the cost-effectiveness of the present program, however, the vocal complaints of the opponents of CBE and the opponents of high costs are at best unfounded. At the same time, common sense makes clear that there will be at least initial higher costs for CBE. After all, the program requires extras, including

1. Paper, paper, and more paper. Self-paced modular instructions have to be provided somehow; usually they are printed on paper. Expect a large increase in budget here.

2. More clerical help for record keeping.
3. Increased mileage cost for staff travel in clinical supervision.
4. Increased use of audiovisual materials, demanding both initial cost and repair.
5. Physical breakdown and theft of software. Films break; even videotapes break. Who knows what pressures cause students to steal, but some inevitably do, so plan on it.
6. Mini-libraries, if used, are expensive. Many institutions when starting spend more than five thousand dollars just on books for a mini-library.
7. Faculty released time for development work.
8. Outside consultant help.

Add all of these up and you have quite a bill. Few institutions can call a moratorium on classes as Weber State did for a year while the program was being developed, so in addition to building you are running another program as well. But where does the money come from? At most institutions the coin of the realm is credit hours. A credit hour *is* money. X students in Y courses multiplied by three credits produces total credit hours. One way to get more money is to increase the number of credit hours. To run a CBE program on the same budget could mean reducing the number of credit hours (either fewer students or fewer courses). Some institutions find that increasing funds by adding credit hours is the best approach. Inservice credit for courses, clinical supervision with student teachers, and courses in schools or through a teacher center operation within a school district are all sources of credit hours. Since graduate credit usually brings in more money per course, this can be a source for increases in spendable funds. To determine faculty load in CBE efforts, one proposal is that a faculty member work half time (perhaps two course equivalents) with students and have at least one graduate course equivalent working with inservice personnel on advanced materials or in seminars. The value of interacting with students on a preservice-inservice continuum cannot be over-stated.

To carry off this approach of generating new funds by adding credit hours is a difficult trick in times of decreasing enrollment. Colleges throughout the nation face a steady decline in students if projective figures are correct. A number of institutions are now losing faculty members because of this. This faculty drain does not serve the purpose of decreasing student-instructor ratios.

Another way to generate money, of course, is through grants. If you are fortunate enough to have a grant for program development we offer only one caution: Make certain that you spend no more for program *operation* than the amount you can count on having from regular funding sources after the grant dries up. Spend the grant on extras, particularly program development and implementation. Do not become dependent on those soft dollars.

Remember also that costs include other items besides money. Time and personal energy are equally precious and equally in demand. Be sure to spend them wisely. And reward the guy whose hide you are taking; it is one of the best investments you can make with your dollars.

SOME OTHER CONCERNS

A key to success in any operation and certainly paramount in the workings of a matrix management system is the fact that the success of the operation depends on the achievement of goals. Program assessment will determine executive and management decisions as well as set policy for future operations. A manager and his organization cannot just exist!!

For a given program this might mean the following goals:

At the end of the first year of operation:

At least 75 percent of the students enrolled in the program will qualify to enter short-term, full-responsibility teaching, and at least 75 percent of those who engage in such teaching will perform to the standards set for it (Schalock, 1973).

At the end of the fourth full semester, at least 60 percent of the students approved for continuation in the program will have completed minimal certification standards.

At the end of the first year of program operation, cost estimates will exceed original by no more than 5 percent and will not exceed the monies available to the college based on regular sources of revenue.

Program decision points are set in advance; post hoc analyses may determine where original predictions were off and why; however, to facilitate program assessment, the goals must be specified in advance.

In addition to program decisions, subparts of the program must be amenable to assessment in the same manner. For example:

After completing the program, 80 percent of the graduates are hired by school districts.

After two years of teaching, 80 percent of the hired teachers are still teaching.

After two years of teaching, ratings from the administrators, supervisors, peer teachers, and students rate the teacher as "above average."

On a smaller scale:

After the program completion, 85 percent of the students who have gone through the program indicate that they think the experience was a positive one.

It was mentioned earlier that a key point in building a workable management system is making certain that it fits with managerial structures already in operation. Some aspects of CBE must be carefully considered, including such things as grading, record keeping, course identification, and tuition. Several of these areas have been covered in other chapters, but some have definite implications for managerial decisions.

In Chapter 3 we discussed grading, pointing out that there are arguments for grading on individual modules or components using an "*A*"–"Incomplete" dichotomy. In at least one institution, the initial flak on this decision did not come from the administration or the students. The flak was generated in the registrar's office. At this institution, if grades are posted at the semester deadline date, the records can be posted by computer. If an "Incomplete" is given, the grade must be changed by hand upon completion of the work. Thus several $2.50-per-hour clerks were tied up in changing grades, and the pressure to stop using "Incompletes" came hard and fast. We recommend that decisions about grading be carefully considered and shared with *all* affected.

A second question arises when one considers tuition. How does a student register for a course? What is a course? At many state-supported institutions, monies are provided to the institution based on course enrollment. But a course is time based; it lasts six, twelve, fourteen, or eighteen weeks. In competency-based programs, how do students register for a "course" they would like to start in the middle of the semester? Furthermore, how does the university get its money from a student who tests out of a course? Does he have to register for it anyway? Can postregistration occur?; Can students sign up for courses after completing them?

These questions are not designed to turn you away from CBE. They have been answered satisfactorily at many institutions. Typically, students can post-register. In most cases, certification is still on a course basis even though the courses may be part of a competency-based effort. Thus, the student must still register. Some places have equated a number of modules with one credit (e.g., fifteen modules = one credit). Depending on the size of the modules, this may work for you. Some institutions have students register in blocks, say fifteen hours, and the self-pacing of modules allows students choices among the sequence of module completion.

Developers of the USOE models spent quite a bit of time looking at the feasibility of their products. In the Georgia feasibility study an interesting operational definition appeared:

> *Credits.* The model program proposes that the normal system of credits in terms of quarter or semester hours be abolished. However, in order to account for students who find it necessary to transfer to other schools or universities and to account for problems associated with election to honor societies and graduation with honors it is necessary to establish a basis for credit.
>
> The feasibility investigation led to the development of the Student Effort Unit (EU) system for establishing credit. An EU is defined as a quantitative approximation of the amount of effort required of an average student to acquire a defined set of specific behaviors. The total number of EUs in the model program is 3,000. Of this total the first 1,000 EUs represent the preprofessional phase, the next 1,000 EUs the specialist phase. . . . The equivalents for an EU are defined as follows:
>
> $\quad$ 1 EU $\quad = 2$ clock hours of effort
> $\quad$ 10 EUs $= 1$ quarter hour of credit
> $\quad$ 15 EUs $= 1$ week of effort (30–45 hours)
> 150 EUs $= 1$ academic quarter (10 weeks of work or 15 quarter hours of credit.
>
> In turn this system can be converted to a semester hour equivalent by multiplying by a factor of $\frac{2}{3}$. That is 10 EUs $= 1$ quarter hour $= \frac{2}{3}$ semester hour.

In CBE programs where students have registered for a number of credit hours, it may in the long run be more efficient to have a second registration for modules within the department or college. An example of this can be seen in Exhibit 9.8. The student's schedule for a semester is blocked out around a 9:00–11:00 A.M. period, four days a week. The student has scheduled five required modules (A, C, D, E, and F) and also scheduled eight other modules, not all of which are of the same value (classroom management, for example, might be worth double credits). In such a scheduling procedure, three weeks are reserved for an internship, and the student even has a free week (No. 13). Each of the noted modules would be offered at different times throughout the semester. If a student did not demonstrate minimal competence, he might have to repeat the module.

There is also a value in this scheduling for the instructor. Suppose

Week ►	1	2	3	4	5	6	7	8	9	10	11	12	13	14	15	16
8-9 a.m.														Internship		
9-11 a.m.	A		Classroom Management				Generic Module		D		Multi-Cultural III					
11 a.m. - 1 p.m.	C		Affective Modules	Multi-Cultural II	Piaget		F & E Component		E	F	Questioning Skills					

This equals twelve credit hours of work. Note: One day each week would be reserved for work in schools. At least one block of three weeks is reserved for every day in the schools—spreading out student teaching over a longer period than one semester.

EXHIBIT 9.8   Student Schedule.

an instructor is a Piagetian specialist. At present in most colleges of education it would be wasteful to offer a three-hour course on Piaget. An instructor, therefore, must "cover" Piaget along with six or eight other topics to make a course. Modular scheduling might allow him to offer his specialty or specialties plus even some optional modules. Instructors could be focusing on their specialties, and the students would be the better for it.

In such a modular operation, student records would have to be considered. In experience-based programs, when a student completes a course, his grade is recorded and the student goes on. In a modular-scheduling program careful bookkeeping must be initiated, keeping track of where students are in their personal programs. One solution proposed by several institutions is the use of computers to keep records on students. Record keeping in such cases involves having individual faculty members submit computer cards or some other kind of completion record to a clerk, secretary, or teaching assistant who places the information in a form that can be handled by a computer. Record files are kept up to date in such a process, making advisement and student files for prospective employers contemporary and correct. While the use of computers may be out of the question for some institutions, the cost is most reasonable for others.[3]

There is also considerable value in differentiated staffing procedures

[3] One excellent prototype system is in operation at the University of Texas at El Paso. Information is available from Dr. J. L. Klingstedt.

necessitated by modular scheduling. Educators for years have been, out of necessity, Jacks and Jills-of-all-trades. In teaming or interdisciplinary programs, perhaps better efforts can be made to focus on the true strengths of professional educators. One problem, of course, with specialization is that there are a few jobs that need to be done for which very few educators are qualified. Generic teaching skills such as classroom management, questioning skills, and set induction techniques may be identified for inclusion in a program. But who will teach them? Who will develop materials for student use in these areas? It has been only in the past few years that Ed.D. or Ph.D. graduates planning on teaching in colleges of education have not needed to specialize in a subject (science, math education, etc.). The requirements for generic teaching faculty members are high now. Subject specialists either will have to be trained in the area of generic skills or new personnel will be hired with these skills. Careful analysis of need might better identify faculty needs and set the stage for recruitment or truly valid inservice efforts.

GUIDING PRINCIPLES FOR THE CBE PROGRAM MANAGER

In this section, we would like to throw theory and models to the wind. Our sole data source will be ideas extrapolated from the extensive experiences of the handful of veterans who have served as CBE adoption agents (internal and external) for a combined total of thirty or more institutions. Like the concepts presented earlier in this chapter, these data are oriented toward the CBE program manager in the trenches.

One data source for our guiding principles is the research of Dick Wallace (1973) who conducted two-day, in-depth interviews with six experienced and successful adoption agents working with teacher education institutions adopting CBE programs. Based on these interviews, analyzed individually in his paper, Wallace draws a very powerful and colorful picture of each of the adoption agents. He then synthesizes a set of commonalities that apply to all six.

> Any attempt to generalize from the six agents interviewed to adoption agents in general (if they exist in great numbers) would clearly be unwarranted. However, one can derive commonalities from reviewing the guidelines provided by our six adoption agents. In brief summary let's highlight a few of them.

1. EACH HIS OWN MAN

It should be abundantly clear from the data presented and from statements from the adoption agents that one must be himself to be effective.

We have seen several of them say that one must know himself, his values, his motives and his goals. This presence of self-knowledge and the all-consuming commitment to the innovation is a prerequisite for successful adoption agents . . . however, it is clearly not enough.

2. DIAGNOSIS

Almost every change agent in some way provides guidelines for diagnosing the situation in which he finds himself. In some instances the diagnosis is relatively short; in other cases it is an ongoing procedure. There is no question that however one defines the problem, whether it be locating decision makers within an institution or determining the motivation pattern of adopters, diagnosis is clearly one of the key skills and strategies that an adoption agent must acquire and practice.

3. KNOW YOUR INNOVATION

There is no question that an adoption agent must know what he is talking about. Preferably he must have experienced the innovation in the trenches as an adopter. Lacking this he must learn vicariously from the experience of others. There is no substitute for knowledge, however. One cannot bluff his way through an adoption interaction with users; to do so is to court disaster.

4. DIFFERENCES BETWEEN INTERNAL AND EXTERNAL ADOPTION AGENTS

It is probably critically important to study the three internal agents and the three external agents differently. . . . One reason for the difference is merely time spent within the user system. The internal agent has more time to work with his faculty and staff and consequently can bide his time and govern his behavior accordingly. An external agent usually has limited time within a user system and therefore he must make effective use of that time. While both agents do not mince words and place great emphasis on communicating with administrators, it is clear in the case of the external agents that communication with administrators must be direct and with "no holds barred."

5. MANIPULATION

As unsettling as it might be to some readers, an effective adoption agent must be an effective manipulator. He must manipulate both people and situations in order to be effective and efficient in innovation adoption. He manipulates people, in a positive sense, by encouraging commitment to an idea through visits with faculty . . . [An adoption agent needs to] effectively [put] people together in order to gain commitment, sanction, or reward to enhance the use of the innovation. As a "benevolent manipulator," the adoption agent is constantly alert to the needs and concerns of users and he attempts to manipulate resources—human, financial, and material—in order to expedite the adoption process. The adoption agent can do this because he has . . . the big picture in mind; he has experienced the innovation and therefore knows the problems that users are likely to encounter. The manipulation strategies used by internal agents are more likely to be of a type that will insure development of ongoing relationships among users that he can monitor on a day-to-day basis. The external agent is more likely to manipulate users as resources to one another; the external agent can often provide sanction and recognition for members of the user system that they cannot or would not provide for themselves.

6. TIME COMMITMENT

The internal adoption agent must work long hours in order to achieve his goals. . . . [He will work] long days, even working during vacation periods to achieve his goals. It takes many hours of hand-holding, listening, supporting, peace-making, planning, and evaluating to promote the adoption of an innovation.

The time commitment of the external agent is less in duration for specific institutions primarily because of the need of the resource system for his services with other adopting institutions. This is not to say that the external agent's time demands are less . . . [for] extensive hours and demanding travel schedules [are required] of the external adoption agent; further the external agent must work hard to make the best of every minute he has in interacting with members of the user system. . . . Making the most of every interaction, including those at social gatherings, is characteristic of effective use of time, a critical variable from the external agent's perspective.

7. PEOPLE VS. PROGRAM ORIENTATION OF ADOPTION AGENTS

At this point it is interesting to view the behavior of the six internal and external change agents [as pertains to] people-oriented versus program-oriented dimensions. . . .

In brief, the external adoption agents are apparently highly concerned for people and greatly concerned for program, but, as [one] put it, people are more important than a program. It would appear that the successful internal adoption agents . . . were really motivated toward program first and then toward personal interactions with their faculty in order to achieve that program orientation.

The following list of principles was developed to synthesize and emphasize some of the points that we feel to be important in managing CBE adoption. These principles are oriented mainly toward looking down the road from the beginning of CBE program adoption. However, it would be worthwhile to keep several of them in mind throughout the adoption process. We offer these for whatever worth they may have. In talking with colleagues who are involved in managing CBE adoption, they have refuted some, agreed with others, and added some. They are offered here as a beginning list with the expectation that others will be added.

1. Change requires an extended period of time. CBE is a change that is not going to be brought about in one semester.

2. One cannot expect to do everything out of his or someone else's

hide. It is not possible to do everything that is being done presently, while adding all the effort needed to build a CBE program.

3. The institution's priorities must be consistent with available resources; the allocation of rewards must be consistent with this effort. The hiring of new personnel must include consideration of the adoption effort. Any new personnel should be selected to fit the program's innovations, priorities, and directions; and new personnel should be so informed when they are being hired.

4. *Active* support and decisive leadership must be provided throughout the adoption process. The maintenance of a consistent direction as it relates to decision making and follow-through on such items as due dates will help reduce low-level concerns and sidetracking.

5. You need to have and use outside resources. You need to know and tap consultants from institutions where things have already been done. Faculty need to be aware of materials that already exist; as was mentioned in Chapter 4, the last thing the world needs is another module on behavioral objectives.

6. In selecting consultants who are experienced with CBE or any other innovation, be wary of which ones you select. Very often project directors may be well known, but in fact they are not involved in the day-to-day operation of their programs. Therefore, depending on your questions and needs, it might be better to get the assistant project director rather than the project director from a particular innovative program.

7. There are some places where it is *really* happening. Look for the hard workers behind the scenes and the staff members at those places where they are really making it go.

8. Everyone will not get everything exactly the way he wants. Everyone will have to give some. There must be an overriding commitment to the idea, to the principles involved. Although you may feel very strongly about certain points, more than likely you will have to give in on some.

9. Things will get worse before they get better. This goes for students as well as faculty, especially in terms of overload, scheduling, and the like.

10. Stay loose. You need to maintain your flexibility, deliberately search out alternatives, and continuously question what you are doing. Don't rule out things until you try them. Also don't reply that you tried it once twenty years ago and it didn't work. Others have already used that reasoning and found that it does not hold much water.

11. Find a "dog robber," appropriations officer, midnight procurement agent, or whatever you wish to call him. If you have a faculty member who has these qualifications or an industrious graduate student, all the better. All sorts of resources are needed, and in many cases they

may be sitting idly by. Everything that is needed can't be bought, unless you really have a big budget. An individual with dog robber skills can be very helpful as part of the support systems for CBE adoption.

12. Beware of extreme adoption strategies such as making decrees. They may result in having many CBE labels and trappings without any of the important depth.

13. You have to get your feet wet. No spectating. You will not learn about establishing a CBE program vicariously. The only way to learn what is entailed is to get involved in doing it yourself.

14. From the beginning all faculty need to know what is happening and that there are continuing opportunities for input and involvement. Communication is essential.

15. A consistent direction needs to be maintained with follow-through on such things as decisions and due dates.

16. If key, higher level administration is not in favor of the innovation and will not actively support it, don't try.

17. The "Hall Principle" has some relevance here as well: If everyone is happy with what you are doing, then you probably are not doing anything. This goes for student feedback as well. Accept it, but not personally.

10

CBE program evaluation and data-based decision making

Establishing a CBE program is obviously a time- and energy-consuming process. Every opportunity to reduce the energy, resources, and time required to build an effective program has to be considered. The word *effective* is a key here. If a CBE program were established and had no identifiable differences in outcome from what went before, the only possible conclusion would be that some really bad decisions were made somewhere.

Wise use of evaluation theory and techniques can significantly enhance the quality of decision making and thereby significantly enhance the potential for efficiently establishing an effective CBE program. As with most systems, evaluation must be approached with sensibility and caution.

Evaluators are capable of presenting a very strong case for evaluating all sorts of needs, outcomes, aptitudes, resources, and aspects of a CBE program. It is highly unlikely, however, that any institution would be able, or would even desire, to support or conduct all of the "needed" evaluation studies. This means that the first decision for the CBE program builder to make is the following: From which aspect(s) of the CBE program do I most need information to assist me in making decisions? That area then becomes the primary focus of the first stages of the evaluation effort. Selecting that area is a task that should not be taken lightly, nor be done in isolation from fellow faculty or without consultation with the evaluators.

Evaluation—its theory, systems, and methodology—is now progressing through an exciting time of examination and development. The alternative theories and approaches within the field of evaluation, along with the leadership of dynamic and conceptually powerful specialists, afford a wide range of knowledge, theory, opinion, and technique for possible application to evaluation of CBE programs. Since the field of evaluation is in flux, there is still no uniform use of terminology, no one common theory of evaluation, nor any single established evaluation system. Instead, several thought-provoking alternatives exist and, to varying degrees, overlap, complement, and compete with each other. It shall not be our purpose here to present a long discourse on any one approach to evaluation but rather to briefly introduce the reader to the literature. This may trigger further reading. We would also like to suggest a framework for applying evaluation theory and systems in establishing and monitoring a CBE program. If you are already familiar with the evaluation literature, feel free to skim over the first section of this chapter. The chapter is organized around the following questions and topics:

WHAT IS EVALUATION?

What evaluation is and is not is an issue by itself. The various experts in the study of evaluation have established definitions of evaluation from their specific frames of reference. In teacher education, several teacher educators and educational researchers have proposed often conflicting definitions and schema for evaluation. CBE program managers should read recent papers by such evaluators as Borich, Provus, Stufflebeam, Guba, Alkin, and Scriven before developing an evaluation plan.

In summary, these professional evaluators see evaluation as a task for persons other than the decision maker. Evaluators collect, analyze, and report their findings to the decision makers who then have a more solid basis for making rational decisions. The pure evaluator collects, synthesizes, and reports but does not *judge* the findings. Evaluation is field based; that is, it is based on the real-world situation rather than employing an ideal experimental design under tight controls. Evaluation is action oriented. It should be designed to *provide* timely data to the decision maker *during* the activity as well as after the fact. Particularly in education it cannot be emphasized enough that evaluation is for decision making during program development as well as deciding about the terminal effects of the program. We feel strongly that during the program building process, evaluation needs to be oriented more toward the implementation and program development needs and effects and less oriented toward the desired treatment effects.

Each of the individuals mentioned above, as well as many of their colleagues, have articulated theories and systems of evaluation that merit study. Their writings acknowledge the complexity of the task and offer useful conceptual schemes for organizing and categorizing the phenomena. Teacher education researchers are also interested in evaluation as is discussed in the next section.

Teacher Educators Look at CBTE Evaluation

Many research-oriented teacher educators have also considered the issue of evaluation in CBTE programs. One difference between the teacher educator's frame of reference and that of the evaluator must be mentioned here. The "pure" evaluators consider themselves to be third parties involved in the orderly collection and reporting of data to the decision makers; but the teacher-educator-oriented evaluators do not appear to make a distinction between who collects and analyzes data and who is doing the judging and decision making. Regardless of their frame of reference, however, they have emphasized many of the basic issues that the "pure" evaluators have identified and have identified some other important issues that are particularly germane to CBTE. For example, Airasian (1973) has emphasized that limiting evaluation to determining which learners have mastered what objectives of instruction is an all-too-limiting definition. He sees evaluation during the implementation stage at least as being much broader:

> . . . a value judgment of merit or worth. . . . The heart of the evaluation process, then, is valuing. Data gathering, be it "hard," objective data or "soft," impressionistic data, is not evaluation. Evaluation takes place when data are compared to some standard or norm and a decision about pass or fail, accept or reject, or good or bad is made.

Airasian goes on to point out:

Despite our wishes to the contrary, decisions about what is good, valu-able, worthy, and desirable are made not in the research domain, but rather spring from our individual philosophies and frames of reference. If I were to ask you to cite three examples of school practices which are based firmly in established research findings, I dare say that you would be hard put to respond. Arguments for and against performance-based education reside, and will continue to reside, in the value domain. The questions asked are not whether one *can* be evaluated on the basis of their students' performance, but whether they *ought* to be. These are issues which are based in philosophy and value orientations and it is in these frameworks that evaluation centers. As a consequence, it is important to consider evaluation issues as they relate to arguments for and against the basic idea of performance-based teacher education.

Airasian proposes that once the assumptions underlying CBTE are accepted, evaluation of the program should include at least the following issues: (1) defining teacher competencies, (2) evaluating student progress, (3) evaluating attainment of competencies, (4) data maintenance, and (5) judging teachers by their students' achievement. Airasian has raised these evaluation issues not so much as a proposed model of evaluation but rather to point out the highly value-laden aspects of evaluation in CBTE programs and that these evaluation issues must be faced by every educational system that becomes involved with CBTE:

. . . the real evaluation questions inherent in performance-based teacher education relate not to constructing objective evidence gathering techniques or measures, but rather to judgments about what data are to be gathered, from whom, and under what conditions. The selection of instruments and techniques is an outgrowth of these prior evaluative decisions. (Airasian, 1973.)

Houston (1973) sees evaluation as it relates to CBTE as follows:

In designing and testing a performance based teacher education program, evaluation serves three purposes: to improve program effectiveness, to improve program organization and management, and to monitor student performance. Evaluation is not something which occurs at the end of the project but is integral to continued development.

Houston sees evaluation as a systemic approach with continual testing and retesting. He goes on to make an important distinction between basic re-search and evaluation:

The reader may note that this systemic, developmental stance is at variance to the research model typical of traditional academic endeavors. In research, a basic set of propositions are assumed, or proven, and with this firm base, further research findings are added. The process is incremental, not developmental. . . . Measurement is an integral part of evaluation; however, evaluation adds the qualitative dimension, the contextual edge to the process.

Houston suggests that improving program effectiveness entails refining both (1) program objectives and (2) instructional resources and procedures. One step toward improving program organization and management entails measuring such variables as the time required to develop various program aspects, the cost of materials and staff required, and the space and other resources required. These first two purposes of evaluation are focused on programmatic development. The third purpose of evaluation that Houston proposes—monitoring student performance—is focused on comparing actual student performance with expected performance as specified in the program goals and objectives. Evaluation of student performance is done not only to assess terminal skills but also to monitor and provide feedback during the program that will enhance student achievement.

Schalock (1974) concurs that the measurement problems are great in CBTE programs, especially since the skills of teaching are so complex. He goes on to point out:

But no matter how complex the performance, measurement is not enough. In addition to the process of measurement *judgments* have to be made about what has been measured, and *decisions* have to be made on the basis of those judgments.

Schalock acknowledges that there needs to be a common language for competency-based teacher education, in general, and for what he calls "assessment" in CBTE programs, in particular:

Specifically, we propose that the term assessment be used to refer to the identification, collection, reduction, analysis, and use of information in service of targeted, adaptive decision-making.

He sees assessment as being a term that incorporates more than measurement and evaluation. Exhibit 10.1 describes the operations that each concept includes as proposed by Schalock.

Schalock has developed a set of characteristics for a CBTE assessment system and has articulated a model of CBTE assessment that is based on

EXHIBIT 10.1

Operation	Measurement	Evaluation	Assessment
Identification of data needed	X	X	X
Collection of data	X	X	X
Reduction and synthesis of data		X	X
Analysis of data in relation to standards		X	X
Analysis of factors affecting data			X
Utilization of data in making decisions			X

"Operations Included in the Proposed Definitions of Measurement, Evaluation, and Assessment," (Schalock, 1974).

these characteristics and criteria. The general characteristics of Schalock's model are as follows:

1. An assessment system should be a decision-serving information system.
2. An assessment system must be a targeted information system.
3. An assessment system needs to be an "open" (adaptive) information system.
4. An assessment system is not necessarily a research-serving information system.

Schalock identifies six components of an assessment system that meet the demands of CBTE programs:

1. In order to service all of the decisions that must be made, families (collections) of decisions must be organized and/or targeted; sub-assessment systems need to be designed.
2. Structures for decision making must be identified and the assessment system structured in accordance with the ways that different decisions are made.
3. The procedures and rules for making decisions need to be spelled out.
4. Participants in each class of decision must be identified and kept in mind in designing and operating an assessment system.
5. Data need to be organized and presented in a form that will insure their being accessible and usable.
6. Performance standards need to be set not only for the learners, but for the staff, program costs, program as a whole, the satisfaction of the participants, etc.

Schalock suggests that if an assessment system is to be operational, at least five functions must be performed: (1) data collection, (2) data reduction, (3) data storage, (4) data retrieval and distribution, and (5) management of the assessment system per se. Schalock also acknowledges that once an assessment system is designed the job is not done, since the assessment system must be integrated with an instructional program and, in the long run, serve the research needs as well.

A SCHEMA FOR DATA-BASED DECISION MAKING

Regardless of the model, all evaluators see evaluation as a continuing activity rather than one engaged in only post hoc. CBE program managers must accept this same stance. Which model or combination of models a particular program employs will to some extent be related to the felt needs of the program decision makers. However, some crucial variables have to be assessed, and some crucial decisions will have to be made if an effective CBE program is to be established. Of course, all variables cannot be systematically studied by any one program, but all CBE program decision makers will be confronted with decisions that might be eased by the availability of some relevant information. We suggest that thought be given to where you believe you already have an adequate data base and also in what areas you do not. Planning for those decisions points before they arrive will significantly enhance your chances for establishing an effective CBE program.

We see evaluation as the gathering, analyzing, and timely reporting of needed information about the CBE program development and adoption processes in objective, orderly, and, when possible, quantitative form. Such steps will ensure that rational decisions can be made about program *development* and *adoption*. Summative evaluation is not excluded, of course, but program development and adoption should be a continuing evolutionary process with any terminal summative evaluation data being used as a basis for making decisions about subsequent changes. We have named this composite process—collecting and reporting data, making value judgments, and selecting a course of action—"data-based decision making."

The whole process of data-based decision making entails more than just collecting data. At least four major clusters of variables can be identified that comprise data-based decision making. The variables, their interactions, and the composite decision-making process are represented in Exhibit 10.2.

Although we are suggesting that decision making should be a rational process, probably the most influential cluster is that of the value and belief system that various involved individuals bring to the process. The implicit and explicit values and beliefs of the decision makers influence all other

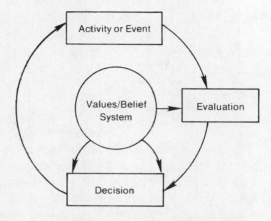

EXHIBIT 10.2   Data-Based Decision Making.

variables, such as the activities or events being considered, evaluation (data collection and analysis), and the decision itself. Values and beliefs affect a decision from the time that a need for a decision is sensed. The actual assignment of decision-making responsibility is normally based on the interests and perceived importance of the decision area rather than who is most qualified by experience, position of authority, or proximity to and knowledge of the problem. Values and beliefs also influence the evaluation activity itself. Although the evaluation may be carried out with complete objectivity, it is quite likely that the original decisions about which activities, events, and variables would be evaluated will be heavily laden with implicit and explicit values and beliefs.

As expert evaluators point out, the actual act of decision making legitimately includes a values-belief component as well as the summarized, relatively objective reporting of the evaluation data. It is at the point of making decisions that the most rational answer is not necessarily the best. However, the decision maker who has evaluation data will be able to make a more calculated decision and probably be more confident in his decisions than if the decision had been completely based on "gut feelings."

As is intimated in Exhibit 10.2, once made, decisions are fed back to the related activity or event (and sometimes others) as well as to the value and belief system. This adaptive process should be a regular operating component of program development and adoption. Deciding on which variables are most in need of evaluation, who will make what decisions, what feedback mechanisms are needed, and who will handle evaluation activities should be settled *before* program development starts. Then, through successive approximations and adaptations to events and data, the evaluation activities should be regularly adjusted.

Unfortunately, this seldom is the case. What seems to be more common is the complete absence of evaluation data to serve decision makers who are in the process of developing and adopting a CBE program. If an "evaluation" activity is ongoing at all during program development and adoption, it is probably one or at the most two quasi-rigorous research studies of a *comparative* nature to determine if, in fact, the students involved in the *first* CBE class are better than or at least different from the students in the "regular" program. Such global analysis of treatment effects resulting from a first trial CBE program is doomed to failure on at least three counts. First, the data are collected on students involved in an experimental program that will never be replicated. Second, the students will need to be followed for several years before any conclusive statements can be made. And third, the data that are collected will be of no assistance to the program developers during the process of getting through that first go-around and will not be available in time to help with decisions about the changes necessary before a second go-around is underway.

Organizing for Decision Making

Exhibit 10.3 is a representation of one way of organizing the decision-making process in a manner that lends itself to ease in handling the issues operationally rather than theoretically. We acknowledge that there are various levels of sophistication to approaching evaluation and decision making. What we propose here is a practitioners' approach, emphasizing those areas where data are most essential for success in CBE program building. The schema is eclectic, emphasizing crucial variables that affect both program development and program adoption.

The schema is organized around two basic dimensions. The first dimension deals with the stages of program development and adoption, while the second dimension categorizes decision areas. Hall (1973) has identified a series of phases that are involved in adoption of new teacher education programs. For our purposes, Hall's six phases have been consolidated into three major stages: (I) *Planning For,* (II) *Implementing,* and (III) *Maintaining* program development and adoption.

As for the second dimension, it is our basic assumption that establishment of a CBE program is not accomplished by a simple decision that "next September there will be a CBE program." Rather, establishment of a program is a developmental process with different issues being considered and decided at each stage. At least four decision areas can be identified: *Outcomes, Resources, Strategies,* and *Costs.*

Each of the matrix cells in Exhibit 10.3 contains some typical questions that need answering. In the Planning For stage, data are needed to predict what resources will be used and to plan how to most efficiently implement

EXHIBIT 10.3 Question Areas for Data-Based Decision Making

Decision Areas	Program Development and Adoption Stages		
	I. Planning for	II. Implementing	III. Maintaining
A. Outcomes Desired Occur	Student Faculty Institution	Why are we not getting what we want? What are the desired outcomes?	Does it look as if we are going to get the outcomes we want? What unexpected outcomes are we getting?	What outcomes are we regularly getting? What unexpected outcomes are we getting? What new needed outcomes have been identified?
B. Resources Have Need	Materials Facilities Skills	What resources do we have? What resources do we need?	Exactly what resources are needed? Will our resources support CBE on a regular basis?	What resources are now freed up? What unexpected resources are being consumed?
C. Strategies Instructional Installation		Which instructional strategy do we want to use? How should we implement? (Which adoption strategy? What training?)	Are the instructional strategies working? What changes must be made in the strategies? Is further faculty training needed? Will everyone be able to do his part?	How effective are the instructional strategies? How effective were the implementing strategies?
D. Costs (Personnel and Resources) Dollars One Time Time Resources Ongoing		How much is it costing to plan? How much will it cost to implement? Once implemented, what will maintenance cost be? How long will materials last? How much staff time to implement?	What is it costing to implement? What do the maintenance costs now look like?	How much is it costing to maintain? How much did it cost to plan for and implement this innovation?

275

the program. During the Implementing stage, data are needed about the actual implementation process and what effect it is having. Implementation data should also be compared with the Planning For stage predictions. In this way program decision makers can anticipate shortages or surpluses of resources or other unexpected changes. During the Maintaining stage, data are needed about the ongoing operation of the CBE program once it is established. Also, the exact planning and implementation costs can then be calculated and be available to others planning to implement a CBE program, as well as be of help in planning future innovative efforts. Several areas of important decisions have to be faced once a CBE program is institutionalized. There are bound to be some unexpected outcomes and expenditures as well as some unexpected gains. Also, the implementation stage probably occupied more resources than does program maintenance. If this is indeed so, then the newly released resources have to be targeted toward some other need, otherwise they are apt to be lost in the ongoing day-to-day activities, thus losing an edge for program renewal or other innovative activities in the future.

The remainder of this chapter is devoted to identifying existing data, data-collection procedures, and expansion of each of the four decision areas. Program developers must make the final decisions; having data and knowing how to get additional data quickly may help reduce the need for ulcer care due to making so many blind decisions.

OUTCOME DECISIONS

Ideally, nearly all decisions to change an educational program should be based on data related to outcomes. The entire program development and adoption cycle should begin and end with assessment of the outcomes being attained and comparison of these with the desired outcomes. Discrepancies between obtained and desired outcomes should serve as the trigger for change.

In appraising outcomes it is important not to limit the scope of the assessment to just those outcomes that are prespecified. Many unanticipated outcomes may be present. The concept of goal-free evaluation that Scriven proposes is important in assessing expected and unexpected outcomes. In addition to assessing student outcomes, it is also important to assess the outcomes being obtained in other areas, such as with faculty and the institution as a whole. If faculty are not learning and growing, and if the institution's goals are not being met or are incongruent with the outcomes being attained, then the probability is high that some changes are in order. Reappraising outcomes should continue throughout the total CBE program development and adoption process. Assessment of learning outcomes in a CBE program was discussed in detail in Chapter 3.

Throughout the program-development process the CBE program development team needs to be provided with benchmark information about outcomes. This information should not be presented as an indictment of failure or testimony of success, but rather should serve as a basis for refinement and redevelopment of the program.

Student outcome data can be readily obtained from module posttests, analysis of audiotapes and videotapes made in the course of completing enabling activities, and direct observation of performance in laboratory and field situations. As was described in Chapter 5, assessment instruments that are administered to children about their teachers also become a data source about student performance. Such nationally available tests as the California Achievement Tests can also serve a useful purpose, although cautions about "norm-referenced" test use must be remembered when assessing teacher effectiveness.

An additional check for each specified outcome is the obvious reporting of the proportion of students who are able to demonstrate the outcome before and at varying intervals following instruction. It is also helpful to relate these proportions to other variables that are of interest. For example, in field testing one set of self-paced materials, one of the authors found that students who were more self-assertive as measured on a standardized personality test did not achieve as well as did students who were more willing to follow directions and have a structure provided for their activities.

Outcome data about faculty and the institution may be a little more difficult to obtain and interpret, but they are also important. Here is an obvious illustration of where value and belief systems heavily influence what data will be collected as well as how they will be interpreted. Before outcome data can be collected in these areas, assumptions, goals, and objectives will need to be explicated. An example of misspent effort would be the analysis of the published program of the annual meeting of a national association as an indicator of the amount of national visibility that an institution has received for its work in CBE when the institution is primarily concerned about its regional visibility and more specifically what its state legislators think. Explication or at least careful speculation about the *real* assumptions, goals, and objectives of the faculty and institution should be undertaken prior to any data collection.

Assessing expected and unexpected outcomes of the program for the students, faculty, and institution should be a continuous cycle. Perhaps the day is not too far off when educational institutions will utilize a specialized group of people whose sole function is assessment of outcomes as a basis for deciding in what areas change and renewal are most needed. This department would have to move far beyond the much-debated instructor-course surveys and begin to assess what has really been learned rather than if students had a good time.

RESOURCE DECISIONS

The decision area involving resources should speak for itself; however, the observed practice in those institutions that receive modest grants to develop programs is that resources are consumed on an immediate-availability basis: while it is here use it; when it is gone something will happen to replace it or forget it.

Resource decisions should be made and anticipated at each stage. Inventory should be taken at the Planning For stage of what resources are available and what resources will be needed. These resources include (1) such *materials* as references, texts, paper for printing, test tubes, and overhead projectors; (2) such *facilities* as classrooms, conference space, computers for managing, field sites, and learning resource centers; and (3), most importantly, such *skills* as counseling, assessment, evaluation, computer programming, instructional development, and packaging.

Locating and effectively organizing these resources to develop and implement a CBE program is not a simple task. Developing and adopting a program based on an overestimation of the capability and extent of the resources will result in staff suffering from battle fatigue, malnourishment, and dejection. This is certain to result in a half-completed program, or one that requires a Rolls Royce budget when only a Volkswagen budget is available.

STRATEGY DECISIONS

During each phase of program development and adoption, decisions must be made about installation strategies to be used. Chapter 9 provides descriptive information about the day-to-day management decisions that will have to be made. Instructional strategies were discussed extensively in Chapters 2, 5, and 6. Decisions about these strategies will have to be both formative and summative. Data collected about outcomes will provide one source of data for these decisions.

In addition to assessing student outcomes, several more subtle questions need to be answered. For example, for each stated outcome that is present in a CBE program, a check should be made to determine if in fact there are enabling activities present to assist learners in attaining the stated outcome. For each outcome that is stated, a check should be made of whether the provided enabling activities offer appropriate practice (see Chapter 4) for the desired outcomes. Having outcomes specified for which no learning experiences are provided is a surprisingly frequent and disastrous happening.

Another area where information is needed has to do with the distribution of objectives and competencies within program components and across the total program. Based on the assumptions and goals of the program, an idealized balance should exist between cognitive, affective, performance, consequence, and expressive objectives. Once this idealized balance is estimated, a tally can be made of the actual distribution of existing objectives and competencies (see Exhibit 10.4). Obtaining these data is relatively simple, yet the finding can greatly assist decision making.

EXHIBIT 10.4   Distribution of Objectives across the Program.

Type of Objective	Phase I Expected	Phase I Actual Count	Phase II Expected	Phase II Actual Count	Phase III Expected	Phase III Actual Count	Phase IV Expected	Phase IV Actual Count
Cognitive	60%	40						
Affective	30%	3						
Performance	0%	2						
Consequence	10%	10						
Expressive	0%	5						
Total	100%							

Another area where regular data are needed deals with evaluation of modules as they are being developed. Information is needed about the amount of time the average student takes to go through the enabling activities, about points of confusion, information gaps, inaccuracies, typographical errors, and so forth. As a regular practice in some CBE programs, students are asked to make notes in the margins and on the backs of pages as they proceed through a module, highlighting points they believe should be brought to the attention of the module developer. To further systematize this process, a module feedback form of the type developed by Englehardt, Gouge, and Hall (1972) can be filled out by students after completing a module (see Exhibit 10.5). By building some parallel items on student and instructor forms, a cross-comparison can also be made. In addition, leaving space after each item enables respondents to add commentary to document their ratings.

Another form that has been of assistance, especially at the maintenance stage, is the simple computer card that is included inside reusable packages such as slide-tape programs (see Exhibit 10.6). These data provide feedback to the LRC staff about the present condition of heavily used materials.

EXHIBIT 10.5   Student Module Feedback Form (Post).

Instructions: In the items below, fill in the blank; circle "yes" or "no"; or place an "X" on the continuum in the appropriate blank.

1. How much time did you spend on the module? _____ hours.

2. How relevant was the topic of the module to you? (Indicate this by placing an "X" in the appropriate blank.)

Irrelevant _____ : _____ : _____ : _____ : _____ Relevant
                                        Somewhat

3. To what extent do you feel the pre- and posttests actually tested the material presented in the module?

Not at all _____ : _____ : _____ : _____ : _____ Completely
                                        Somewhat

4. How helpful was the information presented in the module toward acquiring the competencies described by the objectives?

Confusing _____ : _____ : _____ : _____ : _____ Very helpful
                                        No help

5. How useful were the "objectives" in learning what the module was trying to teach?

Detrimental _____ : _____ : _____ : _____ : _____ Useful
                                        No help

6. How appealing was the overall structural arrangement?

Distracting _____ : _____ : _____ : _____ : _____ Appealing
                                        No effect

7. How helpful were the pictorial illustrations?

Confusing _____ : _____ : _____ : _____ : _____ Facilitation
                                        No help

Please identify confusing or unhelpful illustrations and point out where additional ones are needed.

8. What is the overall level of vocabulary in this module?

Too general _____ : _____ : _____ : _____ : _____ Too technical
                                        Just right

9. What amount of information was provided in this module?

Too little _____ : _____ : _____ : _____ : _____ Too much
                                        Just right

10. In doing this module, how did you feel you were treated?

As a robot _____ : _____ : _____ : _____ : _____ Humanly

11. How much worthwhile information do you believe you learned from having had this modular experience?

None _____ : _____ : _____ : _____ : _____ A great deal
                                        Some

12. How enjoyable did you find this approach to instruction?

Distasteful _____ : _____ : _____ : _____ : _____ Very enjoyable

Indifferent

13. If you had your choice, what percent of your future instruction in this course would you like to have based on a similar module format?

_____ : _____ : _____ : _____ : _____ : _____

0%   20%   40%   60%   80%   100%

14. Did you have the background the module seemed to require?   Yes   No

15. Were you able to skip any sections of the module due to the results of the pretest?   Yes   No
    If yes, did you do it?

16. Did the objectives describe the most important things you could do after experiencing this module?   Yes   No

17. Does the module really teach the objectives it purports to?   Yes   No

18. Were there activity instructions or explanations that were unclear or misleading so that you were unable to proceed and required help?   Yes   No

19. Were there any statements that were inaccurate or inconsistent with respect to your previous knowledge?   Yes   No

20. In the "discussion of responses," were you satisfied with the answers given?   Yes   No

21. Were additional materials needed that were not provided?   Yes   No

22. Except for the pretesting, did the module provide for you as an individual?   Yes   No

23. In doing this module, did you feel a need for alternate routes?   Yes   No

24. How do you feel about filling out questionnaires?

Yuk (#*?@) _____ : _____ : _____ : _____ : _____ Yea

Take it
or
leave it

25. In the space below, please list any suggestions as to how this module might be changed or improved.

Thank you for your help!

RESOURCE EVALUATION AND UTILIZATION

COLLEGE OF EDUCATION   ●   LEARNING RESOURCES CENTER

We rely on each individual using this resource to advise us of its usage and condition. The evaluation is concerned with the quality of the sound and visuals, not with the content. All problems are checked and corrected.

THE NEXT STUDENT AND THE LRC APPRECIATE YOUR COOPERATION

1. Sound quality of resource?	( ) adequate	( ) a problem exists
2. Visual quality of resource?	( ) adequate	( ) a problem exists
3. Is anything missing?	( ) no	( ) yes (explain)

PROBLEMS: (use other side if necessary)

EXHIBIT 10.6

Courtesy of Joe Schroeder, Director of Learning Resources, the University of Houston.

COST DECISIONS

The last decision area, costs, is probably the most important in terms of its effects on the success or failure of any innovation adoption attempt. Do not construe this to mean that all it takes is more money to make an attempt successful. There are other important costs besides money, such as the personnel, time, facilities, and resources required to do the job. At the same time the above is not meant to discredit the importance and necessity of control over a supply of dollars to grease the effort.

Budgets of education departments and colleges are derived in a number of different ways. Seldom does an institution, however, really know how much it costs to certify one of the teachers or doctoral students it graduates. Budgets are usually developed around faculty salaries, graduate assistants, secretaries, materials, and perhaps some travel and other miscellaneous items, occasionally including some monies for media equipment or computer time. All of these figures are assigned to departments. To translate these budget items into instructional costs for an individual student is nearly impossible. The task is compounded because students receive instruction from several different departments and colleges, faculty may have had dual appointments, courses and faculty are not clearly budgeted by degree programs, and so on. These many imponderables make the tasks of predicting and estimating the costs of developing and implementing a CBE program about as reliable as using a crystal ball or a Ouija board. Some attempts have been made, however, and are offered here only as a starting point.

There is a stark absence of data about what it costs to implement and maintain CBE programs (or most other programs for that matter). Distinctions need to be made between one-time "tool-up" costs and ongoing operating costs. Not all costs can be figured in dollars spent. Costs must be tabulated in relation to time spent by faculty and students, as well as the number and kinds of facilities required. CBE programs appear to cost more, but how much more is not clear. In planning to establish and in implementing and maintaining a CBE program, a portion of the resources need to be assigned to obtaining these data, even if no other data are collected. Cost accountability is with us, and those who cannot provide a data-based report of what the returns are for dollars invested will have an ever-increasing problem with getting hard support to do the job.

In a comprehensive review of the effort of five state-supported institutions in the state of Washington to develop PBTE programs, Hite (1973) reports that it was a consensus that the prototype programs were more costly than the traditional programs. Hite has clustered the increased dollar costs around three factors: (1) the resources, manpower, and money needed for program development, (2) the program requirements for individualization of instruction, and (3) the involvement of added personnel, such as school faculty. Hite found that each of these cost factors accounted for about 50 percent of the estimated 150 percent increase in costs over the traditional programs for prototype PBTE programs. Following the initial development phases, he sees costs tapering off. According to Hite, through the use of a slightly heavier student-instructor ratio (18:1) and the use of a field-based supervisor who is a specially trained classroom teacher, the costs can be brought back into line with the costs of most existing programs. Some of the increased costs of materials and other equipment can also be offset to some extent by added income from the increased number of students per faculty member. Hite summarizes his findings thus:

> Initial PBTE budgets will be at least two and a half times standard teacher education programs. After a developmental stage of three or more years, PBTE budgets are likely to be comparable to such existing programs as student teaching, with the exception of providing active participation of teachers and other school personnel.

Hite's estimate of costs is based on five real-world attempts to develop operational PBTE programs. Idealized programs that are developed according to other theories and needs may dictate a cost overrun much higher than Hite's extrapolations. For example, it has been estimated (Burdin and Lanzillotti, 1969) that to fully implement any one of the USOE-funded Comprehensive Elementary Teacher Education models would cost $3 million to $5 million.

Other cost estimates range between these extremes. For example, Joyce (1973, mimeographed, 19 pages), in a paper exploring the various ways and issues involved for a state considering developing competency-based programs, compared the estimated cost of a highly skilled technical team developing and disseminating a CBTE system against having many local centers doing the work and then interrelating the results. Joyce carefully described the task, identifying the systems necessary for having a competency-oriented certification and training program and the organizations needed for creating such a program throughout an entire state. He placed heavy emphasis on computer storage and retrieval of information from assessments, instruction, and meditated components within a highly sophisticated management system. Joyce estimated that it would cost $5 million to $7 million for each local unit within a state to create its own complete system. Just the development of the computer management system was estimated at around one thousand dollars per student, with the most optimal sharing reducing cost down to around five hundred dollars per student. These estimates are based on creating an ideal system from scratch.

For instructional packages that have actually been through an entire research and development cycle, the information is not much more plentiful. The cost of developing one minicourse at the Far West Educational Development Laboratory, where specialized and relatively sophisticated teams are used, is estimated to have been over one hundred thousand dollars for thirty hours of instruction. Joyce also reports that the cost for developing six instructional systems at Teachers College, Columbia University, was slightly over one hundred thousand dollars, or about sixteen thousand dollars per instructional system.

If some of the above figures are anywhere near accurate (and there is reason to believe that they may be conservative), it is apparent that few CBE programs are going to be able to afford to develop the whole system beginning at ground zero. Nor should they. However, the other cost factors (time and facilities) are going to play an expanding role in the program development process, thereby contributing a new round of potential problems. When personnel are asked to continue to give out-of-hide, fatigue, resistance, and frustration are bound to increase.

Estimating and budgeting time and costing out the CBE program development process is badly needed for data-based decision making. One particularly useful system that merits discussion is that of Wallace and Witzke (1972), who have attempted to develop a monitoring system for large-scale programmatic research and development efforts that can easily be adapted to the needs of CBE program managers. The composite system has been named the General Accounting System, or GAS, and was developed to systematically monitor and estimate the time, resources, and dollar costs of R&D in order to have a data base on which to plan and cost out future R&D efforts. Using the entire system requires adjusting the budget reporting and purchasing procedures as well as enlisting the cooperation of the personnel involved.

Each member of the staff is asked to maintain a Labor Accounting Form (LAF) on which he reports the time spent on different tasks that are the major subdivisions of the project effort (see Exhibit 10.7). The kinds of activities that staff members might be doing are listed as work functions (see Exhibit 10.8). For each time interval—an hour, a half hour, or a quarter hour—a work function is assigned to a task. Each staff member categorizes his day's activities according to the agreed-upon work functions and tabulates the amount of time spent on a particular work function for a particular task. Based on these data, the average cost per man-hour of effort for one R&D center was estimated to be sixty-five dollars.

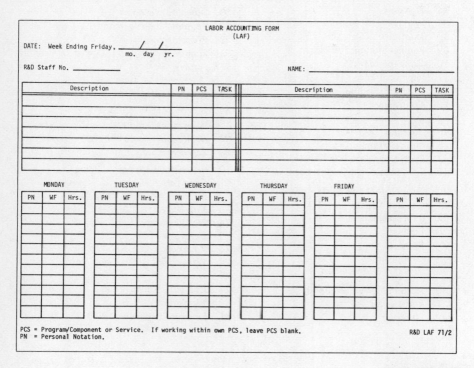

EXHIBIT 10.7

The GAS system can easily lead to paranoia. However, as our counselor friend Bob Ward notes, "It is not paranoia if they are really chasing you." If approached constructively, the resultant data of such a system can be of enormous help in planning future efforts as well as in determining present costs. One of the authors was involved in the use of the GAS for a year and a half and found that once the initial frustration wore off, the task took minimal time and the resultant data were educational, helpful, and, at times, rather alarming. It is amazing how your time *really* gets spent and

EXHIBIT 10.8 LAF Work Functions

Code		Code	
00	Non-R&D Center work	33	Forms Control
01	Meeting/Conference or Personal Interaction	34	General Secretarial/Clerical
		35	Inventory/Supply
02	Planning	36	Mail Handling
03	Proposal Review/Program Production Review	37	Scheduling
		38	Typing
04	Consulting	39	Personnel
05	Reading	40	Telephone Answering
06	Thinking	50	Data Processing
07	Writing	51	Keypunching/Verifying
08	TeleCon	52	Programming
09	Public Relations/Visitors	53	Remote Computer Terminal Operation
10	Correspondence	54	Analysis Review
11	Pilot Testing	55	Machine Operation
12	Behavior Coding	56	Research Design
13	Counseling	60	A/V Production Design
14	Data Coding/Protocol Scoring	61	Equipment Maintenance
15	Training	62	Equipment Operation/A/V Production
16	Budget Planning	63	Engineering
17	Data Collection and Review		
18	Test/Instrument Construction	70	General and Administrative
		71	Class-School
20	Graphic Art and Design	72	Holiday/Compensatory Time
21	Graphic Layout	73	Jury Duty
22	Reproduction	74	Personal Leave
23	Editing	75	Sick Leave
24	Proofreading	76	Vacation
25	Photography	77	Waiting for Assignment/Down Time
26	Visual Aid Production	78	Travel
30	Accounting/Bookkeeping	79	Computer Down Time
31	Bus Driving	80	Teaching
32	Filing	81	Student Conferences

how much that little job you take on just to help out costs in time, dollars, and resources. For example, during the period that the author was involved with the GAS he was also regional president of a small professional organization (six states and around one hundred active members with only one annual two-day meeting). Exhibits 10.9 and 10.10 summarize what it cost in terms of hours of secretaries, professional time, and hard resources for that modest and purely professional effort. If data like these were readily available, legislatures, upper level administrators of universities, students, and the public might have a better idea of how educators spend their time, dollars, and other resources.

EXHIBIT 10.9   Summary of Expenses on a "Minor" Job.

Four-Quarter Summary (January–December 1972)
Unit 42: Inter-Institutional Program
Task 102: Southwest Region Annual Meeting

Man-hours (1,957.5)	$7,778.27
Consultants	120.00
FICA	410.23
Travel (staff)	247.00
Travel (consultant)	24.35
Postage	58.43
Telephone	369.41
Conference expenses	12.68
Office supplies	69.67
Printed materials	3.08
Total	$9,093.12

In planning for, implementing, and monitoring the adopted CBE program, costs need to be projected, accounted for, and analyzed with regard to personnel time. This should be done not only in terms of how long it takes students to go through modules but also in terms of how much faculty, field personnel, and even maintenance personnel time is needed or is being used. The resources needed and spent should also be monitored, along with estimates and actual costs of one-time purchases and ongoing operational costs. With these data in hand future innovators will be much more able to predict costs and consequences.

All of this discussion is not meant as an overly hard push for highly sophisticated data collection and analysis systems. Much of the information can be gotten and handled quite easily. For example, data about the amount of time that students spend on a module can be obtained directly from module feedback forms. In one large-scale field test of a nationally acclaimed instructional module that had twenty-three single-track, self-paced enabling activities for twenty-three cognitive objectives, it was found that the average student was spending in excess of thirty-five hours of instructional time! With the information in hand, decisions were made about the relative economy of the material in mass marketing as well as whether the stated objective encompassed all of the important outcomes. In any CBE program development and adoption effort, much information can be obtained. The issue is to determine the most needed information, how to obtain it quickly and cheaply, and how to organize it so that it is utilitarian.

EXHIBIT 10.10 Breakdown of Man-Hours for "Minor" Job.

Second Summary (January–September 1972)
Unit 42: Inter-Institutional Program
Task 102: Southwest Region Annual Meeting

Work Function	Man-Hours	Cost
Non-R&D Center work	112	$ 560
Meeting-conference	100	500
Planning	10	50
Consulting	1	5
Reading	23	115
Thinking	10	50
Writing	10	50
Telecon	1	5
Public relations	5	25
Training	9	45
Data collection and review	4	20
Graphic art and design	2	10
Filing-reproduction	18	90
Forms control	1	5
General secretarial-clerical	357	1,785
Correspondence	13	65
Inventory-supply	2	10
Mail handling	6	30
Scheduling	14	70
Personnel	21	105
Telephone answering	4	20
Analysis review	24	120
Typing	19	95
General and administrative	335	1,675
Compensatory time	41	205
Jury duty	6	30
Sick leave	26	130
Total	1,174	$5,870

When Do We Do What?

Several criteria can be used in determining which evaluation activities should be undertaken and when. The following is a partial list of points that experience as well as theory suggests are important in prioritizing evaluation activities:

1. Identify the five (you probably cannot afford to collect data on more) crucial decision points that the program development-adoption effort will face during its first trial for measuring.

2. In subsequent trials again identify the five most crucial areas as well as retaining one or two from previous trials.

3. During the program implementation phase it is better to run several "quick and dirty" evaluation studies than one or two experimentally rigorous searches for treatment effects. (Even if you get any significant differences, more than likely you will not be able to clearly account for them or replicate the study.)

4. Evaluation studies need to be timed so that the data will be available and in a concise form when the decision point is reached.

5. Once the program is implemented, a systematic study of treatment effects is a must.

6. If you want to know, ask a direct, closed question. Highly sophisticated instrumentation is a luxury and not a replacement for the straightforward question.

7. If only one area can be evaluated, it should be *costs*.

8. Assessing needs and resources for program implementation during the planning stage is a must.

Evaluation Plan for One Program

The final exhibit of this chapter outlines an expansion of the schema and questions presented above. The exhibit was prepared by Loucks (1974) as an attempt to operationalize the ideas of this chapter for a specific teacher-training institution that was just beginning to develop and adopt a CBE program. Some of the specific questions and data sources should help illustrate and point out the simplicity that is possible in obtaining needed information for data-based decision making if some thought is given to it before the crises occur.

The evaluation questions in Exhibit 10.11 were developed as part of a design for evaluation of the Implementing stage of a particular CBE program. Notice, however, that the specific questions appearing under the heading "What Are Potential Sources of Failure?" apply equally well to the Planning For stage, depending only on when they are asked (before or after initial implementation). Questions appropriate to the Maintaining stage can be written as well, using Exhibit 10.3 for reference and elaborating on subjects and instrument type.

This design is an example of how a model posited by an evaluator (Stufflebeam, in this case) has been utilized for CBE evaluation. In the explanation of the design, Loucks (1974) notes several important features:

1. Stufflebeam's (1971) "process" evaluation, which is most useful

EXHIBIT 10.11 Evaluation Questions.

Global Questions	Sample Specific Questions	Subjects	Kind of Instrument
Total program	What is the quality of inter-personal relationships among staff and students?	Faculty Students Cooperating teachers	Questionnaire
	Are communication channels adequate?	Faculty Students Cooperating teachers	Questionnaire
	Do you always know what is expected of you?	Students	Questionnaire
	Do you know what other team members and cooper-ating teachers are doing with the same students?	Faculty	Questionnaire
	Do you know what students are doing in class?	Cooperating teachers	Questionnaire
	Are resources adequate?	Faculty Students Cooperating teachers LRC staff	Questionnaire
	Are more needed?	Faculty Students Cooperating teachers LRC staff	Questionnaire

Global Questions	Sample Specific Questions	Subjects	Kind of Instrument
	What materials are being used?	LRC staff	Questionnaire Materials use list
	What materials are not being used?	LRC staff	Questionnaire Materials use list
	Are physical facilities adequate?	Faculty Students	Questionnaire Observation *
	Are designated ones being used?	Faculty Students	Questionnaire Observation *
	Is staff adequate?	Faculty Students Cooperating teachers	Questionnaire
	Are there enough faculty members to meet student needs?	Faculty Students Cooperating teachers	Questionnaire
	Do staff members provide good models?	Faculty Students Cooperating teachers	Questionnaire
	Are staff members acting as guides, facilitators, discussion leaders rather than information givers?	Students	Questionnaire

* Observation in schools.
** Observation in seminars.
*** Observation in LRC.

Global Questions	Sample Specific Questions	Subjects	Kind of Instrument
	Is time schedule adequate?	Faculty Students Cooperating teachers	Questionnaire
	How are staff spending time?	Faculty Cooperating teachers	End-of-day reaction sheets given random days once a week
	How are students spending time?	Students	
	Are logistics being handled adequately?	Faculty Students Cooperating teachers LRC staff	Questionnaire
	Are materials available when needed?		
	Are organizational arrangements always worked out in advance?		
	Is LRC meeting needs?		
	Are participants satisfied in general?	Faculty Students Cooperating teachers	Open-ended questionnaire given once a week
	What specific problems are perceived?	Faculty Students Cooperating teachers	Open-ended questionnaire given once a week

Program components: *Is the program being implemented?*

Global Questions	Sample Specific Questions	Subjects	Kind of Instrument
CBTE/Modularized Instruction	Have the competencies been stated?	Faculty	Interview
	Are they public?	Students	Interview
	Do the competencies determine instruction?	Faculty	Interview
	Is the student assessed on attainment of competencies?	Students	Interview
	Are modules being used for instruction?		Observation **
	Are students using modules?	Students LRC staff	Interview Observation ** Materials use list
Faculty teaming	Do faculty share the same students?	Faculty	Interview
	Does the team meet to share planning?	Faculty	Interview Minutes of team meetings
Time blocking	Is student time blocked?	Faculty Students	Interview
	Is the time that is blocked used for instruction or related activity?	Faculty Students Cooperating teachers	Observation End-of-day reaction sheets

* Observation in schools.
** Observation in seminars.
*** Observation in LRC.

	Global Questions	Sample Specific Questions	Subjects	Kind of Instrument
Field based		Do the students spend the majority of time in the schools?	Students	Observation *
		Is instruction related to experiences in the classroom?	Faculty Students	Observation *
		Is time spent with children?	Students	Observation *
Total Program	What is actually taking place?		Faculty Students Cooperating teachers LRC staff	Observation * ** ***

* Observation in schools.
** Observation in seminars.
*** Observation in LRC.

in the Implementation stage, involves three steps: (1) delineating information needs, (2) obtaining information, and (3) providing information. The evaluation questions outlined in Exhibit 10.11 can accomplish the first step, but to be useful they must be determined by, or closely with, the program decision maker(s). Careful consideration must be given to exactly what information is needed, when, how often, and from whom.

2. It is important to look at each program component in order to identify which, if any, is causing a problem (see "Is the Program Being Implemented?"). Be sure to include all program components in the design.

3. People can be interviewed, observed, and asked to fill out forms to such a great extent that the information coming in is no longer meaningful. Be careful not to overburden any one source of information. Random sampling either of individuals or of questions responded to by each individual may be one technique for using questions that must be asked periodically.

11

a look at some exemplary programs

If I criticize others for re-inventing the wheel . . . I'm probably more interested in wheels than invention.[1]

Throughout this book we have looked at CBE as a *process* of development—a process that focuses on a constant feedback system for improvement. We have tried to present some theory and ideas about the movement that might be helpful to you in avoiding pitfalls that could hinder, hurt, or destroy your process, whether it be objective identification or total program implementation. We have made the point, however, that for some areas of concern, you are going to have to "invent" your own solutions.

To help reduce the amount of time you must spend inventing, we offer in this chapter some discussions of existing, total CBTE programs. The chapter is written by program development leaders from six programs now operating in different parts of the country. Each of the described efforts has been through at least pilot trial. The writers have been asked to describe some difficulties and successes they have had in their implementation. Specifically, the writers were asked not to focus on general theory of CBE but to look at the following questions:

[1] Conceived by Dick Barnhart in *Essentiasheet* No. 1, The Evergreen State College, Olympia, Washington.

1. What is the program philosophy? What are your major assumptions?

2. How did the program start? Was there financial support? How many students in pilot efforts? Who started the effort?

3. At the present time, what are the key elements of the program? What is it that program developers are most proud of?

4. What were the major difficulties encountered in building the program? What difficulties remain to be solved?

5. If you had to do it all over again, what would you change?

In the following six sections, each of these questions is answered by the program developer or developers in a specific way. Studying each of the sections should provide the reader with insights into valid and viable program development and adoption processes. Maybe some of the answers will fit questions that you are raising. In any case, the information might give you more time to invent solutions for your own unique problems by giving you a wheel or two to start rolling with.

Descriptions of the following CBTE programs are presented:

Nebraska University Secondary Teacher Education Program

Ward Sybouts

CHAIRMAN OF SECONDARY EDUCATION

The Nebraska Secondary Teacher Education Program (NUSTEP) is a competency-based program that is integrated into a block of time, modularized, team-taught, and field-based. It is a developmental process for improving the preparation program for prospective secondary school teachers. This program came into being partially as a result of several efforts to evaluate the quality of the undergraduate teacher preparation program. The results had generally been consistent: undergraduate students viewed the supervised student-teaching experience as meaningful and worthwhile; two-thirds of them expressed the opinion that methods courses were generally of value, although they were less enthusiastically received than student teaching. The view of other professional courses was less complimentary, to say the least.

The opinions of first-year secondary school teachers who had been graduated from the University of Nebraska were also reviewed by Moller (1968), who found that first-year teachers felt their background and preparation was inadequate with respect to motivating their students and devising meaningful ways to individualize instruction. Other follow-up studies had also provided similar results. Although much that was good was apparent in the preparation of secondary school teachers, there was clearly room for major improvements.

During the mid-1960s, a task force was appointed by the dean of Teachers College, University of Nebraska, to examine the status of teacher preparation and to recommend new approaches for consideration. The following school year a small group of staff members from the Departments of Secondary Education and Educational Psychology and Measurements began plans for establishing a pilot project for the preparation of secondary school teachers. By the second semester of 1969, the first group of 105 prospective teachers entered a pilot teacher education program that was to become known as NUSTEP.

The Larson (1970) study identified several factors as being the most influential in the formulation of NUSTEP:

1. Expressed dissatisfaction with the traditional undergraduate program.
2. Interest on the part of staff members at the university to improve the teacher education program. The fact that the project planners had a particular kind of product in mind influenced the development of the program.
3. Students were involved with the development of the curriculum.
4. By making available techniques and equipment, an inservice project for experienced teachers financed by the Mid-Continent Regional Educational Laboratory influenced the decision to incorporate microteaching into NUSTEP.
5. NUSTEP was financed by reordering the priorities of the Department of Secondary Education and reallocating personnel and materials. No major funding from outside the University of Nebraska was involved.

6. The course structure of the university had a definite influence on the planning process of NUSTEP. The faculty initiated change through existing courses.

7. A rise in enrollments caused curricular expansion and frequent shifts in curriculum emphasis.

Since the first pilot effort in 1969 (in which there were 105 prospective teachers enrolled from the areas of social science education, music education, and science education), the program has gradually expanded to include seven subject areas. In addition to the original three subject areas, the program now includes English education, modern foreign language education, speech education, and selected components of business education. There are continuing plans for adding additional subject areas as materials are developed and staff prepared.

Within the seven subject areas involved in NUSTEP, there has been involved a maximum of approximately 250 students within a given semester and as many as five staff members from Educational Psychology and Measurements and nineteen from Secondary Education. No single staff member was assigned exclusively to NUSTEP. Up to five public school persons have joined the university staff members on joint appointments during a given year, and literally hundreds of public and private school teachers have served as cooperating teachers working with NUSTEP students who were teacher assisting or student teaching.

Program Philosophy

A summary of the basic assumptions and the philosophical base upon which NUSTEP was founded is reflected in the following statement:

The purpose of the school in the American democracy is to foster the development of the capabilities of each individual in a direction and in ways that are both meaningful and satisfying to him and which will lead him to participate effectively, constructively, and on the basis of reason in society both today and tomorrow. It is anticipated that those persons who will be most able to work effectively in society will be those who possess a variety of problem-solving skills which enable them to deal with new situations on a rational, as well as a confluent, basis; who are able to be contributing members of groups; who demonstrate self-initiative; who possess a positive self-image; who are open to new ideas; who respect the rights and opinions of others; and who have acquired basic academic (e.g., reading, mathematical), vocational, and social skills. It seems reasonable to expect the years to come will be years of change. The task of the school is to prepare people for such change through the development of a commitment to inquiry within a framework of concern for both the individual and total welfare and the ability of society to use change in a positive manner.

Although the above summarizing statement is brief, it does contain the implications of many cultural, sociological, and psychological considerations that have an immediate and direct bearing upon the role of the school in our society, and consequently, the role of teacher preparation programs.

As the project staff worked to refine their plans, they set forth several assumptions that were basic to the program. First, the existing teacher education program would serve as the base from which the new program would evolve. Second, student involvement in planning was to be stimulated. Three values of student involvement were envisioned: (1) student ideas were of assistance and value; (2) it would furnish a climate conducive to learning; and (3) it would be an important role for future teachers to learn. The third assumption was that the program should be based on an integration of work in special teaching methods, psychology, philosophy, and the direct application of theory to practice. Finally, it was assumed that teachers in the future will work less as independent and isolated authority figures in the closed classroom and more as a member of a team in which they are involved in diagnosis, planning, prescribing, directing, and evaluating. In addition to these basic assumptions, it was recognized that the program to train teachers must be based on specific objectives that are performance oriented, in a program conducted by teachers who are capable of modeling desired behavior. In order to accomplish the desired outcomes, it was also recognized that a closer and different relationship would have to be built with local school districts in which a more active partnership would exist.

Characteristics of NUSTEP

Students spend approximately sixteen to twenty hours per week in NUSTEP self-instructional, lecture, laboratory, and practice-based activities. One-half of the student's time is spent as a teacher assistant working with a cooperating teacher in the public school settings. Students enroll in NUSTEP during the semester prior to student teaching and are usually second-semester juniors or first-semester seniors. The NUSTEP program provides a minimum of nine hours of academic credit through an integration of three separate courses: an educational psychology course, a subject methods course, and a general course in the principles of secondary education. To accommodate special interests of students, the NUSTEP block may be expanded through the use of independent study.

Materials provided in NUSTEP are arranged into criterion-referenced learning modules and are organized into three sequential stages, referred to as "spirals." The first spiral consists of general learning activities that incorporate basic instructional and psychological principles necessary—in the judgment of the NUSTEP staff—for successful teaching, regardless of subject area. Spiral II activities focus upon the application of skills and principles learned in Spiral I to the specific area of subject-matter preparation in which the student is to be certified for teaching. Spiral I and Spiral II modules are closely integrated so that there is a progression from learning concepts that are general in nature, then relating or applying them to a given subject area and finally testing them in the teacher-assisting and the student-teaching experiences. One or two paperback references are used, but, at this stage of its development, most of NUSTEP's materials are produced by the staff and are printed locally.

Instruction is provided on campus or in learning centers in public school buildings via lectures, small-group discussions, and task work. There is also extensive use of mediated materials, programmed learning activities with the NUSTEP materials, the utilization of individualized learning contracts, and a variety of other approaches. The large-group instruction that does remain is provided on a team-teaching basis; all instruction is planned by instructional teams. Each student also works closely with a single staff member who serves as a proctor for his activities. Microteaching, small-group sessions, and a high level of interaction between staff and pupils are involved. Reliability of proctor assessment of student competence is being validated by the use of the students' performance during student teaching. As the program has developed, there has been a growing emphasis upon monitoring student performance in practice settings through the use of performance contracts. The student, his proctor, and the cooperating teacher from the public school have been involved as equal partners in this process.

Upon the completion of the NUSTEP semester the prospective teacher has been phased into the student-teaching experience. The teacher-assisting activities that are a part of the NUSTEP semester have been highly successful in helping the prospective teacher perform according to the NUSTEP model and move into student teaching with a much higher degree of readiness than was experienced in previous teacher preparation programs (Walter, 1973). The contribution teacher assisting has made in terms of demonstrated competencies, and with regard to moving students into the student-teaching role, is one more illustration of the importance of integrating the various components of the competency-based program.

Some Other Things

NUSTEP has nothing that is new. It has, however, brought together many elements in a CBTE format and integrated them in a way that seems to be making progress. While the utilization of a block of time in which the integration of subject matter, practice, and application is fostered is not unique to NUSTEP, it has been a major emphasis of the program. Instructional materials for NUSTEP were developed by the staff and tailored to fit the specific needs of a group of students in a given institution. Perhaps the NUSTEP staff has one other unique designation—they have probably made more mistakes than most CBTE developers since they have been at it longer than most. They are risk takers and are encouraged never to commit the sin of omission by doing nothing.

The things about NUSTEP of which its developers are most proud have never been formally identified. However, there are some program characteristics that may be worthy of comment. The fact that NUSTEP has been in operation since the second semester of the 1968–69 school year, which makes it one of the oldest programs in existence, and that it was done with minimal funds from outside the regular institutional funds marks it as somewhat unique. The staff is pleased with the results that have been achieved in the short time NUSTEP has been in operation, i.e., (1) Students in NUSTEP tend to demonstrate the competencies prescribed in the NUSTEP model of instruction significantly more than prospective teachers who went through the traditional sequence of courses (Francke, 1971). Student teachers who had experienced NUSTEP and first-year NUSTEP graduates used a wider range of teaching strategies than did traditionally trained teachers (Hughbanks, 1971). (2) NUSTEP students demonstrated an improved self-concept and a much-improved attitude toward their training program when contrasted to students in traditional programs (Kelley and Walter, 1971). (3) Pupils taught by NUSTEP student teachers did better, according to Francke (1971), than pupils taught by student teachers who experienced the traditional sequence of courses. While the Francke study needs to be replicated, it did demonstrate an interesting research application to this area of assessment while it gave preliminary findings to support the contention that the program was moving in a positive direction. These three broadly defined areas of program achievement have been a source of encouragement to the NUSTEP staff.

The relationship with the public and parochial schools has been enhanced by the field-based element of NUSTEP. Strong support is given by administrators and cooperating teachers in public schools. A variety of staff utilization patterns have been accomplished, ranging from simply using cooperating teachers to work with teacher assistants or student teachers up to joint appointments for clinical professors. The public schools have been very supportive and have made numerous and significant contributions to the NUSTEP program.

Major Difficulties Encountered in NUSTEP

No one who enters the process of developing a CBTE program will find a bed of roses. Resources, time, lack of materials, tradition, lack of experience, insufficient research, resistance or attack by resisters or laggards are all items encountered by the NUSTEP staff. Typically, university reward structures do not foster change and the entire system of higher education militates against moving ahead at times. Such frustrations become the daily bread of CBTE program developers.

After several years of operation many problems remain. Staff members can get "burned out" physically and emotionally. Once the Hawthorne effect is gone, as is now the case with NUSTEP, it becomes necessary to carefully design renewal strategies into the process. Evaluation, or the lack of it, remains to hover over the program. Program assessment is an absolute essential and yet it is hard to find the needed resources to accomplish it. A design is currently being developed that is intended to take into consideration learning that (1) is in the cognitive domain, (2) is in the affective domain, (3) reflects demonstrated performance, and (4) is also able to consider consequence objectives. All four categories of learning are then to be considered at various levels that encompass (a) pre-assessment, (b) process feedback, (c) exit or performance criteria at selected points, and, finally, (d) follow-up of graduates. A two-way grid with definable cells is currently being used to plan for future process and product evaluation.

Time and resources are continually overtaxed when developmental and operational efforts must progress simultaneously. Software for CBTE was not totally available from commercial sources or from other institutions. Much of it had to be locally designed, developed, tested, and produced. A staff must, however, recognize that all elements of a CBTE program will not be instantly achieved or acquired. As the program develops and matures, the students and staff will move closer to the specified goals and polish and gradually perfect the process. There seems to be no formula for instant achievement or success.

If Money Grew on Trees . . . and We Could Start Over

To say what could or should have been done differently is somewhat speculative. However, by looking at some feedback there are several indicators that stand out. These include: (1) more inservice training is needed for public school teachers who are to be involved with teacher aides or student teachers, (2) more emphasis is needed on a management and communication system with public schools, (3) more careful attention must be given to internal management systems, and (4) greater emphasis must be placed on developing multiple and mediated options. Actually, all of these items would have been less of a concern if the feedback and evaluation system had been more adequate. Assessment demands a place of high priority.

There are innumerable problems when going into a CBTE program. A staff must develop an attitude that recognizes problems will occur regularly and at the same time recognizes that problems can be solved when people focus attention on "solutions" rather than dwelling on the "problems."

Weber State College Individualized, Performance-Based Teacher Education Program

Blaine P. Parkinson

DEAN, SCHOOL OF EDUCATION

Weber State College is a four-year liberal arts college, with about 8,000 students. Teacher training has been one of the strong departments since WSC attained four-year status in 1963. Between 200 and 300 students are certified in Elementary and Secondary Education each year; this, 500 to 600 students are enrolled in the program. The Individualized, Performance-Based Teacher Education Program (IPT) has been in operation since 1970 and is the only program for certification at the college.

Like many teacher educators, we were discouraged with our track record and concerned with the knowledge that trained teachers didn't seem to perform differently from teachers who hadn't had teacher education. We began to accept the notion that a knowledge of how to teach doesn't necessarily change teaching behavior. Five assumptions emerged as we discussed possibilities for change in the teacher education program.

First, we felt if a technology of teaching did exist, it certainly was not evident, nor was it likely to be known if teacher education and its related approach to research were to continue unchanged.

Second, a new model seemed to be demanded—a model where the focus was on teacher behavior. While there are several reasons for such a focus, the basic reason would be that attention to teacher characteristics and teacher knowledge has not proved productive, yet a program based on teacher consequence would not seem justified in terms of our present knowledge, training, and research skills.

Third, it seemed wise to move from the known to the unknown. We knew independent study was effective; we knew that performance objectives could be clearly specified and training programs set up to achieve them. We felt that human-relations skills were teachable. We felt that because no teacher education curriculum had been validated it would be logical to begin with the present curriculum and change the delivery system to one based upon known, successful practices that would be self-correcting. A validated teacher curriculum, of necessity, must proceed through a series of trials and modifications.

Fourth, we thought it was wise to specify a given set of teacher competencies for all to acquire, rather than to give a choice, for the latter would make it impossible to tell the effect of a certain competency on the behavior of learners. We knew that this would not stereotype a teacher nor prevent him from developing his own style of teaching. It was apparent, also, that an individualized, modularized program significantly increased the necessity of self-selection and self-direction, but it is in the process rather than the product.

Fifth, we recognized the usefulness but also the weakness of a pilot program. Pilot programs often give rise to an unhealthy competition between the pilot and the regular programs, resulting in a less than objective evaluation of the project. It is often thought of as the project director's program, and tends to be evaluated on issues that are not central to the project. It was felt that a program representing such a dramatic change needed full attention of all the faculty and students for an extended period of time to work out the bugs and give it a chance to mature. Our evaluation four years later is that this was one of our wisest decisions.

The project began out of a desire of one faculty member to modularize the educational psychology courses. This initial desire mushroomed until it included the majority of the faculty, with full support from Elementary and Secondary Education, the dean of the School of Education, and the academic vice-president. This solid support was one of the significant factors in the success of the program. Through a series of discussions, first with the faculty, then with public school people, the state Department of Education, and faculties across campus, the idea matured into a plan for a totally new teacher education program. Even though some of the faculty at first were not totally committed to the idea, they were willing to cooperate in the hope that a better teacher education program could be effected.

A grant was subsequently received from the Carnegie Corporation of New York that provided resources to give the total faculty of fifteen released time for a period of nine months to develop modules. During the summer prior to the development work, a committee consisting of the faculty of teacher education, representatives from the public schools— both administrators and teachers, students, and faculty from other schools on the campus agreed upon the basic framework and content for the program. While the committee members from outside teacher education didn't give extensive new input, the public relations payoff of this group was inestimable.

Self-instruction units called WILKITs are used by students in the program. A WILKIT may require from five to thirty hours to complete and carry one-half to one quarter-hour credit. Registration is by blocks of complimentary WILKITs with up to fourteen quarter-hours credit.

Students register for blocks of WILKITs at the beginning of each quarter. However, they may start work on WILKITs any time before or after registration, upon payment of a small fee for the WILKIT and the use of the books in the library that support the WILKITs. They may check out the WILKIT at any time during the quarter. If, at the end of the quarter they have completed the WILKITs in the block, they are given a grade of "CR" (credit). If they have not completed the WILKITs by the end of the quarter in which they register, they are given an "NC" (no credit) on their transcript and must re-register for the block in a subsequent quarter. If a student does not pass a test in a WILKIT, he simply recycles and tries again; there is no failure. There has been absolutely no negative feedback from students relative to the credit–no credit grading system. On the contrary, we have found much support for the system. It eliminates the "grade game-playing" and the pressure and unfairness of the traditional grading system.

The above approach was instigated after a period of time during which we gave a student up to a year to complete the work begun in any one quarter. We found this merely encouraged irresponsibility and procrastination and was not liked by the students. The present system allows adequate flexibility for the average student, and an extension can be given if there is justifiable reason. It cut down the number of noncompletions markedly and does not seem to violate the concept of open time.

In the Secondary Education program of thirty-three quarter-hours, there are about twenty-five WILKITs in addition to one full quarter of student teaching. In the Elementary Education Program of forty-two quarter-hours, there are about fifty WILKITs in addition to student teaching. Teacher education is taken during the junior and senior years, along with other college work.

Students are required to schedule a block of WILKITs in one of three optional hours. Even though there is no class to attend, there are many seminars, films, public school experiences, and checkouts where scheduling time is needed, if the students desire.

We have established an Operations Center that serves as the nerve center for all activities. The Operations director is responsible for scheduling faculty conferences, seminars, films, or other learning activities upon student demand. Objective tests are administered and scored, and student records are maintained. It has become a meeting place, lounge, and study area for students, as well as a "security blanket." It provides the essential continuing contact with students that is lost when there are no regular class meetings. It has proved effective in building cooperation and esprit de corps among students as well as an identity with the program.

The Interaction Laboratory is a unique human-relations training program. It was developed to Weber State College specifications by a division of Thiokol Chemical Corporation of Ogden, Utah (Thiokol, 1973). It is a group experience with twenty-six ninety-minute exercises. The laboratory is experimental, but structured to teach essential human relations skills. Groups consist of about fifteen students with a trainer and a co-trainer. A session usually has a short activity followed by group discussion on its implication for teaching. The Lab has functioned remarkably well. Students say it's the most significant experience they have had in college. They not only feel good but can articulate concepts they have learned. The Lab builds a lot of positive affect, a lot of trust and openness with people. It's established a new student-faculty relationship at Weber State College.

As one might expect, the role of the faculty has changed greatly. A full-time faculty is required to indicate to the Operations director twenty-four hours of each week in which students can be scheduled with the faculty for seminars, private conferences, or individual checkouts. The rest of the faculty's time is spent in revising modules and in other routine campus duties. It appears that the expense for the IPT program is slightly more than that of the traditional one. Even though the faculty appear to work harder, they like it better and say they would never go back to the old system.

We found a remarkable acceptance of our graduates by the public schools. The placement rate continues to be extremely high. Principals and teachers continually comment that our students have skills that student teachers and first-year graduates didn't have in the past. This fact also impresses the faculty, as does the observation that the students now must be self-starters, must plan ahead, initiate activity, and, in general, take responsibility for their education. The students say they *have* to know or be able to perform in order to get through the WILKITs. Many have said they have had to learn to read. While they complain of too much work, there is a general acceptance and approval of the new program among students and a conspicous absence of the old complaint that teacher education is "Mickey Mouse," too theoretical, or not relevant.

In the 1972–73 academic year, four of our regular faculty, along with an evaluation specialist, spent nine months evaluating the teacher education program (Parker, 1974). Evaluation was at three levels. First, they did a technical evaluation of the modules, subjecting each element of the WILKIT to a standard and checking the Learning Experiences and tests against the Objectives. At the second level they gathered data from students going through the program on both the modules and the general program operation. At the third level they gathered field data on the performance of the students, both from our graduates in the field and from cooperating teachers, principals, and faculty supervisors.

A great amount of data has been accumulated and is being used to make program modifications. The data from all levels of the evaluation gives strong support for the new program. However, it is expected, after appropriate revisions are made, that the internal quality of the WILKITs and some operational functions of the program will be improved markedly. Evaluation will continue after revisions and other developmental phases of the program are completed. At that time, it will be appropriate to make more direct comparisons of our graduates with the graduates of other programs.

Surprising to many of the faculty, one of the major problems as we began the developmental work was reducing all the "good things" we had been teaching students to Objectives, highly directed Learning Experiences, and appropriate tests. This experience verified for us that we truly had been in the folklore stage of education and were just now struggling at the beginning of the scientific stage. Other problems were in changing the grading system to credit–no credit and the accounting procedure for faculty time to a student credit-hour average arrived at by dividing total student credit hours by the number of faculty. Library and bookstore rules also had to be rewritten.

We avoided conflict with the College Curriculum Committee and the State Department of Education by simply saying we were teaching the same curriculum as previously approved but were just delivering it in a different way, thus avoiding the problem of new course and program approval.

The first quarter we found that the time requirements for the students were excessive, and we had to cut approximately one-third out of each module. We were fortunate to be able to meet the greatly increased demand for public school experiences due to the efforts of a fine Laboratory Experiences director and receptive public school systems.

A program to utilize an outside consulting group to develop better tests for the modules did not prove workable. Possibly consultation on-site to help our faculty do the work would have been better. We also developed an observation system for in-class objective evaluation of teacher behavior but are not using it due to the complexity of the approach, as well as the fact that it does not give a direct enough measure of student performance on specific competencies.

The IPT program proved ineffective for night school and for inservice, not because of the model, but because the program was developed for a campus population, with the intent to utilize the faculty maximally. Any block of WILKITs may require several faculty to service. The model would lend itself well to evening school or inservice, but the program would have to be written for these groups considering the constraints of time, materials, and personnel.

The major problems in the development and implementation of the IPT program have been: (1) establishing the appropriate field setting in the public schools where our student teachers could apply the skills they have learned in the modules and receive appropriate evaluation and feedback; also (2) the development of the performance assessment instruments to allow either our faculty or the cooperating teachers to do the assessment and give the feedback. The reasons for our not doing this have been time, money, know-how, and public school cooperation. We now have plans for this phase and will soon proceed to accomplish it.

In thinking of how we would do it if we had it to do again, the first impulse would be to have a team of expert writers do the bulk of the writing, with input from the area specialists. This approach suggests both a saving of money and a better quality product. On second thought, however, by having each faculty member, including the administrators, struggle with WILKIT development, a commitment not only to supporting the program but to making it work was gained that may well have offset any waste. This suggests that while there appears to be no need for each school to rediscover the wheel, building a successful, viable PBTE program will require involvement, commitment, and cooperation along with some sound, basic philosophy.

University of Toledo

Richard E. Ishler
ASSOCIATE DEAN, COLLEGE OF EDUCATION

The University of Toledo's CBTE program is predicated on the philosophy that the preservice teacher who completes the program will be prepared to employ teaching behaviors that will help every child:

1. Acquire the greatest possible understanding of himself and an appreciation of his worthiness as a member of society.
2. Acquire understanding and appreciation of persons belonging to social, cultural, and ethnic groups different from his own.
3. Acquire, to the fullest extent possible, mastery of the basic skills in the use of words and numbers.
4. Acquire a positive attitude toward school and toward the learning process.
5. Acquire the habits and attitudes associated with responsible citizenship.
6. Acquire good health habits and an understanding of the conditions necessary for the maintenance of physical and emotional well-being.

7. Acquire opportunity and encouragement to be creative in one or more fields of endeavor.

8. Understand the opportunities open to him for preparing himself for a productive life and enable him to take full advantage of these opportunities.

9. Understand and appreciate as much as he can of human achievement in the natural sciences, the social sciences, the humanities, and the arts.

10. To prepare for a world of rapid changes and unforeseeable demands in which continuing education throughout his adult life should be a normal expectation.[2]

These goals were considered within five contexts. Behavioral objectives were written that would help the preservice teacher attain each. The contexts were:

1. Instructional Organization
2. Educational Technology
3. Contemporary Learning-Teaching Process
4. Societal Factors
5. Research

Each context was further divided into major subjects and topics, and eventually more than 2,000 behavioral objectives were generated. These objectives, after refinement during a feasibility study, became the nucleus of our present competency-based programs.

The specific stipulations upon which the University of Toledo's CBTE programs are based are:

1. The program requires the development and utilization of individually guided education techniques.

2. Elementary teachers are prepared as specialists in one field and as generalists in three other major curricular areas of the elementary school.

3. Teachers are instructed by and taught to utilize the most recent technological and media innovations.

4. The program applies operant conditioning as well as practices dictated by developmental psychology as appropriate.

5. The program requires an awareness of, and appreciation for, the differences existing in society today.

[2] Adapted from a statement on educational goals prepared by the Committee on Quality Education for the State of Pennsylvania.

6. Teachers in the program are expected to assess the effect of their own teaching behavior and style.
7. The program incorporates various levels of experience in order to approximate more ideally the realities of teaching.
8. The public schools serve a vital part of the teacher education program.
9. The university must be changed in ways conducive to the needs of the program and these must precede other activities.
10. Teacher preparation is continuous.

Background of the Program

During the fall of 1967, the University of Toledo, in cooperation with a consortium of the twelve state universities in Ohio and with support of USOE, designed a model elementary teacher education program. This design effort lasted for eight months and resulted in a CBTE program that consisted of the development of instructional modules for the following six target populations:

1. Preschool and prekindergarten teachers
2. Elementary teachers, grades one through six
3. Paraprofessionals
4. Inservice elementary teachers
5. Administrative personnel
6. College and university personnel

Since the original model was developed, it has been expanded to include the secondary program. Currently *all* undergraduate students at Toledo are enrolled in one of several CBTE programs. Each of the University of Toledo's CBTE programs consists of three major components:

1. Career Decisions
2. Professional Year
3. Student Teaching

Career Decisions is a two-quarter, eight-credit-hour program required of all students entering the College of Education. This phase of the CBTE program was implemented in the fall of 1970, with all freshmen (approximately 800 students) who entered the college.

Career Decisions is designed to provide the students with experiences that will enable them to decide whether they wish to pursue a career as a teacher. The student spends two hours per week on campus in small-group classroom instruction and one hour in large-group instruction. In addition, he is required to spend one-half day per week in a related field experience.

Career Decisions is competency-based, modularized, and team taught. The faculty teams serve as teachers and undergraduate advisers. The adviser relationship continues after the student completes Career Decisions until the junior year when he is reassigned to an adviser from the professional year staff.

The *Professional Year* component is the heart of the Toledo CBTE program. Elementary majors take four eight-quarter-hour "courses," and secondary majors take twenty-two quarter-hours (ten quarter-hours one semester, twelve quarter-hours the other). All "courses" are modularized and self-paced. The fundamental principle that underlies the progress of the student through both of the programs is that achievement, not time, should be held constant. A student may work as rapidly or as slowly as he chooses, but he cannot progress to the next module until he has demonstrated competency at the prerequisite stage.

Each course and set of modules is field-based and every effort is made to ensure that what is introduced on campus relates to actual practice. An in-depth experience in a school setting where the student can demonstrate the competencies is required for each set of modules. At the elementary level all field experiences are in multiunit schools, since that program is specifically designed to prepare teachers for that type of school organization. At the secondary level, students are assigned, if possible, to schools that employ team-teaching strategies.

The use of traditional course numbers and credit allocation is observed in order to provide the university registrar with information compatible with the system for recording credit. Currently letter grades are also given for the successful completion of the modules. The faculty wishes to move to a pass-fail system of grading as soon as it can be arranged within the university structure.

Students who do not complete the modules are "recycled." When they fail to complete repeated modules and encounter difficulty with several modules, they are generally counseled out of the program. Currently about 90 percent of all students successfully complete all required modules.

A sixteen-quarter-hour *Student Teaching* experience culminates the CBTE programs at both the elementary and secondary levels. Since the field-based professional year modules give the student opportunities to engage in activities that are normally reserved for student teaching, the student's final laboratory experience (student teaching) more closely approximates that of a regular teacher. He becomes a fully functioning teacher, diagnostician, and decision maker.

Criterion-referenced checklists have been developed to evaluate student teacher performance. These criteria include the terminal performance criteria of the modules that have been taught prior to the student teaching experience. The final determination of whether the student has met the criteria is made by the cooperating teacher and college supervisor on the basis of data collected using the common criteria.

There were approximately 200 elementary student teachers and about 350 secondary student teachers enrolled in the student-teaching modules during the 1973–74 school year.

At the Present Time

The following elements are distinguishing characteristics of Toledo's CBTE programs:

1. Students begin their CBTE program in the freshman year with career-decision opportunities.
2. Total programs are taught by interdisciplinary teams.
3. Elementary students are prepared specifically in and for multi-unit schools.
4. The programs are totally competency-based and there are no alternative programs.
5. The programs are governed and controlled by the College Instructional Improvement Committee (CIIC) which is composed of the dean, team leaders, and department chairmen.
6. Faculty members model the behaviors they expect the students to acquire in the program.
7. The teacher center serves as a vehicle for school university development and revision of the CBTE program.

Program developers are proud of all of the above and the following:

1. The CBTE programs have been developed, by and large, by the faculty working cooperatively with the dean's office.
2. The CBTE programs have been fully implemented without outside funding.
3. Students who are enrolled in the programs have been putting pressure on professors in other colleges within the university to make their objectives and criteria public. We hope this will be the beginning of the development of a competency-based general education component of the program.

Plans for Following Up on Our Graduates

We have a brochure from our Educational Placement office that indicates to prospective employers that our students have been trained in a competency-based program. This has been a successful device for attracting recruiters to our campus to interview our students. A college-wide committee is working on an elaborate follow-up system to determine from employers whether students trained in the CBTE programs perform better on the job than did the graduates of the old program.

Difficulties Encountered

The major difficulty encountered in developing the programs was how to involve all faculty who would ultimately be required to teach in the CBTE program. Due to the dynamic leadership of the dean, the faculty finally determined that they had best help shape their destiny, and they worked diligently and far above and beyond the call of duty to develop the programs.

The following are areas in which we are still seeking answers:

1. What are *the* skills and competencies that are most important for teachers to have?
2. What are the generally agreed-upon knowledge, performance, and product criteria essential in CBTE programs?
3. How are the criteria identified?
4. How are the criteria evaluated?
5. How do you assess teaching behavior and pupil learning?
6. How can a CBTE program in all its complexity be managed?
7. How can the program be best evaluated and by what criteria?
8. Are we preparing *better* teachers in our CBTE programs than the ones we trained in the old program?

These, we believe, are not insurmountable problems. We have developed an extensive evaluation model that will aid us in acquiring the answers to these and other questions. Additional funds and time are needed in order to make the evaluation design operational. We believe that our present implementation efforts are merely our best approximation of the ideal program which was originally designed. Though a series of successive approximations we will ultimately reach the ideal. In the meantime, we continue to strive for it.

If we were to go back and redesign our CBTE program based on what we have learned, there would be very little changed. The stages we went through were important because the program needed to evolve as the faculty's program and not a curricular design laid on them by the administration. Those who are ultimately going to be affected by decisions must be involved in the decision making. Such was the case of faculty involvement in the development of the University of Toledo's CBTE programs.

The Fowler Drive CBTE Program at the University of Georgia

William Capie

DEPARTMENT OF SCIENCE EDUCATION

Competency-based teacher education (CBTE) began at the University of Georgia in 1968 with the development of a program model for preparing elementary teachers. Although specification of program characteristics and feasibility studies were funded by the U.S. Office of Education, implementation was not supported. As a result, implementation is not complete and many of the functioning components operate differently from the methods proposed in the Georgia model.

Implementation, begun at the completion of the feasibility study in 1970, took two simultaneous paths. On one hand, many departments involved in training elementary teachers began specifying goals in performance terms and developing modular training packages. Some departments, such as reading and mathematics, were supported in their development efforts; others, such as science and social studies, were led only by the interests of key faculty and/or graduate students.

Concomitantly, the Division of Elementary Education was initiating a series of field experiences to augment the existing program of study. Four phases of experiences were proposed. Experiences I–III involved groups of about twenty undergraduates enrolled in blocks of courses and assigned to a faculty team and a local school for ten weeks. The team had complete control and flexibility in planning a program for students. Experience IV was a student teaching experience. Students remained together (in a block) only one quarter before moving to a different field experience, faculty team, and school. The desire for more continuous experiences and growth of the CBTE concept led to the development of a pilot program for the 1972–73 academic year. A team of thirty juniors, thirty seniors, twelve university faculty, and approximately forty teachers representing two Athens, Georgia, schools were assembled. That team expanded to approximately 100 students for the 1973–74 year. In addition, key faculty members from the original team were encouraged to initiate two more teams involving another 100 students during the 1973–74 academic year. This summary is devoted to one of the new teams, centered at Fowler Drive Elementary School in Athens.

Assumptions

Shearron and Johnson (1973) identified five assumptions implicit in Georgia CBTE efforts. They are that—

1. most of the competencies needed by teachers can be specified and assessed;
2. teacher education should be field-centered;
3. there will be no significant increases in budget for teacher education;
4. a teacher education program should serve as a model for effective teaching; and
5. teacher education is a joint responsibility of the public schools, state education agency, and teacher preparation institutions.

In addition, all three Georgia programs focus on the development and demonstration of those teaching skills assumed to promote pupil learning.

In establishing a new CBTE team, much concern was devoted to defining the focus of the program. Two kinds of decisions were made. First, teacher roles were described: diagnostician, counselor, planner, manager of the learning environment, and custodian of children. Equipping teachers to fill these roles became the goal of the team. Secondly, practical management decisions reflected the assumption that many deviations from the "ideal" may be necessary in the initial implementation phase. Several examples follow.

Initial enrollment was restricted to forty-four students. This number was sufficient to justify two full-time equivalents of faculty time. In order to keep the faculty team small (and manageable) students with common course needs (as defined by the state-approved program) were recruited. First-quarter juniors were sought so that their official training could start from scratch. The intention was to allow individual differences to produce variations within the group rather than create variability by recruiting students at various levels. It was anticipated that forty new students, several faculty, and the faculty, staff, and pupils of a new school could be incorporated into an existing structure at the beginning of the second year.

One more early management decision was related to numbers. The team was assigned to a small school with only fifteen teachers. Placing all interns in the school at any one time was not feasible. Consequently, interns were rotated into the school causing parallel programs to exist for subgroups within the program.

Distinctive Features

While various management features are unique to this one program at Georgia, significant differences among groups are evident. In our team, for example, the small faculty team has been able to work together quite effectively. During the first quarter, the team appeared to lose ground in many areas, particularly individualization through modular instruction. This caused us to shift to a group-delivery model. The temporary sacrifice of individualization has resulted in greater understanding of respective programs and points of view. Modules are now reappearing along with much more diagnostic testing. The new organization could not have emerged had previously existing components been assembled without the initial exploratory effort.

Beginning with students of one level has enabled the team to focus its efforts. The long-range view has expanded to include four distinctive experiences—*the professional decision, creating an effective teacher-learner encounter, building curriculum,* and *an intensive internship.* The effectiveness of early portions of the model is attested to by the decisions of several interns to major in special education or library education after exploratory internships with appropriate professionals on the team.

Teachers and interns continue to make significant contributions to deciding how and when and what will be taught. While the student still enrolls for blocks of courses, the combinations are different from other programs and none of the courses has retained its original format. *Most* are team planned and taught.

Other distinctive features of the program include emphasis on the human elements. Advisement is kept personal by limiting the number of advisees assigned to each staff member. The role of the advisor extends from signing of computer registration forms, through monitoring field experiences to hand holding when things get tough. Terminal experiences are monitored by a committee consisting of the student, an advisor chosen by the student, a cooperating teacher, and at least one other team member. Thus, the burden of decision making is committed to a group that is well-informed about the intern's capabilities. The human element is fostered in other ways, as well. Counseling and communications training form an integral part of the program (Shearron and Johnson, 1973; Gazda et al., 1973). In addition, student input into program planning has been sought by making students on the steering committee co-equal with university and public school personnel.

One of the strengths of the CBTE program is the impact on school programs and children. The nature of the school changes as more adults are added to the instructional team. More groups of children appear in the halls and media center. Projects abound. While there may be a limit to the number of adults that might be desirable in a school, CBTE has not reached it. Extending the instructional program of the local school is a role for university faculty as well as interns. Their role has extended from demonstration teaching and informal faculty room "inservice" to providing leadership for major curriculum change as in the adaptation of a new science curriculum.

Some Successes . . . Some Failures

The overriding difficulty in establishing a program at the University of Georgia is coping with diffuse lines of decision making. Responsibility for teacher training lies primarily within the College of Education, but art education and music education are part of the College of Arts and Sciences. In the College of Education, more than ten departments are involved in training elementary teachers. Each must be represented whenever students enroll for course credit in that department. Most cannot assign faculty to a team unless students are enrolled in a departmental course. Consequently, care must be taken to budget student credits carefully in order to justify continuous staff assignments.

In addition to interdepartmental problems, Georgia has a variety of "service units" that are involved in teacher training. For example, the Department of Professional Laboratories coordinates field experiences. Therefore, a decision to expand to two schools necessitates their involvement. An Office of Student Personnel Services is a nerve center for student records, requesting course offerings, and various other services. The Elementary Division and The Elementary Advisory Council make policy decisions about programs in elementary education. In short, a CBTE program at Georgia assumes a portion of the responsibility of each of these institutions, the responsibility of communicating with each of the various departments, and the responsibility for controlling forty to 100 undergraduate interns.

Fortunately, the relationship between the Division of Elementary Education and the Clarke County Schools is strong and open so that school negotiations are not a severe problem. Like the university, the district is a complex institution. Delays are most pronounced in both when major decisions such as doubling program size are contemplated. Most decisions involving schools can be made locally once a trust is established between CBTE team members representing both institutions.

Higher-level concerns involve establishing mechanisms for identifying competencies, appropriate indicators, and valid evaluation systems. While it may seem that a CBTE program cannot become operational without complete goal specification, competency specification is a dynamic process that continues throughout the life of a CBTE program. It may be that concern for competency specification does not arise before resolution of lower-level management concerns. Speculating about the changing nature of concerns gives rise to questions about changes in the role of a program coordinator. A program coordinator at Georgia is a generalist who may be expected to serve as administrator, seminar leader, clinical supervisor, counselor, instructional leader, etc. A difficulty facing any CBTE operation is determining if the leadership qualities and style desirable in initiating a program are compatible with complete implementation or sustained operation.

State University College of Arts and Science at Geneseo, New York

Patrick J. DeMarte
ASSISTANT PROFESSOR AND DIRECTOR OF CBTE

The saga of CBTE development at the State University College of Arts and Science at Geneseo can be described only partially. It is an unfinished story of many forces and factors coming together to reach crescendos of fulfillment and the depths of despair on the road to the first pilot trial. This story begins in the fall of 1972, when the Division of Educational Studies critically examined the existing teacher education program and explored alternative models of teacher education. Preservice teachers and collegiate faculty came together in a series of open meetings to discuss common concerns and prospects for future programs.

Two distinct but not separate groups emerged from these meetings: faculty who would take a major role in developing a comprehensive, elementary and secondary, competency-based teacher education program, and faculty who would not wait for proper faculty action to make certain changes in already existing programs. The latter acted first and, in the next semester, developed and implemented a performance-based, modularized format for the two introductory courses in the elementary education sequence. This new development, along with an existing performance-based secondary social studies program, were precursors of the pilot CBTE program scheduled to begin in the fall of 1974.

A third force in this development was a mandate from the New York State Education Department that all certification programs be competency-based and field-centered. The latter provided both motivation and political leverage, though it is only fair to say that the need for change was recognized by the faculty and students alike long before this mandate and that our experience likely would have suggested CBTE. The speed (and ultimately the institutional support) for such an undertaking were strongly influenced by the impending mandate.

Fait accompli would best characterize the method used to create the competency-based, modularized sequence of elementary education courses. In only two months, ten faculty completely designed and operationalized a program for 524 students with little more than moral support from the administration of the Division of Educational Studies. No resources or time was allocated for this revision. Countless hours were volunteered to meet the herculean tasks of rescheduling 524 students into sixty modules, revising (jointly with campus school teachers) the actual prepracticum classroom experiences, readjusting their schedules to meet students' demands for modules, and developing a method of evaluation that was consistent with the performance standards of the modules. Together these represented a dramatic deviation from the traditional instructional format and were possible because this group decided to team teach these courses. Under the shield of academic freedom, this courageous group bypassed official procedures for program revision and within one semester had their innovation "on the books." With one exception, none of the fears held by these individuals regarding this unorthodox method of innovation would have serious repercussion. (The only exception applied to a change in grading.)

The other precursor was the secondary social studies program. Unlike the revised elementary education courses just described, the social studies is a complete certification program and is not modularized. The program involves three courses: two introductory courses blending foundations, active participation in public schools, and methods and a Professional Semester that incorporates methods, measurement, and evaluation, and a seminar into the student teaching experience.

Evaluation of the Pilot

Faced with the need for preparing a proposal for faculty consideration, two faculty members spearheaded the development of a comprehensive, elementary and secondary, competency-based teacher education program. Early in the spring of 1973, while the rationale, goals, and assumptions for the proposed program were being written, the New York State Education Department released a set of "guidelines" for the submission of CBTE proposals. One of these guidelines called for parity between four groups that were to be involved in the development and implementation of any CBTE program: teachers, school administrators, teacher education students, and college faculty. We had already been working with several committees of teachers and administrators from area schools, so there was little difficulty enlisting their support to work on this proposal. A representative group was immediately convened to meet the parity requirement. This group met regularly to consider the rationale, goals, and assumptions set forth for the program, as well as to generate "global" competencies that would act as organizers for more specific performances to be demonstrated by the teacher education students.

In April 1973 a proposal was submitted to the Division Curriculum Review Committee for recommendations. After two lengthy sessions the proposal was passed on to the Division faculty. Again it took two meetings to gain acceptance of this proposal "in principle" and to support further development over the summer, with the proviso that the proposal be resubmitted to the faculty in the fall or before further action.

At this point our efforts were joined by the Science Teachers Association of New York State Trial Project (STP). This was one of twelve projects funded by the New York State Education Department (NYSED) to develop CBTE programs, following the process standards set forth by NYSED in a working paper, "A New Style of Certification" (Division of Teacher Education and Certification, NYSED, 1971). By fall 1971 the Science Trial Project was operating under a strict voting parity of the six agencies involved (school boards, teacher bargaining units, teacher education students, collegiate faculty, STANYS, and a local scientific society), and by the spring of 1973 had succeeded in developing a master set of objectives for teaching science in the secondary school, and "competencies" for teaching science in the secondary school.

STP was, at this time, ready to begin production of self- and instructor-guided modules to assist teacher education students to meet the "competencies." Two faculty members from SUC Geneseo, who were very active in the development of CBTE at Geneseo, were members of this project. This dual membership permitted a bridging of interests. Since both groups were ready to enter the module-preparation phase and the STP group had identified generic as well as specific "competencies," a summer workshop was planned to gain the mutual benefits of each other's experience and budgets.

Eighteen persons worked together in the summer workshop: twelve teachers, three teacher education students, and three collegiate faculty. Over a six-week time span (two weeks of preplanning, three weeks of intensive writing and rewriting, and one week of cleanup) thirty-eight modules were written, edited (by peer review), and rewritten. This experience, as it turned out, was the most enlightening and rewarding in the prepilot development. It was proved conclusively that educators with real diversity could agree on what was important for teacher education and plan a program.

Minimal financial support for this workshop was provided by the following agencies: SUC Geneseo—for three collegiate faculty and two campus school faculty, STP—for seven teachers, and Rockefeller Brothers Foundation, through the Livingston, Steuben County BOCES—for three teachers.

The Rockefeller Foundation money was the remnant of seed money granted to investigate regional CBTE development. Students volunteered their time, and if they *desired to pay,* could earn three credit hours for their experience.

Before the proposal was resubmitted to the faculty in the fall, we had confronted and were able to provide reasonable answers to the most difficult questions relating to implementation: FTE, faculty load, staff, facilities, and credit hours. It became apparent at the faculty meeting that opposition to the proposal stemmed principally from a belief that an untested program was being "railroaded" in to replace the existing program. A compromise motion to "pilot" the program was approved by a vote of sixty-seven to one, with two abstentions.

The next phase was largely political and involved meetings with leaders in the various academic departments on campus to "sell" the program. Four months of political maneuvering culminated in gaining approval of the Faculty Senate for this pilot program on March 19, 1974, one-and-a-half years after the initial meetings. One major compromise was required to gain this approval: instead of a thirty-credit-hour program for both elementary and secondary certification, the faculty would agree to only twenty-four credit hours for secondary certification. This was offset by the acquisition of five of the six credit hours of educational psychology traditionally taught by the psychology department. Under this new arrangement the psychology department teaches a one-credit module developed jointly by faculty from psychology and education.

Although the majority of work done for this program has come out of "hide," the Division of Education Studies did provide two faculty three hours of released time per semester and support for five persons to participate in the first summer workshop. Funds have been allocated for another summer workshop and to hire a full-time director for the project. However, additional support will be required to implement the program as planned. A proposal has been made to the Department of Health, Education and Welfare for funds to defray certain costs of implementation and dissemination. With the possibility of outside support being very slim and with budgets "cut to the bone," funds will be a continuing problem.

Goals and Assumptions of the Proposed Pilot

The primary goal of this program is to develop and examine a sequential, integrated program of expected "competencies" to be demonstrated by teacher education students.

In terms of the individual, the ultimate goal is to produce teachers who are students of human behavior, self-renewing and capable of rational decision making.

More specifically, the program strives to:

1. Maximize and optimize the candidate's involvement in "real-world" educational situations and experiences by employing differentiated strategies and various alternatives on and off campus.
2. Integrate theory and practice.
3. Individualize and personalize instruction based on continuous diagnosis (by self, peer, and instructional specialist's assessment) and prescription of teacher education candidates in terms of their needs and "competencies."
4. Develop a parity between college and public school personnel responsible for teacher education.
5. Identify professional personnal at all levels capable of demonstrating competence and of guiding teacher education candidates toward attainment of that same or greater competence.
6. Set the basis for teacher certification on teacher competence rather than total reliance on college courses.
7. Make public, in advance, to the teacher education student the objectives and "competencies" to be attained for certification and/or a degree.
8. Place the responsibility for attaining competence on the teacher education student.
9. Develop means of assessing teacher competence in terms of observable and measurable performances.
10. Develop a system of management that enables the student and all other agencies involved to keep track of student progress.

This program is based on many fundamental assumptions about learning, formal education, teacher education, and a teacher education program. The scope of this section does not permit a complete listing of these assumptions.

Some of the key assumptions are that:

Learning is personal and idiosyncratic, while formal education is deliberate and systematic.

Formal education is responsible for performing particular specialized tasks that ultimately facilitate the development of the independent learner capable of using independent judgment.

Teacher competence once identified can be learned (and, alternately, can be taught) in a deliberate and systematic manner under the direction of professional educators.

Teacher education students entering and continuing in teacher education proceed through a sequence of describable, observable, and measurable series of concerns: about self, about self as teacher, and about pupils.

A teacher education program can assess the teacher education student's competence, using his performance as the primary source of evidence.

The process of implementing change is normally a slow and arduous process. This need not be so. Change, it was discovered, is actually much easier than often assumed or admitted. When ten faculty members became a "group" and decided to make changes, a synergy developed from which a renewed sense of power emerged. While this group was aware of the possible consequences of taking such action, both in the formal and legal sense and in the informal sense, a feeling of confidence stemmed from the belief that the results were professionally sound and in the best interest of the students. The significance of this "fait accompli" method is that it works! This program was accepted by the administration and our professional colleagues and has been in operation for three semesters. Considering that this represents a radical departure from the conventional two courses it replaced, and was accepted, it seems as though this is a reasonable alternative for implementing change.

Attacking a mainstay of the institution will cause problems. One issue that did stir some administrative concern was that of grading. It is possible that a tactical error caused this to become so volatile an issue. To adopt a model for evaluation that was consistent with the philosophy of the program and with the belief that evaluation, not grading, was best for the students, a pass-fail system in which passes were converted to A's was used. This was an intermediate step prior to gaining approval for a genuine pass-fail system for these two courses. However, the proposal was shelved when the administration of the Division of Educational Studies withdrew support for the proposal and asked that it be withheld until the CBTE proposal was approved. Since the scheme for converting passes to A's was made public to the administration and the students before the semester began, this group decided to proceed as planned. It was not until final grades were in that the administration acted. Although no official action was taken, the administration voiced strong disapproval of the grade distribution for these courses. The procedure for determining grades ultimately reverted to a more traditional grading procedure; students could earn B's as well as A's. The concession was made, not only because of the expressed concern from the administration but because of new additions to the teaching team and a recognition that the grading issue had been made. Continued "violation" of the established grading policy would serve little or no purpose.

No doubt this confrontation could have been avoided by taking a more moderate position from the beginning or by persisting and going through faculty governance procedures. Vindication came three semesters later when the CBTE proposal, employing the pass-fail system of grading, was accepted without comment.

Since CBTE and modules are synonymous in the eyes of many, a few words about our experience with modules are in order. Perhaps the most valuable learning experience resulted from implementing the modules, inasmuch as we learned:

1. that students have difficulty integrating modular experiences without contact, on a regular basis, with each other and an instructor in a situation where they are asked to organize and synthesize these experiences into a holistic framework.
2. that preassessment and counseling are vital.
3. that evaluation, in order to be meaningful, must be nonjudgmental and the emphasis shifted to the student in conjunction with peer and instructor evaluation.
4. that actual classroom experiences are an absolute necessity and that these experiences must be guided by persons who are aware of the entire teacher education program and the nature of the students in it.

Communication and articulation with all persons involved in teacher education are critical factors in the field-centered program. During the first semester in the field, situations arose where a student's difficulties were partially due to the fact that the cooperating teacher did not understand the intent of the program. This created the need for a tremendous amount of additional time and emotional energy for the field supervisor, and certainly, much anxiety for the teacher, to mention nothing of the student who ultimately suffered most. Some teachers became very apprehensive and were reluctant to participate further.

Teachers willing and capable of participating in the training process must be identified. This, it seems, would require nothing more than that cooperating teachers be given the opportunity to clarify their roles as teacher trainers. This may occur from inservice training, or better yet, from active involvement in program development. Internalization of the program and its goals is a *sine qua non*.

Placement of student teachers for the Professional Semester continues to be a real problem. Since the number of placements for the Professional Semester is limited, certain teachers must be repeatedly involved. Aside from the problem of oversaturation, the ability to adequately reward these teachers has become a dilemma. Most of the cooperating teachers already have a master's degree and the standard tuition voucher is of little value and will no longer suffice as remuneration.

This problem will prevail until contractual arrangements for teaching centers are established. The teaching centers would offer opportunities for more and different kinds of rewards, in addition to a place for preservice teacher training and inservice teacher renewal.

The process of developing and gaining approval for this pilot was unusually difficult. The original program outline, which took some five months to write, was submitted to our professional colleagues and accepted "in principle." This may have been a backhanded rejection, but it did permit further development that widened the circle of participation. For the first time college faculty, teachers, and preservice students enjoyed a genuine, cooperative, intense relationship for three weeks identifying performance and assessment procedures for the "Core" of the program.

Buoyed by the experience and possessing more answers than available previously, we reintroduced the proposal to our colleagues. But the "roof caved in." Our colleagues criticized the "lack of theory," the tendency to produce "technicians," the willingness to allow "incompetent" teachers and administrators to make decisions regarding their futures, and the "political pressures" incumbent upon us to develop CBTE. We were regarded as quislings; at the very least, naive. We were abdicating a responsibility that had always been borne by our institutions.

Meetings with colleagues were characterized by divisive, rancorous debates; by charges of "railroading," playing "political games," and jeopardizing students' futures; and by resort to parliamentary tactics to further or retard decision making. Ammunition was provided by some education deans who had petitioned state officials to rescind deadlines for submission of programs and even the mandate to develop CBTE programs.

Thus, we have been subjected to many of the criticisms that plague developers of new programs. However, the critics seem more vitriolic in the case of the CBTE program development. It appears that this type of program, more than others, touches raw nerves (DeMarte, Harke, and Mahood, 1974).

Parting Remarks

While the controversy over CBTE continues to rage, the developers here viewed this movement as an opportunity to make significant changes in our teacher education program. Since a wide variety of perceptions exists as to what CBTE is and what it means, there are, as one would expect, an equal number of teacher education programs claiming to be competency-based. It seems important to keep in mind that only local solutions to program development are meaningful. However, it is not necessary to "re-invent the wheel." We begged, borrowed, and, well, I hope we didn't steal to come up with a rather unique model for teacher education that fits our institution.

We are looking forward to implementing this comprehensive CBTE program. An extensive evaluation design has been prepared, along with modules for instruction and a design for implementation which includes the establishment of teaching centers. Only time will tell if, as James Koerner (1973) predicts, only a "mild meliorism" has occurred.

Brigham Young University Five-Phase Program

Garry R. Hardy and Vern J. Wade
DEPARTMENT OF ELEMENTARY EDUCATION

Brigham Young University is the largest (25,000 students) private institution of higher education in the United States. The College of Education is one of the largest colleges on campus, graduating in excess of 1,000 students each year. Teachers who have received their training at BYU presently teach in every state and in a number of foreign countries. Probably the societal impact of no other group of graduates from BYU would exceed that of the graduates of the College of Education.

There has always been high faculty concern within the Department of Elementary Education at BYU for a quality product. Constant feedback in the products of the program has been received for years. It was this feedback on which the decisions were reached to remodel the program.

In the early 1970s, a survey revealed that public school administrators and teachers as well as students who were a part of the program indicated that the existing program:

1. Contained components that failed to relate to the "real world" of teaching.
2. Contained courses that were redundant.
3. Tended to "lock" students into teaching. By the time some students realized that they were not compatible with the "real world" of classroom teaching, it was too late to change careers without being severely penalized in terms of time and money.
4. Did not provide time for sufficient, meaningful student-professor interaction.
5. Did not provide career and guidance counseling.

It was apparent to our faculty that to resolve these problems, minor modifications of our traditional program would not be sufficient. It was determined that what was needed was a fresh, innovative approach to teacher education.

The following strategies were employed to develop the Five-Phase Elementary Education Program at BYU:

1. Departmental faculty meetings were scheduled for exploratory discussions.
2. New and innovative programs from across the nation were reviewed.
3. Public school teachers and administrators were actively involved in the planning process.
4. Faculty members from other departments and colleges on BYU campus were contacted relative to their concerns about teacher education.
5. Education students participated in surveys and group interaction sessions focusing on program development.

Major Assumptions Underlying BYU's Five-Phase Elementary Program

From the process described above, five major assumptions were generated:

1. Teacher education can modify the prospective teacher's teaching behavior.
2. A majority of teacher education candidates are able to develop acceptable teaching behaviors. However, economy of time, effort, and money for the students as well as the institution suggests that certain candidates might better pursue other career opportunities.
3. Field experiences early in the teacher candidate's program are critical to rational career decision making.
4. Public school personnel have meaningful contributions to make in the design and operation of an effective teacher education program.
5. Awareness of self and acceptance of others are essential to effective teaching.

The Program

Out of a synthesis of the data gathered five logical and sequential components evolved that we felt were necessary for selection and training of effective elementary classroom teachers. These components are:

PHASE I—EDUCATIONAL EXPLORATION. This is a two-credit-hour course usually taken during the second semester of the freshman year or first semester of the sophomore year. Educational Exploration consists of approximately seventy-five hours of in-class activity and provides a two-fold thrust: (1) an examination, by the student, of the teaching profession focusing on the evaluation of self as a potential teacher, and (2) provision for the faculty and counselors to use these relevant data to assist the prospective teacher in making rational career decisions.

Data gathered on the basis of 1,200 students completing the Phase I course indicate that at the end of Phase I approximately 15 percent of the students elect not to continue in the program. Data are presently being analyzed to identify reasons for deselection. However, instructors of the courses do report that most of the students who deselect make the decision because they feel that they would not be happy teaching or have awakened interests to other areas.

PHASE II—TEACHER ASSISTANTSHIP. This is usually taken during first or second semester of the sophomore year (eight semester hours). In order to describe this phase there are three terms that need to be defined:

1. Center school—public elementary school to which twenty to twenty-five teacher assistants have been assigned.
2. University coordinator—a full-time BYU faculty member assigned to a center school for preservice and inservice teacher development.
3. Teacher assistant—a prospective teacher who has completed Phase I and has been assigned to a center school.

During this phase the prospective teacher spends one-half day (8 A.M.–12 noon) for a full semester in a Phase II center school. This experience focuses on the student's developing basic competencies with children.

Functioning as a teaching assistant the student is provided with two seven-week experiences. During one of these experiences the student is placed in a primary-grade classroom and during the other in an intermediate classroom. During concurrent seminars the university coordinator provides instruction in learning theory, child development, and rudimentary generic teaching skills. The classroom provides students with opportunities to observe and/or apply concepts developed in seminars with the university coordinator.

The student who does not demonstrate the required competencies and/ or the student who voluntarily deselects may do so and receive less than the prescribed eight semester hours awarded for successful completion of this phase. Entrance to the college of education and continuation in the five-phase program is contingent on completion of Phases I and II.

PHASE III—METHODS AND STRATEGIES. This is usually taken during the second semester of the junior year. This is an on-campus, eight-credit-hour phase consisting of instruction in generic teaching skills as well as "methods" competencies: reading, language arts, math, science, and social studies. Simulations such as peer teaching, microteaching, and videotape feedback are used as enabling activities and assessment devices.

An important factor in this phase is that instructors model the specific techniques and/or behaviors that they expect students to master.

Another important element of Phase III is the instructional laboratory. Lab instructors help students achieve mastery of competencies and are responsible for the evaluation of specific performance objectives. This allows the student some freedom in pacing himself through the phase.

During Phase III a tentative student teaching assignment is made. This assignment enables the student to prepare during Phase III for his student teaching which takes place the following semester.

PHASE IV—STUDENT TEACHING. This is taken during the senior year. This phase is an eight-week, eight-credit-hour experience taken either half of a given semester. The student is assigned, with eleven other students, to a center school for this experience. The university supervisor, a full-time university faculty member, is responsible for no more than two center schools during a given block. Close clinical supervision allows more individual attention and evaluation of specific competencies assigned to this "real world" experience.

PHASE V. This is taken during the senior year. The final phase of the program is campus-based and consists of approximately twenty one- and two-semester-hour modules. Each student is required to complete eight semester hours to consummate the phase. Three specific modules (four semester hours) are required allowing the student to select modules that make up the remaining four hours. If a need is perceived, it is possible for an instructor of a previous phase to suggest or even require a student to complete specific modules that will better prepare the student for effective teaching.

Modules offered deal with advanced methods of teaching and include language arts, reading, math, science, and social studies. Other modules offered provide instruction in instructional media, education values, learning theory, and classroom management.

Key Elements That We Are Proud Of

1. The program was pilot-tested and is fully operational.
2. Funds expended in program development were minimal.

3. Program design allows for
   a. Early entrance (second semester, freshman year).
   b. Early field experience (sophomore year).
   c. Early career decisions.
   d. Minimal penalty for deselection.
4. Excellent rapport and cooperation with public schools.
5. Students are provided with professional as well as career counseling.

Major Difficulties Encountered in Building the New Program

1. Maintaining our traditional program while designing and operationalizing the new program.
2. Faculty members reaching a consensus concerning design of the new program.
3. The philosophy and operation of the Five-Phase Program required adjustment in course offerings to be made by departments outside the Department of Elementary Education.

If We Were Doing It All Over Again

1. Include in the design of the program a comprehensive data-gathering subsystem.
2. The timely demise or retirement of certain selected faculty members (only kidding, guys).
3. A more systematic approach to program development might have reduced expenditure of time and effort by the program designers.

12

a student's reaction to CBE

In Chapter 11 several program developers focused on their projects. Most of these reports were derived from the perspective of the developers and in only a few was mention made of the reactions of students. In this chapter a student who has completed a CBTE program reflects on his experiences.

The program that Bruce Thompson completed was the first experimental effort at the University of Houston. After a year of development in which some eight faculty and staff members theorized and built instructional materials, sixty-four students began a program designed to produce effective teachers who would be "rational decision makers" and "students of human behavior." Through Bruce Thompson's view of CBE, the reader will be able to gain insight into the Houston effort.

A Student's View of CBE

Bruce Thompson

Despite all the discussions of CBE program development and implementation, despite all the activity and the philosophizing on the causes and consequences of CBE, only a little attention has been given to the reactions of those students for whom the approach was designed. The following is my attempt as a former student in the University of Houston CBE program to speak directly about student evaluation of CBE.

This report is not an attempt to evaluate the abstract philosophy of CBE. True, such judgments may at times be implied by comments on the practical realities of one CBE implementation. Nevertheless, the emphasis here is on portraying some of the thoughts and feelings that evolved out of one student's actual CBE experiences.

Program Recruitment

I first became aware of CBE during the spring of my sophomore year. Late in the semester, I received a brochure describing the CBE concept. The brochure indicated that the University of Houston would soon implement a pilot program that utilized the approach. Should I be interested in hearing more about the pilot program, I could attend a meeting that would provide a more detailed preview of things to come.

I was immediately receptive to the idea of entering the program. It was not that I knew anything about the philosophy of CBE. Nor did I know any of the faculty involved in the project. But I did know that I wanted to teach. I knew that to be certified to teach I would have to take education courses. And I knew that when it came to education courses, "different" inherently meant "better."

My prejudice against education courses had grown out of discussions I had had with many people. Both high school teachers and older teacher education students seemed to agree that education courses generally were "Mickey Mouse" and "busy-work" in nature. Even my liberal arts academic adviser had contributed to my stereotype. He advised that I take my education courses as soon as I could, because other required courses would improve while I passed my time in these.

I went to the meeting described in the brochure to hear more about the pilot program. We saw a brief slide-tape presentation on CBE. We were told that CBE assessment was criterion rather than norm referenced. We were told that modules rather than classes would be the vehicles for our instruction. And we learned that we would work more in the field-experience sites than would the non-CBE students.

The concepts presented in that meeting did not gel in my mind until much later. It was only clear that my competence rather than the passage of time would dictate when I would be certified to teach. This assessment procedure was attractive to me, because I felt that I would fast become a very able teacher.

Staff members cautioned us that this was an experimental program and did not guarantee a problem-free atmosphere. However, we were then told that, if we still wished to enter the program, we would have to be interviewed by a faculty member. We would be accepted or rejected on the basis of this interview. I signed up for an interview.

My interview surprised me. It was not very structured. In essence I was asked to build a case as to why I should be accepted into the program. Why did I want to teach? I want to teach because I believe I can teach well, and because I care about learning. What could I offer the program? I can think. I can articulate my thoughts. I am a good leader. Not long after my interview I received word that I had been accepted into the program.

One other impression I gleaned from these experiences seems noteworthy. During the explanatory meeting the faculty members sat dispersed among the students. During the interviews, the faculty members asked to be called by first name. The faculty were clearly making special efforts to relate with us. I felt a little disoriented. How do you be friends with a faculty member? Was the desire for friendship genuine or ulterior? During my initial interactions with faculty, I felt a little awkward.

The Retreat

Actual participation in program activities did not begin until one week before fall semester classes started. Most of the sixty-four students who had been accepted into the program gathered in a large conference room on campus. We then took a variety of personality tests.

I had very mixed reactions toward being given these tests. I had studied and heard about such tests, but I had not taken any since my freshman year in high school. I was curious about what the tests would reveal. On the other hand, I did not understand how these tests related either to teaching or to the program. Did I have to answer in certain ways to remain in the program? Not being told the purposes of the tests alienated me. It was some time into the semester before we actually learned what the tests were all about.

The tests took three hours to complete. After the testing period we all drove out to a Catholic retreat house. The retreat house was simple and conducive to meditation. It was located in an area heavily wooded with pine trees. Each person had a single room. None of the rooms had locks. The rooms were sparsely furnished, but comfortable.

It was evening by the time all of us arrived at the retreat facility. "We" consisted of about thirty elementary education majors, about thirty secondary education majors, several curriculum and instruction faculty and graduate students, and several counselor education faculty and graduate students. The retreat began in a large room. We sat in a circle about the room's perimeter and were told the rules for the retreat.

The rules were simple enough. No one would be watching over us. We were asked to respect each other's privacy. And we were asked not to leave the premises without what we felt was good cause. Said one person, "You will be treated like adults."

I resented being told I would be treated like an adult. It had been a long time since I had been admonished to act my age. And I felt that I would be perceived as an adult only when it was no longer emphasized that I would be so treated.

Nevertheless, I was, on balance, favorably impressed by the faculty. I again noticed an effort to be warm. I felt the effort stemmed not from a desire to play a role, but originated instead in a genuine attempt to say: "I want to know you as a person. I want to care."

One other impression stood out. True, I didn't know what the retreat would entail. But I did know that it would somehow be very significant.

The retreat began in earnest the next morning. After breakfast we again met in the large meeting room. We were told that we would be grouped into four teams. These teams would work closely together throughout most of the next two years. We would generate these groups ourselves. First, each person would select a partner. Then each pair would join another pair. Fours would connect with other fours. Finally, each eight would join another eight.

We began by performing some sensitivity exercises. These would be used throughout the grouping process. It was emphasized that no one would be forced in any way to participate in any or all of these activities. In fact, several faculty and graduate students watched the group to make sure that no one was participating merely because he was self-conscious about slipping over to the side of the room.

I liked the exercises. They made me feel both afraid and yet secure. At any rate, after a few activities we were told to choose the one person with whom we wished to be paired for the next two years. Elementary and secondary majors could pair together, if they wished to do so. All this seemed incredible. How could we intelligently make such choices after so little time? Yet somehow I knew that this would work. Everyone here seemed special.

The grouping continued until we had formed eights. I felt closer to the members of my four than I did toward the other four in my eight. I had been through more with them. I somehow understood each, and liked each, though we were very different sorts of people.

At this point we were told that we would each have to teach a lesson to the other members of our eight. The lesson would be videotaped and critiqued by the faculty member of our own choosing. But our performances would not be graded nor would they in any way affect our program status. We could do the taping whenever we felt ready to do so. We could teach on any subject. Faculty would assist us in any way they could. They would provide moral support when it was requested. Frightening as the taping was, it was soon done with. Then it was time for the feedback.

The feedback was not to be feared. We were never explicitly told why we were doing the microteaching, but the reasons were apparent. Partly we were doing this to get over the fear of seeing ourselves on tape. But mainly we were being given feedback so that we could infer the thrust of the faculty's interests.

The faculty were concerned about each of us as individual professionals. The feedback emphasized the positive as well as the negative aspects of our performances. The feedback was constructive. Clearly, this experience was intended to establish productive working relationships among faculty and students and to deepen the friendships that had already begun to evolve.

I valued this videotape feedback as I valued feedback I received at other points during my program involvement. The feedback facilitated professional growth, because it was persuasive. Feedback couched in a database of recorded behaviors is difficult to ignore.

But the feedback was also persuasive because an effort was made to recognize and accept student reactions and feelings regarding videotaping. A counselor always assisted the curriculum specialist in giving feedback, partly to insure that student feelings were indeed accepted. The counselors also used their skills in monitoring classroom interactions to provide feedback on the interpersonal dynamics of the performance demonstration. The counselors really contributed a good deal to the entire feedback effort.

By now it was the last day of the retreat. Each group of eight chose one representative. The representatives of each eight then met with some of the faculty in one of the smaller retreat house rooms. We did two things. First, students negotiated among themselves until each eight had joined with another eight to form four teams of about sixteen. Then, with none of the involved faculty present, we negotiated as to which of four faculty would lead each of the four teams for the duration of the program.

Finally, the retreat was over. I think that all of us involved in the retreat left with the feeling that something special had happened. Though leaving the isolation of an idyllic setting, I felt we carried something from what we experienced into the "real world" that we now faced.

Field Experiences Site Selection

During the six weeks that followed, we rotated through each of the six schools that would be the sites for our field experiences. Pairs from each of the four teams of sixteen divided up for the purposes of school visitation. Each week, after spending one afternoon in the school for that week, the pairs would then meet to share impressions and information with fellow members of their team.

The school visits consisted of a visit with the principal, followed by some classroom observation of teaching. But we did more during our visits.

Our task was to get to know the schools we visited, so that we could make intelligent decisions about where we wanted to student teach. Some of us walked the halls. Some of us talked to teachers in the teachers' lounge. Others visited with pupils in the cafeteria during lunch.

Of the six schools we visited, three were elementary schools. Two were high schools. The remaining school was a junior high. The schools varied regarding ethnicity and economic backgrounds of their pupils.

A consensus seemed to emerge from team discussions of our experiences. We were all visiting both elementary and secondary schools. This was good. It gave us the ability to rationally decide whether or not we wanted to seek a different level of certification, or even exit the profession. In fact, several students did choose to seek elementary rather than secondary certification.

One other consensus grew out of our school visits. These inservice professionals were ready to work with us. They felt they could give us much while also learning from us. These were to be working relationships based on mutual respect and interest.

After visiting the six schools, each student chose the school in which he or she would work. But the schools chose us as well. These were negotiated relationships. All parties involved consented to the assignments. Any party could at any time terminate the relationship.

One implication of this field-site selection process bears particular emphasis. Because students could affect field-experience assignments, we could also affect the substance of our experiences. We could choose to work with teachers who would not limit us to performance of only observational or clerical tasks. We could choose to work with teachers who would let us teach and give us constructive feedback on our efforts.

In the end, the school where I chose to work was a high school with pupils of particular diversity. I chose the school because of its diversity and because this diversity gave the school a special quality. Apparently because different groups were so well represented, people seemed especially tolerant of diversity. Everyone seemed open. Here was an ideal place to test different teaching tactics. Here was the place to find myself professionally.

Phase I Experiences

About the third or fourth week into the semester, while we were rotating through the schools, we received feedback on the personality tests we had taken before the retreat. Even then many of us did not yet fully understand how feedback on these tests related to teaching. But we did intuitively appreciate the fact that teaching is an interpersonal activity and that, therefore, personality does affect teaching effectiveness.

There was a more immediate reason why we were no longer alienated by the prospect of being given test feedback. We trusted the faculty. If the faculty said that the results were professionally important for us, we accepted this. Their judgments about the relevance of the tests might be in error, but their intentions were clearly oriented toward doing what they thought would be valuable for us.

I approached my feedback session with two different types of anxiety. I was anxious that I might be hurt. I was at the same time anxious to receive the feedback because I felt it might be a very deep experience for me.

The inputs I received from fellow students who had the feedback before me seemed to justify my anxieties. Students did not share more than general impressions about their sessions. These were highly personal matters. But one consensus did emerge. The counselors were suprisingly able to make special insights on the basis of the test data.

My feedback was an emotional experience for me. I felt a rapport with the counselor from whom I chose to receive the feedback. The conference was not terribly structured. The counselor gave a brief overview of the data, and then floated with my questions and concerns. Some comments related directly to teaching. For example, the counselor asked me if I thought I might have a particular tendency to orient myself toward female rather than male students. Other comments did not directly relate to teaching but were primarily matters the counselor recommended I think about in terms of my personal growth.

During the remaining ten weeks of the first semester, after the school visits and the feedback sessions were over, we then spent about two hours a week in our field-experience sites. We played the role of teacher aides, working with individual pupils or small groups of pupils. Field experience aside, it was anticipated that we would also spend an average of about an additional four hours per week on campus working on the semester I modules.

There was a problem, however. A few of the modules were not ready for distribution, even seven weeks into the semester. There was some sort of a delay at the printing plant. This angered some of the students. We had been told we would determine the pace, manner, and sequencing of our learning. How could we exercise these freedoms when all the modules were not yet available. Finally, the modules were distributed.

In general, we liked the modular approach to learning. Modules emphasize product over process. It's not important how you learn, so much as it is important that in the end you do, indeed, learn. Thus we accepted the freedom to decide what processes we would use in pursuing demonstration of specified competencies. At the same time, we accepted responsibility for the consequences of our learning strategy decisions. If we didn't learn, we had no one to blame but ourselves.

From my perspective, there is special value in such an approach to learning. The approach offers special potential for the personal growth of all concerned. It seems to me that adulthood is nothing more than accepting responsibility for the consequences of one's own freely made decisions. Students may grow in a CBE program that uses modules, because the students have yet another opportunity to explore the nature of assuming responsibility for exercising freedoms.

But this growth should not be unilateral and just on the part of the students. In a truly personalized CBE program, faculty too will grow because they will no longer be required to play authoritarian roles. Faculty need not prod students to do what they as professors know must be done. What authority the professors do exercise is the authority of reason, not the authority of position. Even assessment becomes a process of rationally comparing behaviors against previously specified performance criteria.

In fact, in a really personalized CBE program, the whole growth process is facilitated because faculty and students do not grow separately, but they instead grow together collaboratively. Faculty suggest but do not dictate routes to learning. Faculty and students, in such learning relationships, can know each other and say, "I'm OK. You're OK. Let's relate as adults who are friends, because only through such relationships can we come to know ourselves and each other better."

This type of learning is important, because it's what life is all about. It is relevant to teacher preparation because it is what teaching is all about too. How can I teach elementary or secondary school pupils if I do not know and accept myself? More, really what have I taught my pupils if I haven't helped them better know themselves and their environments?

Discussion of theory on cognitive and personal growth in a CBE program is tolerable because the theory became a reality in our program. We grew contentwise, because we knew ourselves better than our instructors knew us. We had been learning for at least the past twenty years. In CBE we learned optimally because we invested efforts only in those activities from which we knew we would learn the most efficiently.

Some of us chose to work together on our modules. We discussed readings and shared insights. Some of us chose to work alone. It was more efficient to read alone, or to view multimedia presentations alone. The point is, we learned.

We grew personally as well. Students knew each other, and we liked each other. We liked faculty too. Now we could relate as friends with faculty. The time was there, partly because the faculty members were no longer lecturing in classes. We were teaching ourselves, with faculty assistance only where required.

So we learned personal but important things from our relations with each other and faculty. We learned important things through the modules too. Still, the real action was out in the schools.

The little time we spent in the schools was not important simply because it enabled us to field test massive new instructional strategies. The time was most important because our field experiences that semester gave us a feel for what teaching was like.

"Getting a feel for what teaching was like" is an important learning in itself, but there was more involved. Crucially, my off-campus field experiences that semester, as limited as they were, gave me realistic insights into what I needed to learn on campus. One reason I had decided to become a teacher was that I had often thought that I could teach better than could many of my teachers. In a way, I was pretty cocky.

But my experiences that semester gave me an important insight. Teaching is not just the opposite of learning. For example, being able to answer higher-order questions is not the same as being able to teach a lesson using the higher-order questions teaching strategy. Knowing these truths is one thing. Feeling them is another. At the end of the first semester, I felt them.

Semester's end was soon upon us. With it came the startling realization that only one or two of the students had completed all the semester's modules. There were several reasons for this. Due to the printing problem, there had been a delay in distributing some modules. Also, we students had a difficult time learning to pace ourselves when for so long course instructors had performed this function for us. Finally, the faculty had underestimated the time it would take us to complete the modules.

Thus, at semester's end, more than sixty people had not completed all the requirements for the six hours for which we had registered. This was problematic mainly because a decision to give so many Incompletes would not sit too well with the students, much less the registrar. It was decided that students close to completing their work would get A's, contingent upon agreement that the work would later be completed. The remaining students got I's.

These grading decisions seemed arbitrary. What was "close to finishing their work"? How could the implicit contract specifying that grades would be given only upon attainment of the competencies be changed in midstream? Finally, what modules had to be completed to receive credit for each course?

To avoid recurrence of this problem, a committee of students and faculty together specified credit equivalents for completion of different modules. Furthermore, the faculty promised to try to avoid further underestimation of the work the modules required.

Phase II Experiences

Theoretically, during semester II our time investment would be the same as our semester I time investment, but the time would be spent differently. We were to double the time we spent in the field, while halving the time we spent on campus. But since almost none of us had completed all our semester I modules, time investment in modules remained constant while we spent twice as much time in the field. To say the least, this was a rather hard semester.

My work in the field that semester had special value for me. Now I was in my school six hours each week. It was like passing through a quantum level in terms of opening up new horizons of opportunity. Because my appearances were no longer so infrequent that my instruction would seem terribly disjointed to my pupils, my cooperating teacher and I agreed that I would teach Tuesday and Thursday afternoons. I would be fully responsible for determining the content of the lessons I taught. At the end of the quarter, I would assign each pupil two-fifths of his total grade.

I began my classes by telling my pupils: "I want to be a better teacher than other teachers. I want to be different." My pupils liked what I had said. Things looked good.

But what I didn't realize at the time was that my statement meant different things to individual pupils. As we got into lesson content, I soon realized that not all pupils cared about what we were doing. Not all pupils were even learning from the classes. My pupils began to get frustrated because I couldn't produce the perfection I had promised. I became frustrated because I found myself unable to actualize my very high ideals.

It took me a while to realize that my ideals were not going to be met. It took me a while longer to accept this realization. Meanwhile, an atmosphere of frustration and subtle antipathy had begun to emerge in my classes.

This situation was defused, I think, by the visit of two of my professors to one of my classes. I began the lesson in that class period by introducing the two professors. I then told my class: "I am nervous about being observed by my professors. But they are here to watch me, not you. Please try not to be nervous yourselves." Not long into the lesson, I perceived that my pupils were being incredibly attentive. Not a few, or most, but virtually all the pupils were actively involved in the class.

My pupils were attentive not just because I had planned the lesson well. They wanted me to do well in the eyes of my professors. They cared. That seemed important to me. My learning was the insight that pupils would accept less than perfection from me. My high commitment to them was important, even if I didn't always achieve the results I sought. That seems so basic and obvious, but I really only knew it then.

My experiences also made me respect an important characteristic of the competency-based approach to education. Some question how realistic a mode of instruction can be if students can't fail because of the "pass–not yet" philosophy. Yet I had failed when I had committed myself to my students to do the impossible. And I failed when I did not immediately recognize the consequences of my promise.

In fact, CBE is a reality-centered approach to education, because there is more opportunity for failure in any program that so emphasizes performance. Having had this experience, I now attempt to demonstrate competencies until I succeed in doing so, no matter how many attempts I require. Where the program is field-centered, there is more opportunity for me to fail, because I assume greater responsibilities for longer periods of time.

The strength of the CBE assessment process is that failure is not permanently recorded in the summative record of an academic transcript. The system of assessment does not inherently add threatening sanctions to those imposed by reality itself. Failure can be such a learning experience. Why make it a recorded and thus punitive experience? Perhaps this anecdote makes the point. A professor told it to a class once when he failed.

> My mother used to tell me that if you lay an egg, cherish it. It's yours. And there is some beauty in it, because it's yours.

Expressed differently, I like CBE partly because students themselves determine when assessment will occur, while learning progress determines whether assessment will be formative or summative.

All this aside, my Phase II field experiences were soon over. It was a very fruitful experience. I frankly question how much content I taught my pupils. I hope they learned some things they felt were valuable. I know I did.

My most important learning came on the last day of classes. I asked my pupils to comment on me as teacher. Most of the pupils said things like, "Relax, you do better than you think you do." But the comment that meant the most to me was one from a pupil who had not said much during the semester. She wrote: "I have learned more from you than I learned from any teacher I have had before." I knew then that I had made the right decision when I had decided to become a teacher. Teaching is sometimes feeling disappointed, sometimes tired, sometimes angry. But teaching is also sometimes being fulfilled.

Phase III Experiences

The beginning of the third phase of the program the next fall highlighted what for me was a rather sad development in program evolution. Two of the four faculty team leaders were no longer connected with the program. Several students did not return after the summer. All this made it abundantly clear that the cohesiveness of the teams was diminishing.

These personnel changes did not cause the breakdown in the teams, they merely accentuated it. The process had begun much earlier. After the first six weeks of the program, the teams served no practical function other than providing moral support and friendship. True, the feelings of group identity were still there. But these feelings were becoming more latent and less active. This disappointed me, especially considering all the effort and resources that had been invested in building cohesive team units.

My third semester was important for me because I chose to complete Phase III of the program during that period. In other words, I completed the remaining Phase II modules while I did the internship that most students chose to do during the next semester. The consequence objectives of internship assessed our abilities to apply in real settings all the cognitive and performance objectives we had demonstrated earlier.

Internship was very meaningful to me. I felt that I had learned from my earlier experiences. I felt I would teach better than I had before. I was ready. A few weeks into the semester I specified the objectives I would teach my pupils. I would not have proved myself accountable for the learning of my pupils until 100 percent of my pupils achieved these objectives.

I really enjoyed teaching this semester. I felt my pupils were learning a great deal. I felt my pupils and I respected and liked each other. Though my cooperating teacher playfully admonished them not to do so, my pupils called me by my first name whenever they felt it was appropriate to do so. Then one time I was talking with two pupils and one said, "Mr. Thompson, you're really an intellectual person." Then the other pupil said, "Yeah, and that's a lot different from just being intellectual."

After about one month, all my pupils achieved the objectives I had specified earlier. I had successfully demonstrated accountability in the school I had been in for more than one year. I now had to move to a different school to complete a second internship.

The environment of my second internship was very different from my first internship environment. This time I worked in an open concept school. This time I taught government rather than speech. This time my pupils were almost all white, and their economic backgrounds were less varied than were those of my first internship pupils.

Quite frankly, I was assessed less rigorously in my second internship than I had been during my first one. My professors did come to observe me several times. On one occasion they observed a lesson in which I really flopped. This was the first time I was observed when I was doing notably poorly.

After the lesson was over I was given the feedback I expected. My professors didn't come down hard on me, but they didn't exactly praise me either. I felt disappointed in myself. But I felt some other things too. I felt tired. I had been through so much. I had worked so hard. I found it difficult now to motivate myself to work. I needed a rest.

At times being in a CBE program is like being in the middle of a desert. You have been told how many steps it will take you to reach the oasis. But you don't know until you take the steps how difficult each step will be. Some steps are short but you find yourself mired in sand drifts as you take them. As you make your way toward the oasis, it is often tempting to give up. Perseverance is a prerequisite for completion of a CBE program.

I don't think this is necessarily a negative value judgment on CBE programs. If teaching requires a great deal of perseverance, then maybe this is a more realistic approach to teacher preparation. If teaching requires the ability to pace oneself, to make decisions rationally, then maybe again this is a better approach to training. But it's still in many ways a very rigorous method of teacher education.

I was soon done with my second internship, and thus my program involvement. I felt I had grown both personally and professionally as a result of my experiences. My on-campus experiences gave me the theoretical backgrounds and the instructional strategies I needed to teach effectively. My field experiences gave me an informed awareness of what I needed to learn on campus, as well as the opportunity to field test new instructional skills and approaches. It had been a tiring three semesters, but it had definitely been a rewarding three semesters as well.

Some Final Concerns

I care about the CBE method of teacher preparation. I think it can be a better method of teacher training. But because I find the approach so valuable, I also feel bound to be the approach's own strongest critic. Therefore, I mention at least two implementation possibilities that would make a non-perfect approach to teacher education a very imperfect approach to teacher education.

First, there is the danger that CBE may be implemented in response to perceptions that society desires more individualization in education. This is only partially accurate. The development of CBE is largely the result of societal desire for more humanness in education. Humanization of education requires both individualization and personalization of education processes. While personalization of education does imply individualization, individualization does not necessarily imply personalization. The thrusts are not inherently reciprocal. Why individualize instruction if not to acknowledge the human differences in the people who are learners? Will instruction be perceived as being mechanistic if it is individualized only for reasons of efficiency?

How can program implementers foster student perceptions that individualization efforts have their genesis in concern for the person? Students can be given both the freedom to make decisions and the responsibility for accepting the consequences of their decisions. CBE implies student freedom to determine rate, sequence, and method of attaining learning objectives. That's a good beginning.

Crucially, however, the untapped potential for humanizing education (aside from hiring humanistic faculty) lies in also allowing students to affect the content of the objectives they are to pursue. Competency content should partially be determined through negotiation among individual students and individual professors. Negotiation is a humanistic decision-making process, because negotiated decisions are decisions consensually achieved through discussion among persons who as persons are equal.

There is a second significant danger for distorted CBE implementation. Modules must be used to increase professor-student interaction, and not to reduce it. Modules are not bound pages or even sets of alternative learning materials. Modules are only outlines of minimal learning objectives and suggestions of ways to achieve these objectives. Some suggested learning alternatives might include seminars or lectures by professors.

But all modules should both allow and encourage interaction among students and faculty. If the modules don't free instructors to work with students who are having special learning problems, then the modules are dysfunctional. If modules don't also allow students and professors the opportunity to get to know each other as persons, then the modules are twice-over dysfunctional.

CBE has such potential for facilitating growth of more effective and humanistic professionals. Whether CBE achieves this potential will depend on how the education profession responds to the social forces that have brought the evolution of the CBE movement. Hopefully, program implementations will place a consistent and undistorted emphasis on person and reality. After all, what emphases are more compatible with the end purposes and processes of education?

13

CBE and beyond:
some final ideas

What we want to do in this concluding chapter is to describe some of the more nebulous and argumentative issues in CBE and attempt to look into our crystal ball and speculate about what the future may hold.

Rather than throwing out extensive discourses on each of a series of issues, we have chosen to jab briefly at each. Consequently, the flow from topic to topic will not always be smooth. The ideas are plopped with the intent of stimulating thought and speculation on the part of the reader. We will all be vitally interested in looking back in five to ten years and seeing whether CBE has become an even more widespread approach to education or whether the concepts as well as the terminology will have faded from view. We think we see positive consequences from the early stages of the movement—as well as promise in the long view.

Following are the questions and topics to be explored:

THIS BOOK

A Review

In this book we have made an effort to propose some practical as well as theoretical ideas to you as a program developer who is looking at CBE as a prospective training or education model. In Chapter 1 we proposed a simple model to aid us in communicating (see Exhibit 13.1).

Decision Source \ Decision Type	PROGRAM DEVELOPMENT				PROGRAM ADOPTION		
	Assumptions·Goals	Instructional Strategies	Evaluation		Preparing	Implementing	Maintaining
Instructor							
Students							
Profession							
Community							
Negotiated							

EXHIBIT 13.1 Decision Making in CBE Development/Adoption.

In Review

A quick survey of the content of the entire book along the lines of the ideas developed in the model might include:

Competencies-Objectives (discussed in detail in Chapter 2).

1. Are identified by someone (instructor, student, professional), or negotiated.
2. Follow directly from the assumptions values, beliefs, ethics, opinions, and concerns of program builders.

3. Are made public to students before they start working on them.
4. Are constantly reviewed and revised if necessary in light of changing values, beliefs, etc., of program builders and the successes of those students who have completed prior programs.

Instructional Activities (discussed in detail in Chapter 4).

5. Are directly related to competencies and objectives.
6. Consist of various instructional activities for students having different aptitudes, learning modes, cognitive styles, or preferences.
7. Allow for each student to progress at his own pace.
8. Are constantly scrutinized, reviewed, and revised if necessary.

Assessment Procedures (Chapter 3).

9. Reflect the processes used to identify whether individual students have reached specified competencies and objectives.
10. Connote criterion-referenced systems (those that compare student achievement with specified objectives rather than with the achievement of other students).

We also tried to make a case for viewing total program efforts. We viewed CBE development efforts as opportunities to rethink what we are doing rather than simply to modify present programs into another format. Using the best of what we do and using the knowledge, skills, and experiences of others, programs could reflect a higher validity (Chapter 6). To do this calls for coordinated efforts on the part of some people who have not been involved in present program developments. Coordinated efforts call also for changes in faculty and student roles (Chapter 7), as well as coordinated field or practicum settings for CBE in professional schools (Chapter 8). The need for rethinking the adoption process, management strategies, and systems is obvious (Chapter 9).

We proposed ways in which personalization might be reflected in CBE programs (Chapter 5). We also made the point throughout that CBE programs can be as rigid, open, flexible, strict, easy, difficult, demanding, relevant, or useless as any present systems, depending on the values, beliefs, and assumptions of program builders.

We again tried to focus on program implementation, and we presented some ideas from successful program builders around the nation (Chapter 11). We also presented one student's perceptions of a CBE program (Chapter 12).

To us a main ingredient of successful competency-based education is the thrust toward self-renewal; to this end we tried to focus on program evaluation and data-based decision making in Chapter 10.

Authors rarely take time to contemplate the title of their book in public. We would like to do it here. Our title, *Competency-Based Education—A Process for the Improvement of Education,* seemed catchy when we first proposed it to Prentice-Hall. To us it still is. What is the process for the improvement of education? Obviously, having a CBE program does not in itself improve education any more than adding a course to a syllabus improves anything. The following anti-illustrations may help.

1. On the way to work on August 6, 1973, one of us heard the following (as best as he can remember) over the "CBS Morning Radio News": "The American Bar Association has expressed concern over the large number of lawyers involved in the Watergate cover-up. The association did not project a solution but did indicate that perhaps laws schools should offer more courses in ethics."
2. Bill Drummond of the University of Florida has pointed out, "You can slice baloney many different ways, but you still have baloney."
3. We were talking to a faculty member at a small school not long ago and he told us that he used modules and that "CBE stuff" and the students didn't like it as well as his lectures. He indicated that he would not be interested in further trial.

The point we are trying to illustrate is that CBE as a name does nothing. It can mean something, however, if attempts are made to continually monitor our successes and failures and to act accordingly.

We believe that the key to the CBE movement is the constant assessment of goal achievement. Are students learning what is expected of them? Are students satisfied with their experiences and outcomes? Is there general satisfaction on the part of instructors? Are the selected goals and objectives of the program not only being met but are they relevant to the needs of students and to the needs of their future clients?

By most people's admission, CBE causes everyone to work harder. Students, faculty, registrars, and others comment on the work load increasing. It is no wonder that students like lectures more than some in-depth modules if the work load is greater and the outcomes are no more compelling. In teacher education it is a heck of a lot easier to listen to someone talk on motor-skill development of children than to be held accountable for the development of motor coordination of pupils in public schools. Yet most prospective teachers would prefer to leave a teacher education program feeling prepared to teach rather than go through a "nonrelevant" set of experiences.

Another colleague noted recently that she was not interested in CBE either. She had already identified the objectives that were necessary for the teaching of foreign languages and told her students what was expected of them. Incidentally, this same instructor also permits students to self-pace and does not award any grade until they have completed minimal expectations (stated in advance). This same faculty member also has an elaborate system to generate feedback on her course and changes the course based on student and colleague input as well as a national organization's guidelines for effective programs in foreign language education. She doesn't want CBE though. It's just a shame that she is against the process that she uses.

Admittedly, many, in fact, most of the examples provided in this book relate to teacher education (CBTE), our field. We are convinced that the application of the principle to other fields is equally possible. It has already been demonstrated that in engineering (cf. the work of Wales et al. at West Virginia), subject-matter courses of all types (cf. Keller method experiences), and other professional schools (dental and medical schools especially) it has worked. Courses and some programs are now using mastery learning experiences, specifying outcomes in advance, and continually changing as a result of feedback and effectiveness of graduates. It is the rare college that does not have some form of effort in this area.

Similar comments apply equally to elementary and secondary schools. Individualized efforts with mastery learning, self-pacing, and, in some cases, personalization exist throughout the nation.

These efforts grew as a result of program developers' looking at what they were doing and comparing what they found with what they wanted. Successful efforts, those that constantly reflect an improvement of some form of education, never stop this scrutinizing. That's the improvement we are referring to in the title.

As we have emphasized throughout this book, CBE is *not* some sort of product or innovative "box" that is procured and installed like a new textbook and then life is allowed to return to its normal routine. CBE is a *process,* a catalyst for change. Introducing CBE does not prescribe what the program will be like. However, introducing CBE often unleashes many and diverse actions, events, and consequences. These outcomes cannot be totally predicted or controlled. One thing is certain: maintaining the preexistent inertia is nearly impossible. CBE often serves as such a powerful catalyst that those who have paranoid tendencies may fear that CBE is a subversive plot to induce change and undermine the way things are, and they may be right.

CBE with its built-in feedback systems appears to have the potential to aid institutions not only in initiating change but also in creating a climate of continual, gradual, and controlled renewal. It would be quite difficult to institutionalize a totally static CBE program that contained only published modules, fixed organizational structures, and repetitive normalized routines and roles. The feedback systems would prohibit this by continually providing data for use in deciding on necessary modifications as well as pointing out the need for the introduction of yet undeveloped innovations. CBE does not have to be a closed system, and we believe that CBE has the potential for maintaining openness, and in fact requiring it, if fully operationalized and institutionalized.

One short-term outcome of CBE is obviously the stimulation of much discussion and examination of what one is doing and what others are doing. Many exciting alternatives to the traditional three-credit-hour course based on forty-two clock hours of teacher talk and three one-hour exams are being experimented with. The outcome of all this talk and experimentation can't be all bad. Just the increased awareness of what others are doing is a significant improvement. In addition, it appears that the accumulation of course credits as the basis for certification is being seriously questioned. There is also an obvious increased emphasis on clinical experiences, including early experiences.

The long-term outcomes of CBE will not be known for four to ten years from the inception of any CBE program. The obvious and often forgotten reason for considering CBE or any other innovation is the improvement it can make in the clients. In teacher education, CBTE is aimed toward developing more effective teachers who will be able to increase desired learning outcomes in children. In the health sciences the desired outcome is better-trained health science personnel who can provide improved health care. Whether these and other desired long-term goals will come to pass, only time and research will show. We and others believe that at worst CBE will compare favorably with the existing alternative(s).

EFFECTS AND AFFECTS OF CBE

Stimulation

Somewhere in an airplane we ran across a quotation that said, "The innovation that sooner or later arouses no resistance must be extremely trivial." Based upon this, CBE must be of some importance. No single movement in education has effected and affected educators as CBE has. Although a survey made by AACTE in 1972 found that more than 70 percent of the teacher education institutions in the nation were considering some form of CBE, the arguments raged. Some critics felt that there was no theory behind CBE; others felt that there was no research evidence that CBE was better than anything else. One critic claimed that CBTE was anti-intellectual.

One obvious effect of the movement has been to divide educators as few other things have. Yet a countereffect seems to indicate that with all the antis, the pros are making headway. It has been pointed out that it takes roughly twenty years for an innovation to work into the mainstream of American education. Someone seems to have short-circuited the mainstream with CBE, and there have been a few electrocutions on both sides.

These effects and affects are both nationwide and local. In efforts where CBE seems to be working, there are some local effects that cannot go unmentioned here. These effects are not limited to clients. Most operating CBE programs report closer relationships between faculty and students. Most also report that there is less competition between students and considerably more cooperation as students recognize that they are not being compared with each other. A key to operating CBE efforts seems to be the growing concept of *andergogy* (the teacher as only one of a number of learning resources) and the lessening of the concept of *pedagogy* (the teacher as the single learning source and master). Most CBE efforts report a different and improved relationship between administration and faculty as well.

These changes in faculty, students, administrators, and community come about through what Emily Girault (1974) and others refer to as system ownership rather than individual proprietorships. Because of the opened-up communication channels and the investment that all must make to develop and adopt a CBE program, most members of the institution(s) have a share in the ownership of the resultant program. This means that they also have higher intensity concerns about its maintenance and improvement. The consequence is increased commitment and, therefore, increased pressure for support of the program.

Growth consequences of CBE have not been limited to those who have attempted CBE development. Many who normally sit on the fence and watch the swing of the pendulum have been drawn into the fray. CBE is a concept so sophisticated that to attack it first requires intensive analysis and description of one's position. Analyzing one's position to defend it has to result in new clarity of reason and purpose. This stimulation of thought, discussion, and debate is priceless in and of itself and should be much more a part of our professional lives.

An Administrative System for CBE

To be able to effectively maintain a once-implemented CBE program and to allow for ongoing renewal requires that policies and support systems like administrative structures, and allocation of resources, be adaptive. In fact, for institutional viability, support systems in the future will need to be adaptive systems that respond to the needs of the institution's productive efforts rather than always adapting production to fit the support systems.

If a support system with an evolving structure is used, the administrative structure would be capable of regularly adapting to the needs of the evolving program. Rather than having to adapt a program to fit existing administrative structures while waiting for pressure and courage to build to the point where another cataclysmic reorganization can take place, an evolving management system *can* be developed. A starting point would be simply having a "five years hence" picture of what the ideal support system structures should look like and gradually moving toward this goal with the ideal being modified each year to fit the existing realities.

There is, of course, a risk in having an evolving support system structure. There is a tendency for increased instability and malfunctioning. However, to maintain a viable institution with viable programs, continually evolving support system structures seem to be much more stable and supportive than massive reorganization every five to eight years. Give it some thought.

Death of Educational Institutions

Changing a university is like trying to rearrange a cemetery (attributed to S. Freud).

Let's take a look at some realities for the future of educational institutions, especially in higher education. During the early 1970s many new institutions of higher education were established without intentionally abolishing or changing the mission of any of the existing institutions. In teacher education alone in the state of Texas there were at last count sixty-six institutions that could recommend certification to the state. Other states have equally large numbers of institutions with the same mission. Networks of community colleges and junior colleges, new medical and dental schools, and state universities and branch campuses of already established colleges and universities have all been added. While this institutional expansion has been underway, the dollar support has not kept pace. School boards, legislatures, and trustees are not able to procure as many dollars as are needed or were promised. Nor has the number of students entering college increased at the expected rate.

The funding basis for most public institutions is usually some sort of "head count" formula that necessitates maintaining a high and ever-increasing enrollment. In addition, in most cases to add a new faculty member requires adding a larger number of students than need to be lost to justify the elimination of a faculty position. For example, to add a faculty member may require an increase of twenty-four full-time students, whereas the budget for a faculty member is lost when the enrollment drops by eighteen full-time students. Since students are now a valuable commodity, the demand for students has increased. Many campuses have established specialized offices for recruiting students. On those campuses where the number of students is declining, the number of faculty is declining at an even faster rate due to the budgeting formulas. What all this means is that the faculty-student ratio is increasing on many campuses and the time and resources available for innovation are decreasing.

Another symptom of the problem is that many high-level administrators employ the "fingernail hang" survival strategy in hard times. The we-will-take-a-deep-breath-and-hold-on—the-next-biennium-will-be-better stance is often little more than a cop-out. Things are not getting better. *No* decision *is* a decision.

Meanwhile, at some institutions, risk-taking administrators and faculty are innovating. While some administrators search for ways of increasing enrollment by altering or removing admission standards, others work on programs, making them more relevant and of better quality for students. Students now and in the future will be, more than ever, selecting schools rather than schools' selecting students. Just how careful and informed students will be as purchasers remains to be seen; however, we believe that the pressure on educational institutions that do not attempt to improve the quality of the learning opportunities will become oppressive to some (assuming, of course, that they don't have winning football teams).

An interesting statistic is that in 1972, 3.5 million children entered first grade in the United States. In 1974, there were only 3.1 million births. The impact of this continuing decline in quantity of available students as the wave rolls through our educational institutions is going to be interesting to watch. Fewer learners could mean an unheard of opportunity for improving the quality of learning experiences. It could also mean higher salaries for fewer educational personnel or, even more remotely, lower taxes.

At a very real point in time, the critical mass of many educational institutions will drop below the threshold required for efficient functioning and survival. We believe strongly that many educational institutions, unless they develop more relevant and effective programs (not necessarily CBE), are going to die. To test our predictive powers we have developed a private list of nominee institutions around the country, many of which are public, state-supported colleges and universities, that appear to be in late stages of rigor mortis. Many will not make another five years. At one of these institutions, located in the Midwest, one of the authors was talking with a faculty member and asked him what he thought the state would do with the buildings once the institution closed. The faculty member quickly responded that it would brick up the windows and use the buildings for grain elevators.

At several spots in this book we have made the point that students in CBE programs do not have to compete with each other as in a norm-referenced program. Evaluations are made based on what the student is able to do with respect to a specified objective or competency. Some faculty note that this is sort of Pollyanna-ish in that students are going into the real world where competition is a way of life. It is our opinion that this competition has done more to ensure human alienation than it has done for human development, but that's not really our point here. Most CBE efforts do find students cooperating. It is a common practice for students to share sources, papers, references, and the like.

Sharing in CBE is not limited to students, however. Faculty members also seem to be more open and willing to share. It wasn't always this way, we might add. In the late sixties there was a very careful guarding of modules, program specifications, and the like. Often all the sharing got for the sharer was the enmity of the sharee. Worse yet, in several instances the sharee got credit for the sharer's work by publishing it first. But this stage seems to have turned around. More and more people are willing to look at sharing as a positive feature.

Within some CBE programs faculty share time and instructional resources by using blocked scheduling and topic or modular instruction rather than having independent courses. Many CBE programs utilize faculty teaming for sharing, planning, scheduling, and knowledge of students. Sharing also goes on between programs and between institutions on a national scale. CBE program faculty openly share ideas, prototype materials, and how-to-do-it knowledge whenever they come into contact with fellow CBEers. Thus, people in the states of Oregon and Washington are aware of what is being tried and developed not just in their own states but also in Utah, Texas, Florida, Georgia, and New York. Through the many CBE conferences and the regular professional meetings, faculty members involved in CBE are continually being appraised of what others are learning and doing rather than everyone trying to hide from everyone else what and how they are doing. This sharing includes being open about the things that are not going well. Any program has its bad spots, and these are not kept secret but are pointed out as areas that need improvement or as an illustration of the consequences of a wrong decision.

This sharing by faculty involved in CBE is somewhat paradoxical and, certainly, most faculty feel uncomfortable at first. An explanation for the discomfort is readily available. Look at the background and selection pressures that have operated on the average faculty member. He was selected for admission to graduate school because he had higher grades than his peers. During graduate school he was expected to get higher grades, and to (independently of any others) design, conduct, and report a research study for his dissertation. Upon becoming an assistant professor, rewards and advancement were based on staying in one's office and writing single-author papers, corralling a bunch of graduate students, and out-hustling the other guy for grant money, travel money, and secretarial support. Obviously, the illustration could go on. However, the point is that the average faculty member in an educational institution is selected and continually rewarded for his ability to function as an *autonomous* individual, deliberately competing with and holding back from fully communicating with his colleagues. Now CBE and the times in general are pushing for faculty sharing. People who were recruited and advanced because they were effective nonsharers are now being required to share. Developing these skills is not easily accomplished, and the increased self-concerns of faculty involved in the process should not be considered as only an irritation.

Consequences of Sharing for Institutional Viability

The consequences of this sharing within and between CBE program faculty have critical implications for institutional viability. If you accept a developmental and evolutionary process of change within a social system, then either those institutions that are refusing to develop CBE programs or those that are developing CBE programs are making an expensive and perhaps fatal decision. We believe that because of the catalytic nature of CBE for generating new ideas, concepts, processes, and products, those involved in CBE are renewing themselves and their institutions at an ever-increasing rate. This increasing rate of renewal and adaptiveness is further enhanced by the sharing. Those CBE programs that are tied in to one or the other of the national CBE grapevines are not having to reinvent the module. When one program has an idea that works, others have access to it to accept, reject, or change based on their values. When a program runs into one of those many dead ends, the others learn of this also and do not have to repeat the same mistake.

Not participating in this ever-increasing rate of renewal that CBE catalyzes may be a dead end. Certainly, nonparticipating institutions are not going to find many shortcuts to establishing a CBE program when they get around to it. It will still take three to six years of concentrated effort. Meanwhile those institutions that have already begun establishing CBE programs and those that have been at it for three years or longer have the potential for breaking out into still uncharted worlds that require the CBE program development and adoption experience as prerequisites, if for no other reason than for the faculty and administrator development that has gone on when developing and adopting a CBE program.

The ever-increasing rate of renewal, the sharing, and the required development time means that the "early" institutions are moving away from the "later" institutions at an ever-increasing rate. If these institutions and individuals on the crest of the wave develop capabilities, knowledge, and insight that can only be fully developed and utilized by going through the CBE process, they will be at a decided advantage as the survival pressure on institutions continues to grow.

If indeed those institutions and individuals that are first to develop advanced CBE programs do have a critical potential that non-CBE institutions do not have, there may result a critical difference in viability. If so, an interesting question will arise. Do we let natural selection take its course, or do CBE institutions in some way aid others in developing the needed capabilities?

Cost versus Quality

The reader, if he hasn't gagged over some of the expenses projected for CBE found in Chapters 9 and 10, must still feel a bit uneasy about the economics of the movement. Most people recognize that CBE is going to cost more. Cost can of course get in the way. It is our experience that with the exception of the health sciences and some law schools, the choice between economics and degree of sophistication and safeness is really no choice. Economics wins. Regardless of the school, laymen still pay the bills. Taxes, endowments, and grants pay for colleges to operate. The health sciences and the legal profession have done a better job of convincing the laymen that they need the money.

Teacher education, for this reason, has been stuck with a quantity model. We needed more and more teachers for the growing population. But weird as it may seem, a growing population needs more doctors also. Yet in 1910 the famous Flexner Report (Flexner, 1910) appeared, noting that quality was only possible with fewer prospective doctors. The Flexner Report shaped medical education for sixty years and, according to Silberman, has resulted in the shortage of doctors that we have today.[1] The Flexner Report is only one example where the health sciences have done a more thorough job of impressing the funding bodies than teacher education. Teacher education has its own Flexner Report coming, though. It's called the demand for accountability.

For a moment let's think about the preparation and role of a general practitioner physician in comparison with the preparation and role of an elementary school teacher. The physician has to have extensive and intensive

[1] A. Flexner, *Medical Education in the United States and Canada* (New York: Carnegie Foundation for the Advancement of Teaching, 1910), Bulletin #4.

training first as an undergraduate premed student. Those students selected for medical school then receive three to four years of concentrated training and a two-year internship. The elementary school teacher receives three years of liberal arts course work as an undergraduate that is not in the least controlled by the professional teacher educators and one year of an often haphazard collection of professional education courses. The physician, following his professional training and being certified as "safe" to begin practice, establishes a practice where his clients *select him*. At the most, all he does is cut them with a knife once or twice in their lifetime. The teacher, after his training, is certified as "safe" and is hired by a school system as a full-fledged elementary teacher. His clients are thirty pupils who are *assigned* to him. He then lives with them in one room for thirty hours a week for forty weeks each year. He does not carry a knife in his hand, but he does carry the potential for rendering even more deadly harm with a psychological knife, daily cutting at minds at the rate of thirty a year.

It would seem that there are some arguments here for the improvement of professional teacher education. Just because little was spent in the past on an area does not mean that it was necessarily right then or that it should hold today and tomorrow.

The cost versus quality issue also focuses on individuals. For example, as we mentioned, educational institutions almost always go for the cheapest route, whether it be acquiring a new classroom facility or replacing a retired distinguished faculty member. On the quality side, faculty involved in professional education programs are seldom rewarded for their performance in the classroom. Rather it is their work with graduate students, the number of publications, and their membership on committees that reap rewards. Is not teaching as creative a performance for the teacher educator as carving a sculpture is for the artist or performing a musical composition is for the musician? Why is it not legitimate for faculty to demonstrate their creativity in teaching, especially those involved in professional education programs?

NEXT STEPS FOR CBE

Need for Research

There is always need for research. It seems that every research report begins with two or three paragraphs describing a few related research studies. This is followed by a paragraph that invariably begins, "However, there is no research done that explores the relationship between . . ." As we have illustrated throughout this book, the research opportunities related to CBE are abundant. Those who have reservations about CBE and its advocates are all saying that research data are needed related to CBE. The number of research questions within the program development process alone is nearly infinite, while, sad to say, the many research questions on the program adoption side are equally pressing and there is even less known. The questions range from "What kind of graduates will be needed in tomorrow's world?" to "What kind of enabling activities are appropriate for what kinds of skills and competencies, and how do these relate to individual learners?" The big question, however, is, "What competencies does a practicing professional need, to what level of proficiency, and how do these relate to client outcomes?"

As is reflected in reviewing the proceedings of the 1974 National Conference on Research in Competency-Based Teacher Education (Houston et al., 1974) the preoccupation of the majority of researchers in CBTE has converged on the "big" question—the attempt to identify which competencies are related to learning outcomes. We acknowledge that this question is obviously crucial. However, to bet nearly all of the research efforts on this question is premature. There is reason to doubt that this question is answerable in a meaningful way now, and answers to many of the smaller questions could be obtained and applied with some of the effort that is being focused on the big question.

Certainly, one of the reasons that the CBTE advocates have converged on this big question is out of self-defense. Many of the critics are demanding that CBTE not be adopted by others until the answer to this question is in. They seem to neglect the fact that the present programs have no better support for their being. However, as always, the established way does not need to justify its being. The potential danger to CBTE from preoccupation with collecting teacher effectiveness research studies is that the results will probably not be clear cut. CBTE has many other strengths besides training for competencies that research suggests are important. Pursuing the big question at the instigation of the CBTE critics will only reinforce the "life-or-death" struggle that is explicit behind some critics' attacks. We believe that conducting coordinated research on several fronts is well worth consideration.

While we are on the topic of research, we want to make a point about local research. Somehow in the United States we have developed a club membership in research studies. Stanford, Chicago, Indiana, Texas, and any number of "name" schools have the reputation for research. One need only look at the AERA program each year to identify a very small and elite list. Our point is that made by Bob Soar and Don Medley at an AACTE regional conference in Phoenix in 1974: "We have met the researcher and he is us." Locally, for continued program regeneration, we are it. Findings by the nationwide researchers Norbert Frelb, Irving Glotz, and Thelonius Garth at Prestige U will probably do little to help remold professional efforts at home. Keep that in mind.

The Fallacy of Us versus Them

CBE, in the short time it has been in existence as a set of concepts, has generated more than its share of activity. Unfortunately, CBE is not filling a void—there are other professional programs. To survive, CBE must take the place of something—something that is the product of people who have heavily invested in its development. CBE cannot help but be viewed as a threat to these establishments.

Rather than viewing CBE as an alternative, as an evolutionary step, or as something that might enhance what is already in existence, more than one critic has attempted to set up a life-or-death struggle with CBE. Some of the criticisms are valid. Many facets of CBE are rationally appealing but personally disturbing. Accountability, student independence, nonmandatory attendance, all raise the flags. CBE forces us to rethink some ideas about education that have been embedded in a lifetime of educational experiences. People can overlook the increased one-to-one contact with students when "behavioral objectives" are mentioned. They can also ignore the unique ways that students put together their own variation of competence when "subdivision into microscopic skills" is mentioned. We guess it is just human nature to selectively ignore and emphasize things in our own personal game of "Blemish." One thing is certain, if a polar life-or-death struggle continues, we are all going to lose.

It may be that criticism of CBE stems not so much from ideological differences between proponents and opponents of the movement as it does from miscommunication. Our good friend Jack Gant of Florida State University has provided a useful way of looking at some of the problems in establishing competency-based teacher education.

To accept an educational change, Jack says, the potential adopter must be involved in identifying the goals of the movement. If he is not involved, the goals and the assumptions will not be his, no matter what they are. When this occurs the challenge is thrown down, and innovation developer and potential adopter take opposite sides in an adversary relationship. The only way that adversaries can gain additional support is to "sell" their respective views to others who are not already decided on the value of the innovation. Such selling must necessarily take place through a common language, through the use of a terminology that is known to the buyer. In competency-based teacher education, the terms became CBTE versus Traditional. When the lines were thus drawn, both sides began to oversell. Opponents pointed to mechanization, behavioral objectives, all teachers looking alike, dehumanization, and so forth. Proponents pointed to personalization potential, cost-effectiveness, accountability, humane treatment of pupils in schools by competent teachers. The issue became *good* versus *bad, evil* versus *wonderful.*

In win-lose situations such as this, where one side is out to destroy the other, both sides lose. The real tragedy is that few of those involved in the fray have stopped swinging long enough to examine, side by side, the goals of the CBTE and non-CBTE factions.
We see them thus:

Non-CBTE: The development of programs that will educate teachers who are able to function for the best ends of their pupils.

CBTE: The development of programs that will educate teachers who are able to function for the best ends of their pupils.

The point we hope to make here is that educators must become collaborators, not competitors. CBE is not a religion—it is a tool. The tool may be of use in the development of a more realistic, valid, and reliable educational program. Perhaps this book will help us to use the tool effectively. But *remember,* CBE is only a tool.

The political pressures for and against CBE have been tremendous. After it had barely been conceptualized, CBE had been either legislatively or administratively mandated as *the* way or an alternative way to train teachers for certification in some twenty states. CBE has been under serious study in many of the other states, and most colleges and universities at least acknowledge having heard of CBE. Any time you mandate something, the potential for resistance increases by at least a factor of one hundred. In Texas, for example, once the attempt was made to mandate CBTE for certification, all sorts of academicians who had never before taken any particular interest in teacher education began an intensive political and oratory campaign to have the mandate reversed or set aside. A summary of the positions and events of each side is well presented in the January 1974 issue of *Phi Delta Kappan.* The fascinating thing about the mandate is that even the most pro-CBEers in the state did not want it. Bob Howsam makes the point: "We are more in danger from our 'friends' than from our 'enemies.' " Later, in the spring of 1974, the attorney general of Texas ruled on a request of the Texas Education Agency about TEA's right to require CBTE as the single basis for certification. Due to precedent decisions and existing laws, the attorney general ruled that TEA could not require any particular kind of program; furthermore, the ruling noted that TEA's function was to approve whatever programs the colleges and universities developed.

Rather than the decision being pro- or anti-CBTE, it was a legal one. Thus in this case many of the CBTE advocates were pleased, since they believed that mandating would result in ineffective CBTE programs, and the anti-CBTE forces were off the hook on a statewide level.

CBE has in its short existence gained surprisingly widespread attention and, sometimes, support. CBE is actively being considered by institutions of higher education, schools, state education agencies, professional associations, and legislatures. We doubt that the momentum that has been developed will be easily brought to a halt. Rather, as was suggested earlier in this chapter, we see those who become involved with CBE as learning and creating at an increasing rate in comparison with those who are refusing to entertain CBE tenets as alternative catalysts for change. The intermediate-range consequence may well be that those institutions and individuals who have been actively involved for an extended period of time in developing, adopting, and researching CBE will become the cutting edge of creativity and development in education. This will be the case, not because CBE is any final answer but rather because the activity catalyzed by CBE is something that institutions and individuals not involved with CBE have no alternative for. Thus a future map of the reference point institutions in professional education and the *who's who* of professional educators and administrators will be heavily laden with those that were earliest and were carefully and most intensively involved in developing, adopting, and researching CBE programs.

Beyond CBE

Looking beyond CBE from near its inception is, at best, a risky proposition. CBE could still turn out to be nothing more than a short-life-span attention getter and irritant. However, we think that CBE is going to be seen as much more. To illustrate *how* much more requires that we draw way back from viewing the day-to-day activity and attempt to look at the broad picture of the advancement of formal education, as a scientific discipline and process for formal learning.

An important book by Thomas S. Kuhn titled *The Structure of Scientific Revolutions* (1970) provides an important theory on which to base where we see CBE fitting into the evolution of education. In his book Kuhn theorizes that the advancement of a science is not accomplished merely by the accumulation of knowledge, as is commonly believed. Rather, a science advances when all of its members *share a common paradigm* around which their research efforts are oriented. The research efforts are then based on and related to this common paradigm and oriented toward testing various aspects of the paradigm, accumulating information that supports the paradigm and perhaps extending its boundaries.

Kuhn suggests that in any discipline, prior to the acceptance of a common or shared paradigm, there are many alternative and sometimes competing paradigms that researchers and practitioners in the field hold allegiance to and study. These various schools of thought attempt to account for what is known and attempt to advance their own paradigms. The net result is not so much the advancement of knowledge as an attempt to have one's own paradigm accepted by others. Kuhn uses as an example the state of physical optics before and after Newton developed the first paradigm acceptable to nearly all researchers in the field:

> Being able to take no common body of belief for granted, each writer on physical optics felt forced to build his field anew from its foundations. In doing so, his choice of supporting observation and experiment was relatively free, for there was no standard set of methods or of phenomena that every optical writer felt forced to employ and explain. Under these circumstances, the diologue of the resulting books was often directed as much to the members of other schools as it was to nature. That pattern is not unfamiliar in a number of creative fields today, nor is it incompatible with significant discovery and invention. It is not, however, the pattern of development that physical optics acquired after Newton and that other natural sciences make familiar today.[2]

Kuhn suggests that once a shared paradigm exists within a field of study, only then can that field be a science as we think of the investigative process for gathering knowledge and creating new frontiers:

> Men whose research is based on shared paradigms are committed to the same rules and standards for scientific practice. That commitment and the apparent consensus it produces are prerequisites for normal science, i.e., for the genesis and continuation of a particular research tradition.

Once a paradigm is shared across most of a field, scientific investigation of the paradigm can begin. This period of paradigm investigation Kuhn sees as a time of "normal science":

> Normal science consists in the actualization of that promise, an actualization achieved by extending the knowledge of those facts that the paradigm displays as particularly revealing, by increasing the extent of the match between those facts and the paradigm's predictions, and by further articulation of the paradigm itself.

The shared paradigm only comes into disfavor and needs to be replaced when an anomaly occurs or is "discovered" that does not fit the paradigm. When information is provided that the paradigm cannot account for and a new paradigm is required what Kuhn labels a "scientific revolution" occurs:

> And when it does—when, that is, the profession can no longer evade

anomalies that subvert the existing tradition of scientific practice—then begin the extraordinary investigations that lead the profession at last to a new set of commitments, a new basis for the practice of science. The extraordinary episodes in which that shift of professional commitments occurs are the ones known in this essay as scientific revolutions. They are the tradition-shattering complements to the tradition-bound activity of normal science.

Thus Kuhn theorizes that a true science for investigating a field of study does not exist until that time when there is a shared paradigm that nearly all are investigating from the same frame of reference. Instead of having to research and to promote one's own paradigm, investigations are conducted to support, test, and advance a common frame of reference. Scientific revolutions occur when an accepted paradigm is fatally challenged by new information.

Back to CBE and education. We suggest that CBE just may be the first shared paradigm by a critical mass of the factions involved with formal education. This does not mean to say that there is close agreement and understanding of what CBE is, but rather that for the first time there is a paradigm of sorts that educators, researchers, certifying agencies, students, unions, professional organizations, state education agencies, schools, and colleges are talking about, exploring, operationalizing, and even researching. Thus we think that a significant critical mass has coalesced for the first time in education. There are a shared, common paradigm and language upon which scientific investigations can be pursued for the sake of testing the paradigm rather than pursuing investigations for the purpose of promoting one's own school of thought and refuting another school's paradigm.

CBE as a paradigm shared by a significant mass does not at all mean to suggest that CBE is any kind of final word. It is the first crude step toward establishing the processes of formal learning as a field of scientific study and practice rather than a collection of competing schools. In Kuhn's language, CBE may do for education what Newton did for physical optics. The result will not be a science as in the natural sciences, but the beginning of the development and advancement through periods of "normal science" and "scientific revolutions" of the science of education, learning, and instruction.

We suspect that the anomalies will come at a furious rate as a result of there being a common paradigm in education. Thus, what educational research or learning in the classroom of the near future will look like will probably be beyond our fondest dreams and greatest fears and in directions as yet unimagined. The field is enormous; the number of researchers, practitioners, and clients is enormous; the potential payoff defies description.

LAST WORDS

We have learned a great deal from our involvement in CBE and from sharing ideas and experiences with others involved in it. We see the potential for some exciting things from CBE. Whether or not CBE or any other paradigm will make contributions depends upon the readiness and willingness of all to thoughtfully consider its potentials and to be willing to personally take some risks. Trying some different things just on the chance that some worthwhile outcomes will be attained will be challenging. Becoming so personally involved to the point where life-and-death, us-versus-them confrontations are the only interchanges will make losers of us all. We have attempted to report and describe in what ways we see CBE as having promise. None of this promise will materialize for any of us unless we become more tolerant and accepting of experimentation and of mistakes. We invite you to identify two or three ideas that have been suggested here and try them out. Don't just make a "go–no go" decision. That is too easy to do. Afterward, share your experience, good or bad, with some others.

Earlier in this chapter we mentioned that in the short circuit necessitated by CBE involvement there were a few electrocutions. The reader will have to answer for himself whether the risks are worth it. They may just be. This book contains a few of the reasons why we think they are. We hope you have a few.

bibliography

ABBOTT, A. R. (Ed.) *Florida center review: A report to Florida teacher educators on competency-based teacher training and protocol materials.* Coral Gables, Florida: Florida Center for Teacher Training Materials, University of Miami.

AIRASIAN, P. W. Performance-Based Teacher Education: Evaluation issues. In T. E. Andrews (Ed.), *Assessment.* Albany: New York State Education Department, Division of Teacher Education and Certification, and Multi-State Consortium on Performance-Based Teacher Education, 1974.

ALEXANDER, L. T., & YELON, S. L. *Instructional development agencies in higher education.* East Lansing: Michigan State University at East Lansing, 1972.

ALLEN, W. H. Instructional media research: Past, present and future. *Audiovisual Communication Review,* 1971, *19* (1), 5–17.

AMERICAN ASSOCIATION FOR THE ADVANCEMENT OF SCIENCE. *Preservice science education of elementary school teachers: Guidelines, standards and recommendations for research and development.* Washington, D.C.: American Association for the Advancement of Science, 1969.

AMIDON, E. J., & HOUGH, J. B. *Interaction analysis: Theory, research and application.* Reading, Mass.: Addison-Wesley Publishing Co., 1967.

ANDREWS, T. E. (Ed.) *PBTE.* Albany: New York State Education Department, Division of Teacher Education and Certification, and Multi-State Consortium on Performance-Based Teacher Education.

Annotated listing of competency-based modules. Coral Gables, Fla.: Florida Center for Teacher Training Materials, University of Miami, 1972.

Annotated listing of competency-based modules (Addendum A). Coral Gables, Fla.: Florida Center for Teacher Training Materials, University of Miami, 1973.

AUSUBEL, D. P. *The psychology of meaningful verbal learning.* New York: Grune and Stratton, 1963.

AYERS, J. B., & SHEARRON, G. F. Feasibility of the management subsystem components. In C. E. Johnson & G. F. Shearron, *The feasibility of the Georgia educational model for teacher preparation—elementary* (Vol. I) U. S. Office of Education 9–0477). Washington, D.C.: U. S. Government Printing Office, 1970.

BENNIS, W. G., BENNE, K. D., & CHIN, R. *The planning of change.* New York: Holt, Rinehart and Winston, 1961.

BERNE, E. *Games people play.* New York: Ballantine Books, 1964.

BHOLA, H. S. Configuration of change. An engineering theory of innovation diffusion, planned change and development. Paper presented at the Ohio State University—USOE Conference on Strategies of Educational Change, November, 1965.

BLOOM, B. S. Learning for Mastery. *Evaluation Comment,* May 1968, *1* (2), 1–3.

BLOOM, B. S., HASTINGS, J. T., & MADAUS G. F. *Handbook of summative and formative evaluation of student learning.* New York: McGraw-Hill, 1971.

BOERRIGHTER, G. C. (Ed.) Elementary teacher education models, Phase II: Feasibility. *Journal of Research and Development in Education,* Spring 1970, *3* (3), 2.

BORGERS, S. B., & WARD, G. R. *Affective modules.* Houston: The University of Houston, 1972.

BORGERS, S. B., & WARD, G. R. *Affective 12.0: Professional ethics for the educator.* Houston: The University of Houston, 1973.

BOWEN, L. S. The use of Flanders' interaction analysis system. In C. W. Beegle & R. M. Brandt (Eds.), *Observational methods in the classroom.* Washington, D.C.: Association for Supervision and Curriculum Development, 1973.

BROUDY, H. S. *A critique of performance-based education.* Washington, D.C.: American Association of Colleges for Teacher Education, 1972.

BROWN, G. G., & MENAKER, S. L. *Personalization impact on students and faculty* (R&D Report Series #65). Austin: Research and Development Center for Teacher Education, the University of Texas, 1972.

BRUNER, J. S. *A symposium on the training of teachers for elementary school.* Melbourne, Florida: I/D/E/A, 1968.

BURDIN, J. L. (Ed.) *AACTE Bulletin.* Washington, D.C.: American Association of Colleges for Teacher Education.

BURDIN, J. L., & LANZILLOTTI, K. *A readers guide to the comprehensive models for preparing elementary teachers* (SP003–421). Washington, D.C.: ERIC Clearinghouse on Teacher Education and AACTE, 1969. (Library of Congress No. NO–108426.)

CARLSON, R. O. *Adoption of educational innovations.* Eugene, Oregon: University of Oregon Press, 1965.

CARROLL, J. A model for school learning. *Teachers College Record,* 1963, *64,* 723–33.

CARTER, R. *Help! These kids are driving me crazy.* Champaign, Illinois: Research Press, 1972.

A catalog of protocol materials in teacher education (rev. ed.). Tallahassee, Florida: State Department of Education, Division of Elementary and Secondary Education, 1972.

CBTE proficiency analysis rating: An evaluation guide for certification of CBTE interns. Houston: Competency-Based Teacher Center, University of Houston, 1973.

CBTE STEERING COMMITTEE, WESTERN KENTUCKY UNIVERSITY. *Sequence of school roles.* CBTE Working Paper, 1974.

CHARTERS, W. W., JR., EVERHART, R. B., JONES, J. E., PACKARD, J. S., PELLEGRIN, R. J., REYNOLDS, L. J., & WACASTER, C .T. *The process of planned change in the school's instructional organization* (CASEA Monograph No. 25). Eugene, Ore.: Center for the Advanced Study of Educational Administration, the University of Oregon, 1973.

COMBS, A. W. Educational accountability from a humanistic perspective. *Educational Researcher,* September 1973, *2* (9).

COMPETENCY ASSESSMENT, RESEARCH AND EVALUATION—A report of a national conference March 12–15, 1974. Available from the American Association of Colleges for Teacher Education, Washington, D.C., or the National Dissemination Center for Performance-Based Education, Syracuse University.

COOPER, J. M., & WEBER, W. A. A competency-based systems approach to teacher education. In J. M. Cooper, W. A. Weber, & C. E. Johnson, *A systems approach to program design.* Berkeley, Calif.: McCutchan, 1973.

COOPER, J. M., JONES, H. L., & WEBER, W. A. Specifying teacher competencies. *Journal of Teacher Education,* Spring 1973, *24* (3), 17–18.

CURWIN, R. L., & FUHRMANN, B. S. *Discovering your teaching self: Humanistic approaches to effective teaching.* Englewood Cliffs, N.J.: Prentice-Hall, Inc., 1975.

DARLAND, D. D. Preparation in the governance of the profession. In B. O. Smith (Ed.), *Teachers for the real world.* Washington, D.C.: American Association of Colleges for Teacher Education, 1968.

DEMARTE, P. J., HARKE, D. J., & MAHOOD, R. W. A peck of troubles: Developing a competency-based teacher education program. Paper presented at the Eighth Conference on Value Inquiry, Geneseo, New York, 1974.

DILLNER, M. *Employment opportunities for elementary teachers* (trial ed.). Houston: The University of Houston, 1973.

DIMOND, E. G. A safe physician. *Arch. Intern. Med.,* January 1972, 129–30.

ELAM, S. *Performance-based teacher education: What is the state of the art?* Washington, D.C.: American Association of Colleges for Teacher Education, 1971.

ENGELHARDT, J., GOUGE, C., & HALL, G. E. *A measure for developmental evaluation of instructional modules.* Austin: Research and Development Center for Teacher Education, the University of Texas, 1972.

FARRINGTON, J. A., & WALLACE, R. C., JR. *Position paper for the PTE basic program plan.* Austin: Research and Development Center for Teacher Education, the University of Texas, 1972.

FLANDERS, N. A. *Teacher influence, pupil attitudes, and achievement* (U. S. Office of Education Cooperative Research Project No. 397). Minneapolis: University of Minnesota, 1960. (*Mimeograph.*)

FLEXNER, A. *Medical education in the United States and Canada* (Bulletin 4). New York: Carnegie Foundation for the Advancement of Teaching, 1910.

FOSTER, R. L. A critical analysis of our schools. In J. G. Saylor (Ed.), *The school of the future now.* Washington, D.C.: Association for Supervision and Curriculum Development, 1972.

FOX, R., LUSZKI, M., & SCHMUCK, R. *Diagnosing classroom learning environments.* Chicago: Science Research Associates, 1966.

FRANCKE, E. L. *Pupil achievement and teacher behaviors: A formative evaluation of an undergraduate program in teacher preparation.*

Doctoral dissertation, University of Nebraska at Lincoln, 1971.

FULLER, F. F. *Becoming a born teacher: A conceptual framework of personal education for teachers and other students.* Austin: Research and Development Center for Teacher Education, the University of Texas, 1973.

FULLER, F. F. Concerns of teachers: A developmental conceptualization. *American Educational Research Journal,* March 1969, *6* (2), 207–226.

FULLER, F. F. *Personalized education for teachers, an introduction for teacher educators.* Austin: Research and Development Center for Teacher Education, the University of Texas, 1970.

FULLER, F. F. *Putting it all together: An attempt to integrate theory and research about self-confrontation in teacher education.* Austin: Research and Development Center for Teacher Education, the University of Texas, 1972.

FULLER, F. F., & BOWN, O. H. *Becoming a teacher.* In *Seventy-fourth Yearbook of the National Society for the Study of Education.* Chicago: The National Society for the Study of Education, 1975.

FULLER, F. F., & CASE, C. *A manual for scoring the Teacher Concerns Statement.* Austin: Research and Development Center for Teacher Education, the University of Texas, 1972.

FULLER, F. F., & MANNING, B. A. Self-confrontation reviewed: A conceptualization for video playback in teacher education. *Review of Educational Research,* 1973, *43* (4), 469–528.

FULLER, F. F., PECK, R. F., BOWN, O. H., MENAKER, S. L., WHITE, M. M., & VELDMAN, D. J. *Effects of personalized feedback during teacher preparation on teacher personality and teaching behavior* (R&D Report Series #4). Austin: Research and Development Center for Teacher Education, the University of Texas, 1969.

GABRIEL, J. *Emotional problems of the teacher in the classroom.* London: Angus & Robertson, Ltd., 1957.

GAGE, N. L. *Teacher effectiveness and teacher education.* Palo Alto, Calif.: Pacific Books, 1972.

GAGNÉ, R. M. *The conditions of learning* (2nd ed.). New York: Holt, Rinehart and Winston, 1970.

GAZDA, G. M., ASBURY, F. R., BALZER, F. J., CHILDERS, W. C., DESSELLS, R. E., & WALTERS, R. P. *Human relations development, a manual for educators.* Boston: Allyn and Bacon, 1973.

GELATT, H. D., VARENHORST, B., CAREY, R., & MILLER, G. P. *Decisions and outcomes.* New York: College Entrance Examining Board, 1973.

GENTRY, C. G. *Heuristics for the development of a CBTE program.* Toledo, Ohio: University of Toledo, 1971.

GEORGE, A. Analysis of five hypothesized factors on the Teacher Concerns Checklist, Form B. Paper presented at the annual meeting of the American Educational Research Association, Chicago, 1974.

GINOTT, H. G. *Between parent and child.* New York: Macmillan, 1965.

GINOTT, H. G. *Between parent and teenager.* New York: Macmillan, 1969.

GINOTT, H. G. *Teacher and child.* New York: Macmillan, 1972.

GIRAULT, E. S. Development, implementation and stabilization in preservice teacher education, or: Who owns the action? Paper presented at the NSTA/NSF Symposium, Washington, D.C. May 1974.

GLASSER, W. *Reality therapy: A new approach to psychiatry.* New York: Harper and Row, 1965.

GLASSER, W. *Schools without failure.* New York: Harper and Row, 1969.

GUTHRIE, J. W. A survey of school effectiveness studies. In U. S. Office of Education, *Do Teachers Make a Difference?* (Catalog No. HE 5.258.58042). Washington, D.C.: U. S. Government Printing Office, 1970.

HAAK, R. A., KLEIBER, D. A., & PECK, R. F. *Student evaluation of teacher instrument II.* Austin: Research and Development Center for Teacher Education, the University of Texas, 1972.

HALL, G. E. *Analysis of teaching behavior, an instructor module.* Austin: Research and Development Center for Teacher Education, the University of Texas, 1969.

HALL, G. E. *Computer processing and feedback of interaction analysis data for teachers.* Austin: Research and Development Center for Teacher Education, the University of Texas, 1973.

HALL, G. E. *A manual for users of the IAST v.2: A system of interaction analysis.* Austin: Research and Development Center for Teacher Education, the University of Texas, 1972.

HALL, G. E. *Phases in the adoption of educational innovations in teacher training institutions.* Austin: Research and Development Center for Teacher Education, the University of Texas, 1974.

HALL, G. E., LOUCKS, S. F., MANNING, B. A., PENDLETON, J. K., PENNINGTON, R. E., WALLACE, R. C., JR., & WITZKE, D. B. *A workshop for interdisciplinary faculty teaming.* Austin: Research and Development Center for Teacher Education, the University of Texas, 1974.

HALL, G. E., PENDLETON, J. K., & LOUCKS, S. F. *Modules and their role in personalized programs, a teacher educator workshop.* Austin: Research and Development Center for Teacher Education, the University of Texas, 1973.

HALL, G. E., WALLACE, R. C., JR., & DOSSETT, W. F. *A developmental conceptualization of the adoption process within educational institutions.* Austin: Research and Development Center for Teacher Education, the University of Texas, 1973.

HAVELOCK, R. G., GUSKIN, A., FROHMAN, M., HAVELOCK, M., HILL, M., & HUBER, J. *Planning for innovation through dissemination and utilization of knowledge.* Ann Arbor: Center for Research on Utilization of Scientific Knowledge, Institute for Social Research, the University of Michigan, 1971.

HERNDON, J. *The way it's spozed to be.* New York: Simon and Schuster, 1954.

HITE, H. The cost of performance-based teacher

education. *Journal of Teacher Education,* Fall 1973, *24* (3), 221–24.

HOUSTON, W. R. Behavioral science teacher education program, feasibility study summary. In G. C. Boerrighter (Ed.), Elementary teacher feasibility models, Phase II—feasibility. *Journal of Research and Development in Education,* Spring 1970, *3* (3), 45–55.

HOUSTON, W. R. *Resources for performance-based education.* Albany: The University of the State of New York, and the State Education Department, Division of Teacher Education and Certification, 1973.

HOUSTON, W. R. *Strategies and resources for developing a competency-based teacher education program.* Albany: New York State Education Department, Division of Teacher Education and Certification, and Multi-State Consortium on Performance-Based Teacher Education, 1972.

HOUSTON, W. R., & BAIN, R. J. *Houston needs assessment system.* Houston: University of Houston, 1973.

HOUSTON, W. R., HOLLIS, L. Y., JONES, H. L., WHITE, S. J., PACE, A., & EDWARDS, D. *Developing instructional modules.* Houston: The University of Houston, 1972.

HOWSAM, R. B. Management of PBTE programs. *Journal of Teacher Education,* Fall 1973, *24* (3), 213–20.

HUGHBANKS, W. M. *A study of the relationship between the student teaching behavior of TEPS and the teaching skills which they have been taught in the NUSTEP program.* Doctoral dissertation, University of Nebraska at Lincoln, 1971.

HYMES, J. L., JR. *Behavior and misbehavior, a teacher's guide to action.* Englewood Cliffs, N.J.: Prentice-Hall, Inc., 1955.

Inner-city simulation laboratory. Chicago: Science Research Associates, 1969.

Interaction laboratory for teacher development (3rd ed.). Ogden, Utah: Thiokol Chemical Corporation, 1973.

JERSILD, A. *When teachers face themselves.* New York: Teachers College Press, 1954.

JOHNSON, C. E. A guide to Georgia educational model specifications for the preparation of elementary teachers. In G. C. Boerrighter (Ed.), Elementary teacher feasibility models, Phase II—feasibility. *Journal of Research and Development in Education,* Spring 1970, *3* (3), 159–95.

JOHNSON, C. E. A guide to Georgia educational model specifications for the preparation of elementary teachers. In J. Burdin & K. Lanzillotti, *A readers guide to comprehensive models for preparing elementary teachers* (SP003–421). Washington, D.C.: ERIC Clearinghouse on Teacher Education and AACTE, 1969. (Library of Congress No. NO–108426)

JOHNSON, L. V., & BANY, M. A. *Classroom management: Theory and skill training.* New York: Macmillan, 1970.

JONES, H. L. *Piaget and education.* Houston: The University of Houston, 1972.

JONES, H. L. *Using set induction.* Trial module for University of Houston CBTE program, 1972.

JONES, H. L., & WEBER, W. A. *Psychological foundations II: Phenomenological learning.*

Houston: The University of Houston, 1972.

JOYCE, B. P. *Estimating costs of competency orientation.* Unpublished paper, Teachers College, Columbia University, New York, 1973.

JOYCE, B. P. Teachers College, Columbia University, A guide to the teacher-innovator: A program to prepare teachers. In J. L. Burdin & K. Lanzillotti (Eds.), *A readers guide to the comprehensive models for preparing elementary teachers* (SP003–421). Washington, D.C.: ERIC Clearinghouse on Teacher Education and AACTE, 1969. (Library of Congress No. NO–108426.)

JOYCE, B. P., & WEIL, M. *Models of teaching.* Englewood Cliffs, N.J.: Prentice-Hall, Inc., 1972.

JUNG, C., HOWARD, R., EMORY, R., & PINO, R. *Interpersonal communications.* Portland, Ore.: Northwest Regional Educational Laboratory, 1971.

JUNG, C., PINO, R., & EMORY, R. *RUPS: Research utilizing problem solving.* Portland, Ore.: Northwest Regional Educational Laboratory, 1970.

KAMPSNIDER, J. J. (Ed.). *Interaction laboratory for teacher development.* Ogden, Utah: Thiokol Chemical Corporation, 1971.

KASS, MIRIAM. Doctor's unlikely cholera diagnosis saves a life. Houston: *The Houston Post,* September 9, 1973.

KAUFMAN, B. *Up the down staircase.* Englewood Cliffs, N.J.: Prentice-Hall, Inc., 1964.

KELLER, F. S. Goodbye teacher. . . . *Journal of Applied Behavioral Analysis,* Spring 1968, *1* (1), 79–89.

KELLEY, E. A., & ANDREWS, L. (Ed.) *Social studies education learning tasks.* Lincoln, Nebraska: NUSTEP learning materials for Performance-Based Teacher Education, University of Nebraska, 1973.

KELLEY, E. A., & WALTER, L. J. *Student attitudes toward the teacher preparation program of the University of Nebraska-Lincoln.* Lincoln: Department of Secondary Education, University of Nebraska, 1971.

KENNEDY, D. A. Some philosophical and practical problems of PBTE performance-based teacher education. *PBTE Newsletter,* November 1973, *2* (5), 15.

KLEIBER, D., VELDMAN, D. J., & MENAKER, S. L. The multidimensionality of locus of control. *Journal of Clinical Psychology,* October 1973, *29* (4), 411–16.

KOERNER, J. Governance of teacher education. In D. J. McCarty (Ed.), *New perspectives on teacher education.* San Francisco: Jossey-Bass Publishers, 1973.

KUHN, T. S. *The structure of scientific revolutions* (2nd ed.). Chicago: International Encyclopedia of Unified Science, the University of Chicago Press, 1970.

LARSON, C. O. *A description of a curriculum development project in teacher education.* Doctor's thesis, University of Nebraska at Lincoln, 1972.

LOUCKS, S. F. *An evaluation design for implementation of a CBE program.* Austin: Research and Development Center for Teacher Education, the University of Texas, 1974.

MCNEIL, J. D., & POPHAM, W. J. The assessment

of teacher competency. In *The second handbook of research on teaching.* Chicago: Rand McNally and Company, 1973.

MAGER, R. *Preparing instructional objectives.* Palo Alto, Calif.: Consulting Psychologists Press, 1962.

MAGUIRE, L. M. *An annotated bibliography of the literature on change.* Philadelphia, Pa.: Research for Better Schools, Inc., 1970.

MERWIN, J. C. *Performance-based teacher education: Some measurement and decision-making considerations.* Washington, D.C.: American Association of Colleges for Teacher Education, 1973.

MILES, M. B. (Ed.) *Innovation in education.* New York: Teachers College Press, Columbia University, 1971.

MOLLER, G. *A comprehensive study of the problems of beginning teachers in selected large senior high schools.* Unpublished doctoral thesis, University of Nebraska at Lincoln, 1968.

MOOD, A. M. Do teachers make a difference? In U. S. Office of Education, *Do Teachers Make a Difference?* (Catalog No. HE 5.258.58042). Washington, D.C.: U. S. Government Printing Office, 1970.

Mutable principles of organization, *Public Administration News, Management Forum,* February 1967, *17* (1), Section II.

NEISWORTH, J. T., DENO, S., & JENKINS, J. R. *Student motivation and classroom management: A behavioralistic approach.* Newark, Dela.: Behavior Technics, Inc., 1969.

NEWLOVE, B. W., & PENDLETON, J. K. *Participant handbook videotape feedback in a personalized program.* Austin: Research and Development Center for Teacher Education, the University of Texas, 1974.

OFFICE OF EDUCATION. *How teachers make a difference.* (Catalog No. HE 5.258.58042). Washington, D.C.: U. S. Government Printing Office, 1970.

PARKER, R. Weber State College evaluates IPTE after three years. *Phi Delta Kappan,* January 1974, *55* (5), 320.

PENNINGTON, R. E., & GOUGE, C. *User's manual for the analysis of teaching behavior computer program.* Austin: Research and Development Center for Teacher Education, the University of Texas, 1973.

Perceiving, behaving, becoming: A new focus for education. Washington, D.C.: Association for Supervision and Curriculum Development, 1962.

PETERSON, G. T. Conceptualizing the learning center. *Audio Visual Instruction,* 1973, *18* (3), 67–72.

PFEIFFER, J. W., & JONES, J. E. *A handbook of structural experiences for human relations training* (4 vols.). Iowa City: University Associates Publishers and Consultants, 1969, 1970, 1971, 1973.

POPHAM, W. J. Alternative teacher assessment strategies. Paper prepared for meeting of the Multi-State Consortium of Performance-Based Teacher Education, New Orleans, February 1973.

POPHAM, W. J. California's precedent-setting teacher evaluation law. *Educational Researcher,* July 1972, 13–15.

POPHAM, W. J. Performance tests of teaching proficiency: Rationale, development, and validation. *AERA Journal,* January 1971, 105–17.

POPHAM, W. J. Teaching improvement kit (Forms A, B, C). Los Angeles: Instructional Appraisal Services, 1972.

POPHAM, W. J. Teaching skill under scrutiny. *Phi Delta Kappan,* June 1971, 599–602.

POPHAM, W. J., & BAKER, E. L. *Planning an instructional sequence.* Englewood Cliffs, N.J.: Prentice-Hall, Inc., 1970.

POSTLETHWAITE, S. N. A system approach to botany. *Audio Visual Instruction,* April 1963, *8,* 243–44.

PROGRAM FOR INSTRUCTIONAL SPECIALISTS IN CONTINUING EDUCATION (Vol. I). CERLI, July 1969.

PROGRAM ON TEACHING EFFECTIVENESS. *Teacher training products: The state of the field.* (National Institute of Education Contract No. NE–C–00–3–0061). Palo Alto, Calif.: School of Education, Stanford University. (Research and Development Memorandum No. 116, January 1974.)

RATHS, L. E., HARMIN, M., & SIMON, S. B. *Values and teaching.* Columbus, Ohio: Charles E. Merrill Publishing Co., 1966.

ROGERS, C. *Freedom to learn.* Columbus, Ohio: Charles E. Merrill Publishing Co., 1969.

ROGERS, E. M., & SHOEMAKER, F. F. *Communications of innovations—A cross-cultural approach* (2nd ed.). New York: The Free Press, 1971.

ROSENSHINE, B., & FURST, N. Research on teacher performance criteria. In B. O. Smith (Ed.), *Research on teacher education: A symposium.* Englewood Cliffs, N.J.: Prentice-Hall, Inc., 1971.

ROSENSHINE, B., & FURST, N. The use of direct observation to study teaching. In *The second handbook of research on teaching.* Chicago: Rand McNally and Co., 1973.

RUTHERFORD, W. L. *Guidelines for establishing field-based teacher education programs.* Austin: Research and Development Center for Teacher Education, the University of Texas, 1973.

SCHALOCK, H. D. A guide to a competency-based, field-centered systems approach to elementary teacher education. In J. Burdin & K. Lanzillotti, *A readers guide to comprehensive models for preparing elementary teachers.* Washington, D.C.: ERIC Clearinghouse for Teacher Education and AACTE, 1969.

SCHALOCK, H. D. Notes on a model of assessments that meets the requirements of CBTE. In W. R. Houston (Ed.), *Exploring competency-based education.* Berkeley, Calif.: McCutchan Publishing Corporation, 1974.

SCHALOCK, H. D. *Notes on a model of assessments that meets the requirements of competency-based teacher education.* Monmouth, Ore.: Oregon College of Education, 1973.

SCHMIEDER, A. A. *Competency-based education: The state of the scene.* Washington, D.C.: ERIC Clearinghouse on Teacher Education, AACTE, and NCIES, 1973.

SCHMIEDER, A. A., & YARGER, S. J. Teacher/teaching centering in America. *Journal of Teacher Education*, Spring 1974, *25* (1), 5–12.

SCHMUCK, R. A., RUNKEL, P. J., SATUREN, S. L., MARTELL, R. T., & DERR, C. B. *Handbook of organization development in schools.* Eugene, Ore.: National Press Books, 1972.

SHEARRON, G. F., & JOHNSON, C. E. A CBTE program in action: University of Georgia. *Journal of Teacher Education,* Fall 1973, *24* (3).

SHOSTAK, R. The field experience component in PBTE. *PBTE Newsletter,* November 1973, *2* (5).

SILBERMAN, C. E. *Crisis in the classroom: The remaking of American education.* New York: Random House, 1970.

SIMON, S. B., HOWE, L. W., & KIRSCHENBAUM, H. *Values clarification: A handbook of practical strategies for teachers and students.* New York: Hart Publishing Co., Inc., 1972.

SKINNER, B. F. *The technology of teaching.* Englewood Cliff, N.J.: Prentice-Hall, Inc., 1968.

SMITH, B. O. Introduction. In B. O. Smith (Ed.), *Research in teacher education.* Englewood Cliffs, N.J.: Prentice-Hall, Inc., 1971.

STUFFLEBEAM, D. L., FOLEY, W. J., GEPHART, W. J., GUBA, E. G., HAMMOND, R. J., MERRIMAN, H. O., & PROVUS, M. M. *Educational evaluation and decision-making.* Itasca, Ill.: F. E. Peacock, 1971.

TABA, H. *Teachers' handbook for elementary social studies.* Reading, Mass.: Addison-Wesley, 1967.

TAYLOR, C., SMITH, W. R., & GHISELIN, B. The creative and other contributions of one sample of research scientists. In C. W. Taylor & F. Barron (Eds.), *Scientific creativity: Its recognition and development.* New York: Wiley, 1963.

THORNDIKE, R. L., & HAGEN, E. *10,000 careers.* New York: Wiley, 1959.

TURNER, R. L. Levels of criteria. In B. Rosner, *The power of competency-based teacher education.* Boston: Allyn and Bacon, Inc., 1972.

VELDMAN, D. J. *Initial assessment battery.* Austin: Research and Development Center for Teacher Education, the University of Texas, 1970.

VELDMAN, D. J. *Teacher evaluation form.* Austin: Research and Development Center for Teacher Education, the University of Texas, 1964.

VELDMAN, D. J. *Student evaluation of teaching* (Research Methodology Monograph No. 10). Austin: Research and Development Center for Teacher Education, the University of Texas, 1970.

WALLACE, R. C., JR. *Each his own man: The role of adoption agents in the implementation of personalized teacher education.* Austin: Research and Development Center for Teacher Education, the University of Texas, 1973.

WALLACE, R. C., JR., and WITZKE, D. *A general accounting system for programmatic research and development.* Planning document. Austin, Texas: Research and Development Center for Teacher Education, The University of Texas, 1972.

WALTER, L. J. *An assessment of the teacher assisting component of the Nebraska University secondary teachers education program.* Unpublished doctoral thesis, University of Nebraska at Lincoln, 1973.

WEBER, W. A., & RATHBONE, C. A study of the feasibility of the Syracuse University model for the preservice and inservice education of elementary school teachers. In G. C. Boerrighter (Ed.), Elementary teacher feasibility models, Phase II—feasibility. *Journal of Research and Development in Education,* Spring 1970, *3* (3), 80–93.

WEIGAND, J. (Ed.) *Developing teacher competencies.* Englewood Cliffs, N.J.: Prentice-Hall, Inc., 1971.

WILSON, D., SEYMOUR, J., & KEARL, S. *Concerns of teachers* (MTRIPP slide-tape program). Austin: Research and Development Center for Teacher Education, the University of Texas, 1973.

name index

subject index

This pioneering book covers both the theory and implications for practice that have been developed and discovered in building CBE programs. Much of its content arises from the authors' experience in developing competency-based programs in many institutions. They provide exciting illustrations from real-world CBE programs, and much of each chapter deals with the problems and solutions encountered in program development. Several successful CBE program efforts are described in detail.

Hall and Jones present the theory and present state of the art of competency-based education. A balance of attention is given to the criticisms as well as the strengths of CBE, with a special chapter on personalization of CBE programs. They define, explain, and challenge CBE and guide the way to new horizons and goals through the proven effectiveness of CBE programs. All educators will be stimulated by their book and welcome its fresh ideas so clearly directed and explained.

Gene E. Hall, Ph.D., Syracuse University, is Director of the Procedures for Adopting Educational Innovations Project of the Research and Develop-